REGIME CONSEQUENCES

Regime Consequences
Methodological Challenges and Research Strategies

by

Arild Underdal
University of Oslo,
Oslo, Norway

and

Oran R. Young
University of California,
Santa Barbara, California, U.S.A.

Arild Underdal is the Rector and a Professor of Political Science at the University of Oslo. Oran Young is a Professor of Environmental Science and Management at the Donald Bren School of Environmental Science and Management at the University of California at Santa Barbara. Most of the work on this project was completed while the editors were in residence as research fellows at the Centre for Advanced Study in Oslo, Norway.

KLUWER ACADEMIC PUBLISHERS

DORDRECHT / BOSTON / LONDON

A C.I.P. Catalogue record for this book is available from the Library of Congress.

ISBN 1-4020-2070-8 (HB)
ISBN 1-4020-2208-5 (e-book)

Published by Kluwer Academic Publishers,
P.O. Box 17, 3300 AA Dordrecht, The Netherlands.

Sold and distributed in North, Central and South America
by Kluwer Academic Publishers,
101 Philip Drive, Norwell, MA 02061, U.S.A.

In all other countries, sold and distributed
by Kluwer Academic Publishers,
P.O. Box 322, 3300 AH Dordrecht, The Netherlands.

Printed on acid-free paper.

All rights reserved.
© 2004 Kluwer Academic Publishers
No part of this work may be reproduced, stored in a retrieval system, or transmitted
in any form or by any means, electronic, mechanical, photocopying, microfilming, recording
or otherwise, without written permission from the Publisher, with the exception of any material supplied specifically for the purpose of being entered and executed on a computer system,
for exclusive use by the purchaser of the work.

Printed in the Netherlands.

Contents

Contributing Authors — vii

Preface — 1

Chapter 1 The Consequences of International Regimes — 3
   ORAN YOUNG

Part I: Simple Effectiveness — 25

Chapter 2 Methodological Challenges in the Study of Regime Effectiveness — 27
   ARILD UNDERDAL

Chapter 3 Case Studies of the Effectiveness of International Environmental Regimes — 49
   STEINAR ANDRESEN AND JØRGEN WETTESTAD

Chapter 4 Causal Mechanisms and the Study of International Environmental Regimes — 71
   JON HOVI

Chapter 5 Boolean Analysis, Mechanisms, and the Study of Regime Effectiveness — 87
   OLAV SCHRAM STOKKE

Chapter 6   A Quantitative Approach to Evaluating International
            Environmental Regimes   121
    RONALD B. MITCHELL

Chapter 7   Formal Theory and Regime Effectiveness:
            Rational Players, Irrational Regimes   151
    HUGH WARD, GRANK GRUNDIG AND ETHAN ZORICK

Chapter 8   Does Regime Robustness Require a Fair Distribution of
            The Gains from Cooperation?   183
    ANDREAS HASENCLEVER, PETER MAYER,
    AND VOLKER RITTBERGER

Part II: Broader Consequences   217

Chapter 9   Methodological Issues in the Study of Broader
            Consequences   219
    THOMAS GEHRING

Chapter 10 Exploring Regime Interaction   247
    THOMAS GEHRING AND SEBASTIAN OBERTHÜR

Chapter 11 International Regimes And Democracy   281
    HELMUT BREITMEIER

Chapter 12 Into the Methodological Void   307
    GREGOR WALTER, MICHAEL ZÜRN

Chapter 13 Regimes and Social Transformation   335
    BARRY B. HUGHES

Part III: Conclusion   359

Chapter 14 Research Strategies for the Future   361
    ARILD UNDERDAL AND ORAN R. YOUNG

Index   381

Contributing Authors

Steinar Andresen, Helmut Breitmeier, Thomas Gehring, Grank Grundig, Andreas Hasenclever, Jon Hovi, Barry B. Hughes, Peter Mayer, Ronald B. Mitchell, Sebastian Oberthür, Volker Rittberger, Olav Schram Stokke, Arild Underdal, Gregor Walter, Hugh Ward, Jørgen Wettestad, Oran Young, Ethan Zorick, Michael Zürn

Preface

This volume has a long and distinguished pedigree. It is the product of an effort to devise clear and unambiguous methods for demonstrating that international regimes make a difference stretching back at least to the early 1990s. What has transpired in the meantime is the development of a suite of useful techniques of analysis rather than the creation of a single, correct methodology for use in this field of study. Our assumption is that we can be relatively confident regarding assessments of the consequences of individual regimes when those employing a variety of methods converge on the same conclusions. When different methods yield divergent conclusions, on the other hand, we can take this as a signal that more work is needed to arrive at convincing judgments regarding the consequences of the regimes in question.

Along the way, we came to understand that there is an important distinction between what we describe in this book as simple effectiveness and broader consequences. Most analyses of the effectiveness of international regimes focus on individual cases and seek to assess the performance of regimes on a case-by-case basis. This is entirely understandable. Yet it is now clear that individual regimes not only interact with one another but also operate in and affect broader settings. The study of these broader consequences is less mature than research on the effectiveness of individual regimes. But it points to a line of analysis that is destined to become increasingly prominent during the foreseeable future. We therefore devote a large portion of this book to a consideration of ways to think about the emerging issue of broader consequences.

This volume concentrates on matters of methodology, modeling, and measurement. It is not likely to become a best seller. Yet the issues it addresses are critical to the fate of regime analysis. If we can make substantial headway in efforts to evaluate regime consequences, the future of this field of study will be bright. If not, regime analysis will go the way of many other fashions in the study of international relations. As a result, we expect this book to be read and referred to frequently both by established scholars in the field and by graduate students seeking guidance in the development of topics for their theses.

The bulk of the substantive work on this volume was done during the academic year 1999-2000, when we were both fellows of the Centre for Advanced Study located at the Norwegian Academy of Science and Letters in Oslo, Norway. Early in the year, we organized a workshop at the Centre where authors presented preliminary drafts of the papers included in the volume. We then had the pleasure of holding a follow-up workshop during the spring of 2000 to discuss revised drafts and to receive input from a number of other colleagues. Since then, all the authors have engaged in several rounds of revisions of the papers that form the chapters of this volume.

We owe a large debt of gratitude to the Centre for Advanced Study for providing the support needed to engage in work of this kind and for trusting us to come up with a significant product in the absence of any active supervision. It is a pleasure to acknowledge this support.

Arild Underdal
Oran R. Young

Chapter 1

THE CONSEQUENCES OF INTERNATIONAL REGIMES
A Framework for Analysis

ORAN YOUNG
Donald Bren School of Environmental Science and Management, University of California (Santa Barbara)

The debate about whether international regimes matter is essentially over. Despite periodic rearguard actions (Mearsheimer 1994/1995) and occasional outbreaks of self-doubt, a consensus has emerged that regimes and more generally social institutions do make a difference—sometimes a big difference—in international society (Levy, Young, and Zürn 1995; Young 1999, Miles et al. 2002). Lest anyone be tempted to see this as the end of a line of enquiry, however, we hasten to point out that the emergence of this consensus opens up a large and important research agenda for those interested in the roles that institutions play in international society. While regimes matter, the ways in which they matter, the extent to which they matter, and the conditions under which they matter are variables whose values range widely over the universe of cases. Moreover, the effort to explain variance in these terms is fraught with a number of analytic and methodological problems ensuring that efforts to pin down the consequences of regimes under real-world conditions will remain high on the list of challenges confronting those engaged in research on international regimes during the foreseeable future.

The purpose of this introductory chapter is to set the stage for a concerted effort to advance our knowledge of the consequences of international regimes and, in the process, to provide context for the substantive papers included in this volume. The discussion to follow directs attention to two distinct dimensions of this subject. One dimension is substantive; it is based on a key distinction among types or categories of consequences flowing from the operation of regimes. A major objective of this discussion is to broaden the range of effects or impacts of regimes that analysts consider in endeavoring to assess the consequences that these arrangements produce. The second dimension is analytic and methodological; it highlights a series of challenges facing those seeking to produce convincing conclusions about the consequences of international regimes. An important goal in this connection is to enlarge the current debate in this field by expanding the tool kit available to those seeking to enhance our understanding of the consequences of regimes. The boundaries among types of consequences and especially among types of research challenges are not hard and fast; they should be treated simply as points of departure for this exercise. Even so, it may help to juxtapose the two dimensions, a procedure that yields a 2x3 table (see Table 1.1) in which the rows feature different types of consequences and the columns emphasize major categories of analytic and methodological challenges.

Efforts to contribute to our understanding of the roles regimes play in international society may proceed by focusing either on the rows or the columns of this matrix; they may also concentrate more intensively on individual cells in the matrix. The conference that gave rise to the papers in this volume proceeded by establishing row teams on the grounds that what drives the study of international regimes is, first and foremost, an interest in understanding the ways in which these arrangements affect the course of world affairs. Each row team then coordinated the efforts of its members to examine the analytic and methodological issues arising in the three columns. This procedure worked well at the conference, and we have carried it over as an organizing principle for the papers included in this volume.

Table 1.1. *Consequences and Challenges.*

TYPES OF CONSEQUENCES	ANALYTIC/METHODOLOGICAL CHALLENGES		
	Concepts/ Hypotheses	Causal Connections	Data Issues
Simple Effectiveness			
Broader Consequences			

1. TYPES OF REGIME CONSEQUENCES

For the most part, recent studies of the effectiveness of international regimes have treated these arrangements as responses to relatively well-defined problems and directed attention to internal effects or effects occurring within the behavioral complexes where specific problems are located (Underdal, 1992; Young 1992; Haas, Keohane, and Levy 1993; Young and von Moltke 1994; Weiss and Jacobson 1998; Victor, Raustiala, and Skolnikoff 1998; Young 1999a, Miles et al. 2002). Thus, the ozone regime addresses the problem posed by the impacts of chlorofluorocarbons (CFCs) and several related families of chemicals on the stratospheric ozone layer. The goal of the regime is to protect humans and other organisms from adverse effects of increased UV-B radiation resulting from a thinning of the ozone layer, and it makes sense to evaluate this regime's performance in terms of progress toward achieving this goal. The objective of the regime for biological diversity is to prevent losses of biodiversity occurring as side effects or externalities of actions designed to promote economic development and other similar objectives. The natural way to assess the performance of this regime is to evaluate its impact on rates of change in losses of biodiversity at the genetic, species, and ecosystem levels. Much the same is true of the regime dealing with desertification where the problem is to retard or even reverse land degradation in arid regions of the world. There is nothing wrong with this problem-oriented approach to the consequences of international regimes. There is room for a steady stream of useful studies that adopt this perspective. Nonetheless, this procedure has the effect of truncating the analysis of regime consequences. To understand the meaning of this observation, consider the content of the rows included in Matrix 1.

1.1 Simple Effectiveness

The relationship between regimes and issue areas is a complex one both because issue areas are socially constructed and because there is generally substantial scope for judgment in specifying the boundaries of individual regimes as well as of the issues they address. In some cases, regimes simply follow widely accepted ways of delimiting issue areas. The GATT/WTO regime, for instance, deals in a rather comprehensive manner with international trade which is normally treated as a well-defined issue area in its own right (von Moltke 1997). Much the same is true of the regime covering marine issues as articulated in the 1982 Convention on the Law of the Sea together with a variety of more specific arrangements subsequently nested into this institutional framework (Friedheim 1993). Nonetheless, the relationship between regimes and issue areas is often subject to divergent interpretations that are not easy to reconcile in any simple way. Is transboundary air pollution an issue area such that the European regime on long-range transboundary air pollution (LRTAP) covers only a subset of this range of concerns? Or are we better off treating transboundary air pollution in Europe as an issue area in its own right? And what should we make of the fact that the LRTAP regime, which originally focused on sulfur dioxide and nitrogen oxides, has steadily broadened its coverage to encompass volatile organic compounds, persistent organic pollutants, heavy metals, and the combined effects of multiple pollutants? Similar concerns are common in other domains. Is the protection of whales an issue area in its own right, for instance, or is it merely a subset of a broader issue area encompassing human interactions with marine mammals? Alternatively, is there a case for treating marine mammals as one among a number of interrelated concerns arising in large marine ecosystems? The resolution of these matters is complicated not only by the fact that delineating the scope of regimes is almost invariably a political process which has consequences for the interests of particular players but also by the fact that there is no terminological consensus about such matters within the scientific community.

However we resolve these concerns, it is important not to confine the analysis of issue area consequences to problem solving in any narrow sense of that term. Some problems (e.g. resolving jurisdictional disputes relating to areas like Svalbard or Antarctica) are solvable in the sense that the results are generally accepted and the issues are unlikely to be reopened under any foreseeable circumstances. But other problems (e.g. managing consumptive uses of living marine or terrestrial resources) cannot be solved in any ordinary sense of the term. They require ongoing efforts and, more often then not, periodic adjustments in governing arrangements to ensure that they are properly adapted to changing circumstances. In other cases, the operation of regimes gives rise to new insights about the problems at stake or even to new ways of defining or framing the problems in contrast to yielding decisive solutions to the problems as originally framed. Most observers would concur, for instance, with the observation that one of the main consequences of the LRTAP regime has been a sizable contribution to our understanding of the causes and consequences of transboundary air pollution as an environmental problem. Beyond this lies a group of cases in which the participants in regimes do not even share a common understanding of the nature of the problem to be solved. Consider the differences between the perspectives of conservationists and preservationists with regard to the regime for whales and whaling as a case in point. Not surprisingly, adherents to these divergent perspectives have opposing views regarding the performance of this regime during the 1980s and 1990s (Friedheim 2001; Miles et al. 2002).

It is worth noting as well that internal effects may vary in terms of their directness and in terms of the extent to which they produce positive or negative results (Young 1999b). The matter of directness concerns the length of the causal chain linking the operation of a regime and the effects of its operation on the problem to be solved. In general, the difficulties involved in tracing regime effects grow—often dramatically—as the length of the causal chain increases. It is relatively easy, for example, to show that the entry into force of the 1992 UN Framework Convention on Climate Change (UNFCCC) caused many member states to pass implementing legislation. It is far more difficult to demonstrate that the operation of this regime has brought about changes in the behavior of specific agents, such as operators of coal-fired power plants or drivers of gasoline-powered automobiles. There is, as well, the possibility that specific regimes will generate effects that are negative rather than positive from the perspective of problem solving. A regime intended to protect biological diversity that triggers a major shift from regulated legal markets to flourishing and largely unregulated black markets in plants and animals, for instance, may do more harm than good with regard to the goal of preventing losses of biological diversity. It is fair to say that most studies of simple effectiveness have directed attention to regime consequences that are internal, direct, and positive. There is nothing wrong with a focus of this sort. But it is important to bear in mind that this is a somewhat restricted perspective on the roles that regimes play as causal agents in international society.

1.2   Broader Consequences

Given the pronounced tendency to look upon regimes as devices intended to solve more-or-less well-defined problems, it is understandable that studies of effectiveness typically focus on the consequences of these arrangements within their own behavioral complexes or issue areas. Do regimes dealing with living resources serve to prevent the occurrence of the tragedy of the commons? Do regimes dealing with pollution serve to protect large atmospheric, marine, and terrestrial ecosystems? But in most cases, answers to these questions—even convincing ones—do not tell the whole story with regard to the consequences of international regimes. Regimes can and often do produce consequences whose effects are felt beyond their own issue areas, whether or not they succeed in solving the problems that motivate their creators to form them. These broader consequences may encompass a relatively wide range of effects, and there is as yet no standard taxonomy available for identifying and describing these consequences. But it may help, for starters, to differentiate among (a) cross-regime effects, (b) domestic consequences, (c) systemic consequences, and (d) impacts on international society.

Given their complexity, it is understandable that those seeking to come to terms with the roles that regimes play have directed their attention primarily to simple effectiveness. Recently, however, we have become aware that individual regimes do not operate in an institutional vacuum. As the number and variety of regimes operating in international society increase, we can expect cross-regime effects or what some have labeled institutional interplay to become a topic of growing concern (Young et al. 1999; Young 2002). Already, we have become aware of the significance of institutional interactions among regimes dealing with trade and the environment (Runge 1994). Trade regimes may have far-reaching consequences both for the incidence and for the severity of the environmental impacts of economic activities. Concern about these effects led directly to the drive to negotiate an environmental side agreement linked to the North American Free Trade Area (NAFTA) Agreement. One of the most telling criticisms of the 1994 GATT/WTO agreement concerns its relative insensitivity to the environmental impacts of this system for managing international trade in an era of globalization. It is unlikely that additional agreements dealing with international trade will prove acceptable in the absence of a careful consideration of their probable impacts on major environmental regimes. Similarly, many criticisms of the International Tropical Timber Agreement (ITTA) are based on the proposition that this regime appears to be concerned more with encouraging trade in tropical wood products than with the impacts of this trade on environmental regimes, such as the arrangement dealing with biological diversity articulated in the Convention on Biological Diversity (CBD). But note that the flow of consequences may go in the opposite direction as well. There is a growing tendency for international environmental regimes to include provisions that place restrictions on or otherwise affect international trade. This is true, for instance, of the regimes dealing with trade in endangered species of wild fauna and flora, transboundary movements of hazardous wastes, the regulation of substances that deplete the ozone layer, and emissions of greenhouse gases. In each of these cases, arrangements designed to solve problems that are predominantly environmental in nature can produce consequences that have substantial implications for the operation of institutional arrangements pertaining to trade.

Nor are cross-regime consequences confined to matters involving interactions between environment and trade. There are obvious possibilities for impacts of this sort to occur between regimes focused on sustainable uses of living resources and regimes concerned mainly with air and water pollution. However conservative or risk averse managers may be in setting allowable harvest levels and regulating by-catches, regimes dealing with the harvesting of fish and wildlife may be unable to achieve sustainable results in settings where there are no effective restraints on activities (e.g. the use of chemical fertilizers and pesticides) that give rise to serious air and water pollution. Given the propensity of many pollutants, such as persistent organic pollutants (POPs), to migrate over long distances from their points of origin and to reside in atmospheric, marine, and terrestrial systems for protracted periods of time, the potential problems associated with cross-regime consequences in such cases are serious. One way to deal with matters of this sort is to promote mergers in which all the relevant activities (e.g. fishing and farming) are covered by the same overarching regime. But the legal and political impediments to successful applications of this strategy at the international level are always significant and often insurmountable, a fact that reinforces the importance of thinking systematically about institutional interplay in the study of regime consequences.

Whatever their consequences with regard to simple effectiveness or cross-regime effects, the rise of international institutions can also have consequences for domestic affairs and (especially) political processes occurring within member states. Sometimes these consequences are direct and focused. International regimes that require individual members to comply with rules dealing with human rights within their own jurisdictions or to refrain from certain forms of economic development in the interests of protecting biological diversity, for instance, seek to circumscribe the traditional freedom of action enjoyed by states within their domestic jurisdictions. In other cases, the domestic consequences take the form of impacts on the allocation of material and political resources within member states. Because such resources are always scarce, an international regime that becomes a controversial issue in domestic politics or requires a sizable commitment of resources can generate substantial opportunity costs at the domestic level. Beyond this lie the domestic consequences arising from the impacts of the growing collection of international regimes in contrast to the effects of individual regimes. It is the prospect that states will become enmeshed in an expanding web of international regimes that they can neither control nor ignore, for instance, that has led some observers to raise questions about the effects of the growth of international regimes on the operation of democratic political systems within member states.

The idea of systemic effects, by contrast, leads us to ask whether the operation of international regimes—singly or in combination—produces consequences that show up in a variety of aggregate measures of human welfare. Can we detect the signal of the operation of international regimes in social transformations involving such matters as demographic shifts (e.g.

declines in fertility rates, increases in life expectancy), trends in levels of economic (in)equality at the international level, or the diffusion of democratic political systems from one part of the world to another. The impact of regimes, on this account, is likely to be indirect, and there is every reason to expect that regimes will constitute only one among a number of driving forces associated with various systemic occurrences. Given the significance of these largescale developments both for human welfare and for the Earth's carrying capacity, however, this category of broader consequences seems worthy of serious consideration, even if the impact of regimes accounts for only a small fraction of the empirically observable variance in demographic, economic, and political trends.

It is well understood that issue-specific regimes operate within an overarching social setting defined by the constitutive rules or the deep structure of international society (Bull 1977). General rules pertaining to the identity of states and the nature of their interactions with one another form an institutional substrate on which more specific rules pertaining to matters such as pollution, trade, human rights and the proliferation of various weapons systems rest. This does not mean that the constitutive rules of international society are fixed and unchanging. On the contrary, major forces for change such as globalization have made the current era a period of considerable dynamism regarding the basic character of international society. Among the more striking results of this dynamism are the rise of influential nonstate actors (e.g. multinational corporations, environmental NGOs) and the growth of social networks that some observers see as constituting a basis for the emergence of a global civil society (Princen and Finger 1994; Wapner 1997; Reinicke 1998). Clearly, these trends have important implications not only for the processes involved in forming international regimes but also for the performance of these arrangements once they are put in place.

Of particular importance in the context of this discussion, however, are the societal consequences flowing from the creation and operation of issue-specific regimes. In some cases, these consequences may be conservative in the sense that they serve to reinforce or prop up prevailing constitutive arrangements (e.g. the organization of international society as a society of territorially-defined states). Membership in many regimes, for instance, is limited to states whose authority to exercise control over the activities of other actors operating within their jurisdiction is affirmed and reinforced by the substantive provisions of the regimes in question. Some observers see the GATT/WTO regime, to take a specific example, as a state-centric arrangement that can be expected to shore up the ability of states to manage their own economic affairs in an era marked by growing challenges both to the authority of states to manage economic relations and to the capacity of states to control the activities of actors that are able and willing to exploit new technologies to minimize their susceptibility to state control (Reinicke 1998). In other cases, the creation and operation of regimes can trigger processes that lead to substantial changes measured in societal terms, quite apart from their performance as devices designed to solve specific problems. Nowhere is this more apparent than in the realm of environmental affairs where specific regimes regularly provide opportunities for nonstate actors to play influential roles and give rise to complex practices organized around bioregions that cut across the jurisdictional boundaries of states or around global systems (e.g. the Earth's climate system) that are largely beyond the reach of the jurisdiction of individual states. Although these societal consequences are often indirect and the behavioral mechanisms that produce them are typically hard to track in a convincing manner, it is perfectly possible that consequences of this sort will ultimately prove more far-reaching than the impacts that arise in connection with simple effectiveness and that constitute the focus of most current studies of the consequences of international regimes.

2. ANALYTIC AND METHODOLOGICAL CHALLENGES

Just as any effort to produce a comprehensive account of the consequences of international regimes must distinguish among several types of regime consequences, those engaged in this research program must devise ways to meet a number of distinct analytic and methodological challenges. The methodological challenges in this field of research are unusually severe. Partly, this is an outgrowth of complications confronting efforts to measure the effectiveness of regimes within their own issue areas, much less to pinpoint broader consequences arising from the operation of these arrangements. In part, it is a result of characteristics of the relevant universe of cases which make it difficult to use familiar empirical and especially statistical techniques for drawing inferences as methods for arriving at convincing conclusions about the consequences of regimes (Young et al. 1999).

Because any effort to come to terms with analytic and methodological challenges should be motivated by overarching goals rather than becoming an end in itself, we asked the teams concerned with simple effectiveness and with broader consequences to begin with an overview of the research agenda or, in other words, an account of the current state of play in efforts to understand the consequences of international regimes. These statements appear as the opening chapters of the two major sections of this book. Not surprisingly, there are significant areas of overlap in these statements. In both cases, the agenda includes: questions about causation or the roles that regimes play as determinants of collective outcomes; questions about performance or the factors that govern the effectiveness of regimes, and questions about design or the prospects for constructing regimes to achieve identifiable goals.

Beyond this, however, lie three sets of analytic and methodological challenges dealing with: (1) concept formation, hypothesis development, and model construction, (2) causal inference, and (3) data collection and management. The boundaries among these sets of concerns are not hard-and-fast; they are simply clusters of issues that loom large in efforts to make headway in adding to our understanding of regime consequences. Nor is there any reason to expect the allocation of time and energy among these concerns to be the same among those dealing with simple effectiveness and those focusing on broader consequences. Nonetheless, the principal distinctions introduced here will serve to lend an element of comparability to the papers included in the substantive sections of this book.

2.1 Concept Formation, Hypothesis Development and Model Construction

The analysis of simple effectiveness is clearly more advanced than the study of broader consequences. Yet even among those concerned with the internal effects of regimes, a number of conceptual issues remain to be resolved. First and foremost is the need to pin down the dependent variable(s). Although most analysts concerned with simple effectiveness would agree with the idea of problem solving as the ultimate target of analysis, delineating the causal role of regimes in solving well-defined problems is a tall order. One response to this difficulty is to introduce a distinction—familiar to students of public policy—among outputs, outcomes, and impacts (Easton 1965). The study of outputs, which directs attention to matters like the promulgation of regulations designed to operationalize rules and the development of policy instruments intended to guide the behavior of key actors, appeals to lawyers and political scientists who are typically concerned with matters of implementation and compliance (Chayes and Chayes 1995; Weiss and Jacobson 1998). Outcomes, by contrast, involve measurable changes in the behavior of regime members and those subject to their jurisdiction. Researchers whose intellectual roots lie in the behavioral sciences generally prefer to direct attention to the outcomes associated with regimes (Levy, Young, and Zürn 1995; Young 1999b). For their part, impacts are best construed as the contributions regimes make to solving the problems that lead to their creation in the first place. Those whose interest in regimes stems from a deep-seated concern for solving environmental problems, for instance, will emphasize this approach to the conceptualization of the dependent variable (Barrett 2003).

There is as well some debate among students of simple effectiveness regarding the relative merits of measuring the effects that regimes produce in terms of movement away from the status quo ante or the probable outcome in the absence of regime creation or in terms of movement toward some collective optimum with regard to the problem at hand (Miles et al. 2002). One conceptually elegant way to deal with this issue is to combine the two perspectives on effectiveness so that we can construct an index of effectiveness that measures the proportion of the distance from the no regime outcome to the collective optimum that a regime has moved the relevant system over various periods of time. An attraction of this procedure is that it produces an index that varies between 0 and 1 and that can be compared across regimes in efforts to assess relative effectiveness (Helm and Sprinz 1999; Sprinz and Helm 1999). Nevertheless, this approach to the dependent variable requires the acceptance of controversial assumptions, and it is certainly correct to say that it has not been used in any systematic way by those seeking to assess simple effectiveness (Young 2001a). At this stage, it is probably accurate to say that the center of gravity in research on effectiveness lies in efforts to assess the behavioral consequences of individual regimes within their own issue areas.

Although most students of regimes have directed their attention to simple effectiveness, the discussion in the preceding section makes it clear that there is also a need to find ways to define and measure broader consequences. Whether these broader consequences are properly understood as unintended side effects of the operation of regimes or as products of indirect efforts to influence either domestic or international affairs, describing these effects will require procedures that extend beyond the realm of problem solving in the usual sense of the term. With regard to systemic and societal consequences, in particular, the domain of possible effects is extensive, ranging all the way from the generation of new issue areas through the management of persistent conflicts to significant alterations in the character of international society as a whole. Ideally, this research program should spawn a suite of measures or ways to think about regime consequences that bear some relationship to one another but that also can be analyzed independently. But it is clear, at this stage, that whereas there are debates about specific formulations of the dependent variable in the analysis of simple effectiveness, the study of broader consequences will involve a range of dependent variables many of which are just beginning to come into focus.

When we turn to the formulation of hypotheses, there is ample room for alternative approaches as well. In this connection, three distinct issues merit particular attention. We want to know how much of the variance in outputs, outcomes, and impacts is attributable to the character of a regime itself in contrast to various exogenous factors, including the nature of the problem to be solved and the nature of the social context in which a regime operates. Second, we are interested in exploring the relative importance of the major categories of driving forces that occupy the attention of social scientists (e.g. power, interests, knowledge) when it comes to explaining or predicting either simple effectiveness or the broader consequences of regimes. In addition, we seek to understand not only the relative weights of different variables in generating regime consequences but also the ways in which differentiable drivers—non-anthropogenic as well as anthropogenic—interact with one another in the process of generating regime consequences.

Moreover, this concern with the formulation of hypotheses raises a larger set of questions about the role of models in research on regime consequences. Specifically, it directs attention to the problem of sorting out the relative merits of collective-action models (Rutherford 1994), which construe regimes as rules and procedures designed to solve social dilemmas arising from individualistic behavior under conditions of interactive decisionmaking and which emphasize the logic of consequences, and of social-practice models (Scott 1995), which envision regimes as cognitive and culturally-determined constructs that lend identity to participating actors, structure the discourses in terms of which they think about problems, and highlight the logic of appropriateness (March and Olsen 1998; Young et al. 1999; Young 2001b). Those favoring one or another of these perspectives on regimes may not only differ in their thinking about the determinants of regime consequences, they may also delineate the universe of cases or, in other words, the set of arrangements included under the rubric of regimes in different ways.

2.2 Causal Connections

However we choose to conceptualize regime consequences and to frame hypotheses about the forces that govern these consequences, progress in this field of study will require a sustained effort to demonstrate the existence and content of the causal links between the creation and operation of regimes and the various consequences we associate with them. This problem is hardly unique to this field of study. It is a central feature of every effort to evaluate the consequences—both intended and unintended—arising from the adoption and implementation of public policies (Pressman and Wildavsky 1973). And analogous concerns arise well beyond the realm of the social sciences. Consider the difficulties bedeviling the efforts of those seeking to show unambiguous links between increases in atmospheric concentrations of greenhouse gases and changes in the Earth's climate system or particular features of this system, such as inter-annual variability in temperatures, precipitation patterns, or the behavior of sea ice. In all these cases, complex multivariate relationships are the norm, and there is an ever present danger that what appear to be significant consequences will turn out on further inspection to be nothing more than spurious correlations.

How, then, should we approach the issue of drawing causal inferences about the consequences of international regimes? In one sense, all efforts to answer this question involve exercises in what may be called counterfactual analysis. That is, we want to know how and to what extent actual outcomes differ from those that would have occurred in the absence of a regime or in the presence of a different type of regime. Yet there is a range of procedures for addressing issues of this sort, and it is important to identify the relative merits of these procedures in the specific case of efforts to pin down the consequences of international regimes.

Undoubtedly, it makes sense to take advantage of all the leverage we can get from correlational or variation-finding techniques in this realm. But the occurrence of three problems imposes significant limitations on such efforts. The universe of cases is small. In most situations, we are likely to be limited to analyses based on dozens of cases rather than hundreds or thousands of cases. Heterogeneity among the members of this universe is great. That is, we must contend with the fact that the differences among regimes are more significant that the differences among individual members of many other universes of cases. In addition, contingent relationships are of central importance in efforts to understand the effectiveness of regimes. To illustrate, factors like the number of actors, transparency, or learning capacity appear to be critical to the effectiveness of regimes under some circumstances but not under others. There is nothing unusual about this phenomenon in conceptual terms. In situations where universes of cases are large, the obvious response to the occurrence of contingencies of this sort is to subdivide the universe of cases into two or more smaller subsets in order to control for the effects of certain factors (e.g. group size, incentives to cheat, or responsiveness to changing circumstances).

Where (initial) universes of cases are small, two contrasting responses are worth exploring. One response focuses on procedures designed to expand the universe of cases. Thus, it is possible to come up with universes containing several hundred cases when dependent variables are conceptualized in terms of differences in the behavior of individual regime members, in the behavior of the same members over time, or in factors like annual percentage changes in well-defined environmental concerns (e.g.

emissions of greenhouse gases).[1] This way of thinking leads to analyses in which statistical procedures (e.g. regression analysis) are brought to bear to account for the extent to which regime features (as well as other factors) can account for variance in the dependent variables. Beyond this, the arguments of those who focus on "scientific inference in qualitative research" apply to the study of regime effectiveness, just as they do in other realms of social inquiry (King, Keohane, and Verba 1994). Thus, it makes sense to follow many of the rules associated with inductive forms of analysis, even when the universe of cases is not large enough to meet the formal requirements of standard statistical procedures.

Still, there is no denying that the limitations identified above are serious ones. Under the circumstances, it makes sense to supplement variation-finding approaches to causal inference with other procedures, such as tendency-finding analysis (Dessler 1992) and the search for behavioral mechanisms or pathways (Haas, Keohane, and Levy 1993; Young 1999b). Tendency-finding analysis asks: how is it possible for a particular regime to be effective? It leads to the construction of what philosophers of science often call genetic explanations that provide convincing accounts of outcomes occurring in specific cases in contrast to generalizations that seek to identify invariant relationships between regime effectiveness treated as a dependent variable and a variety of other conditions that are treated as determinants of effectiveness (Nagel 1961). Since regimes are not actors in their own right, moreover, this way of thinking highlights the need to identify the behavioral mechanisms through which these institutional arrangements influence the behavior of those who are actors and, as a result, affect the content of collective outcomes in international society. If we are able to trace step-by-step the pathways through which the operation of a regime influences the behavior of its members as well as those operating under the jurisdiction of members, there is some basis for drawing inferences about the effectiveness of the regime, even if it is not possible to assess the case in terms of the application of some recognizable covering law.

This sort of thinking increases the significance of the debate between those who see regimes as responses to collective-action problems and approach regime members as unitary and self-interested utility maximizers, on the one hand, and those who look upon regimes as constitutive arrangements and interpret the behavior of regime members in terms of what has become known the logic of appropriateness, on the other (March and Olsen 1998, Young 1999b). Naturally, these analytic techniques are not meant to supplant the use of variation-finding procedures. On the contrary, the goal is to build up a set of procedures that, taken together, can enrich our understanding of regime consequences.

Although these underlying epistemological—and even ontological—concerns are ultimately critical, there is as well a need to consider the strengths and weaknesses of a number of specific tools that those seeking to understand regime consequences can and do deploy either singly or in combination in order to demonstrate causal connections. In the first instance, this is a matter of reviewing the familiar range of quantitative and qualitative methods with an eye toward their utility in efforts to address the specific subject of regime consequences. Are certain statistical procedures more or less useful in this context, given central features of the subject matter such as the need to work with ordinal rather than interval scales? Are there opportunities to conduct informative natural experiments—in contrast to controlled experiments—in drawing inferences about the consequences of regimes? Are there special problems associated with efforts to apply the logic of scientific inference to the analysis of qualitative data of the sort we have to work with in many analyses of regime consequences? Are there new approaches to the methodology of conducting case studies that merit particular attention on the part of those seeking to understand the consequences flowing from the operation of specific regimes (Bates et al. 1998; Mitchell and Bernauer 1998)? These questions will all be familiar to those engaged in social science research in any of a number of fields. Nonetheless, they deserve self-conscious and systematic consideration on the part of participants in ongoing and collaborative efforts to enhance our understanding of the consequences arising from the operation of international regimes.

To these familiar tools, we need to add a number of additional procedures that have generated considerable interest among students of international affairs in recent years. One of these is a collection of procedures centering on process tracing and thick description (Geertz 1997) and on the conduct of thought experiments or counterfactuals in the narrower sense of the term discussed by James Fearon and others (Fearon 1991; Tetlock and Belkin eds. 1996). In essence, these methods center on an effort both to probe beneath the surface and to impose a certain rigor on the conduct of case studies. A second supplementary method involves the use of simulations to understand the dynamics of institutional arrangements treated as complex and dynamic systems. Some simulations (e.g. Robert Axelrod's computer tournaments) feature highly simplified thought experiments designed to explore central puzzles in a controlled manner (Axelrod 1984). Others are oriented toward probing the sensitivity of institutional arrangements to small changes in specific rules or decisionmaking procedures (e.g. systems of implementation review or noncompliance procedures). Yet another tool that has recently captured the imagination of some students of international regimes centers on Charles Ragin's method of using Boolean algebra to develop what he and his colleagues describe as qualitative comparative analysis (Ragin 1987; Ragin 1997). In essence, this technique features the construction of truth tables which are intended to identify factors or combinations of factors that are sufficient (and, less often, necessary) to produce effective regimes or other well-defined outcomes. The purpose here is not to replace traditional quantitative and qualitative methods as tools for the study of regime consequences. Rather, the goal is to devise a collection of methods that can be deployed in various combinations to maximize the persuasiveness of our conclusions about the consequences arising from the operation of regimes.

2.3 Data Collection and Management

As the preceding discussion suggests, the study of regime consequences will require the use of both qualitative and quantitative data. Several distinct concerns pertaining to the acquisition and handling of data arise in all efforts to assess regime consequences. One centers on the selection of dependent variables and the development of procedures to operationalize them. First and foremost, this is a matter of devising one or more indices of regime effectiveness or, more broadly, regime consequences that would allow us to make meaningful comparisons regarding the results flowing from different regimes or the results flowing from the operation of the same regime under different socioeconomic conditions or at different points in time. Although the development of interval scales obviously would be desirable in this connection, this goal may be beyond our reach, at least for the foreseeable future. As a result, efforts to make progress regarding the challenge of index construction should focus at this stage on the construction of relatively simple ordinal measures that can be used to rank the effectiveness of regimes on a scale running from dead letters to arrangements that solve problems in a more or less decisive fashion (Underdal 2002).

Another concern involves the need for harmonization or standardization with regard to measures of the principal independent variables of interest to students of regime consequences. Given the history of regime analysis as a field of study based largely on discrete case studies conducted by researchers who devise their own conceptual frameworks, it is easy to explain the lack of standardization in this realm. But in the absence of agreed upon definitions and measurement procedures, there is little prospect that we will be able to make significant progress toward the overarching goal of explaining and predicting variations in the effectiveness of international regimes. To be more specific, we need to reach consensus on what we mean in talking about the roles of problem structure, actor attributes, and social context as factors influencing the effectiveness of regimes. As recent debates regarding the concept of problem structure make clear, we have a considerable distance to go in the development of agreed measures of these (suites of) variables (Young 1999a). Yet it is beyond doubt that standardization is necessary to any effort to construct conclusive tests of a variety of hypotheses pertaining to matters like the role of power, interests, and ideas as determinants of effectiveness or, more generally, the consequences flowing from the operation of regimes.

Yet another concern in this area focuses on data management and, specifically, on the need to create repositories of data structured to allow individual researchers to gain access to those data needed to explore a wide range of hypotheses and designed to benefit from contributions of new data resulting from compatible research projects. Clearly, such data repositories should be accessible electronically and managed in such a way that all qualified researchers can use the data they contain at minimum cost. Public utilities of this sort are expensive to create and difficult to sell to funders who have little experience with the development of data and information systems for the social sciences. The place to begin in this connection may well be with the International Regimes Database (IRD), an electronic database developed initially under the auspices of the International Institute for Applied Systems Analysis (IIASA) and currently funded by the German Science Foundation (Breitmeier, Levy, Young, and Zürn 1996a; Breitmeier, Levy, Young, and Zürn 1996b). But other efforts to construct databases relevant to the study of regime consequences are worthy of consideration as well (Mitchell 1999; Underdal 2002). What is needed at this stage is a careful review of the status of these endeavors and an assessment of their relevance to future efforts to advance our understanding of the consequences of international regimes. This should result both in adjustments of existing databases to enhance their usefulness for this stream of research and in the identification of data needs that cannot be met using currently available data sets. A set of well-grounded recommendations pertaining to data and information needs should emerge from this process.

3. PLAN OF THE BOOK

An earlier version of the framework set forth in the preceding sections served as the conceptual roadmap for the international conference on The Study of Regime Consequences: Methodological Challenges and Research Strategies held in Oslo, Norway during November 1999; the current version provides the architecture for this volume of essays. The two main sections of the book deal, respectively, with simple effectiveness and with broader consequences. In each case, the section begins with a paper intended to introduce the principal issues at stake and to give some sense of the state of play regarding the study of these issues. These chapters are followed by a set of more specific papers exploring and evaluating the usefulness of a variety of research strategies treated as procedures for expanding our knowledge of regime consequences. Given the current status of studies of regime consequences, there is an unavoidable and significant asymmetry between the two substantive sections. While students of international regimes have been wrestling with the problem of assessing simple effectiveness for some time, systematic work on issues relating to broader consequences is just getting underway. A major consequence of this asymmetry is that there is an emphasis in the section dealing with simple effectiveness on the strengths and weaknesses of different strategies for demonstrating causal connections, whereas the section dealing with broader consequences directs attention more to conceptual matters involving the specification of the major dependent variables. Needless to say, readers should bear this asymmetry in mind in reading the papers included in this volume. So long as it is understood as a reflection of the current state of the art rather than as a bias on the part of the editors, however, we do not see the existence of this asymmetry as a problem.

The concluding chapter that together with this introductory chapter brackets the substantive sections of the volume, seeks to take stock of the study of regime consequences in the aftermath of the Oslo conference. It reviews areas in which we have made significant progress and identifies areas in which we are in need of significant conceptual and empirical advances. It emphasizes the judgments of the editors regarding assignments for the next phase both of research on simple effectiveness and of studies of broader consequences. And it compares this endeavor to other efforts in the field of international relations to promote large-scale coordinated research dealing with relatively well-defined research agendas (Alker 1996; Singer 1990). Although successful ventures involving large-scale coordinated research are still uncommon in the field of international relations, we believe that the current prospects for moving forward are favorable in the case of research on the consequences of international regimes.

NOTES

[1] As Mitchell's essay in this volume makes clear, it is possible to introduce procedures that result in relatively large universes of cases. Consider the issue of compliance as an example. If the (non)compliant behavior of each member of a regime for each year the regime is in place is taken as a case, the universe of cases can become quite large.

REFERENCES

Alker, H. R. (1996) *Rediscoveries and Reformulations: Humanistic Methodologies for International Studies,* Cambridge University Press.
Axelrod, R. (1984) *The Evolution of Cooperation,* Basic Books, New York.
Barrett, S. (2002) *Environment and Statecraft. The Strategy of Environmental Treaty-Making,* Oxford University Press.
Bates, R. H., Avner, G., Levi, M., Rosenthal, J. and Weingast, B. R. (1998) *Analytic Narratives,* Princeton University Press.
Breitmeier, H., Levy, M. A., Young, O.R. and Zürn, M. (1996a) International Regimes Database (IRD): Data Protocol, *IIASA WP,* 96–154.
Breitmeier, H., Levy, M. A., Young, O. R. and Zürn, M. (1996b) The International Regimes Database as a Tool for the Study of International Cooperation, *IIASA WP* 196–260.
Bull, H. (1977) *The Anarchical Society: A Study of Order in World Politics,* Columbia University Press, New York.
Chayes, A. and Chayes, A. H. (1995) *The New Sovereignty: Compliance with International Regulatory Agreements,* Harvard University Press, Cambridge.
Dessler, D. (1992) The Architecture of Causal Analysis, paper presented at the Harvard Center for International Affairs.
Easton, D. (1965) *A Systems Analysis of Political Life,* John Wiley & Sons, New York.
Fearon, J. (1991) Counterfactuals and Hypothesis Testing in Political Science, *World Politics* 43: 169–95.
Friedheim, R. L. (1993) *Negotiating the New Ocean Regime,* University of South Carolina Press, New York.
Friedheim, R. L. (ed.) (2001) *Toward a Sustainable Whaling Regime,* University of Washington Press, Seattle.
Geertz, C. (1973) *The Interpretation of Cultures: Selected Essays,* Basic Books, New York.
Haas, P. M., Keohane, R. O. and Levy, M. A. (eds.) (1993) *Institutions for the Earth: Sources of Effective Environmental Protection,* MIT Press, Cambridge.
Helm, C. and Sprinz, D. (1999) Measuring the Effectiveness of International Environmental Regimes, *PIK Report* 52.
King, G., Keohane, R. O. and Verba, S. (1994) *Designing Social Inquiry: Scientific Inference in Qualitative Research,* Princeton University Press.
Levy, M. A., Young, O. R., and Zürn, M. (1995) The Study of International Regimes, *European Journal of International Relations* 1: 267–330.
March, J. G. and Olsen, J. P. (1998) The Institutional Dynamics of International Political Orders, *International Organization* 52: 943–69.
Mearsheimer, J. J. (1994/1995) The False Promise of International Institutions, *International Security* 19: 5–49.
Miles, E. L., Underdal, A., Steinar, A., Wettestad, J., Skjaerseth, J. B., and Carlin, E. M. (2002) *Explaining Regime Effectiveness: Confronting Theory with Evidence,* MIT Press, Cambridge.
Mitchell, R. B. (1999) Situation Structure and Regime Implementation Strategies, paper prepared for the annual meeting of the American Political Science Association.
Mitchell, R. B. and Bernauer, T. (1998) Empirical Research on International Environmental Policy: Designing Qualitative Case Studies, *Journal of Environmental and Development* 7: 4–31.

Nagel, E. (1961) *The Structure of Science: Problems in the Logic of Scientific Explanation,* Harcourt, Brace and World, New York.
Pressman, J. and Wildavsky. A. (1973) *Implementation,* University of California Press, Berkeley.
Princen, Thomas, and Finger, M. (1994) *Environmental NGOs in World Politics: Linking the Local and the Global,* Routledge, London.
Ragin, C. C. (1987) *The Comparative Method: Moving Beyond Qualitative and Quantitative Strategies,* University of California Press, Berkeley.
Ragin, C. C. (1997) *Fuzzy-Set Social Science,* University of Chicago Press, Chicago.
Reinicke, W. (1998) *Global Public Policy: Governing without government?* D.C.: Brookings Institution, Washington.
Runge, C. F. (1994) *Freer Trade, Protected Environment: Balancing Trade Liberalization and Environmental Interests,* Council on Foreign Relations, New York.
Rutherford, M. (1994) *Institutions in Economics: The Old and the New Institutionalism,* Cambridge University Press, Cambridge.
Scott, W. R. (1995) *Institutions and Organizations,* Sage Publications, CA.
Singer, J. D. (1990) *Models, Methods, and Progress in World Politics: A Peace Research Odyssey,* Westview Press, Boulder, Colorado.
Sprinz, D. and Helm, C. (1999) The Effect of Global Environmental Regimes: A Measurement Concept, *International Political Science Review* 20: 359–69.
Tetlock, P. E. and Belkin, A. (eds.) (1996) *Counterfactual Thought Experiments in World Politics: Logical, Methodological, and Psychological Perspectives,* Princeton University Press.
Underdal, A. (1992) The Concept of Regime Effectiveness, *Cooperation and Conflict,* 27: 227–40.
Underdal, A. (2002) One Question, Two Answers, in E. L. Miles et al., *Explaining Regime Effectiveness: Confronting Theory with Evidence,* MIT Press, Cambridge, 3–45.
Victor, D. G., Raustiala, K. and Skolnikoff, E. B. (eds.) (1998) *The Implementation and Effectiveness of International Environmental Commitments,* MIT Press, Cambridge.
von Moltke, K. (1997) Institutional Interactions: The Structure of Regimes for Trade and the Environment, in O. R. Young (ed.) *Global Governance: Drawing Insights from the Environmental Experience,* MIT Press, Cambridge, 247–72.
Wapner, P. (1997) Governance in Global Civil Society, in O. R. Young (ed.) *Global Governance: Drawing Insights from the Environmental Experience,* MIT Press, Cambridge, 65–84.
Weiss, E. Brown and Jacobson, H. K. (eds.) (1998) *Engaging Countries: Strengthening Compliance with International Environmental Accords,* MIT Press, Cambridge.
Young, O. R. (1992) The Effectiveness of International Institutions: Hard Cases and Critical Variables, in J. N. Rosenau and E.-O. Czempiel (eds.) *Governance without Government: Order and Change in World Politics,* Cambridge University Press, Cambridge, 160–194.
Young, O. R. (1999a) *Governance in World Affairs,* Cornell University Press, Ithaca, New York.
Young, O. R. (ed.) (1999b) *The Effectiveness of International Environmental Regimes: Causal Connections and Behavioral Pathways,* MIT Press, Cambridge MA.
Young, O. R. (2001a) Inferences and Indices: Evaluating the Effectiveness of International Environmental Regimes, *Global Environmental Politic* 1: 99–121.
Young, O. R. (2001b) The Behavioral Effects of Environmental Regimes: Collective-Action vs. Social-Practice Models, *International Environmental Agreements* 1: 9–29.

Young, O. R. and von Moltke, K. (1994) The Consequences of International Environmental Regimes: Report from the Barcelona Workshop, *International Environmental Affairs* 6: 348–70.

Young, O. R. with contributions from A. Agrawal, L. A. King, P. H. Sand, A. Underdal and M. Wasson (1999) Institutional Dimensions of Global Environmental Change (IDGEC) Science Plan, *IHDP Report No. 9,* IHDP, Bonn.

PART I

SIMPLE EFFECTIVENESS

Chapter 2

METHODOLOGICAL CHALLENGES IN THE STUDY OF REGIME EFFECTIVENESS

ARILD UNDERDAL
Department of Political Science, University of Oslo

1. EFFECTIVENESS AND RELATED CONCEPTS

The study of regime *effectiveness* can be considered a sub-field of the broader study of regime *consequences*. This sub-field is distinguished first and foremost by the *perspective* it adopts: regimes are assessed in terms of how well they perform a particular function or the extent to which they achieve their purpose.[1] The notion of effectiveness implies the idea of regimes as (potential) *tools*, and like all other tools regimes can be evaluated in terms of their usefulness in helping us carry out a particular task. In adopting this instrumental perspective, students of regime effectiveness concentrate their attention on a *subset* of consequences; notably those that are germane to the function or purpose assigned to the regime in focus. Other consequences—side effects—are of interest only in so far as they have a direct or indirect bearing on this task or purpose. Moreover, in assessing effectiveness the *costs* incurred in establishing and operating the regime are usually left out of the equation. Effectiveness thus becomes a matter of gross rather than net achievement, and should not be confused with *efficiency*. Finally, in evaluating a regime in terms of the extent to which it achieves its official purpose or solves the problem that motivated its establishment, we should keep in mind that regimes are normally designed to promote the values or interests of their (dominant) *members*. If these interests and values differ significantly from those of non-members, a regime may well serve a useful function for its members at the expense of creating a serious problem for others. As defined here, effectiveness does not imply fairness.

These limitations have important implications for the normative status of the concept. Since neither side effects nor costs are included in the assessment, we cannot assume that a high score on "effectiveness" implies a positive contribution to net social welfare, let alone *global* welfare.[2] To be sure, students of international regimes normally think of effectiveness as something to be desired. Moreover, policy-makers presumably try to design regimes so that they can accomplish something worthwhile. Yet it should be clearly understood that effectiveness is a good thing only in the narrow sense of implying success in performing a particular function or solving a certain problem.

A first encounter with the literature on regime effectiveness may well leave an impression of profound confusion (Bernauer, 1995). One source of confusion is the fact that the same *label* ("effectiveness") is used to refer to different *concepts* (compare e.g. Sand (1992) with Underdal (1992)), while different labels (such as "strength" and "effectiveness") sometimes are used for what seem to be rather similar concepts. On the basis of his extensive reading of the literature, Young (1994:142-52) distinguishes six meanings of "effectiveness", and indicates that there may well be more. Two of the six—referred to as "constitutive" and "evaluative" effectiveness—cannot be subsumed under the notion that I have described above.[3] To make things even worse, the latter of these categories is in fact a huge basket including very different notions such as efficiency, sustainability and equity. The inevitable conclusion to be drawn from inventories laying out the full range of concepts in use is that the study of regime effectiveness lacks a common and precisely defined core. And without such a core the prospects for cumulative research and theory development seem poor indeed.

Now, while this conclusion is hard to challenge if we look only at the *range* of variation for the field at large, it misses the fact that within this wide span we find a pronounced tendency towards *convergence* on a much smaller set of concepts.[4] Moreover, difference does not necessarily mean *chaos*. I will argue that most research in this field works with a small set of key concepts that can be related to each other in a meaningful order. Let me begin substantiating this argument by examining two notions that cannot be subsumed under the concept of effectiveness as I have defined it above. I will refer to these two as *strength* and *robustness*.

1.1 Strength

The *strength* of a regime is usually defined in terms of the extent to which it constrains the freedom of legitimate choice open to the individual member (see e.g. Aggarwal, Haggard and Simmons).[5] This notion of strength can be applied to the substantive as well as to the procedural component of regimes (see Donnelly, 1986; Vogler, 1995). In terms of the former, a "strong" regime is one whose substantive norms, rules and regulations significantly constrain the range of behaviour that qualifies as legal or appropriate. The closer a regime comes to saying "anything goes", the weaker it is, in this particular sense. This perspective leads to a preoccupation with aspects such as the stringency, legal status, normative compellence and legitimacy of regime provisions. In terms of its procedural component, a regime is strong to the extent that it subjects a system of activity to *collective* governance rather than individual decision-making. The more authority is centralised, the stronger the regime. Strength in this latter sense then becomes partly a matter of the scope and inclusiveness of regime domains—i.e. "how much" of a particular system of activity is made subject to collective governance—and partly a matter of the decision rules, specifying the minimal size and/or composition of a "winning coalition".

This notion of regime strength differs from the notion of effectiveness first and foremost in the fact that it focuses upon properties of the regime itself rather than on the consequences it produces. These properties can be of considerable interest in themselves, from a legal as well as an ethical perspective. At the same time it seems that part of the rationale for studying strength hinges on the assumption that it is an important determinant of performance; more precisely that strength enhances effectiveness. This seems an intuitively plausible assumption. At the very least we can easily see that—insofar as we focus on consequences produced by the regime itself rather than by the *processes* through which it is established and managed—a certain minimum of strength is a *necessary* condition for effectiveness. To be effective a regime must influence behaviour, and it cannot do so unless it limits the set of options or provide guidelines for the choice among these options. It is, however, equally clear that strength is not a *sufficient* condition for effectiveness. Stringent rules enhance effectiveness only to the extent that they prescribe or encourage behaviour that alleviates the problem (or proscribe or discourage behaviour that causes or aggravates the problem), *and* are complied with. These are non-trivial conditions; stringency itself guarantees neither sensibility nor compliance.[6] Even if both conditions are met, the relationship between strength and effectiveness is not a linear one. To begin with, strength enhances effectiveness. However, as we reach some upper threshold, further regulation of behaviour and centralisation of governance is likely to prove counterproductive, particularly when it comes to dealing with complex and rapidly changing systems. Where flexibility is required, minimising the discretion left to each party is hardly a good recipe for maximising effectiveness.

1.2 Robustness

A regime is *robust* to the extent that it is able to cope with challenges and survive stress with its functioning capacity intact (see e.g. Hasenclever, Mayer and Rittberger, 1996:4; see also their contribution to this volume).[7] Robustness should not be interpreted as capacity to resist all kinds of change. On the contrary, the ability of an institution to survive is—like that of any species in the biosphere—dependent upon its ability to *adapt* to changing (task) environments. The relationship between robustness and adaptability is, however, a complex one, and raises intricate analytical questions at two levels. First, there is the conceptual issue of what has to remain constant for an institution to "survive". The conventional answer has been to define survival in terms of persistence of the "essential" or "constitutive" characteristics—"…those that best define the way in which the system operates" (Easton 1965:92). We can easily see, however, that the distinction between "essential" and "non-essential" features can be difficult to draw in a given case. Second, there is the empirical question of the causal link between adaptability and robustness. To what extent does the ability to adapt "non-constitutive" elements to changes in its task environment increase the chances that the "core" of a regime will survive? Put differently, what is the "optimal" level of adaptability? These are hard questions to answer, but at least it is abundantly clear that extreme rigidity is rarely if ever a good recipe for survival in a changing environment.

What, then, is the relationship between robustness and effectiveness? Other things being equal, (perceived) effectiveness seems to be an important source of support. In the long run a certain minimum of effectiveness comes close to being a necessary condition for survival. It is, though, hardly a sufficient condition. Robustness depends also on several other factors, *legitimacy* probably being the most critical. The higher the general legitimacy of a regime, the less vulnerable it will be to temporary performance failures, and the longer it can survive even more endurable "malfunctioning". The impact of robustness on effectiveness is somewhat more complex. To be effective an institution must be able to survive encounters with the kind(s) of problems it has been established to solve or alleviate. This is so particularly in domains where producing the desired effects is a matter of continuous influence. In this particular sense effectiveness requires robustness. It is, however, equally obvious that effectiveness can be enhanced by the ability to adapt quickly and constructively to new challenges and changing environments. "The problem" is usually a moving target, and institutions are often "a static force" (Morgenthau, 1985:106; see also Goldmann, 1988). Constructive adaptation may involve change also in "constitutive" elements. The general conclusion to be drawn from these two observations is that effectiveness requires a particular *combination* of resilience and adaptability. Determining more precisely what constitutes an "optimal" balance can, though, be a difficult task, and the answer seems to depend on, inter alia, characteristics of the system to be regulated.

This analysis leaves us with three concepts that are all used for describing the "clout" or "importance" of international regimes. These concepts are different in contents, but also linked in important and complex relationships (Figure 2.1), and these relationships are yet poorly understood aspects of the functioning of international regimes. This article is, though, not the place to pursue that topic. The remainder of this paper will focus exclusively on effectiveness. In narrowing the focus, we should, however, recognize that a significant amount of the literature on international regimes deals with what I have called "strength" while a few other studies focus on "robustness".

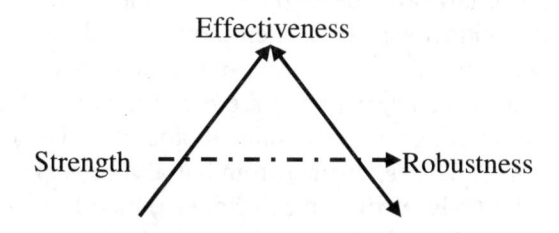

Figure 2.1. *Related notions of regime "importance."*

2. ASSESSING REGIME EFFECTIVENESS

From a methodological perspective, assessing the effectiveness of an institution means comparing its observed or predicted performance against some standard of "success". Any attempt at developing a methodological framework for such an exercise must, then, address at least three main questions. First, what precisely is the *object* to be assessed? Second, against which *standard* is this object to be evaluated? And, third, *how* do we—in operational terms—go about comparing that object to the standard we have defined? Methodological approaches to the study of regime effectiveness can be described and distinguished in terms of their answers to these three questions.

2.1 The object

The question about the object to be assessed may at first thought appear trivial; the object must clearly be the regime in focus! On second thought, however, we can easily see that this answer does not take us very far. Further clarification is required on at least two dimensions: First, what exactly do we study the consequences *of*? Do we focus only on the norms, rules and regulations that make up the regime itself, or do we include also the political *processes* through which it is established and operated? Second, *where* in the chain of consequences do we enter to assess effectiveness? Let us briefly examine the main options and explore the implications of the choices we make.

A regime is conventionally defined as a set of norms, rules and regulations supposed to govern a particular system of activities. All research on regime effectiveness tries to determine to what extent and how this body of norms and rules influence the behaviour of parties and target groups. Students of international law often begin by deriving the (legal) implications of these rules, while political scientists often move directly to the study of behavioural responses—including active resistance and covert cheating as well as positive compliance. International regimes are political constructs, developed and operated through a set of political processes. These *processes* generate their own consequences, distinct from but also related to those that can be attributed to the body of rules they establish, modify or implement. International negotiations tend, for instance, to generate their own stakes for the governments involved, inter alia, in the form of incentives to do well in the eyes of domestic constituencies and important others. Similarly, international negotiations are often large-scale exercises in social learning, leading at least some of the parties involved to change their perception of the problem and their evaluation of alternative policy options. As a consequence, parties may well make *unilateral* adjustments of behaviour, even in the absence of any legal or political obligation to do so. The aggregate importance of these process-generated effects may well be as great as the significance of any convention or protocol signed at the end (see Underdal, 1994). Furthermore, the operation of regimes often provides opportunities for individuals, agencies and companies to get access to new resources, enhance their own status, or strengthen their competitive edge. Some actors are therefore likely to value a regime as much for the private benefits it brings as for the contribution it makes to fulfilling its official purpose.

We can now see that the distinction between effects that can be attributed to the regime itself and those that can be attributed to regime formation and operation *processes* is not merely a matter of academic hair-splitting. Not only may the score we end up with depend critically on whether we include process-generated effects or not; also the advice we would give to policy-makers may well depend on which of these perspectives we adopt.[8]

The default option is to focus only or at least primarily on consequences that can be attributed to the regime itself. This tendency is particularly pronounced in legal studies, but most political science research seems to follow the same path. This is, of course, a perfectly legitimate choice. Moreover, it offers a perspective that is conceptually clean (in the sense that it unambiguously concentrates attention on consequences of "the regime" itself) and methodologically attractive (in that it permits us to avoid the pitfalls involved in tracing more elusive process effects). We should, though, be aware of its implications, and make sure that our choice is explicit and transparent. A more ambitious goal for the longer term should be to improve our analytical and methodological grasp also on process-generated effects.

To complicate things further, our actual *unit of analysis* is not always what we think it is. Most assessments of regime effectiveness focus on one single regime, considered largely as a stand-alone arrangement. What we in fact observe are, however, often consequences of a connected *complex* of regimes, or—more precisely—the effectiveness of the regime in focus *as amplified or conditioned by the institutional context in which it is embedded.*[9]

To illustrate, assume that we want to determine to what extent the Barents Sea fisheries regime accomplishes its purpose. On closer inspection, we will discover that the Barents Sea fisheries regime is embedded in a much more comprehensive Law of the Sea "super-regime". If we pursue this line of reasoning further, we will see that the Law of the Sea regime is, in turn, embedded in an even more fundamental system of rights and rules, including, inter alia, the principle of state sovereignty. What at first appears to be effects of a regional fisheries regime may, therefore, more appropriately be understood as consequences produced by this multilayered *complex* of regimes. This does not mean that the current practice of assessing single regimes is inherently flawed. Analytically, context can be treated as a *ceteris paribus* condition. Nor should it necessarily lead us to call for greater efforts or more sophisticated techniques for *separating* the effects of the regime in focus from those of the institutional context in which it is embedded. I am not particularly optimistic about the pay-off we can expect from such an exercise. Rather, the most important implication of the argument is simply that in making assessments we should recognise that the consequences we attribute to a particular regime will often be "co-products" in the sense described above. Whenever this is the case, there is no guarantee that a particular regime design that has worked well in one institutional context will work equally well in another. The phenomenon of embeddedness can be ignored only at the risk of erring in causal inference as well as in regime design.

Most regimes produce a *chain* of consequences, and effectiveness can be measured at different points in this chain. To simplify matters, we can draw a distinction between effects on human behaviour (here referred to as *outcome*) and effects on the problem allegedly caused by this behaviour (*impact*). For example, when we are dealing with an environmental regime it makes sense to distinguish between its effect on (target group) behaviour (e.g. industry emissions of polluting substances) and its impact upon the state of the environment. A regime cannot improve the state of the environment without changing human behaviour, but it may well change human behaviour—even as intended—without improving the state of the environment. Similarly, an arms control regime may succeed in limiting the production, purchase or deployment of certain types of weapons without enhancing the security of its members or contributing to a more stable peace. In these and many other cases the score of effectiveness that we would assign to a regime would obviously depend on our choice of entry point; assessments referring to outcomes would show higher effectiveness than assessments of impact.

Impact is, presumably, the ultimate concern of decision-makers and stakeholders. Yet, most assessments of effectiveness focus mainly or exclusively on changes in human behaviour. Good reasons can be given for this order of priorities. One is simply that whatever the ultimate purpose, human behaviour is always the immediate target of regulation. Change in human behaviour is a necessary condition for problem-solving. Moreover, for political scientists thinking about regimes in terms of governance—and even more for lawyers and others focusing on the sub-problem of compliance—success in changing human behaviour as intended is indeed a sensible notion of effectiveness. If success in achieving the behavioural change intended does not bring about improvement in the state of affairs that motivated the parties to establish the regime, the remaining problem is—as seen from this perspective—one of diagnostic error rather than of ineffective governance.

Another reason is that assessing effectiveness becomes increasingly difficult the further out we move in the chain of consequences. One problem is that assessing impact will often require substantial expertise in other disciplines. For example, in order to determine whether LRTAP regulations have improved the health of European forests and lakes, we need to know not only whether they led to reductions in the emissions targeted, but also how changes in emissions of particular substances affect bio-production and other aspects of ecosystem "health". The latter requires expertise in fields of natural science. Moreover, the further out we move, the more difficult it becomes to distinguish effects caused by the regime from "noise" caused by other factors. As we shall see, the causal inference problem can be intricate enough for behavioural change, but difficulties tend to increase substantially if we try to determine impact on complex social or biophysical systems.

Third, by focusing on behavioural change we can study regime effects at the *micro* level. Regimes often exert greater influence on some parties than on others, and such differentials can be as interesting and important as aggregate levels of change.

Finally, while changes in human behaviour can normally be detected at an early stage, impact on complex systems can sometimes be determined only long after the regime has been established. Such time lags seem to be particularly long for some environmental regimes; Nature often takes years—sometimes decades or even centuries—to respond to changes in human behaviour. Observers as well as policy-makers often want to assess regime effects before impact on the problem itself can be determined. This is probably the main reason why assessments of effectiveness most often focus on the immediate target rather than the ultimate purpose.

2.2 The standard

To be able to assign a score of effectiveness to a particular regime we need a standard of evaluation. Such a standard should fulfil two important functions. First, it should define a point or trajectory against which actual performance can (easily) be compared.[10] Second, it should provide a common metric of measurement that can be applied across a wide range of cases. It seems fair to say that the tools we have at present perform the former function better than the latter.

With regard to points of reference, there seems at the most general level to be two principal alternatives. One is the hypothetical state of affairs that would have come about had the regime not existed. This is clearly the standard we have in mind when arguing that "regimes matter" or "improve" a particular state of affairs. The other option is to evaluate achievements against some idea of what constitutes a "good" or "optimal" solution.[11] This is the appropriate standard if we want to know whether and to what extent a problem is in fact "solved" under present arrangements. These two standards can easily be combined, as suggested by Helm and Sprinz (1999; see also Sprinz and Helm, 1999). Their formula (see below) conceptualises the effectiveness of a regime in terms of the extent to which it *in fact* accomplishes all that *can be* accomplished.

> *Actual regime solution—non-co-operative outcome*
> *Collective optimum—non-co-operative outcome*

Before we move on to consider the methodological challenges involved in applying these standards in practice, three remarks seem appropriate to clarify the relationship between them.

Most obviously, they are different in terms of points of reference and may therefore yield different scores. A regime can significantly improve a "bad" situation without achieving anything close to a "perfect" solution. Conversely, if the non-co-operative outcome is "good", the change needed to reach the "collective optimum" will be marginal. The main implication for the field at large is that we need to be able to play with *both* of these notions without confusing them.

Second, although distinctly different, they are not *mutually independent* options. To be more precise: it makes perfect sense to ask whether a regime made a difference without necessarily comparing its performance against some notion of a "good" or "ideal" solution. However, once we ask whether it *improved* the state of affairs, we need an idea of what constitutes "positive" change.[12] In this particular sense, the former standard implies some notion of the latter. Conversely, since the concept of effectiveness implies *attributing* a certain effect to the existence or operation of the regime, rating a regime as effective with reference to some "ideal" solution implies a claim that it makes a significant difference.[13] And that difference is to be measured against the hypothetical situation that would have existed in its absence.

These two observations lead to a third: the collective optimum is clearly the more demanding standard, in two different respects. For one thing, it simply takes more to be "perfect" than to make a positive difference. Secondly, the "optimum" standard confronts us with all the methodological challenges involved in assessing improvement *plus* the intriguing problems of determining what constitutes an "optimal" solution and measuring the distance between that optimum and what is actually accomplished.[14] Against this background, it should be no surprise that most studies of regime effectiveness focus exclusively or at least primarily on improvement over the non-co-operative outcome. This is by no means to say that the notion of "good" or "optimal" solutions is absent from the literature. On the contrary, particularly in policy oriented research it seems to pop up like weed—quite often in unspecified and inverted form, such as statements saying or at least implying that a particular solution "fails to solve" the problem (see e.g. Caldwell, 1990:36f; Susskind, 1994: chapter 2).[15] The point is, though, that only a few studies—such as Helm and Sprinz (1999) and Miles et al. (2002)—"dare" try to use this demanding standard explicitly and systematically for purposes of *comparative* empirical research. Not surprisingly, these few attempts all seem to be vulnerable targets of criticism.

Developing a standard is also a matter of defining a *metric* of measurement that can be used to fill notions of "more", "the same" and "less". If we are to take measurement seriously, there is no escape; there can be no measurement without some metric. Moreover, whenever we engage in comparative or statistical research, we need a yardstick that can be *standardised* and applied across a certain range of cases.

It is abundantly clear that prevailing practice in regime analysis does not aspire to top rating by the canons of scientific measurement. On the positive side, we may note that many single-case studies do measure effects systematically in terms of standardised indicators such as emission volumes, concentration of pollutants, or catch levels. As long as we are studying *intra-regime* change in effectiveness over time, we may legitimately claim to engage in something that can—at least with some generosity—pass as "measurement". The situation becomes much more complicated if we try to compare regimes across issue-areas. We clearly do not have a common "unit of effectiveness" that can be applied to e.g. fisheries, arms control and human rights regimes. Yet, comparisons of regime effectiveness across issue-areas are in fact made, almost as a matter of routine (see e.g. Young, 1999b). Through what kind(s) of intellectual operations can such comparisons be made?

The answer seems to be that we compare regimes in terms of some notion of *relative* effectiveness. The Sprinz and Helms formula makes the logic transparent. In saying that regime X is more effective than regime Y we say that X tapped more of the joint gain potential than Y. Actual and potential achievement are measured in terms of values specific to each particular case; what we compare across regimes are the *proportions* of potential gain that each regime has in fact achieved (or some other notion of relative improvement). This is—in principle—a perfectly sensible operation. Actual practice does, however, leave much to be desired. The problem is not so much that regime scores in most cases are assigned on the basis of crude, qualitative assessments rather than systematic, quantitative measurement. Even the most ardent behaviouralist would have to admit that the problems involved in applying the canons of scientific measurement in this particular field are substantial. Moreover, Hedley Bull's (1966:366) stern warning that the study of international politics can be badly impoverished by a "fetish for measurement" is relevant in this context as well. The main problem is lack of *transparency*; too often we simply cannot determine *how* a particular conclusion has been derived. And without transparency we have no basis for determining whether we are in fact engaged in the same exercise. Before investing additional energy in searching for quantitative indicators or in computing precise coefficients, we should try to do better in terms of specifying the standards and procedures we use in assessing effectiveness.

2.3 Operational procedures

Let us assume that we know the state of affairs that obtains with the regime in place, and that we have some metric that enables us to assess effectiveness in crude ordinal-scale terms, i.e., to distinguish "less" from "more". The remaining challenge, then, is to determine whether, in what respects, and to what degree the state of affairs that we observe with the regime in existence differs from the hypothetical state of affairs that would have come about in its absence (and, perhaps, also from an "ideal" solution).

This is a question that can be answered only through counterfactual analysis, in two steps. First, we have to determine what *"order"* would have existed in the absence of the present regime. The default option is to assume that the order that existed immediately prior to the establishment of the present regime would have continued unchanged. There is nothing substantively compelling about this assumption; it is, for example, not at all obvious that if the present "ozone regime" had not been in force we would have been stuck with the previous order. Nor is it obvious that the alternative order would necessarily have been "weaker" or less effective; the closest competitor may well in some cases be a stronger and more effective regime. It is, however, a convenient and often plausible assumption, and I will adopt it here for exactly those reasons. That leaves me free to concentrate on the second step, which is that of determining what would have happened under the previous order.[16]

There are two main categories of methodological approaches to this latter question. One relies on simple *extrapolation*. The key assumption here is that the future will be a linear extension of the past. This assumption is most often specified in terms of *trends*; the direction and rate of change is assumed to be constant.[17] This assumption permits us to derive the state of affairs that would have occurred at time t_{+n} had the previous order continued, as a linear extension of the trend observed during (the last years of) its existence (period $t_o - t_{-n}$). What makes this approach attractive is its combination of operational feasibility and intuitive plausibility. With appropriate time series data, linear extrapolation is technically a very straightforward exercise. Moreover, most systems of activity seem in fact to be fairly stable most of the time. This suggests that as long as it is used cautiously for short time spans, linear extrapolation should more often than not produce plausible estimates. The obvious problem with this method is that it is devoid of theoretical substance; it specifies no driving forces or feedback mechanisms. In fact, the underlying "model" has *time* as its only independent variable. This is clearly not a satisfactory solution. Even though most systems are fairly stable most of the time, non-linearity and inflection

METHODOLOGICAL CHALLENGES

points are too important phenomena to be ruled out by definition (see Doran, 1999).

The only alternative that enables us to deal systematically with non-linearity is an approach that builds on some kind of model identifying what we assume to be the main determinants of change and stability in the system of activities we study. If we are dealing with a pollution control regime such a model should, ideally, identify the critical factors assumed to affect emissions of the substances targeted, and specify how these factors—individually and jointly—determine the volume of emissions. In terms of theoretical merit, this kind of approach is clearly superior to that of linear extrapolation. It is, however, also a more demanding approach; constructing and applying a model that meets both of the two requirements specified above can be a tall order, often requiring expertise well beyond the discipline of political science (or, for that matter, law or economics).

When that challenge becomes overwhelming—as it most often does—two less demanding options are available. One is to look for model-based estimates that have already been made by competent experts in the particular field. In a number of cases—the emission of greenhouse gases being one example—fairly sophisticated business-as-usual scenarios are available. The other option is to simplify things, i.e. come up with a recipe that remains true to the basic logic of counterfactual analysis but redefines the task so that it becomes manageable. Such a redefinition of the task involves a subtle change of perspective. Instead of asking what consequences would have flowed from a continuation of the previous order, researchers pursuing this path ask what *changes* (if any) have been brought about by the present regime. To answer the latter question they must first of all determine in what respects and to what degree the present regime differs from the previous order. This is the easy part. Then they must determine the consequences of this marginal *difference* in institutional properties for target group behaviour and/or the "health of the patient". The latter requires first of all that we can identify the causal *mechanisms* or pathways through which a regime—or particular properties of a regime—*can* influence behaviour.[18] Regime analysis has made significant progress on that front over the last decade (see e.g. Haas, Keohane and Levy, 1993; and Young, 1999a). Identifying and describing mechanisms is not enough, however; we must also determine what consequences were in fact produced by these mechanisms in a particular case. As we shall see in a moment, the latter ultimately takes us back to "square one".

This approach has, at least on first thought, some very attractive features. First of all, for the political scientist it shifts the game to "home turf" in the sense that it focuses directly on the significance of *institutions*. Second, it seems to provide a most welcome shortcut in the sense that it leads us straight to the consequences of the *change* in institutional arrangements brought about by the establishment of the present regime. On second thought, however, we realise that the latter holds true only if we assume that everything else remains constant. And that assumption would bring us right back into the linear extrapolation mode of analysis that we tried to transcend. Recognising that this is where the "shortcut" in fact leads, students normally move on to examine changes in *other* variables that might significantly affect behaviour or the state of the problem itself. To be able to do so systematically we would, though, need at least a crude theory-based model identifying the main independent variables and specifying their general impact. In the absence of such a model, the fallback strategy seems to be to engage in backward reasoning, centred on two key questions: (1) what *else* has changed? (2) Can the changes in those *other* variables plausibly account for the change observed in human behaviour or in the "health of the patient"? This is a perfectly sensible approach, and it may well be the best feasible solution in many cases. In current practice, however, it often boils down to a low-priority exercise in ad hoc reasoning. In that format it can provide only "counterfactuals light". One may also wonder whether a strategy that focuses so much attention on pathways through which *institutions* (can) affect behaviour leaves the student prone to underestimate the influence of *other* factors. The strength of the strategy described in this paragraph lies clearly in its contribution to our understanding of *how* institutions (can) affect behaviour—not in distinguishing the effects they actually produce from consequences caused by other factors.[19]

3. EXPLAINING REGIME EFFECTIVENESS

However we conceptualise and measure "effectiveness", some regimes no doubt qualify for higher scores than others. As important as assessing effectiveness is therefore the task of predicting and explaining variance. This is not the place to review or evaluate the attempts that have been made to address the latter question,[20] but a few words about the methodological challenges involved and the main options available are in order.

Any attempt at explaining variance must first of all try to identify the critical "determinants" of effectiveness. Previous research has identified a wide range of independent variables that seem to have made a significant difference in some particular case(s). To simplify things, we can categorise most of these variables into three main clusters: the nature of the *problem*, characteristics of the *group of parties*, and properties of the *regime itself*.

Few would dispute the general proposition that some problems are harder to solve than others. The challenge is to specify precisely what makes a problem "difficult" to solve, and to determine to what extent specific problems in fact exhibit these features. Somewhat different answers to the former question have been suggested (see e.g. Efinger and Zürn, 1990; Stein, 1982; Underdal, 2002; Zürn 1992),[21] but these answers seem at least largely compatible. Even though further work is needed to refine distinctions and test related propositions, it seems fair to say that we have at this stage at least some useful analytic tools and a fair amount of substantive knowledge about what distinguishes "difficult" from "easy" problems.

A second path of research departs from the assumption that some groups of actors have greater *capacity* for collective action than other groups. The challenge here becomes to determine more precisely which group characteristics enhance that capacity, and to what extent particular groups possess these characteristics. Again, somewhat different suggestions have been made—some playing with the inclusive concept of "social capital" (in particular Ostrom, 1995), others focusing on more specific aspects such as formal organisation (e.g. Wettestad, 1998), overall "closeness" and "friendliness" of relations, the distribution of power, and the supply of instrumental leadership.[22]

Finally, effectiveness depends to some degree on properties of the regime itself. For example, some regimes provide stronger (selective) incentives for co-operative behaviour than others. Some contribute through providing procedures, arenas or other facilities that enable parties to develop a base of consensual knowledge and shared beliefs. Other attributes of regimes—or, to be more precise, of *perceptions* of regimes—that can enhance effectiveness include legitimacy and normative compellence (Franck, 1990; Stokke and Vidas, 1998). To the policy-maker, regime characteristics are particularly interesting dimensions since they can, at least in principle, be deliberately manipulated and used as instruments. If the study of regime effectiveness is to provide important inputs to praxis, it will have to do so first and foremost through producing knowledge that can be used as a basis for *designing* effective institutions.

Now, the significance of problem "malignancy", group capacity, and regime characteristics cannot be determined by treating them as mutually independent factors. Beyond a fairly high level of generality, capacity can be defined and determined only with reference to a particular function or type of problems. Similarly, to be able to design a regime so that it effectively induces or fosters effective problem-solving one needs to know what kind of problem it has to cope with and the state of the group it is supposed to serve. The student of regime effectiveness is, in other words, faced with a web of contingencies (indicated in Figure 2.2) that calls for careful *differentiation* of statements about "conducive" regime properties or group characteristics. What works well in one context may produce very different results in another context. There is nothing peculiar about this; medical doctors, policy-makers and many others work with contingent recipes all the time, as a matter of routine. Also students of international regimes are, of course, familiar with contingency relationships. Even so, it seems fair to admit that much analytical and empirical work remains to be done before we can present accumulated knowledge about regime effectiveness succinctly in those terms.

```
              Regime
                /\
               /  \
              /    \
   Problem   /_____\   Group (of members)
```

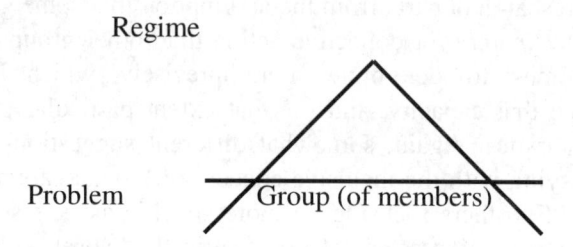

Figure 2.2. *The triangular complex of determinants.*

The important question in the context of this paper is whether this image of a causal *complex* has implications for research strategies and designs. The answer seems to be yes; at the very least it suggests that the methodological challenge before us can best be described as one of understanding a particular kind of *interplay*. If the impact of one factor is contingent upon one or more other variables, the familiar task of isolating the influence of one factor by controlling for others must be supplemented by an approach inviting us to express effectiveness as a function of *configurations* of conditions. The latter does not necessarily favour one particular *technique* of analysis over another—although something can be said in favour of Ragin's (1987) claim that Boolean logic is particularly well suited for identifying causal conjunctures. It does, however, generate a suit of other suggestions—first and foremost for the way we specify our research questions and interpret our findings, but also for the way we think about different methodological approaches. Let me conclude this section by making two observations pertaining to the latter aspect.

First of all, it seems that our ability to deal with causal complexes can be enhanced if we can find creative ways of combining methodological strategies that are sometimes seen as competing and embedded in incompatible epistemological positions. Among these strategies are intensive diachronic tracing of causal mechanisms and pathways, extensive comparative or statistical analysis designed to reveal patterns of variance, and deductive and quasi-experimental techniques enabling us to explore the basic "logic" of situations and games. Instead of engaging in the sometimes heated controversy over the relative merits of "qualitative", "quantitative" and "formal" methods, I take the ecumenical view that each of these strategies has its own distinct comparative advantages and provides opportunities that the others can not offer, at least not to the same degree. The study of regime effectiveness can make good use of them all. Furthermore, I see these approaches as building on the same basic logic of scientific inquiry, meaning that the very substantial differences that separate them do not constitute fundamental incompatibilities preventing us from combining them (King, Keohane and Verba, 1994:4).

There can be no doubt that we still have quite some distance to go before we can claim to have utilised the methodological repertoire of the social sciences to its full potential in this field. At present, the study of international regimes is characterised by a pronounced tendency towards polarisation. Nearly all of the empirical research reported so far is in the mode of intensive process tracing, examining one or a few cases in depth. At the opposite end of the spectre, we have a fair amount of formal game theory analysis. In between we have lots of almost empty space. To be sure, both in-depth case studies and the deductive analysis of games have contributed substantially to our accumulated fund of knowledge about international regimes, and will most likely continue to do in the future. Yet, there are important functions that neither of them is well suited to perform. For example, in order to determine whether a particular conclusion based on the study of one single case can be generalised to a wider range of regimes we would need more extensive and rigorous comparative or statistical analysis. Similarly, in order to examine systematically how particular regime characteristics—e.g. decision rules, particularly rules not currently in use – influence effectiveness we could make good use of simulations. Both of these approaches have their own limitations, and neither of them can *replace* those that dominate the field today. They can, however, fill gaps. For that reason alone, the appropriate amount of investment in such supplementary modes of analysis should be significantly above zero.

A somewhat related observation is that the current rate of knowledge accumulation in the field seems to be rather low. The reasons are obvious: in the absence of a common explanatory model, a common conceptual framework, and inter-calibrated tools of measurement it can be very hard to relate the findings reported in one study to those described in another. Although some progress is being made, at least on the first and second of these fronts, I see little hope of *fundamental* change in the near future.[23] This suggests that we should explore less demanding strategies for getting more mileage out of our growing reservoir of case studies. In this regard, there may be a useful role for systematic *re*-analysis of observations and findings reported in a set of existing studies. The problems involved are substantial, and building from scratch may well turn out to be a more cost-effective strategy. Before we draw the latter conclusion, however, opportunities as well as obstacles deserve to be systematically explored.

4. A CONCLUDING REFLECTION

This paper has probably done a better job in describing problems than in suggesting constructive solutions. This discrepancy can safely be taken as an indication that the author himself has more hard homework to do. There is, however, also another plausible interpretation, namely that there is no quick fix to our methodological malaise. The problems we are coping with are multifaceted and complex, and the recipe for progress may well be equally complex. At several junctures we have seen that progress in dealing with methodological challenges will require progress in developing more precise conceptual tools and a better understanding of complex causal pathways. In this sense, constructive use of methodological tools is intimately linked with theory development. This makes the task ahead all the more demanding.

Acknowledgement: This chapter has benefited substantially from comments and suggestions from participants in the Oslo workshop, 19-20 November, 1999. I am particularly grateful to Albert Weale for taking the time to provide detailed written comments.

NOTES

1 In this paper I use the word "function" to refer to any role or task by which the observer assesses effectiveness. The "function" assigned by the observer may or may not correspond to the "official purpose" of the regime, nor to the private concerns or goals of individual parties. The default option is, though, to assess the effectiveness of a regime with reference to its official purpose, and to assume that this purpose is also what in fact motivated its members to create and maintain it.
2 A cynic might even argue that the contribution of international regimes to net social welfare tends to be constant and close to zero (see e.g. Johansen, 1979): whatever may be gained in terms of more stringent rules and regulations tends to be offset by lower levels of compliance and higher transaction costs.
3 In particular, "constitutive" effectiveness seems remote from the concept that I have introduced here. As defined by Young (1994:147-8) a regime is effective in the "constitutive" sense if "...its formation gives rise to a social practice involving the expenditure of time, energy, and resources on the part of its members". Expenditure of time and effort means that members find it worthwhile to participate, so presumably they

get something back. In itself, however, the notion of effectiveness as (transaction) expenditures is likely to appear peculiar to anyone assessing regimes as problem-solving tools, and to economists in particular.

4 Besides, at the micro level the situation is quite different. Even though the level of precision still leaves something to be desired, most of the recent projects that I know of have a reasonably clear idea of what they are talking about.

5 The word "constraints" usually carries negative associations, suggesting that actors are deprived of one or more attractive options. I use it here, however, with no such implications of a "welfare loss". Particularly in situations characterised by fear that accommodative moves can be exploited by others, or that one's partners lack information or knowledge required to understand what is in their own best interest, constraints will often provide positive assurance that a preferred option can safely be chosen. In such circumstances, constraints enable parties to switch to a more preferred course of action that they otherwise would have found too risky.

6 As Downs, Rocke, and Barsoom (1996) have shown, compliance is – except for benign problems of co-ordination – likely to be inversely related to the amount of behavioral change required.

7 As defined here, robustness has an internal as well as an external dimension. A regime is robust in the former sense if it exhibits a pronounced tendency to return to some equilibrium state in the wake of perturbations or distortions brought about by its own operations. An international fisheries regime that is able to weather a period of severe internal conflict and defection generated or fueled by its own regulations, and then resume "normal" functioning, meets this requirement. For good reasons, external challenges seem, though, to be the principal concern; Hasenclever, Mayer, and Rittberger (1996) even define "robustness" in terms of "exogenous" challenges.

8 For example, the study of process-generated stakes and effects can offer interesting suggestions for the design of arenas and procedures, and for the management of negotiations and other regime-related processes.

9 For a finer set of distinctions between different kinds of regime linkages, see Young (1996). I use the word "embedded" in a somewhat looser sense here, including also what Young refers to as "nesting".

10 In this formulation the standard supervenes upon the putative consequences, meaning that we first ask what consequences have resulted and then ask how valuable those consequences are. A standard may, however, also guide the analysis of consequences. I am grateful to Albert Weale for helping me see this distinction.

11 As the formulation above suggests, this option actually includes a range of somewhat different standards. I use the words "good" and "optimal" to indicate that the standard may be defined in terms of "satisficing" as well as "maximizing". To complicate things further, there are different concepts of "maximization", adapted to different decision rules. What they all have in common, though, is that they compare actual results against some notion of the "best" solution that could have been accomplished.

12 I am grateful to Olav S. Stokke for helping me see this link clearly. Arguably, the notion of "improvement" implies even an idea of an "optimal" solution. In many situations, change in what is at the outset a positive direction can go "too far". If it does, it can no longer be considered "improvement".

13 One can, of course, compare the state of affairs obtained with the regime in place with the "collective optimum" or some other notion of a "good" solution, but in itself the result of that exercise tells us nothing about regime effectiveness. Assessing effectiveness involves causal inference.

14 In generalised form, the same observation applies also to less ambitious notions of a "good" or "satisfactory" solution. Shifting from "maximising" to "satisficing" does not make the standard less demanding as an analytic tool for the researcher.
15 Such statements at least imply a notion of what it would take to "solve" a problem; without knowing "x", we cannot conclude that something is "non-x".
16 Counterfactual analysis may well require further specification of conditions. What Helm and Sprinz (1999) refer to as the non-co-operative outcome may be sensitive to a number of more precise assumptions about e.g. the amount of information available to the actors and their time horizons ("the shadow of the future"). I am grateful to Jon Hovi for helping me see this aspect more clearly.
17 Alternatively, one can assume that the state of affairs that existed immediately prior to the establishment of the regime would have continued unchanged. Except when we are dealing with systems that has a consistent record of high stability, and examine very short time spans, this is, however, a less plausible assumption.
18 This is a distinct and important contribution that the other approaches do not provide.
19 This applies to research focusing on causal mechanisms and pathways more generally; the focus is on how a particularly mechanism works rather than on what it produces. The two are, of course, related, but answers to the "what" question cannot be inferred (only) from information about "how". Even the most detailed and accurate description of how an engine produces energy does not in itself tell us whether or how far it moved the vessel.
20 Excellent state of the art reviews are already available; see e.g. Levy, Young and Zürn (1995), and Hasenclever, Mayer and Rittberger (1997).
21 For a critique of two of these scales, see Young (2000, chapter 3).
22 In addition, various types of resources (e.g. financial) and capabilities (e.g. technological) can, of course, be important components of capacity (see e.g. VanDeveer, 2000).
23 Arguably, such disparity may have advantages as well, particularly in terms of providing a fertile ground for innovation. On the other hand, it may be instructive to compare the situation in the case study literature with that in formal game theory analysis, where a common analytic framework makes it much easier to "compare notes" and build on the work done by others.

REFERENCES

Aggarwal, V. (1985) *Liberal Protectionism: The International Politics of the Organized Textile Trade,* University of California Press, Berkeley.
Bernauer, T. (1995) International Institutions and the Environment, *International Organization* 49: 351–377.
Bull, H. (1966) International Theory: The Case for a Classical Approach, *World Politics* 38: 361–377.
Caldwell, L. K. (1990) *International Environmental Policy,* Duke University Press, Durham.
Donnelly, J. (1986) International Human Rights: A Regime Analysis, *International Organization* 40: 599–642.
Doran, C. F. (1999) Why Forecasts Fail: The Limits and Potential of Forecasting in International Relations and Economics, *International Studies Review* 1: 11–41.
Downs, G. W., Rocke, D. M. and Barsoom P.N. (1996) Is the Good News about Compliance Good News about Cooperation? *International Organization* 50: 379–406.
Efinger, M. and Zürn, M. (1990) Explaining Conflict Management in East-West Relations:

A Quantitative Test of Problem-Structural Typologies, in V. Rittberger (ed.) *International Regimes in East-West Politics*, Pinter, London.
Easton, D. (1965) *A Systems Analysis of Political Life,* John Wiley & Sons, New York.
Franck, T. M. (1990) *The Power of Legitimacy among Nations,* Oxford University Press, New York.
Goldmann, K. (1988) *Change and Stability in Foreign Policy,* Princeton University Press.
Haas, P. M., Keohane, R. O. and Levy, M. A. (eds.) (1993) *Institutions for the Earth: Sources of Effective International Environmental Protection,* MIT Press, Cambridge, MA.
Haggard, S. and Simmons, B.A. (1987) Theories of International Regimes, *International Organization* 41: 491–517.
Hasenclever, A, Mayer, P. and Rittberger, V. (1993) *Justice, Equality, and the Robustness of International Regimes,* Tübingen University, Tübingen, Tübinger Arbeitspapiere zur Internationalen Politik und Friedensforschung 25.
Hasenclever, A., Mayer, P. and Rittberger, V. (1997) *Theories of International Regimes,* Cambridge University Press.
Helm, C. and Sprinz, D.F. (1998) *Measuring the Effectiveness of International Environmental Regimes,* Potsdam Institute for Climate Impact Research, Potsdam, PIK Report 52.
Johansen, L. (1979) The Bargaining Society and the Inefficiency of Bargaining, Kyklos 32: 497–522.
King, G., Keohane, R. O. and Verba, S.(1994) *Designing Social Inquiry: Scientific Inference in Qualitative Research,* Princeton University Press.
Levy, M. A., Young, O. R. and Zürn, M. (1995) The Study of International Regimes, *European Journal of International Relations* 1: 267–330.
Miles, E. L. et al. 2002. *Environmental Regime Effectiveness: Confronting Theory with Evidence,* MIT Press, Cambridge, MA.
Morgenthau, H. J. (1985) *Politics Among Nations,* Sixth edition, revised by K.W. Thompson, Knopf, New York.
Ostrom, E. (1995) Constituting Social Capital and Collective Action, in R. O. Keohane and E. Ostrom (eds.) *Local Commons and Global Interdependence,* Sage, CA.
Ragin, C. (1987) *The Comparative Method,* University of California Press, Berkeley.
Sand, P. H. (ed.) (1992) *The Effectiveness of International Environmental Agreements: A Survey of Existing Legal Instruments,* Grotius Publications, Cambridge.
Sprinz, D. F., and Helm, C. (1999) The Effect of Global Environmental Regimes: A Measurement Concept, *International Political Science Review* 20: 359 – 69.
Stein, A. (1982) Coordination and Collaboration: Regimes in an Anarchic World, *International Organization* 36: 299–324.
Stokke, O. S. and Vidas, D. (eds.) 1996. *Governing the Antarctic: The Effectiveness and Legitimacy of the Antarctic Treaty System,* Cambridge University Press, Cambridge.
Susskind, L. E. (1994) *Environmental Diplomacy: Negotiating More Effective Global Agreements,* Oxford University Press, New York and Oxford.
Tetlock, P. E. and Belkin, A. (eds.) (1996) *Counterfactual Thought Experiments in World Politics,* Princeton University Press.
Underdal, A. (2002) One Question, Two Answers, in E. L. Miles, et al., *Environmental Regime Effectiveness: Confronting Theory with Evidence,* MIT Press, Cambridge, MA.
Underdal, A. (1994) Progress in the Absence of Substantive Joint Decisions? In T. Hanisch, (ed.) *Climate Change and the Agenda for Research,* Westview Press, Boulder, CO.
Underdal, A. (1992) The Concept of Regime "Effectiveness," *Cooperation and Conflict* 27: 227–240.

VanDeveer, S. (2000) Protecting Europe's Seas, *Environment* 42: 10–26.
Vogler, J. (1995) *The Global Commons: A Regime Analysis*, John Wiley & Sons, Chichester.
Wettestad, J. (1998) *Designing Effective Environmental Regimes*, Edward Elgar, Cheltenham.
Young, O. R. (2000) *Governance in World Affairs*, Cornell University Press, Ithaca, New York.
Young, O. R. (ed.) (1999a) *The Effectiveness of International Environmental Regimes: Causal Connections and Behavioural Mechanisms*, MIT Press, Cambridge, MA.
Young, O. R. (1999b) Hitting the Mark, *Environment* 41: 20–29.
Young, O. R. (1996) Institutional Linkages in International Society: Polar Perspectives, *Global Governance* 2: 1–23.
Young, O. R. (1994) *International Governance*, Cornell University Press, Ithaca, New York.
Zürn, M. (1992) *Interessen und Institutionen in der internationalen Politik: Grundlegung und Andwendung des situationsstrukturellen Ansatzes*, Leske +Budrich, Opladen.

Chapter 3

CASE STUDIES OF THE EFFECTIVENESS OF INTERNATIONAL ENVIRONMENTAL REGIMES
Balancing Textbook Ideals and Feasibility Concerns

STEINAR ANDRESEN AND JØRGEN WETTESTAD
The Fridtjof Nansen Institute

1. INTRODUCTION[1]

In the paper presented at the conference on "Methodological Approaches to the Study of Regime Consequences" we focused mainly on our experiences acquired over more than a decade as case study workers on the effectiveness of international environmental regimes. Although we have not been among the chief architects conceptually or theoretically in this field, we believe that few others have as much experience in testing out the fruitfulness of various perspectives through case study work. It could be useful, therefore, to sum up in an explicit manner some of the lessons we have learnt on this long journey. Moreover, we believe that an *interaction* between "theorists" and "practitioners" who try out the theories is crucial in advancing the study of regime effectiveness.

In section two of this report we will deal with the principal challenges of case study research in this field, related to issues such as case selection, causation, data-gathering, regime-linkages and qualitative versus quantitative approaches. The third and main section of this report is a chronological journey through seven projects dealing with various aspects of regime effectiveness. As far as possible our experiences are related to the methodological issues and challenges identified in section two. This review places more emphasis on the more or less conscious methodological choices than on the actual findings of the projects discussed. In this account we will also reflect on how some related projects have dealt with these common challenges.

In the final section (four) we will contrast our approach with the "textbook ideals" introduced in section two. In other words, according to the textbook how *should* we in fact have conducted our research? As will be seen, there is a considerable discrepancy between these two approaches. The question is, however, how close can we get to the ideal under real-world circumstances, and what can we gain in extra insight? If we were to start again, would we have conducted research in a totally different manner? What are the trade-offs between the ideals and real-world constraints such as time and costs and finally, what are the implications of deviating from the textbook wisdom?

2. "TEXTBOOK IDEALS": A BRIEF SUMMARY OF SOME PRINCIPAL CHALLENGES.[2]

In this section we will briefly address certain principal challenges confronted by every researcher entering the complex terrain of regime effectiveness. The first challenge pertains to the issue of *case selection*. Careful selection can help us maximise what Bernauer and Mitchell (1998) call "internal" and "external validity." Internal validity involves making "within-case" causal relationships as plausible as possible. External validity has to with the explicit identification of "the boundaries between the population of cases with which the findings can be validly generalised and beyond which valid generalisations are unlikely" (op. cit. p. 8). Since high internal validity can be seen as a necessary condition for high external validity, and since there is often a need for a trade-off between these ideals, much can be said for letting internal validity take precedence over external validity. How, then, are cases to be selected in order that internal validity be maximised? Some general principles can be outlined: first, one should focus initially on the theory and select empirical cases later. This will contribute to a reduced risk of achieving biased results. Second, look for cases where the values of the independent variable(s) vary, and third, look for more cases than explanatory variables. This makes it easier to hold specific, exogenous (control) variables constant and generally enhances analytical oversight and control. A fourth important recommendation is to try to find particularly "difficult" or "easy" cases in which the control variables either make it very unlikely or very likely that the explanatory variable will produce the theoretically predicted value of the dependent variable.

Thus, although selecting cases to hold the value of certain variables constant increases internal validity, it also automatically limits the range of cases to which one can validly refer (external validity). This paradox can be reduced and external validity increased by using the "difficult"/"easy" case logic mentioned above. Moreover, additional case studies can be conducted in which the control variable has a different value. Finally, by linking own cases and research to past and ongoing research (programs), the logic of literal or theoretical replication can collectively produce results with a wider relevance.

In addition to selecting cases and key variables, a second principal challenge pertains to *operationalisation and data gathering*. A ground rule here is to record and report explicitly and openly the process by which data is generated in order to make data and analyses as replicable as possible. Variables should be defined and operationalised so that the data relate to the theoretical constructs as accurately as possible. However, because appropriate, reliable and observable indicators of complex conceptual variables often prove difficult to find, and this is certainly the case in the regime effectiveness field, it is often necessary to identify various indicators and multiple proxies. In order to give such indicators substance, various types of data should be collected and utilised. This includes reviews of primary and secondary literature, structured or open interviews and surveys, direct or participant observation, or the collection of quantitative data. In practice, due to resource and time constraints, researchers will often rely heavily or entirely on some of these types of data and the strengths and weaknesses of such data "skews" should be explicitly discussed.

When cases have been selected, hypotheses formulated, and data gathered in the process of analysis, it is a central challenge not only to establish correlation between variables but also to make *sound causal inferences*. This was touched upon in the discussion on case selection, where such selection can serve to strengthen internal validity. But case selection is only part of the picture. Several other aspects and tools need to be mentioned. Central tools in going "beyond correlation" are process-tracing of causal pathways and the careful examination of rival hypotheses. The first of these closely related tools is, by nature, qualitative and not least useful in tracing the paths of institutions' influence on regime effectiveness. The second tool can be utilised either in a qualitative and intensive manner, or in a quantitative manner (relying on statistical techniques). Used qualitatively, the method of counterfactual reasoning can be helpful. For instance, had a regime commitment not been adopted, would other factors like economic fluctuations and energy switching nevertheless have led to reduced emissions?

This touches on an ongoing discussion among students of international relations relating to the use of *qualitative* versus *quantitative* methods. In their seminal contribution on the issue, King, Keohane and Verba (1994) advocate the many merits of the quantitative approach. Others argue more strongly in favour of the qualitative approach. If conducted properly, the key challenge of trying to demonstrate causation may well be done by the soft-case study approach.² One illustrative example of the applicability of the case-story approach under real world circumstances is the practice used in a court of law. "In such proceedings judges or juries are asked to make judgements about causation and intent based quite literally on a single case." (McKeown, 1999:167). To a large extent, the approach used depends upon what you want to know more about and both approaches have shortcomings as well as assets.

A final methodological challenge refers to *the unit of analysis*. Studies of the effectiveness of international regimes will easily zoom in on how individual regimes deal with individual problems. Understanding this is a tall order in itself. However, as environmental problems are often interrelated in intricate ways, and policies adopted in one regime context affect policy-making in other regime contexts, a narrow one-regime – one-problem focus may easily lead us to ignore important questions of interplay, context and linkages. (Young, 1999b, Stokke, 2000)

In the next section we will relate these methodological challenges to the manner in which we have conducted our work on effectiveness of international environmental regimes.

3. "INEFFECTIVE STRUGGLING WITH EFFECTIVENESS?" SOME MAIN PRACTICAL CHALLENGES

3.1 Point of Departure: Ignoring Oran's Caveat...

In 1982 Oran Young wrote: "... there are severe limitations to what we can expect from efforts to evaluate regimes in terms of the outcome they produce... this suggests the importance of giving some consideration to non-consequentalist approaches to the evaluation of regimes." (Young, 1982:138). In a recent review of the status in this research field, he puts far more emphasis on remaining challenges and uncertainties than on the considerable achievements made so far (Young, 2000). Considering this status after a decade of research by a number of able scholars, maybe he was right? Maybe all of us should have followed his early advice and never embarked upon this avenue. For our part, we are glad that he, as well as the rest of us, did *not* listen to this early word of caution. Our knowledge today is perhaps not as extensive as we expected naïvely a decade ago, but we surely know a lot more than if we had never embarked upon this effort. For example, we are now in a much better position to correct someone unqualified who boasts of the success of a regime. Even if our optimism has been naïve, it has also been productive. If nothing else, it has got us involved in a number of interesting research projects, as will be seen below.

3.2 Overview of Relevant Effectiveness Projects

We have been involved in the following projects that deal, more or less directly, with the effectiveness of international environmental and resource regimes:

1. Miles et al. Phase I 1989-90, "Science, Technology and International Collaboration: Conditions for Effective Global and Regional Action Concerning the Problem of Global Climate Change"; not finished as planned.
2. Related to Miles et al I: FNI effectiveness project (with Underdal) 1990-92 (with some later outputs).
3. Project at the International Institute for Applied Systems Analysis (IIASA) on The Implementation and Effectiveness of International Environmental Commitments (IEC), 1993-96.
4. Project led by Underdal and Hanf on the domestic implementation of acid rain commitments, 1993-95.
5. Project on Science and Politics in International Environmental Regimes, CICERO-FNI collaboration, phase I: 1993-94; phase II: 1997-1999.
6. The Effectiveness of Multilateral Environmental Agreements (MEAs), Nordic project, 1994-95.[3]
7. Project on the Designing of Effective Environmental Regimes, carried out by Wettestad, on and off 1993-98.
8. Miles et al. phase II, 1994-2000.[4]

Almost all our work within these projects has been case-study oriented. Arild Underdal has provided most of the intellectual capital to the majority of these projects. While he discusses the overall perspective in this book, a more practical "street-level" story may bring some useful complementary insights.

3.3 The Initial Miles Project': Where It All Began...[5]

It all started with a project initiated by Professor Ed Miles called "Science, Technology and International Collaboration: Conditions for Effective Global and Regional Action concerning the Problem of Global Climate Change".[6] Two main project phases were envisaged, with the first one summing up main lessons from the field, and the second and main phase applying these lessons to the then fresh and exciting issue of how to address global warming. Based on these lessons, how should the climate regime be designed?[7] In terms of the key concept of effectiveness, although the project title talked about "effective action", it seems right to say that we – like virtually all others at the time – started out with a perspective geared largely towards *outputs* produced by regimes. This probably explains why "level of collaboration" figured as a central dependent variable in the early project talks. Much time within this project was spent on achieving a shared understanding of the basic model – i.e. main variables, relationships between variables, the formulation of hypotheses, and how the variables and hypotheses were based on various strands of International Relations theory.[8] The only methodological issue, in a strict sense, that was discussed in some depth during the initial project meetings referred to *case selection*. The need to cover as many and varied cases as possible was stressed by the initiator of the project. The main criteria for assigning research work were existence and availability of competence: which regimes had the various collaborators already conducted work on or had fairly easy access to relevant data on. Feasibility and pragmatism were the keywords.

In line with textbook ideals, we started out with a main emphasis on theory. However, with the benefit of hindsight, we did not pay enough attention to the link between theory and case selection, apart from aiming at a large number of (varied) regimes. Theoretically, as well as empirically, the project was very ambitious, as is often the case when real-world constraints do not receive sufficient attention. As it turned out, the original Miles et al. project did not obtain US financial support.[9] A more modest and simplified version of the *first* part of the initial project is now near completion (see Miles et al. II) – more than a decade after it started…

For their part, the FNI team obtained a modest two-year grant to start on a simplified version of the eclectic and comprehensive analytical approach presented in the common project note. The basic conceptual work was developed by Arild Underdal in several draft notes and the main ideas were circulated as a working paper in 1990. The dependent variable ("effectiveness") had here been developed further than in the initial project note and the independent variables had been simplified through the two key concepts of "problem structure" and "problem solving capacity".[10] This seminal model and concepts have no doubt continued to influence much FNI work on this subject up to the present. Moreover, we think it is also safe to conclude that these basic early ideas have had significant impact over time on the thinking of large parts of the "effectiveness community". Again, the textbook was followed by the elaboration of theory as a first step, and this time a seemingly simpler and more unified approach paved the way for the empirical research.[11] However, when we started selecting cases in 1990, we sinned against the textbook ideal again, since our case selection primarily grew out of the pragmatic thinking of the Seattle-Oslo project context. It was *not* extensive discussions over internal and external validity that formed the basis for selecting the five cases to be studied: The whaling regime, the acid rain regime, the Paris Convention on land-based marine pollution (PARCON), the Oslo Dumping Convention (OSCON), and the international regime to conserve the marine resources in the Southern Ocean (CCAMLR). The first three were selected because we were very familiar with these while the two remaining regimes were new to us. In general, not much systematic research had been undertaken on these regimes at the time. Moreover, we saw some interesting differences between them. For instance, two of them dealt with marine living resources, three of them with the environment; two of them were global and three were regional; some were rather inaccessible and "closed", while others were more "open"; and we also expected disparities in terms of effectiveness.

The issues of data collection and causation are closely linked in this case since real-world working conditions and perhaps intellectual limitations did not allow much in-depth case study research.[12] Somewhat paradoxically, a master's dissertation on the (North Sea) Oslo Commission was the only case study that could fully take on the formidable empirical and analytical challenges presented in the analytical structure. In terms of main sources and data, the authors of this chapter largely used second-hand sources; primarily books and articles. Although some first-hand sources from regime meetings etc. were consulted, this vast array of information was not systematically utilised. These sources were complemented by a "semi-structured" questionnaire sent out to "expert panels" consisting of regime parties and a select group of more independent observers (including NGOs and scientists).[13] In addition, a few interviews were conducted. Maybe the single most important shortcoming was that most cases in this early phase were not detailed enough to allow us to address the crucial question of causation in a fairly meaningful manner.

Finally, a few words on some of the problems we encountered when trying to apply the theoretical approach. Although the approach was elegant as well as useful, all concepts were not easy to apply. This was especially true for one of the effectiveness indicators, "distance to collective optimum". As has been pointed out quite recently, this criterion is not easy to apply, even under ideal circumstances (Young, 2000), and with our limited data, application was somewhat random and ad hoc. Another unperceived aspect of the theoretical approach was that it devoted little explicit attention to the role of domestic institutions and policy.[14] This was possibly due to the fact that Underdal's paper was geared towards understanding the negotiation of effective solutions, naturally downplaying the role of the domestic scene

(Underdal, 1990). But other factors also contributed to our "domestic neglect". Important implementation processes had just started in several of the regimes we studied. As some of these regimes were less than a decade old, the ink had only just dried on important protocols and declarations Thus, some of the cases were premature in terms of tracing behavioural impacts – which of course should have been given more consideration when cases were selected. With the benefit of hindsight, with this rather slim empirical background and the short time elapsed, it did not make much sense to bring in the even more complicated impact issue, i.e. whether the regime in question had an impact on the problem at hand. But this is exactly what we did. In fact, since we more or less skipped the domestic scene, we moved directly from output to impact.

With regard to explaining effectiveness, we assumed that problem structure was the most important perspective. This perspective contained many sub-dimensions that required considerable analytical attention. The issues of problem-solving capacity and institutional design, more analytically interesting as such factors may be more easily changed and manipulated, were overall given a short shrift in this first phase. In our "summing up so far" article from 1995 (Andresen and Wettestad, 1995), we emphasised the need for more attention, not least to the domestic processes but also to the questions of institutional design and problem-solving capacity. At least four projects were underway at this point which addressed these concerns and in which we were involved. Let us first briefly sum up two "domestic" projects before reviewing two "institutional" projects.

3.4 Domestic Implementation and Behavioural Change: The IIASA/IEC Project and the Hanf/Underdal Acid Rain Project.

It has been maintained that the study of domestic implementation of international environmental commitments is a side-track to the study of effectiveness of regimes (Young, 1998). In our opinion this depends on how one defines domestic implementation. If it is perceived as the formal process of transforming international rules into national legislation, we agree. If, however, target groups define it as regime-related behavioural change this is at the very heart of effectiveness studies.[15] In fact, defined this way, we will argue that in order to conduct process tracing, find causal pathways, and undertake counterfactual analysis, the detailed study of domestic implementation processes offers an excellent opportunity. Since we had more or less neglected these processes in our first-generation effectiveness studies, the chance to participate in two "implementation" projects, the IIASA project and the Hanf/Underdal project, offered a promising opportunity to delve deeper into our understanding of effectiveness from this perspective.

Turning first to the project led by Ken Hanf and Arild Underdal, we have less to add here than for some other projects we have participated in, since we were not much involved with designing the theoretical framework or with selecting the cases. From our perspective, the project was sound, fairly straightforward and simple from a methodological point of view. There was one key regime – the acid rain regime: what effect did this regime have on domestic implementation in ten selected member countries? The acid rain regime stood forth as a natural choice, considering it was comparatively mature. The first protocol was adopted back in 1985; quite a lot seemed to have been accomplished by the regime and new protocols were being added. This rather narrow approach in terms of issue area and regime implied that some of the "big" questions we had dealt with within the multi-regimes projects, such as the comparison between regimes and the more complicated issue of case selection, were not touched upon. This is *not* to say that the approach adopted within this project was smooth and easy to deal with in terms of analytical perspectives and method. One key issue within the project was whether a quantitative or a qualitative approach should be adopted.[16] In the end, the final product was essentially of a qualitative nature.[17]

We think that there is much to say for this rather simple approach. Since there was *one single* regime common to as many as ten countries, and the case studies were mostly carried out by scholars from the country in question, fairly solid cross-country comparisons were possible. More important from our perspective was the possibility to study the issue of causation in more detail, i.e. the causal significance of the regime for the implementation process in each country. This approach contributed more than most effectiveness projects we are familiar with in explaining the effectiveness of a single regime in terms of behavioural change. By using rival hypotheses, we were able to demonstrate in the case of Sweden and Norway (for which we were responsible), that the regime had not been the main driving force in the initial reductions in SO_2 emissions, but sooner unrelated factors[19]. In the case of Norway, it was concluded that "... a closer look at the measures reveals that only a few of them can be said to have involved any cost to Norway, and they were not introduced as result of international agreements, nor motivated by acidification."[20] This finding would have been hard to discover without detailed process tracing based on high-quality case study work.[21]

The main weakness of this project was not related to what was achieved, but to the missed opportunity to conduct a closer investigation of inter-linkages between related institutional contexts, i.e. the European Union (EU) and the Convention on Long-range Transboundary Air Pollution (CLRTAP). For various reasons this was not pursued as envisioned in the application. Some of the case studies indicated that for some (laggard) countries, EU Directives were more important than CLRTAP commitments. Elaborating more systematically on the links between the two regimes could have been one of the first main contributions in this field. Subsequently the links between the EU and CLRTAP on this issue have only grown in importance (Wettestad, 2002).

The project carried out at the Institute for Applied Systems Analysis (IIASA) was much more than case-study work. Still, it seems fair to say that this was the major part of the project and it constitutes the main core of the IIASA effectiveness project book.[22] (Victor et al., 1998). In terms of what we should do and how we should do it, this was a much more open-ended and process-oriented project than the acid rain project. This certainly made the initial, rather long, process exciting since we all had some influence on where we were moving.[23] The project application made it clear that a main module should deal with domestic implementation, but not much was said about particular regimes, countries and more specific approaches.

Turning first to the question of case-selection, this was finally done in the same way as in all international research projects that we have participated in: rather pragmatically – based on expertise and preferences of the team members.[24] Since IIASA is a more political organisation than most other research institutions we are familiar with, there was an East-West dimension to the project, affecting approaches and case selection. Initially a much more "ideal" approach was conceived, but as usual time went faster than expected and money was in shorter supply than envisaged at the outset. Thus, we all ended up writing accounts about the cases that we were familiar with; the acid rain regime, the whaling regime, the London dumping regime and the North Sea regime. The Russian case study participants chose a similar approach.[25]

Although this is not according to the textbook, there may also be certain advantages in applying such a pragmatic approach, since it increases the chances of achieving rather good case-stories. By and large we think this was true of the IIASA project. Thus, causation, process-tracing, as well as rival hypotheses were discussed fairly systematically in most cases. Moreover, there is no doubt that the Baltic regime[26], the North Sea regime and the acid rain regime are appropriate for studies of domestic implementation. It is more doubtful whether the same goes for the whaling regime.[27] It may also be argued that the three regional regimes mentioned are a bit too similar along many dimensions. All of them are regional regimes, with fairly limited participation and involving only developed countries. Two of them include both Eastern and Western European countries. Some more variation would have added more analytical mileage. Considering the resources and the personnel involved in this project, it should in principle have been possible to initially choose a more ideal strategy from a methodological perspective.

As for the analytical approach, we were searching for a niche, to make it easier to produce a simple "take home" message. After long discussions in the hot summer of 1994, we ended up with *access and participation*. According to one of the reviewers of the IIASA book, this was not a happy choice, and to some extent we agree. With the benefit of hindsight, it might have been better to basically compare the implementation processes of East and West in a systematic fashion – considering the composition of the teams and the regimes chosen. Still, looking at it more from a process perspective, it did provide us with a more specific focus. It also had obvious connections to very seminal political science debates, touching upon some core democracy issues and discussions. However, within the complex world of "regimes, states and societies"[28], the approach sort of melted in our hands – although subsequent summers were not quite that hot. By some, we were (rightfully) accused of providing "waffling" messages – and we (rightfully) responded that the access and participation issue was a waffling one. A simpler approach would probably have functioned better for the majority of case study authors who could not link the IIASA work to deep-diving dissertation work.[29] But that doesn't mean that our work didn't produce interesting results. For instance, although the IWC was no ideal case, the work on this regime questioned several generally held assumptions in this field; both that maximum transparency and NGO involvement is always good, and that NGOs and states are always on the opposite side of the floor. Finally, work within the IIASA project provided helpful inputs to other projects that we were involved in at the time, such as the project on the science-politics interface, Wettestad's institutional design project as well as Skjærseth's Ph.D study on the North Sea.

3.5 "High ambitions": Two Projects Addressing the Complex Issue of Institutional Design

Wettestad and Andresen (1991) had already concluded that there was a need for closer study of problem-solving capacity and especially the intriguing question of institutional design. Based on a couple of preliminary papers/ articles written jointly by Andresen/Wettestad,[30] Wettestad started on a more comprehensive "institutional" project during his 1993 sabbatical. In order to benefit from and provide further inputs to the Miles/Underdal effectiveness project, both the dependent variable ("effectiveness") and the "problem structure" explanatory perspective were quite similar to the "Miles/Underdal" model. The main differences lay in 1) the institutional specification; and 2) the treatment of the problem structure perspective as a "rival hypothesis" control perspective. With regard to the institutional specification, six main institutional variables were identified and discussed in the 1995 preliminary project note (Wettestad 1995): access procedures and participation issues; decision-making rules; the role of the secretariat; the structuring of the agenda; the organisation of the science-politics interface; and verification and compliance mechanisms. Case selection was again done pragmatically, based on what could be utilised from own research and from other contributions from the FNI. Eventually, the project ended up by focusing on three main cases (OSCON/PARCON; CLRTAP; ozone regime) and a fourth, rough analysis of the organisation of the climate regime so far (Wettestad 1999). Although these cases offered a certain variation both in terms of effectiveness and the focused institutional variables, the selection of other cases could undoubtedly have increased this variation.

On the institutional side, the main new source of information in addition to earlier efforts was a series of institutionally focused interviews with central Norwegian participants in the regime processes under scrutiny. Although ideally far more interviews – and in several key countries – should of course have been carried out, given the complex character of the institutional issues, the author was quite satisfied with this "fewer, but deeper" approach as regards the interviews. In terms of overall methodology, the high ambitions of the project were reflected in an effort to carry out a systematic institutional comparative effort. Although comparing three/four environmental regimes may not sound like a tall order to some, for one researcher alone it turned out to be a very tall order indeed.[31] One basic problem, of course, is that in order to carry out meaningful comparisons, you first need to have a pretty good understanding of the components you are seeking to compare. Take, for example, the decision-making/ratification requirements within the ozone regime: It is hard enough to grasp all the nuances in texts and differences between the procedures related to the Convention, Protocol and amendments. Add then, first, the task of verifying the practical, causal impact of these nuances and differences in the vast number of processes and for the large number of actors. A safe bet for political scientists is "not very much practical impact", but safe bets may sometimes turn out to be terribly wrong. Then, add the need to understand the operation of the decision-making procedures in relation to the rest of the complex ozone regime machinery. Hence, the importance of *context* and *conditioning factors* became the main, general lesson that stood forth from the author's efforts to juggle all these processes, actors and procedures. There is no "effective regime design" as such. Factors like problem types (e.g. conflicts over interests versus conflicts over values), phase in the development of the regime (e.g. the early confidence-building phase versus the more mature, "confident" phase) and process types (e.g. processes of preparation versus negotiation versus implementation) need to be taken into consideration.

The other institutionally-focused project started in 1993 as a collaboration project between CICERO and FNI on the organisation of the *science-politics interface in international environmental regimes*. Given the many complexities related "only" to this institutional issue, this alone indicates the folly in taking on the vast agenda indicated above. As to analytical approach, we singled out one small piece of the explanatory perspective used in the broader effectiveness projects. Regarding the dependent variable we used a three-level indicator related to acceptance and adoption of scientific input. Based on previous research, we did not expect scientific input to be among the main premises determining policy. A wide range of other factors may be more important. We therefore decided to check the significance of some other key variables: i.e. state of knowledge, political malignancy and public saliency. Again, we think our analytical approach was quite solid, based on a template mainly produced by Underdal, but the team effort was central for this result as well as the final outcome.[32]

But the link between the theoretical point of departure and case selection was basically pragmatic. Due to previous work and the case study work within the Miles/Underdal context, it was again tempting to "bet on the old horses" for the FNI-team, which meant PARCON/North Sea Conferences, CLRTAP and IWC/whaling. Tora Skodvin from CICERO brought some fresh ideas to the group, and added the climate change regime as a new case in addition to the ozone regime. But selection was equally pragmatic on her part.[33] Nevertheless, again we expected a significant variance between the regimes on a number of dimensions, including the importance of how the scientific input is organised. As to data gathering, we could to some extent build on previous science-policy research carried out at the FNI (e.g. Andresen/Østreng, eds., 1989; Wettestad, 1989, Andresen, 1989). That is, we were already familiar with the broad lines of the science policy interplay within the regimes. Still, some time had elapsed and the science-politics relationship was by no means static. Moreover, as this project was geared more specifically towards the *institutional design* issue, it was more demanding than our previous research on the general relationship between science and politics. This implied that we had to collect new data, not least through a series of interviews with scientists and policy makers within the different regimes.

During the final phase of the project (1997-99), we think it is fair to say that we acquired more and better data, although there was some variance between the cases in this regard.[34] The most important improvement from a methodological point of view was the combination of fairly detailed case studies and a more systematic and quantitative comparative effort. Others must judge whether this was successful, but we think it made good sense to contribute to bridging differences between various academic traditions. We also think that such an approach gives added insight and forces us to be more transparent as well as systematic.

As to main findings, we concluded that, overall, the state of knowledge was more important than the design of this process. Still, the institutionalisation of the science-policy interface made a difference under certain circumstances. As expected, institutional design within the regimes was geared towards maintaining a certain balance between scientific integrity and involvement/feasibility. However, the balance was more tilted towards involvement than we expected. But the fact that advice was not always strictly independent caused fewer problems than we had predicted. This was perhaps not much of a general take-away message, but such a message is not always easy to find when one attempts to delve deeply into a complex issue. A simple, blunter, message would be that knowledge often seems to mean little and how the knowledge-making process is designed means even less to the effectiveness of international regimes, but this is also not much of a "take-home" message.

3.6 The Miles Project, Phase II (1994-2000): "Confronting Theory with Evidence"

Several factors have made it possible for us to improve our "Miles" case studies during the second and final project phase. Since we had worked on most of the cases for a long time, we now had a better knowledge of our cases.[35] The work of others, both conceptually and empirically, has also contributed to improving our understanding. We were therefore in a much better position to estimate the real causal effects of the regimes, compared to other factors. The process by which data-gathering took place and causation was discussed, had improved considerably. From a methodological and analytical perspective this is clearly the most ambitious effectiveness project we have been involved in, both in scope and depth. Nevertheless, the pragmatic approach has essentially been used during case selection, building on the first phase of the project. But the number of cases is considerably higher than in other projects we are familiar with. The number of regimes is 14 (FNI 7 regimes and Miles et al. 7 regimes), but the number of cases is "thirty-something" as the cases are split into regime phases and components.[36] Still, even in comparison to a not-so-large universe, the number of cases is far too small and not meant to be representative. Hence, no substantial conclusions in a statistical sense can be drawn. But compared to other effectiveness projects, there is a rather unique combination of significant quantitative analytical element and many in-depth case studies. Since the standardisation of the cases has improved considerably, we think this project will make a significant contribution to bringing research on the issue one step forward.[37] As case study workers we find the "hard-soft" approach appealing, although we have yet to tap the full potential of the aggregate findings from the soft approach. Still, compared to our feeble start, we are now in a better position to shed light on why some regimes fail and others succeed.

After these somewhat self-congratulatory remarks, it is time to make the reader aware of some of the problems that still remain. Young (2000) is right when he remarks that the subjective judgement of the individual analyst when explaining and evaluating the effectiveness of various regimes is crucial. This is a weak point that is hard to get around. The problem is compounded when the project has stretched out so long and the number of analysts has been fairly large. We have tried to control for this by intensive group coding, but are far from certain that we have been successful. Cultural differences, personal opinions, preferences, styles, experiences and biases are bound to have an effect. But at least we are transparent and present all our scores in a separate appendix.

A final point on our (semi-) statistical approach: in principle there should be nothing mysterious about applying numbers to something that has already been described in prose. Nevertheless, from the perspective of those having to decide whether the score on some complex dimension should be "two" or "three" on a five-point scale, this can be a very painful process. Maybe it is because we belong to a more qualitative tradition that we find it much more comfortable to describe and analyse in prose. In addition, the increased transparency related to quantification makes us all the more vulnerable, since we know there are many out there who disagree with us – often with good reason. You will now all be able to judge what score you will assign to our main product (Miles et al., 2001).

4. CONCLUSION: BALANCING TEXTBOOK IDEALS AND FEASIBILITY CONCERNS

Let us first briefly sum up of our work related to methodological approach. Generally, we have been true to the textbook ideal by starting out with a more general analytical approach, but have not been able to follow this up in relation to case-selection. Our most persistent sin has been in the selection of cases. In none of our projects have discussions of external and internal validity formed the basis for case selection. Although our arsenal of cases has expanded over the years, all cases have generally been chosen pragmatically. As for the issues of causation and data collection there have been considerable improvements over time. This, however, has partly been the result of a learning process, as we have become more familiar with some key cases over time. In our opinion neither the qualitative nor the quantitative approach is superior to the other. There is no "correct" method in this regard; they clearly supplement each other – and we need both. At heart we are qualitative caseworkers, but this may be the result of training, lacking skills and tradition rather than of principles. The attempt at bridging the two approaches introduced by professor Underdal has been somewhat painful but also stimulating. Finally, to the question of analysis units and regime linkages and interplay. This is a rather recent fad, but one aspect that we would been able to explore better at a much earlier stage, if we had we been true to our initial focus on complex problems rather than single regimes. However, in a complex reality, we found that regimes were much easier to pin down compared to changing and comprehensive "problem structures". In the most recent project, however, this broader perspective has been included to some extent.

Turning then to the seminal question of "what would we have done differently had we known then what we know now?", posed to us by the editors of this book in a review of our original paper, at least two points stand out. First, we should have set aside some (more) time to study and discuss methodology – not a common subject at the FNI a decade ago. Even though time and resources are always limiting factors, this could have reduced some of the initial shortcomings. Second, rather than starting out with five cases, we should probably have started out with one or two. Considering our ambitious analytical approach, with the benefit of hindsight, we really stood no chance of answering the questions we set out to answer for so many cases. The best approach would probably have been to have carefully singled out only one case as a "pilot case" to test our perspective. Then we would have been in a much more favourable position regarding process tracing, domestic implementation, data collection etc. Also, we would have been able to test the fruitfulness of the analytical perspective much more systematically. To illustrate this point, it can be noted that two of the doctoral theses produced at the FNI within the "effectiveness and implementation" tradition in the 1990s both used around four years to study these questions within *one* regime. No wonder then that especially our initial effectiveness research had some of the weaknesses we have shared with you in the previous section.

Secondly, is there a trade-off between textbook ideals and feasibility concerns? In research institutions not part of the university system we think the answer is generally "yes". But we hope that this chapter has shown that after careful deliberation of theoretical and methodological challenges in the early project phase, combined with an open discussion of the concessions to feasibility, the final trade-off may produce both interesting and reliable results. Although we have been quite humble about the limitations of our findings due to the lack of methodological considerations, maybe authors of textbooks in methodology should also consider real-world constraints to a larger extent. If not, they may tend to be rather lofty publications without much practical significance for empirical research.

Finally, to the final question raised by the reviewers of the original paper, the implications of deviating from the textbook wisdom. In our case this primarily relates to case selection. We have already touched upon one alternative route: to dive deeper down into one case and do that more thoroughly before expanding to consider new cases. An alternative route would be to start out by mapping the "universe" of international environmental – and resource regimes. Even though this is only a small subset of all international regimes, there are considerable methodological challenges in delimiting them from other regimes as the borderlines between them are often not that clear-cut.[38] Leaving this challenge aside, it is quite clear that we now know a lot about a rather small number of regimes. Apart from the ones we have discussed here, the climate regime, the biodiversity regime and a few others are the main candidates.[39] Thus, we know little or nothing about the large majority of international environmental and resource regimes. The reason for this selection bias is of course that the regimes which are studied most are considered to be the most important both from a political and analytical point of view. Still, this is troublesome from a methodological perspective as they may not be representative for all cases. The most ambitious effort to correct this is the large-scale so-called "IIASA-database-project.[40]" It has proven very time-consuming and not easy to finance, but the effort should be commended, even though we don not yet know the final outcome.

NOTES

[1] This chapter is a revised version of a paper presented at the workshop on 'Methodological Approaches to the Study on Regime Consequences', held at the Centre for Advanced Study, Oslo, November 19-20, 1999. Thanks to Rigmor Hjorth, Maryanne Rygg and Anne Christine Thestrup for language and editing assistance.

[2] This section draws first and foremost upon King, Keohane and Verba (1994) and Bernauer and Mitchell (1998).

[3] See for example McKeown, (1999).

[4] The final publication from the project is Stendahl-Rechardt et.al. (eds.), (1996). We covered CLRTAP (Wettestad) and the North Sea (Andresen). We learned a lot about the differences between international lawyers and political scientists concerning how to deal

5 with effectiveness, but since we did not gain much additional insight compared to other projects we have participated in, we will not discuss this project here.
5 FNI has also conducted or been involved in a number of other effectiveness projects that will not be discussed here. E.g. Skjærseth (2000), Rosendal (2000), Stokke and Vidas (1996) and Young et.al. (1999a).
6 See also Andresen and Wettestad (1995).
7 Andresen spent his sabbatical at the University of Washington at the time, thereby facilitating the link to the FNI.
8 An early attempt at applying this perspective was reported in Andresen and Wettestad (1992).
9 As this was Professor Miles' baby in the first place, he spent much time in the cupboard at the first meetings; 'drawing and explaining' while the FNI delegation listened and made notes.
10 For a fascinating account of the history of this (and other) Miles' projects, see Miles (1997). Suffice it here to explain that one reason why financing was not obtained was the link to these 'environmentally radical' Norwegians. Recall that the official US climate policy at the time was not very progressive. See Agrawala and Andresen (1999).
11 Since we assume these concepts are explained by the founding father in this book, we see no reason for a more systematic elaboration here.
12 The FNI team was strengthened by Jon Birger Skjærseth, a graduate student at the time. He has been on our team off and on throughout the entire period and concluded his Ph.D thesis on the North Sea co-operation in 1999.
13 Given FNI's very applied nature (at the time) and soft financing structure, we were never able to concentrate our full attention on this project. Still, and maybe fortunately, strict financial project accounting had not yet been introduced at the FNI, allowing us to spend more time on this project than we actually had funding for.
14 In the case of CLRTAP we received eight replies from the group of parties and four from observers. The response was good as regards the IWC, but was not much use due to the polarisation of the whaling issue.
15 It was Skjærseth's (1991) more detailed study that first brought this problem to the fore.
16 In our work we have focused on target groups in a narrow sense. Others have defined it more broadly, see Stokke and Vidas (1996).
17 On a continuum from soft to hard, Dr. Sprinz was at one end and Dr. Boehmer-Christiansen on the other while Professor Underdal was the chief mediator as he had a foot in both camps.
18 This applied to the report sent to the Commission, as well as the later book version (Hanf and Underdal, 2000).
19 Because Norway had made such progress in emissions reductions, they had a moral upper hand and were quite successful in using CLRTAP strategically to push more reluctant parties in the initial phase (Laugen, 1995).
20 Hanf et.al (1996:75).
21 We can say this since we were not the ones who actually wrote the reports. This was done by two very talented young scholars from Norway and Sweden.
22 We are mainly addressing the final main part of the book, dealing with domestic implementation.
23 Some 15 researchers from a number of countries were involved in the project.
24 We are not familiar with all major research projects carried out over the last decade. The selection process may have been much more 'ideal' in the 'Tubingen-project' and the 'Jacobsen – Brown Weiss' project, as we know little about the internal life of these.

Although we have not been a part of the Young et.al. effectiveness project (Young, 1999), based on the expertise and interests of the members and the cases covered, they seem to have used a pragmatic approach as well.

[25] The same procedure was used to some extent in the other main part of the project dealing with international review mechanisms, (IRM) but due to the tremendous work capacity of Dr. Victor, this team may have been able to use a somewhat more ideal approach.

[26] See Roginko (1998) and Hjort (1998).

[27] Since Andresen wrote this piece, we are in a position to say this without hurting anybody's feelings. The reason why the whaling regime is not so suitable for such studies is that there was not much domestic implementation in the traditional sense. As the situation was at the time, the cases were selected too late in the process to have done this differently.

[28] These were the three key words in the so-called 'Think Piece' produced by the core FNI team (Andresen et al. 1995).

[29] Skjærseth was in such a position, and he proved that it might not have been the niche that was wrong but the ability to 'deliver' on the part of the rest of the team.

[30] Andresen and Wettestad (1992), (1993).

[31] However, projects with *several* researchers addressing the complex institutional issues automatically run into problems of inter-subjectivity with regard to interpretation of concepts, and measurements and assessments

[32] The final product is now published, Andresen/Skodvin/Underdal/Wettestad, (2000).

[33] Skodvin worked on her Ph.D thesis on IPCC/the climate regime (Skodvin, 1999).

[34] Personal attendance at some of the relevant negotiation meetings was an additional important source of data.

[35] We guess a cynic's comment would be: 'that's about time!' And that may be true, but the more we work on these regimes the more we understand how complex they are.

[36] Not all the reviewers in the last round (i.e. spring 2000) were happy with our many phases and regime components, but we consider this approach to be essential to analyse the evolving nature of regimes.

[37] Some of the reviewers did not find the standardisation good enough in the first round. We agreed and have improved it, and overall we think the standardisation is better than in most comparative projects.

[38] For an overview of the number and growth of environmental regimes compared to other regimes, see Agrawala, 1999 (Ph.D thesis). For a discussion of the difficult borderline between environmental - and other types of regimes, see Andresen, 2000.

[39] It should be noted, however, that some of the reviewers of the Miles II project have complimented the fact that Professor Miles in particular has brought in some new cases. See Miles et al., 2001.

[40] For some information on this project, see Breitmeier et al, 1996.

REFERENCES

Agrawala, S. (1999) *Science Advisory Mechanisms in Multilateral Decision-making: Three Models From the Global Climate Change Regime,* Ph.D. thesis, Woodrow Wilson School, Princeton University.

Agrawala, S., and Andresen, S. (1999) Indispensability and indefensibility? The United States in the Climate Treaty Negotiations, *Global Governance* 5: 457–82.

Andresen, S. (1989) Science and Politics in the International Management of Whales, *Marine Policy* 13, 2: 99–118.

Andresen, S. (2001) Global Environmental Governance: UN Fragmentation and Co-ordination, *Yearbook of International Co-operation on Environment and Development 2001/2002,* O. S. Stokke and Ø. B. Thommessen (eds.) Earthscan Publications, London and Sterling, VA.

Andresen, S. and Wettestad, J. (1992) International Resource Cooperation and the Greenhouse Problem, *Global Environmental Change* 2, 4: 277–91.

Andorka, R. and Kolosi, T. (1984) The effectiveness of international resource cooperation: some preliminary notes on institutional design. *International Challenges* 13, 2: 61–75.

Andresen, S. and Wettestad, J. (1995) International problem-solving effectiveness: the Oslo Project story so far. *International Environmental Affairs* 7, 2: 127–50.

Andresen, S., and Østreng, W. (eds.) (1989) *International Resource Management*, Belhaven Press, London.

Andresen, S., Skjærseth, J. B., and Wettestad, J. (1995) *Regime, the State and Society: Analysing the Implementation of International Environmental Commitments*, Laxenburg, IIASA Working Paper WP-95-43.

Andresen, S., Skodvin, T., Underdal, A. and Wettestad, J. (2000) *Science and Politics in International Environmental Regimes: Between Integrity and Involvement*, Manchester University Press.

Breitmeier, H., Levy, M., Young, O.R., and Zürn, M. (1996) *The International Regimes Database as a Tool for the Study of International Cooperation*, Laxenburg, IIASA Working Paper WP-96-160.

Hanf, K., (ed.) (1996) *The Domestic Basis of International Environmental Agreements: Modelling National/International Linkages,* Final report to the European Commission, EC Contract EVSV-CT92-0185.

Hanf, K. and Underdal, A. (eds.) (2000) *International Environmental Agreements and Domestic Politics: The Case of Acid Rain,* Ashgate, Aldershot.

Hjort, R. (1998) Implementation of Baltic Sea Pollution Commitments in Poland: A review of the Literature, in D.G. Victor, K. Raustiala and E.B. Skolnikoff (eds.) *The Implementation and Effectiveness of International Environmental Commitments*, MIT Press, Cambridge, MA, 639–59.

King, G., Keohane, R. and Verba, S. (1994) *Designing Social Inquiry: Scientific Inference in Qualitative Research*, Princeton University Press.

Laugen, T. (1995) *Compliance with International Environmental Agreements – Norway and the Acid Rain Convention,* FNI Report 003–1995, Lysaker, The Fridtjof Nansen Institute.

McKeown, T. J. (1999) Case Study and the Statistical Worldview, in review of King, Keohane and Verba's Designing Social Inquiry: Scientific Inference in Qualitative Research, *International Organization* 53, 1:161–90.

Miles, E.M., Underdal, A., Andresen, S., Wettestad, J., Skjærseth, J. B. and Carlin, E. M. (2001) *Environmental Regime Effectiveness – Confronting Theory with Evidence*, MIT Press, Cambridge, MA.

Mitchell, R. and Bernauer, T. (1998) Empirical Research on International Environmental Policy: Designing Qualitative Case Studies, *Journal of Environment and Development* 7, 1: 4–31.

Roginko, A. (1998) Domestic Implementation of Baltic Sea Pollution Commitments in Russia and the Baltic States, in D.G.Victor, K. Raustiala and E.B. Skolnikoff (eds.) *The Implementation and Effectiveness of International Environmental Commitments*, MIT Press, Cambridge MA.

Rosendal, G. K. (2000) *The Convention on Biological Diversity and Developing Countries*, Kluwer Academic Publishers, Dordrecht/Boston/London.

Stendahl-Rechardt, K. (ed.) (1996) *The Effectiveness of Multilateral Environmental Agreements*, Nordic Council of Ministers Report 18.

Skjærseth, J.B. (1991) *Effektivitet, problem-typer og løsningskapasitet: en studie av Oslo-samarbeidets takling av dumping i Nordsjøen og Nordøstatlanteren*, FNI Report R:009–1991, Lysaker, The Fridtjof Nansen Institute.

Skjærseth, J.B. (2000) *North Sea Cooperation: Linking International and Domestic Pollution Control*, Manchester University Press.

Skodvin, T. (1999) *Structure and Agent in the Scientific Diplomacy of Climate Change*, dr. polit. thesis, Department of Political Science, University of Oslo.

Stokke, O.S. and D. Vidas (1996) *Governing the Antarctic: The Effectiveness and Legitimacy of the Antarctic Treaty System*, Cambridge University Press.

Stokke, O.S. (2000) Managing Straddling Stocks: The Interplay of Global and Regional Regimes, *Ocean and Coastal Management* 43: 205–34.

Underdal, A. (1990) *Negotiating Effective Solutions: The Art and Science of Political Engineering*, unpublished paper, University of Oslo.

Victor, D.G., Raustiala, K. and Skolnikoff, E.B. (eds.) (1998) *The Implementation and Effectiveness of International Environmental Commitments*, MIT Press, Cambridge MA.

Wettestad, J. (1989) *Uncertain Science and Matching Policies: Science, Politics and the Organization of North Sea Cooperation*, FNI Report R:003 – 1989, Lysaker, The Fridtjof Nansen Institute.

Wettestad, J. (1995) *Nuts and Bolts for Environmental Negotiators? Institutional Design and the Effectiveness of International Environmental Regimes*, FNI Note N:001–1995. Lysaker, The Fridtjof Nansen Institute.

Wettestad, J. (1999) *Designing Effective Environmental Regimes – The Key Conditions*, Edward Elgar, Cheltenham.

Wettestad, J. (2002) *Clearing the Air – European Advances in Tackling Acid Rain and Atmospheric Pollution*, Ashgate, Aldershot.

Wettestad, J. and Andresen S. (1991) *The Effectiveness of International Resource Cooperation: Some Preliminary Findings*, FNI Report R:007–1991, Lysaker, The Fridtjof Nansen Institute.

Young, O. R. (1982) *Resource Regimes Natural Resources and Social Institutions*, University of California Press.

Young, O. R. (1998) *The Effectiveness of International Environmental Regimes: What We Know and What We Need to know*, paper produced for annual meeting of the American Association for the Advancement of Science, 1998, February 12–17, Philadelphia.

Young, O. R. (2000) Epilogue: Indices and Causal Inferences: Exploring the Effectiveness of International Regimes, in J. Wettestad (ed.) *The Effectiveness of Global and Regional Environmental Agreements: Proceedings from the 1999 Oslo Concerted Action Workshop*, FNI Report 001–2000, Lysaker, The Fridtjof Nansen Institute, 49–62.

Young, O. R. and Levy, M. (eds.) (1999) *The Effectiveness of International Environmental Regimes*, MIT Press, Cambridge, MA.

Young, O. R. and Underdal, A. (1999) Science Plan for the Project on the Institutional Dimensions of Global Environmental Change, *The International Human Dimensions Programme of Global Environmental Change*, IHDP, Bonn.

Chapter 4

CAUSAL MECHANISMS AND THE STUDY OF INTERNATIONAL ENVIRONMENTAL REGIMES

JON HOVI
Department of Political Science, University of Oslo, and CICERO

1. INTRODUCTION

Over the past two decades or so, the idea of causal "mechanisms" has become extremely widespread in both the philosophy of the social sciences and in applied social science. Recently, it has also turned up in the literature on international environmental regimes. A common motivation for invoking the concept seems to be a desire to open up the black box between a cause and its effect, that is, to analyze in detail exactly *how* the cause relates to the effect. On closer inspection, however, it turns out that those using the term have a number of different things in mind. This leaves a somewhat confusing picture of what a causal mechanism is and what it means for explanation in the social sciences.

The purpose of this chapter is to review and discuss some of the ways in which the concept is being used. A main concern is to compare applications in the literature on international environmental regimes to definitions found in the philosophy of the social sciences. The chapter is organized as follows: Section 2 describes and elaborates on three influential definitions found in the philosophy of the social sciences. Similarly, section 3 considers three definitions from the literature on international regimes. Section 4 compares the various definitions from sections 2 and 3 and points out a number of sources of disagreement. Finally, the concluding section asks what, if anything, should be done about the current, somewhat confusing state of affairs that is created by the multitude of existing definitions.

2. MECHANISMS IN THE PHILOSOPHY OF SCIENCE LITERATURE

Before I go on to discuss how the term "mechanism" is used in the literature on international regimes, I will first discuss how it is conceptualized within the philosophy of social sciences. Three definitions in particular have influenced scholarly thinking in the field. The first, which is due to Arthur L. Stinchcombe,[1] contrasts the idea of a mechanism with that of a black box:

> As I will use the word, "mechanism" means (1) a piece of scientific reasoning which is independently verifiable and independently gives rise to theoretical reasoning, which (2) gives knowledge about a component process (generally one with units at a "lower level") of another theory (ordinarily a theory with units at a different "higher" level). (Stinchombe 1991: 367)

By this account, explaining by mechanisms means accounting for "complex phenomena in terms of their individual components" and thus becomes a program for reductionism that might be linked to methodological individualism (Elster 1998: 47). In the words of Daniel Little, "there is no such thing as autonomous social causation; there are no social causal mechanisms that do not supervene upon the structured choices and behavior of individuals" (Little 1995: 35). Causal mechanisms are here taken to provide microfoundations for social causal explanations. Moreover, this is done by way of theorizing about a component process in the causal chain, typically at a lower level. If the explanandum is at the group level, the mechanism helps us understand how individual agents are led to act in a manner that makes the causal chain hold at the group level. According to Little, the basis for this kind of theorizing is most likely to be found in "rational choice theory, theory of institutions and organizations, public choice theory, analytical Marxism, or, perhaps, social psychology," since "these fields have in common…a commitment to providing microfoundations for social explanations" (Little 1995: 35).

The above conceptualization of "mechanism" is largely congruent with the one presented in a recent volume called *Social Mechanisms* (Hedström and Swedberg 1998), where a number of authors (including Stinchcombe) offer their views on mechanisms in the social sciences. For example, in one chapter, Thomas C. Schelling describes a social mechanism as

> a plausible hypothesis, or set of hypotheses, that could be the explanation of some social phenomenon, the explanation being in terms of interactions between individuals and other individuals, or between individuals and some social aggregate (Schelling 1998: 32 – 33).[2]

Schelling's notion of mechanism strongly resembles Stinchcombe's. Both insist that mechanismic explanations for social phenomena must be sought at the individual level. By the account of both authors, then, "mechanism" essentially means "*social* mechanism."

The second definition says that mechanisms are "frequently occurring and easily recognizable causal patterns that are triggered under generally unknown conditions or with indeterminate consequences" (Elster 1998: 45). This conception of mechanism reflects the everyday notion that in certain situations, things "could go both ways." By this view, the opposite of a mechanism is a scientific law. Thus, explaining by mechanism replaces "If A, then always B" with "If A, then *sometimes B*." Note that statements of the latter type can provide a basis for explanation, but not for prediction. One of Elster's favorite examples is that "[e]x ante, we cannot predict when [people] will engage in wishful thinking—but when they do, we can recognize it after the fact" (Elster 1998: 48). According to the second definition, then, one of the defining characteristics of a mechanism is an element of *indeterminacy*.

Elster proceeds to distinguish two types of mechanism, depending on the kind of indeterminacy involved. A mechanism of *type A* exists when two (or more) mutually exclusive causal chains can be triggered under approximately identical conditions. Consider the situation in Serbia in the fall of 1999, when one observer noted that "as winter tightens its grip, nobody can predict whether hardship will make the Serbs angrier or more passive" (*The Economist* 25.1999:42).

In a mechanism of *type B*, two (or more) causal chains operate simultaneously. Moreover, these causal chains have opposite effects on the dependent variable, so that the net result is indeterminate. Consider the use of economic sanctions in order to extract political concessions. Sanctions increase the hardship of the population in the target country, which tends to reduce the endurance of the target. But sanctions also generate defiance and can even enable decision makers in the target state to profit personally, via control over illegal smuggling. This pulls in the opposite direction. Without a theory explaining the conditions under which each of these casual chains is likely to prevail, we cannot predict in a given case whether sanctions are going to succeed.

A third definition of mechanism stems from Mario Bunge:

> We stipulate that a mechanism is a process in a concrete system, such that it is capable of bringing about or preventing some change in the system as a whole or in some of its subsystems. (Bunge 1997: 414)

A "concrete system" is "a bundle of real things held together by some bonds or forces, behaving as a unit in some respects and (except for the universe as a whole) embedded in some environment" (Bunge 1997: 415). Natural, social, and technical systems are concrete, while conceptual systems (such as theory) or semiotic systems (such as language) are not. Mechanisms, then, are (bundles of) processes in natural, social, or mechanical systems:

> For example, a physiological mechanism is a collection of processes inside an organism, and a political mechanism—such as popular mobilization against a proposed bill—is a collection of processes within a polity or among polities (Bunge 1997: 414).

For convenience, I shall link the first of these three definitions to the name of Arthur Stinchcombe, the second to that of Jon Elster, and the third to that of Mario Bunge.[3]

3. MECHANISMS IN THE INTERNATIONAL REGIMES LITERATURE

So far, attention has been restricted to definitions used in the philosophy of the social sciences. However, as already noticed, the term "mechanism" also has been used recently in a number of books and articles on international regimes. At least three ways of using the concept may be distinguished in this literature, all of which differ in one way or another from each of the definitions discussed in the previous section.

According to one common use of the term, a "mechanism" simply refers to a set of rules, an institutional body, or an institutional procedure. For example, this is the case in labels such as the "Clean Development Mechanism" of the Kyoto Protocol, the "Trade Policy Review Mechanism" of the World Trade Organization, or the "Exchange Rate Mechanism" of the former European Monetary System. Similarly, de Senarclens (1998) talks about the "mechanisms of international regulation," when he simply seems to mean international institutions. And Daves and Nammack (1998) refer to the American Endangered Species Act and the Convention on International Trade in Endangered Species (CITES) as "mechanisms" for protection of sharks.[4]

A second meaning of the term is found in a recent volume edited by Young (1999). Young equates "mechanism" with "behavioral pathway," defined as "the generative source of behavior on the part of the states and other actors—intergovernmental organizations, nongovernmental organizations, corporations, and even individuals—whose behavior contributes to outcomes in the issue areas under consideration" (Young and Levy 1999: 21). Specifically, the authors list six different models of how regimes influence behavior. The "mechanisms" are the driving forces in these models: rational self-interest, social norms, social learning, the operation of social roles, and internal politics.[5]

Finally, a second recent volume on international regimes that invokes the term "mechanism" is Stokke and Vidas (1996). In the latter book, the term "mechanism" refers to "intermediate processes" between the design of the Antarctic Treaty System (ATS) on the one hand and regime effectiveness on the other. The authors discuss five specific mechanisms. The first is "that of generating a *productive deadlock phobia* among the Consultative Parties when addressing politically sensitive matters." The second is the role of "the ATS serving to *decouple* mutually beneficial cooperative practices from conflictual matters which otherwise would impede them." The third, "crucial for its ability to accommodate external criticism, is to provide means for *cooptation*," that is positive incentives for those who support the regime. The fourth, "important for its ability to protect scientific activities in the Antarctic, and also for balancing utilisation and conservation in the region, is to *elevate science* as an instrument by which to achieve collective decisions on various uses of the Antarctic." Finally, "a fifth specific mechanism of the ATS is that it provides a pool of acceptable solutions to difficult political puzzles in the Antarctic" (Stokke and Vidas 1996:452 – 454).

4. SOURCES OF DISAGREEMENT

In previous sections, six different definitions of mechanism have been identified—three from the philosophy of science literature and three from the international regimes literature. The current section elaborates on the differences between these various definitions. There seem to be at least seven sources of disagreement. The first has to do with the normative status of explaining by mechanisms. The second relates to how the notion of a mechanism connects with that of a causal chain. The third is whether mechanisms are bits of theory or something in the real world. The fourth is if a mechanism must always be located at a lower social level than the explanandum. The fifth concerns the possible relation of explaining by mechanisms to the program of methodological individualism. The sixth has to do with whether theorizing about mechanisms necessarily adds realism to the underlying model. Finally, a seventh source of disagreement stems from the alleged generality or specificity of a mechanism.

4.1   Normative Status

Elster explicitly states that he does *not* advance explanation by mechanisms as an ideal or a norm. On the contrary, he says, "[e]xplanation by laws is better—but also more difficult, usually too difficult" (Elster 1998: 51 – 52). Thus, Elster's view is not that explanation by mechanisms is in any way superior to explanation by laws. Rather, he advocates mechanism – based explanation as a matter of *necessity*.

By contrast, Stinchcombe strongly emphasizes that the main purpose of theorizing about mechanisms is to *improve the higher-level theory* by adding to the latter's "suppleness, precision, complexity, elegance, or believability" (Stinchcombe 1991: 367). Thus, explaining by mechanisms is clearly presented as an ideal. This is also the view of Bunge, although for different reasons. While Elster argues that law-based explanation is too difficult, Bunge claims that it is not *enough*. According to Bunge, covering-law explanations are simply not very enlightening unless the underlying mechanism is specified:

> For example, it is not very illuminating to reason that someone is bound to die eventually because he or she is human, and it so happens that all humans are mortal. Though logically impeccable, this argument is unilluminating because it does not point to any mechanisms. Some scientists are trying to uncover the senescence and death mechanisms, such as repeated DNA damage and rearrangement, as well as apoptosis (genetically programmed death), to understand why humans must die. (Bunge 1997: 412)

Similarly, it does not shed much light on the termination of the conflict in Kosovo to say (1) that all wars end,[6] (2) that this conflict was a war, and (3) that therefore the conflict in Kosovo ended. In short, Bunge's view is that any covering-law explanation needs to be supplemented by specification of the underlying mechanism. In other words, only mechanism-based explanation can add significantly to our understanding of real-world phenomena.

A similar view seems to underlie studies of mechanisms in the regime literature. Indeed, one of the principal ideas in the Young and Stokke and Vidas volumes seems to be precisely that theorizing about mechanisms adds to our understanding of the effects of international regimes.

4.2 Mechanisms: Elements of a Causal Chain or Vice Versa?

A second difference between the various definitions is the way they relate the idea of a causal mechanism to that of a *causal chain* (or causal pathway). There are at least three ways of looking at this relationship. First, according to Bunge's and Little's definitions, there is a close resemblance between the two concepts. In Little's formulation, the resemblance approaches identity: "A causal mechanism . . . is a series of events governed by lawlike regularities that lead from the explanans to the explanandum" (Little 1991: 15). Similarly, Stokke and Vidas equate a mechanism with an "intermediate process," which appears to be something closely related to a causal chain.

A second view is inherent in Stinchcombe's definition, which allows several mechanisms within a single causal chain. Indeed, Stinchcombe's view is that in a given theory, the role of a mechanism is to substantiate the claim that a causal relationship exists between a given pair of variables in a causal chain. One therefore ideally should propose a mechanism for every link in the chain (including feedback loops). By this view, "causal mechanism" is a more basic concept than "causal chain," in the sense that a single causal chain may involve more than one mechanism. Thus, a causal chain from X via Z to Y involves at least two mechanisms.

Finally, Elster's definition implies the reverse relationship—that is, that "causal chain" is a more basic concept than "causal mechanism" since it allows a single mechanism to consist of several causal chains. This is particularly clear from Elster's definition of a type B mechanism, where the point is precisely that (at least) two causal chains operate simultaneously, with opposite effects on the dependent variable. Thus, a mechanism of type B *always* consists of at least two causal chains.

4.3 Bits of Theory or Pieces of the Real World?

Bunge points out a third source of disagreement. It is whether mechanisms belong to the real world or to the abstract realm of theory:

> [C]ontrary to Stinchcombe (1991)..., in my view—which is that prevailing among natural scientists and engineers—mechanisms are not pieces of reasoning but pieces of the furniture of the real world. (Bunge 1997: 414)

Recall that Stinchcombe sees mechanisms as "bits of theory," while Schelling refers to them as "plausible hypotheses." By both accounts, then, a mechanism is a piece of reasoning. By contrast, Bunge emphasizes that mechanisms are real-world processes. Although Elster does not address the issue explicitly, it follows directly from his formulation that mechanisms are "frequently occurring causal patterns" that he too uses the concept to refer to real-world phenomena. Similarly, Young's identification of mechanisms with behavioral pathways and Stokke and Vidas's emphasis on intermediate processes place these contributions in the camp of Bunge and Elster on this issue.

Granted, this apparent disagreement may be at least partly spurious. On closer inspection, Stinchcombe's terminology turns out to be inconsistent, as he sometimes refers to "theories of mechanisms" in a way that clearly suggests that he has in mind theories of something in the real world—not theories of "pieces of scientific reasoning" (e.g., Stinchcombe 1991: 384 – 385). However, there may well remain a hard core of real disagreement, since in Schelling's terminology, "mechanisms" consistently refer to models or hypotheses, rather than to the real-world phenomena that these models or hypotheses are intended to describe.

4.4 Lower-level Phenomena?

A fourth source of disagreement concerns the level of analysis at which mechanisms may be identified. We have seen how Stinchcombe and Schelling insist that mechanisms are invariably found at a lower level than the explanandum. Young and Levy's use of the term also seems to be consistent with this view. While regime effectiveness is a phenomenon at the inter-state level, Young and Levy's mechanisms are the driving forces underlying the actions and interaction of states as well as lower-level agents.

By contrast, the definitions of Elster and Bunge make no particular claims that the mechanism must be at a different level than the explanandum. Moreover, Stokke and Vidas's identification of mechanisms with *processes* suggests that they are using the term in a way similar to that of Bunge. Indeed, the Antarctic treaty system may be seen precisely as a concrete system in Bunge's sense, and the mechanisms discussed by Stokke and Vidas as the processes that "make this concrete system tick" (cf. Bunge 1997: 410). However, since the mechanisms of Stokke and Vidas are at the same (inter-state) level as the explanandum (i.e., regime effectiveness), it is clear that their use of the term does not conform to Stinchcombe's definition.

4.5 Methodological Individualism?

Little (1991, 1995) and Stinchcombe (1991) agree that mechanisms provide microfoundations for higher-level causal relationships. The same is true for Schelling's notion of a social mechanism. In other words, these authors hold macro-level law-like statements to be inadequate for explanation, unless some micro-level mechanism is specified. This view links the search for mechanisms to the program of methodological individualism, which holds that "to explain social institutions and social change is to show how they arise as the result of the action and interaction of individuals" (Elster 1989: 13).

The claim that law-like relationships at the social-level are unable to explain is a controversial one. For example, it has been vigorously attacked by Harold Kincaid:

> On either of the two most influential accounts of explanation—the covering law model of Hempel and the question model of van Fraassen and others—well-confirmed macro-level laws seem to explain. Hempel's hypothetical deductive account does not restrict explanation to laws at some given level. Events subsumed under well-confirmed laws are thereby explained. If there are confirmed laws relating macro-level variables, then they would serve to explain. Similarly, if I ask why the output of a given industry has expanded and request an answer citing known causal regularities, then social laws also explain on the van Fraassen model. Social laws answer questions and thus explain. (Kincaid 1994/1990: 115)

How would an adherent to methodological individualism respond to this line of attack? One possibility is to invoke the claim that social-level covering-law explanations are *incomplete* unless the underlying individual-level mechanism is identified. An alternative line of defense may be developed on the basis of the distinction between "halfway" and "rock-bottom" explanations. Consider the following, oft-cited passage from one of the most prominent spokespersons for methodological individualism:

> There may be unfinished or halfway explanations of large-scale social phenomena (say, inflation) in terms of other large-scale social phenomena (say, full employment); but we shall not have arrived at rock-bottom explanations of such phenomena until we have deduced an account of them from statements about the dispositions, beliefs, resources, and interrelations of individuals (Watkins 1994/1957: 442).

According to this view, then, the search for (social) mechanisms is best seen as a quest for *rock-bottom* explanations of social phenomena. While other types of explanation are not deemed worthless, they are seen as unfinished explanations that are less than fully satisfactory and that can (in principle) only serve a preliminary purpose until a rock-bottom explanation—based on individual action and interaction—is eventually reached.

An interesting question is whether there is a way around the apparent link between mechanisms and the program of methodological individualism. In fact, there are at least two ways in which this link may be broken. The first is consistent with Stinchcombe's definition, in the sense that it admits the view that mechanisms must be found at a lower level than the explanandum. Consider the theory explaining the Cold War arms race as a process of action and reaction between the United States and the Soviet Union. This theory depicts a mechanism in the sense of Stinchcombe, since an inter-state ("social") phenomenon is explained in terms of a lower-level theory, namely a theory of interaction between two states. However, it would not satisfy a methodological individualist who is likely to insist that a rock-bottom explanation must be given in terms of individuals' actions and interaction. According to the latter view, then, the action/reaction model of the arms race would at best qualify as a halfway explanation.

A more radical break between explanation by mechanisms and methodological individualism is provided by Bunge. Indeed, one of Bunge's reasons for rejecting Stinchcombe's definition is precisely that, in his view, lower-level explanations represent only one of several possible categories of mechanisms. He rejects methodological individualism, as well as methodological holism, in favor of "systemism":

> I suggest that the most adequate reductive explanations are combinations of the two basic types (i.e., individualism and holism)—such as when a political event is explained as the outcome of the concerted actions of a number of individuals in response to an irreducibly social issue, such as high

unemployment, inflation, or political oppression. The combination of microreduction with macroreduction is characteristic of the *systemic* (or systems-theoretic) approach. According to systemism, to explain how a system works—that is, to unveil its mechanism—one must not only take it to bits (microreduction) but also show how the bits fit together, giving rise to emergent features (macroreduction) (Bunge 1998: 441).

Bunge summarizes the three perspectives as shown in Figure 4.1 (Bunge 1997: 441).

Individualism	Holism	Systemism
Microreductionist or bottom-up	Macroreductionist or top-down	Micro-cum macro-reductionist or bottom-up cum top-down
Macrolevel ↑ Microlevel	Macrolevel ↓ Microlevel	Macrolevel ↑↓ Microlevel

Figure 4.1.

According to Bunge, then, the idea of explaining by mechanisms provides no clear-cut advice as to where to look for the relevant mechanism in a given case. It might be found at a lower level, but it could also reside at a higher level or in a combination of the two.

4.6 Added Realism?

A sixth point of disagreement among the various proposed definitions relates to the extent to which a focus on mechanisms is believed to add to the realism of a model or a theory. In the literature on international regimes, there is a tendency to identify mechanisms through what is sometimes called "process tracing." For example, according to King, Keohane, and Verba,

> Identifying causal mechanisms is a popular way of doing empirical analyses. It has been called, in slightly different forms, "process tracing" […], "historical analysis," and "detailed case studies" (King et al. 1994: 86).

The idea seems to be that a focus on mechanisms serves to structure the research process so that the causal process can be followed—or traced—step by step. This way, the researcher is believed to come closer to how things "really" are connected than he or she would be with some alternative method of inference. Indeed, it seems that in this literature an important motive for explaining by mechanisms is precisely that this enables us to increase the realism of theoretical models as well as the detail and richness of empirical studies.

By contrast, Stinchcombe makes a strong argument that theories about mechanisms can be highly useful even if they are *not* particularly realistic:

> While ultimately it would be nice if all parts of our theories on the aggregate or structural level were true and complete at the level of components, my argument is that quite often very imperfect theories of mechanisms are very useful at the aggregate level. "Assumption mongering," showing that the theories of the mechanisms are not true, is therefore seldom a useful strategy in scientific theorizing at an aggregate level. Just as statistical mechanics is still useful even if molecules of gases are not little round elastic balls, so assumptions that all people can calculate at a level two standard deviations above the mean may not be far enough wrong *in relevant ways* to undermine assumptions of rationality in economics. (Stinchcombe 1991: 384, emphasis in original)

Stinchcombe's argument is that a model that is unrealistic at the individual level may nevertheless work well at the group level. There are at least three reasons why this may be the case. First, provided that the effects are not systematic, deviations at the lower level may cancel out at the higher level. Second, some effects are small, even if they are systematic. They may then safely be neglected at the aggregate level, although they could be of great interest at the lower level. For example, Stinchcombe argues that the studies of Kahneman and Tversky (e.g., 1979) may largely be ignored by economics even if they are theoretically crucial for psychology. Finally, there may be compensating effects that prevent the micro-level deviations from having a bearing on the macro-level outcome. Stinchcombe's example is the calculating of internal transfer prices in American businesses, which could probably not be carried out by at least 90 percent of the working population in the United States. However, this fact largely may be ignored by economists working in this field. They can safely continue to rely on the assumption that the calculations are carried out correctly, since if a corporation needs to calculate such prices, it will simply hire someone who is able to do the job (Stinchcome 1991: 383).[7]

4.7 Specific or General?

A final source of disagreement concerns the relative specificity of a mechanism. While some authors use the term to refer to very specific causal relationships, others have quite general driving forces in mind. To illustrate, consider the difference between Young and Levy on the one hand and Schelling on the other. Recall that in the language of Young and Levy, a mechanism is a "behavioral pathway." This means that the mechanisms of Young and Levy are far more general phenomena than those of Schelling, since the latter has in mind very specific models of action. Calling for a catalogue of mechanisms, Schelling (1998: 40) suggests that his well-known distinction between "thermostats," "lemons," and other families of models could provide a starting point, or at least be a contribution to such a taxonomy (Schelling 1978). Note that Schelling (1998) refers to these categories as *families* of mechanisms. Since all of these mechanisms are based on the assumption that people act rationally, it is clear that they all belong in a single one of Young and Levy's categories. According to Schelling's view, therefore, the behavioral pathways of Young and Levy must be seen as (very) broad categories, which may in turn be broken down into families of mechanisms.

5. CONCLUSION

As the discussion in this chapter has shown, the term "mechanism" currently is being used in a number of different ways. This is true for scholars working in the philosophy of the social sciences as well as for scholars specializing in the field of international regimes. The various definitions disagree over a number of important issues, including (1) the normative status of explaining by mechanisms; (2) how the concept of causal mechanism relates to that of causal chain; (3) whether mechanisms are bits of theory or something in the real world; (4) whether mechanisms are necessarily found at a lower level than the explanandum; (5) how mechanism-based explanation relates to methodological individualism; (6) whether thinking in terms of mechanisms necessarily means enhanced realism or if even highly unrealistic theories can work well in an explanation based on mechanisms; and (7) whether a mechanism is a specific model or rather a large family of models. This leaves a fairly confusing picture of what a mechanism is and what exactly it means to "explain by mechanisms" in the social sciences.

What should we make of this state of affairs? There seem to be three main answers. A first response is to try to build a consensus over a single definition. This definition could be one of the existing alternatives, or it might be a new proposal. For example, one might try to extract a common core from the various existing definitions, and, on that basis, proceed to propose yet another definition. Many of the definitions referred to in this chapter seem to conceive of a mechanism as something "in between" a cause and its effect. Thus, it is conceivable that this could be a basis on which to develop a new definition. However, there are exceptions. For example, Elster's definition sees a mechanism as a frequently occurring causal pattern. Thus, in his view, a mechanism includes not only something in between a cause and its effect, but also the cause and the effect themselves.

Still, an optimistic view would be that a new definition could eventually replace the existing ones, and that the current disagreement over the meaning of a mechanism would evaporate. However, it is hardly necessary to point out that things might not actually work out this way. An equally likely possibility is that no consensus emerges and that the new definition merely adds to the existing confusion.

A second way to alleviate the situation could be to drop the term "mechanism" entirely. Proponents of this strategy are likely to ask how a term used in so many different meanings could possibly add to the precision and clarity of a scientific discipline. Why not call a lower-level theory just that, instead of invoking the less precise concept of a mechanism? Or, if one has a behavioral pathway in mind, why not simply stick to that term, instead of calling it a mechanism? Similarly, "causal pattern," "intermediate process," or "institution" may not be perfectly well-defined concepts, but is there really anything to be gained by renaming them "mechanisms"? One might add that the social sciences already contain too many terms that, although sometimes highly fashionable in use, do not carry sufficient precision to justify that they are accepted as scientific terminology.

A third option is simply to leave things as they are. In support of this view, it can be argued that it is not uncommon for multiple definitions of a single term to co-exist alongside each other. A similar state of affairs exists for several other methodological terms that are widely used in the social sciences. "Model" and "theory" are but two simple examples. According to this position, therefore, the above discussion simply provides yet another reminder that it is important to give an explicit definition whenever an otherwise ambiguous concept is invoked.

It is hardly necessary to stress that the latter position stands out as the most sober. To convince the community of social science scholars that one particular definition of mechanism is more appropriate or fruitful than the others is likely to be a formidable task, considering the current jungle of options. No less challenging is the ambition to convince one's colleagues to drop the concept entirely. It seems more than likely that in the future we shall continue to see the term used in different meanings. The best we can hope for is probably that whenever the idea of a causal mechanism is introduced, scholars will be careful to explain in a precise manner what exactly it is that they have in mind.

NOTES

1 This formulation largely paraphrases the editors' own definition.
2 I concede that this may be somewhat unfair. Elster used a variant of the first definition in earlier work (e.g., Elster 1983, 1985), and there are other authors as well who apparently use the first definition, or one closely related to it, independently of Stinchcombe (e.g., Little 1991, 1995).
3 This way of using the concept seems to be strongly related to the one found in the general literature on public goods provision. For example, Miller and Hammond (1994) speak of incentive-compatible procedures for provision of public goods as "mechanisms." Their work is part of a larger tradition, rooted in economics, which is sometimes called "games of mechanism design" (Fudenberg & Tirole 1994:244; see also Binmore 1992:523ff. and Rasmusen 1989:173-175). In these games, a "mechanism" is a procedure that enables a principal to induce one or several agents to reveal private information truthfully.
4 Although Young and Levy describe six different models, they specify only five different mechanisms. The explanation is that two of the models rely on the same "mechanism," namely utility maximizing.
5 This law paraphrases the title of Fred Charles Iklé's insightful book Every War Must End (Iklé 1991).
6 I have argued elsewhere that, for a number of reasons, unrealistic models can be useful for empirical research (Hovi 1998). Stinchcombe's argument adds yet another reason to the list.
7 No doubt it is also true for scholars working in other applied fields.

REFERENCES

Binmore, K. (1992) *Fun and Games: A Text on Game Theory*, D.C. Heath and Company, Lexington, MA.
Bunge, M. (1997) Mechanism and Explanation, *Philosophy of the Social Sciences*, 27: 410–465.
Daves, N. K. and M. F. Nammack (1998) US and International Mechanisms for Protecting and Managing Shark Resources, *Fisheries Research* 39: 223–228.
de Senarclens, P. (1998) Governance and the Crisis in the International Mechanisms of Regulation, *International Social Science Journal* 50, 1: 91–104.
Elster, J. (1983) *Explaining Technical Change*, Cambridge University Press.
Elster, J. (1985) *Making Sense of Marx*, Cambridge University Press.
Elster, J. (1989) *Nuts and Bolts for the Social Sciences*, Cambridge University Press.
Elster, J. (1998) A Plea for Mechanisms, in P. Hedström and R. Swedberg (eds.) *Social Mechanisms: An Analytical Approach to Social Theory*, Cambridge University Press, 45–73.

Fudenberg, D. and Tirole, J. (1994) *Game Theory*, MIT Press, Cambridge, MA.
Hedström, P. and Swedberg, R. (1997) Social Mechanisms, *Acta Sociologica* 39: 281–308.
Hedström, P. and Swedberg, R. (eds.) (1998) *Social Mechanisms: An Analytical Approach to Social Theory*, Cambridge University Press.
Hovi, J. (1998) The Relevance of Unrealistic Models for Empirical Political Science, *Homo Oeconomicus* 15: 41–56.
Iklé, F.C. (1991) *Every War Must End*, revised edition, Columbia University Press, New York.
Kahneman, D. and Tversky, A. (1979) Prospect Theory: An Analysis of Decision Under Risk, *Econometrica* 47: 263 – 91.
Kincaid, H. (1994/1990) Defending Laws in the Social Sciences, in M. Martin and L.C. McIntyre (eds.) *Readings in the Philosophy of Social Science*, MIT Press, Cambridge, MA, 111–130.
King, G., R., Keohane, O. and Verba, S. (1994) *Designing Social Inquiry: Scientific Inference in Qualitative Research*, Princeton University Press.
Little, D. (1991) *Varieties of Social Explanation: An Introduction to the Philosophy of the Social Sciences*, Westview Press, Boulder, CO.
Little, D. (1995) Causal Explanation in the Social Sciences, *The Southern Journal of Philosophy* 34 (Supplement): 31–56.
Miller, G. and Hammond, T. (1994) Why Politics is More Fundamental than Economics: Incentive-Compatible Mechanisms Are Not Credible, *Journal of Theoretical Politics*, 6: 5–26.
Rasmusen, E. (1989) *Games and Information*, Blackwell, Oxford.
Schelling, T. C. (1978) *Micromotives and Macrobehavior*, W.W. Norton, New York.
Schelling, T. C. (1998) Social Mechanisms and Social Dynamics in P. Hedström and Richard Swedberg (eds.) *Social Mechanisms: An Analytical Approach to Social Theory*, Cambridge University Press, 32–44.
Stinchcombe, A. (1991) The Conditions of Fruitfulness of Theorizing about Mechanisms in Social Science, *Philosophy of the Social Sciences,* 21: 367–388.
Stokke, O. S. and Vidas., D. (1996) *Governing the Antarctic: The Effectiveness and Legitimacy of the Antarctic Treaty System,* Cambridge University Press.
Watkins, J. W. N. (1994/1957) Historical Explanations in the Social Sciences, in M. Martin & L.C. McIntyre (eds.) *Readings in the Philosophy of Social Science*, MIT Press, Cambridge, MA: 441–450.
Young, O. (ed.) (1999) *The Effectiveness of International Environmental Regimes: Causal Connections and Behavioral Mechanisms,* MIT Press, Cambridge, MA.
Young, O., and Levy, M. A. (1999) The Effectiveness of International Environmental Regimes, in O. Young, (ed.) 1999. *The Effectiveness of International EnvironmentalRegimes, Causal Connections and Behavioral Mechanisms*, MIT Press, Cambridge, MA.

Chapter 5

BOOLEAN ANALYSIS, MECHANISMS, AND THE STUDY OF REGIME EFFECTIVENESS

OLAV SCHRAM STOKKE
The Fridtjof Nansen Institute

1. INTRODUCTION

Can we make better comparative use than today of existing case-oriented studies of regime effectiveness to develop better explanations of this phenomenon?[1] In this chapter, I argue that one way to enhance cumulation of knowledge here is to narrow in on the causal processes, or mechanisms, invoked in such studies and investigate comparatively the conditions under which they succeed in changing problem-related behaviour. A set-theoretic comparative technique developed by Charles Ragin, Qualitative Comparative Analysis (QCA), seems particularly well suited for this purpose because it permits analytical reduction even when the number of cases is too small to carry statistical analysis. The emphasis here is on the Boolean, or crisp-set version of QCA, with some discussion of the more recent extension to fuzzy sets.[2]

Empirical studies of regime effectiveness so far have largely turned on one or a handful of case-studies of individual regimes at work, narratively compared.[3] Very few attempts have been made to compare the performance of numbers of regimes that would permit statistical procedures.[4] This is in part due to the fairly recent appearance of regime effectiveness analysis implying that key concepts and theories are still in a formative stage and thus frequently difficult to adapt and apply meaningfully outside of the issue area in which they were developed—let alone a long series of issue areas. A frequently articulated complaint about case-oriented research, however, is that it tends to incorporate too much of the specific context of the case into the causal accounts to permit inferences to other cases: it tends to be weak on external validity. Others question the internal validity as well, arguing that case studies are often "over-determined" in the sense that the researcher is unable to choose between various possible or plausible explanations. In variable-oriented research, this is coined a degree-of-freedom or "small-N" problem—there are too few observations relative to the set of variables under consideration to determine the relative significance of the causal factors.[5] In an influential critique of the case-study approach, King et al. argue categorically that "nothing whatsoever can be learned about the causes of the dependent variable without taking into account other instances when the dependent variable takes on other values".[6]

For their part, many qualitative researchers maintain that the intensive approach taken in qualitative research allows privileged interpretive access to the complexity of the causal processes that are played out in any given case. From this point of view, the term "small-N problem" misrepresents the challenge confronting case-oriented research:

> Thus it is not the number of relevant cases that limits the selection of method... but the nature of the method that limits the number of cases and the number of different causal conditions that the investigator is able to consider.[7]

The QCA technique is Ragin's response to the latter challenge. The original, crisp-set version builds upon the binary language developed by George Boole in the mid-1800s, which also forms the mathematical basis of computer technology. Boolean algebra does not manipulate numbers but rather systematizes logical expressions in order to sort data and create a list of the configurations of circumstances associated with a given outcome. The systematic formalization inherent in QCA helps overcome two limitations of the *logical* analysis of causality that was elaborated by Boole's contemporary, John Stuart Mill.[8] Specifically, the logical operations involved in Mill's methods of agreement and difference become (1) increasingly complicated when the number of cases or variables grows beyond a handful, and (2) in practice, invalidated in situations of multiple or conjunctural causation, i.e., when recurrent events may be caused by *any* of several circumstances or *combinations* of circumstances.[9] Boolean algebra permits careful inspection of such configurations even when the number of cases is high; and this ability is particularly important in case-oriented research which is much less inclined than variable-oriented research to address the effect of each causal condition in isolation.[10]

In this chapter, I present, discuss and apply QCA to a series of cases of international marine living resource management—in the Barents Sea, the

Northwest Atlantic, and the Southern Ocean. Throughout the discussion, contrastive side-glances are made to the most common variable-oriented approaches to causal inference: structured and focused comparison, which has marked regime effectiveness studies to date,[11] and statistical inference based on larger data-sets.

2. CAUSAL MECHANISMS AND REGIME EFFECTIVENESS

An interesting feature of the case-studies of regime effectiveness generated so far is that a great many of them embrace a 'mechanism approach" to identify and substantiate causal claims about international institutions.[12] For instance, in a project directed by Young, contributors agreed to "frame a set of models that appear important on theoretic grounds and then turn to the case studies to assess the relevance and relative importance of the behavioural mechanisms associated with each of the models under real-world conditions".[13] Similarly, a project headed by Keohane and associates organized their causal analysis around "concrete mechanisms around which institutions can alter the behaviour of state actors, and in turn improve environmental quality".[14] In the same vein, Stokke and Vidas instructed case-study contributors to a project on Antarctic regimes to bring out the fine details of how a particular outcome came about, noting that "[d]ifferent mechanisms can be invoked when spelling out this process, accounting for *how* international regimes may affect behaviour".[15]

The purpose of introducing mechanisms in regime research, (and in this chapter) is partly to allow detailed examination of the various ways in which regimes may affect behaviour: this could be coined a *magnifying* purpose. The second objective is the *methodological* one of facilitating systematic comparison of cases by constituting them in ways that make them sufficiently homogeneous to permit employment of available comparative techniques.

While mechanisms figure prominently in regime analysis, none of the effectiveness projects mentioned here discuss in any depth exactly how they conceive of "mechanisms" and the role it may play in causal explanation.[16] It could be helpful, therefore, to pay some initial attention to the broader conceptual and methodological social science literature on mechanisms.[17] There is broad agreement in this literature that a *definition* of mechanisms must include causality, simplicity, and microscopic domain. According to Stinchcombe, for instance, a mechanism is an independently verifiable, pragmatically simplified model of micro phenomena designed to improve a theory at a macro level by enhancing its suppleness or elegance or by generating new and testable implications.[18] Substantively compatible but less restrictive as to rationale, other authors have described a mechanism as a "continuous and contiguous chain of intentional or causal links;"[19] "a series of events governed by law-like regularities that lead from the *explanans* to the *explanandum*";[20] or a fine-grained, agent-sensitive coupling between cause and effect that cannot be expected to apply beyond a limited range of circumstances.[21]

The microscopic character of mechanisms may turn on causal *agency*.[22] For instance, a theory of state behaviour is typically propped up by mechanisms modelling, e.g., how bureaucratic organizations tick, whereas one of organizational behaviour would highlight typical individual responses to organizational features like standard operating procedures.[23] But mechanisms can also be microscopic in *sequential* terms in that the theoretical capsules invoked highlight determinants of certain events in previous events. Take the notion of path-dependency, implying that earlier events structure the set of options available or considered at subsequent decision points. A simple and compelling "lock-in mechanism" identified in this line of inquiry is sunk costs, including specific investments in one particular technical or institutional solution that serves to discourage exploration of other options.[24]

While authors agree in conceiving of mechanisms as explanatory capsules—simple sometimes-true theories at a microscopic level that form parts of an aggregate explanation—they differ radically as to *how* the mechanisms relate to the aggregate theory. To Stinchcombe, mechanisms are used as pragmatic simplifying *assumptions* made in order to "let the higher-level theory go"[25] without exploding the data requirements. In other words, mechanisms are used as "grey-boxes" offering a somewhat sketchy glimpse into a hypothesized process but little elaboration or substantiation. Indeed, Stinchcombe insists that the empirical tenability of the micro-level theory in any given context is not decisive to its fruitfulness because even if it should not hold, the error introduced is likely to be small, unsystematic or evened out by a compensating aggregate-level mechanism. To illustrate, while the assumption that individual shopkeepers are profit-seekers may not always hold, the exceptions are likely to be few—and if there are many, a macro-level mechanism called the market would compensate the initial error by driving most exceptions out of business.[26] In this usage, resort to mechanisms is meant to relieve the scholar of the burden of micro-level investigation—and is thus helpful only when its boundary conditions can be specified at the aggregate level.[27]

Elster, by contrast, is much less sanguine about the causal reliability of mechanisms. Indeed, his emphasis on conjunctions of mechanisms often working in opposite directions prohibits high stakes on aggregate outcomes without close scrutiny of the "nuts and bolts" in motion. In this usage, the key purpose of mechanisms in evaluation of theories remains to permit an opening of the "black-box" to *expose* the fine grains of the process—or several reinforcing or counteracting processes—which mediate between a causal situation and a given outcome. Thus, mechanisms enable empirical explanations at an intermediate level of abstraction whenever law-like generalizations do not hold—something which happens more often than not.[28]

In regime analysis, the usage of mechanisms is primarily Elster's rather than Stinchcombe's. The general tendency is to go microscopic not only in theorizing but also in empirical substantiation. As one would expect, most of the mechanisms hypothesized in this literature turn on processes that link features of institutions and individual perception or behaviour.[29] Such mechanisms can be conceived at different levels of generality. In the study of environmental regimes, for instance, a host of specific variants have been invoked of the general mechanism that regimes may affect problem-related behaviour by altering the incentive structure of states—including by shaming, trade sanctions, or transfer of clean-production technologies. Each of those specific variants of the more general mechanism invites different hypotheses about contextual conditions. For instance, shaming presupposes attentiveness among groups whose opinion matters to the decision-maker. Trade sanctions may require legal provisions authorizing or obliging such linkages between issue areas. And transfers of technology can only occur when someone is prepared to pay for it.

When deciding upon the level of abstraction at which a mechanism is analysed and compared across cases, pragmatic trade-offs are in order between cross-case homogeneity, which requires specificity, and extensiveness within each category which might call for wider categories.[30] In this chapter, shaming has been selected for purpose of illustrating Boolean analysis because along with a few other mechanisms shaming has been salient in a number of resource-management cases previously examined by the author. It is highly possible that investigation of another set of management cases would have highlighted other mechanisms. This type of diversity would only demonstrate that social causation tends to be multiple. If, in contrast, the difference would turn not on the mechanisms invoked but on the conditions under which they succeed, it would suggest limits to the travelling capacity of the findings—the extent to which they can be expected to hold beyond the set of cases examined.[31]

In the remainder of this chapter, we shall be mostly concerned with the use of systematic comparison to pursue parsimonious causal statements without jeopardizing the *internal* validity—that is, reach the simplest causal claims that can be substantiated about the cases included in the analysis.

3. MILL, SET THEORY, AND QUALITATIVE COMPARATIVE ANALYSIS

Basic to QCA are the two logics of qualitative comparison systematized by Mill and termed the methods of agreement and of difference.[32] Mill's method of agreement is the search for a single common condition among cases agreeing on the outcome; such conditions can be relevant to a discussion of necessity. His method of difference is the search for a single distinguishing feature among cases disagreeing on the outcome—i.e., experimental design.[33] While both may be important to the discovery of connections between phenomena, only the method of difference is reliable for substantiating causality.[34] Equipped only with the method of agreement, the investigator cannot differentiate cause from effect and will be hard put to rule out spuriosity, i.e., co-variation induced by a common dependence on a non-modelled antecedent variable.

On the other hand, it is only rarely possible outside the laboratory to ascertain that two cases, or observations, are similar in all respects save one. Thus, in the many cases when variables cannot be manipulated by the researcher, the method of difference in its direct and rigorous form is unavailable. That is why recourse is often taken to the *indirect* method of difference, which is a sequential application of the method of agreement first on positive cases (to identify a causal candidate) and then on negative ones (to ascertain that the causal candidate is absent). This method is one of difference because it identifies differentiating features among positive and negative cases. And it is indirect because it does not proceed by examining the effects of an actual change in the causal candidate but by searching for sets of cases which agree in every respect except for the outcome and the causal candidate.[35] To the extent that the cases actually do agree in all other relevant respects, the indirect method of difference approximates the laboratory situation and provides a "natural experiment" which allows the investigator to observe the effect of presence or absence of the factor analysed. But because the number of potentially relevant factors is infinite, the approximation is never complete.[36]

The main new element provided by the QCA is set-theoretic algebra, which provides the formalization required to apply Mill's logic reliably even to a large number of observations. The original formulation of QCA uses crisp (or Boolean) sets, implying that cases are either inside or outside a given category. For instance, when coding a fisheries management regime with respect to transparency of decision-making—a factor widely held to be relevant to regime effectiveness—the only values available would be presence and absence. More recently, the technique has been extended to fuzzy sets which permit differentiation among cases with regard to their degree of membership in such categories.[37] To illustrate, a management regime which allows non-governmental organizations to participate as observers at regulatory meetings is more transparent than one which only publishes *post facto* reports—although none of them can be described as non-transparent.

The first step of a QCA analysis is to determine the set of cases to be included, which is frequently no straightforward matter. If the research question is how international regimes can reinforce shaming efforts in international resource management, exactly what activities should count as shaming—and when can such activities be said to be regime-based? Would it suffice that non-governmental organizations criticize management practices with reference to regime standards, or should we require that regime bodies explicitly reprimand the practices in question? Such conceptual clarification is an important part of case constitution and usually proceeds in tandem with identification of causal conditions believed to influence the effectiveness of shaming efforts. A movement back and forth occurs between the cases themselves and the concepts and theories which inform the study. That movement revolves around the building of a *truth table*, an ordering device which on the one hand lists all possible combinations of the causal conditions believed to be salient—the property space—and, on the other hand, variation in outcome among empirically observed combinations.[38] The distribution of cases on the truth table can be used to evaluate the appropriateness of the initial model. If the model fails to align cases in reasonably comparable groupings, such heterogeneity may provide clues to refinement of the causal model. One notable occasion for such refinement is when the preliminary table displays "contradictory" cases, i.e., the same configurations yield opposite outcomes in different cases. Sometimes such contradictions can be removed by adding a new causal condition. This way, the QCA procedure guides the elaboration of the causal model by confronting initial ideas with findings from the cases, thus connecting the features of a single case with the patterns displayed across cases.

The next step is to use the truth table to evaluate propositions about necessary and sufficient conditions for the phenomenon that is studied. Factors which are either present or absent for *all* cases with a given outcome may, if corrobarated by other knowledge, be relevant to claims about necessary conditions for that outcome. In contrast, propositions about sufficient conditions can be explored by identifying causal configurations which are present for at least *one* case with that outcome but in none of the cases with a different outcome.[39] This initial list of configurations uniquely present in cases with a given outcome can then be minimized by means of set-theoretic algebra to reach the most general formulation of sufficient conditions that is compatible with the cases examined. The various ways of minimization are detailed in the analysis below; essentially, it is done by removing redundant conditions and terms found in the initial configuration.

A final step supported by QCA is the introduction of *simplifying assumptions* whenever the analysis is impeded by limited diversity. Limited diversity refers to insufficient variation in the causal variables included: empty cells in a variable-oriented data matrix or, in Boolean analysis, that the empirical cases at hand do not exhaust the number of logically possible combinations of the causal factors involved. In such situations, the researcher cannot know how the non-existing cases would have influenced the necessity or sufficiency tests of causal configurations sketched above. A frequent effect of limited diversity is to render the analysis less conclusive. In variable-oriented analysis, this shows up as inability to impose statistical or comparative control on competing variables. In Boolean analysis, limited diversity usually implies that set-theoretic minimization is inhibited by the fact that few configurations are identical in all respects save one.[40] An important feature of QCA is that it allows substantive inspection and evaluation of the assumptions that must be made about non-existing configurations in order to proceed beyond the minimization that is possible on the basis of existing cases.[41]

Another troubling aspect of limited diversity concerns external validity, or the relationship between the set of cases analysed and the wider population for which the causal propositions are sometimes meant to apply. While, as noted, the focus of this chapter is internal validity, it is worth noting that set-theoretic reduction can explicate the generalization problem by producing a compact statement about the causal combinations that are absent in the material and for which the causal propositions reached cannot readily be assumed to apply. That statement expresses the substantive boundaries of the analysis.[42] The compactness of such a statement can support a discussion, based on other substantive and theoretical knowledge, of what outcome they likely would have generated had the researcher been able to study them.[43]

4. SHAMING IN INTERNATIONAL RESOURCE MANAGEMENT: CROSS-CASE ANALYSIS

The number of cases selected for illustrative comparative analysis in this chapter is ten. Since the emphasis is on the analytical procedure and not on the substance of analysis, neither case constitution nor model specification are given the attention they would otherwise receive. All cases have been pinned down in intensive case studies reported elsewhere and will be rather sketchily recounted here.[44] They all revolve around international regimes serving as platforms for efforts to shape, by means of public exposure, problem-relevant behaviour in one of the three realms of resource management: science, regulation, and compliance stimulation. Some of the cases reviewed here portray different phases of a controversial issue addressed under a regime. The rationale for conceiving these phases as separate cases is that the causal configuration has shifted in that at least one of the conditions modelled in the truth table has changed its value; recall that configurative analysis conceives cases as ensembles of conditions.[45]

4.1 Shaming and How It Can be Modelled

The one mechanism analysed here, shaming, highlights attempts to bring about a change in problem-related behaviour not by material rewards or punishment but by *exposing* certain practices to third parties whose opinion matters to the target of shaming. International regimes facilitate shaming to the extent that they provide, i.a., authoritative standards to which behaviour can be compared or enhanced transparency regarding that behaviour.[46] All cases sketched below involve shaming efforts on the part of either regime bodies, other state parties, or non-governmental organizations interested in resource management. The extent to which this shaming is regime-based, however, varies along two dimensions: (1) Whether the shamers can substantiate their criticism by reference to explicit recommendations by the regime's scientific advisory body; and (2) whether the target behaviour violates a conservation measure adopted by the regime's decision-making body. The second condition, commitment, is defined inclusively to capture not only legally binding conservation rules. This is because most fisheries management regimes provide members with either the power of veto in decisions on binding conservation measures or an opting-out clause which allows them to remain legally uncommitted even if the measure is adopted. As for instance Norway and Japan have experienced in the case of whaling, such reservations cannot protect them from intensive shaming strongly anchored in conservation measures adopted by the International Whaling Commission, of which they are both members.[47]

When seeking to identify other conditions likely to influence the successfulness of shaming efforts—that is whether or not the target adapts its behaviour in response to shaming—earlier work on the subject alerts us to at least two causal pathways.[48] One is an international path, by which the target state is concerned with the costs associated with loss of reputation as a reliable partner. (3) A condition worth examining therefore, frequently coined the "shadow of the future", is the perceived need of the target for striking new deals under the regime and whether such beneficial deals are likely to be jeopardized if the criticism is ignored. (4) Presumably, the target would also consider the inconvenience of the behavioural change shamers are trying to accomplish. (5) A final factor is highlighted by the domestic politics pathway, i.e., the political costs that may ensue on the domestic scene for being scandalized as a culprit under the regime: there is much to suggest that shaming is more likely to succeed if there is a strong domestic constituency reverberating the particular criticism voiced internationally.[49]

These five proposed conditions are hardly daring. They simply reflect the pervasive expectation that governmental behaviour will be guided by political costs associated with the options available, either in relations with other states or domestically—and that such costs are likely to be higher if shaming efforts can be buttressed by authoritative scientific advice or a conservation measure adopted by an institution that counts among its members the target of shaming.

4.2   The Constitution of Cases

The regime mechanism studied here, shaming, is particularly effective in identifying cases: since appeals to third parties require a level of publicity or political row, the researcher is likely to discover shaming whenever it occurs. Beyond this, the constitution of cases that go into a QCA analysis proceeds in a way that combines features of the two approaches that inspired it—variable- and case-oriented research. According to the rules of the former, case selection should primarily be guided by the model that is put up for test. This calls for appropriate variation in the dependent variable and all the causal conditions included. Moreover, the number of cases should permit comparative or statistical control of rival conditions; and if the population of cases permits, they should be picked randomly to avoid systematic influence of non-modelled conditions. In contrast, case-driven narrative analyses usually start out with a few well-known cases featuring the phenomenon under scrutiny and seen as being sufficiently similar to warrant comparison.[50] The explanatory model is then developed in a step-wise manner as understanding of the cases deepens, in part by examining their similarities and dissimilarities.[51]

As we have seen, the case-oriented movement back and forth between model and evidence is characteristic of QCA analysis as well. In the process, new cases may be added whereas others could drop out. In our context, this could happen because the role of shaming in some cases proved more marginal than initially believed, or because the focus in the meantime had been narrowed down to one of the versions of shaming indicated above—domestic and international. Although a QCA researcher would probably be more inclined to add a causal condition deemed as substantively interesting even if this should lead to empty data-matrix cells, important canons of variable-oriented research are nevertheless heeded. Received theoretical and substantive knowledge is important to the initial specification of the model, thus relating the study to a broader set of investigations of the matter discussed.[52] The truth table directs attention to missing configurations, and the analytical constraints associated with limited diversity induce a search for a set of cases with adequate variance in the causal conditions. Moreover, since sufficiency statements are based on causal configurations that differentiate among positive and negative outcomes, the QCA procedure concurs with the variable-oriented rule that causal analysis is supported by variation in the dependent variable as well.[53]

Meaningful comparison also requires a level of homogeneity among the cases with regard to non-modelled conditions. In this study, for instance, we would like to be reasonably sure that what we observe when examining shaming efforts and a behavioural response is the success or failure of shaming, and not of some other strategy designed to affect behaviour. Accordingly, cases were not included in the study if they displayed a high score on other factors known to be powerful in inducing behavioural change. Important examples in our context would be cases where mechanisms such as compensation or punishment loom large. Thus, whereas Iceland's protracted rejection of Norwegian–Russian management rules in high-seas areas of the Barents Sea is recorded as a case of failed shaming, Iceland's ultimate acceptance of those rules in 1999 is *not* seen as constituting a case of successful shaming because of the linkage made in the relevant agreement between backing down on continued non-regulated high-seas fisheries and gaining access to the national waters of the coastal states.[54] This pragmatic selection is motivated by a desire to keep the model as simple as possible; including cases featuring non-shaming inducements could be handled by adding conditions to the model. The cost of simplicity, judged as bearable in this study, is that the effect of shaming cannot be studied in conjunction with such other inducements.

4.3   Ten Cases of Shaming

In this section the ideas represented in the model are applied in a number of management processes. While the detailing of each case is hopefully sufficient to lend some plausibility to the subsequent coding, it is of course inadequate for actually substantiating the codings. It will be recalled that the purpose of this chapter is not to test a model but to explore a methodological technique.

A first instance turns on *overfishing* of Barents Sea cod, managed jointly by Norway and the Soviet Union, later Russia, since the evolution of exclusive economic zones in the late 1970s.[55] While the total allowable catch is set by a Joint Fisheries Commission on the basis of scientific advice from the International Council for the Exploration of the Sea (ICES), annual agreements allowed Norwegian coastal fishermen to continue operations with traditional, fixed gear even after the quota had been taken. This provision was a part of the compromise on how to divide the cod quota and was much appreciated by coastal fishermen in Northern Norway. From 1980 onwards, however, the abundance of fish within reach of small coastal vessels increased dramatically, pushing Norwegian overfishing of their share of the scientifically recommended cap to levels ranging from 40 to 100 percent. The Soviets, unsurprisingly, expressed deep concern at a series of Commission meetings; and the trawler-based part of the Norwegian industry, which fished on the same stock, was also unhappy about the situation. Mismanagemen of such proportions undermined the credibility of the regime as an instrument of reciprocal restraint, implying that the shadow of the future loomed large. Norwegian regulations were soon sharpened, and when those measures were criticised in the parliament, the government justified them by reference to conservation needs as well as Soviet complaints. In 1984, the coastal-fisherman's right to continue fishing after the cap had been reached, was removed without compensation: the shaming had been successful. The Boolean coding for this and the following nine cases are provided in the table found in section 4.4 below.[56]

A contrasting instance concerns *mesh-size* regulations. Citing a series of ICES recommendations that the mesh-size be enlarged, Norway required this of its own fishermen in the Barents Sea and throughout the 1980s urged Soviet authorities to do the same. The main arguments for larger mesh-size in the trawl bags is protection of juveniles and the fact that for any given catch level, targeting bigger fish removes fewer individuals from the spawning stock. Moscow had been much less enthusiastic about this measure than the Norwegians, however, presumably in part because migration patterns make the average size of groundfish taken off the Norwegian coast larger than those taken off of Russia. Larger mesh-size will tend to reduce the efficiency of harvesting off the Russian coast and shift more of the effort to the distant-water fishing grounds further to the west. The Soviet position was bolstered by an argument promoted by Soviet researchers that smaller fish do not in fact escape trawl-bags whatever the mesh-size, due to the density of other fish, and that alternative measures would be more effective. Whatever the merits of such competing scientific views, the mesh-size dispute was hardly grave enough for Moscow to fear that it would disrupt cooperative relations with Norway in the fisheries sector. Among the predicaments created by the 1982 Law of the Sea Convention is that states sharing fish stocks are stuck with each other—exclusive authority inside their respective zones implies that none of them can hope to achieve sustainable management on their own.[57] In the early period of this dispute, there were virtually no civil society groups in the Soviet Union independent of the state apparatus to reprimand management practices if appropriate. The fisheries industry, in contrast, was well incorporated into the national and international management system, and Norwegian science-based shaming efforts were rejected.

From the late 1980s, especially after Chernobyl and towards the dissolution of the Union, complaints over environmental malpractices were increasingly accepted and even encouraged. In this period, Soviet fisheries scientists outside of the departmental structure published a series of reports and articles vehemently attacking the management approach taken by the Joint Fisheries Commission. Adding to the potential domestic reverberation of foreign criticism was the fact that by then, the traditional supremacy of the Soviet fisheries bureaucracy was challenged by the State Committee on the Environment which, around the turn of the decade, formally if not in practice, were in charge of both domestic quota allocation and the compliance control apparatus.[58] Despite this change on the domestic scene, the Soviet position on the mesh-size issue remained firm.[59]

One of the consequences of the gradual liberalization of foreign trade in the Soviet Union, which exploded with the dissolution of that state and the appearance of Russia as legal successor in the region, was a crippling of the traditional Soviet *compliance control* system. This system had been based on comparison of catch reports by vessels with delivery reports by processors. From the early 1990s, most of the Russian harvest was delivered in Western ports, especially in Norway, which created an enforcement deficit in waters where Russian-licenced vessels could not be inspected by the Norwegian Coast Guard.[60] According to ICES, as much as a quarter of the harvest in 1992 was taken in excess of allocated quotas and went unreported, the lion's share taken by Russian vessels. Norwegian authorities, the harvesting sector, and fisheries press were highly critical of the way Russian quota commitments were implemented. The hard currency obtained from deliveries in the West was much in demand in Russia's contracting economy, however, so there were powerful counterforces to reform of the compliance system. Norwegian concern grew further when Faroese vessels were allowed to buy parts of the already substantially overfished Russian quotas and operate, virtually uncontrolled, in large parts of the Barents Sea. As in the case of Norwegian overfishing a decade earlier, but this time with Russia as the culprit, the entire value of the Joint Fisheries Commission as a vehicle for reciprocal cooperation was at stake. Soon after the Norwegian complaints had been substantiated, the Faroese were thrown out of Russian waters even though in the meantime they had bought additional quotas. Moreover, a whole menu of Norwegian proposals to enhance the transparency of Russian operations in its own waters were accepted by Moscow, including routinized exchange of information on landings and inspection reports, direct lines of communication between inspection vessels of the two states, and collaboration on the development of a positional tracking system for the entire Barents Sea.[61]

The regional management system was soon to be challenged from another side, however. While the cod had been loyal to coastal-state management aspirations for decades and remained within national waters, around 1990 a change in the migration pattern made it increasingly available in the so-called *Loophole*, a sector of international waters located in between the Norwegian and the Russian zones. Icelandic vessels, troubled by poor harvests in domestic waters, began a substantial fishery here, with their flag state highlighting the fact that coastal states are obliged by international law to cooperate with other user states in the management of stocks straddling national waters into the high seas.[62] A period of intense shaming began, in which Norway and Russia refused to negotiate the issue with Iceland and in a range of fora portrayed the Icelanders as having recklessly overfished their own stocks and now being out to grab the fruits of coastal-state restraint in the Barents Sea. Since the newcomer was not at the time incorporated in the regional regime, however, the coastal states were unable to link their criticism to Icelandic commitments to scientific or regulatory regime outputs. Indeed, the coastal-state insistence that Iceland had no rights whatsoever with regard to Barents Sea cod polarized the issue further and reduced the political clout of those in Iceland who were uneasy about the rapid shift implied from coastal-state frontrunner to distant-water hardliner.[63] From the Icelandic perspective, moreover, the shadow cast by this Norwegian and Russian wrath was hardly more than slightly chilling as they had no previous fishing interest in the region to jeopardize. On the contrary, by ignoring the coastal-state complaints, which in any case were shaky on legal grounds, Iceland actually gained a level of historical fishing that would come in handy in future negotiations. The Loophole case is one of failed shaming: an agreement was finally drawn up in 1999 but Iceland's acceptance of coastal-state management primacy was contingent upon Icelandic access to cod in the Norwegian and Russian zones.[64]

On the other side of the North Atlantic, the coastal state Canada had for years faced similar problems with fishermen from the European Community (EC) operating on *unilateral quotas* in the Nose and Tail of the Grand Banks—a high-seas area adjacent to Canada's national waters and managed under the Northwest Atlantic Fisheries Organization (NAFO). Since 1986, the EC had taken considerable diplomatic beating from Canada for ignoring a high-seas cod moratorium recommeded by the organization's Scientific Council and adopted by the regulatory Commission. Instead, the EC had set quotas for itself that were taken beyond Canada's jurisdiction. Due to an opting-out clause in the NAFO Convention, such unilateral quotas were allowed; the Canadian argument was that this undermined the collective enterprise of managing the stocks. There is no question that this conflict severely threatened cohesion within NAFO, with two potential costs to the target of shaming. The Canadians might—and actually did—close their own waters to EC vessels; and other NAFO members would likely ask why they should stay within their quotas when another major player did not. For its part, the EC portrayed NAFO as a tool for projection of Canadian management authority and excessively cautious management principles, into high-seas areas. There is much to suggest that the Northern cod stock in these waters had been pinpointed by the EC as one of the more promising bases for boosting Community catches—vital due to the simultaneous entry of Spain and Portugal which had considerably enhanced EC harvesting capacity.[65] Other EC states also held strong stakes in this solution because of their determination to keep large parts of the Iberian distant-water fleets outside of Community waters—and Canada's complaints were for years rejected by the EC.[66]

By 1992, however, the situation had changed in one important way: the stocks had collapsed, implying that going along with coastal-state demands would not be as inconvenient as in the past. For some years, the Community accepted NAFO quotas and re-established cooperative ties with Canada.[67]

The last three cases of shaming outlined here turn on management of *krill* in the Southern Ocean. Until the decline in the activity of Eastern European states associated with their transition to market economies, the Antarctic krill had fed the largest crustacean fishery in the world. Commercially, krill has been by far the most significant species taken in the region since the adoption of the 1980 Convention on the Conservation of Antarctic Marine Living Resources (CCAMLR)—but also one of the last to be regulated. While demands for restrictions had surfaced at the CCAMLR Commission meetings early on—spurred by fears that in some areas the fishery might critically interfere with the food situation for predatory species such as albatross and penguins—no agreement could be reached in the Scientific Committee until 1991 when quantitative caps were recommended and acted upon by the Commission.[68]

The process which yielded this outcome provides an interesting glimpse of the dynamic relationship between scientific investigations, political shaming, and regulatory advances in the Antarctic context. The initial position of the major fishing states, especially Japan and the Soviet Union, had been that there was no scientific evidence that the krill stocks or associated species were threatened by the fishery. Accordingly, from their perspective, catch restrictions would be inconvenient not only by constraining krill harvestors but also by violating the principle that conservation measures should be science-based. There was rising wariness in these states that CCAMLR, like the International Whaling Commission before it, would grow into a preservationist regime.[69] In other words, to the extent that the user states worried about how this contested issue would impact on future cooperation, the long-term costs of accommodating the shamers would seem to be higher than those associated with defiance.[70] Both states were accomplished distant-water fishing nations, and the Antarctic option was not questioned at home. The affairs of the Seventh Continent are usually rather obscure in the domestic politics of member states and largely handled by a thin and scarcely monitored bureaucratic layer. Hence, attempts by the conservationist majority in CCAMLR to push Japan and the Soviet Union to assume commitments on the basis of possible but unsubstantiated ecosystemic effects were rejected out of hand.[71]

In response, the non-fishing majority in CCAMLR shifted the focus of the debate from conservation measures to information measures. More specifically, they successfully induced the Scientific Committee to request sharper and more fine-scaled reporting requirements regarding effort and harvest, especially in certain areas designated by a working group on ecosystem monitoring. The initial reluctance on the part of the fishing nations, essentially on grounds that it would be excessively inconvenient for the fishermen to maintain detailed logs of where and when, and with what result, the trawl-bags were dragged, proved difficult to defend, especially when considering their general insistence that regulations should be based on firm scientific evidence. The cooperative atmosphere within this regime had been considerably improved in the mid-1980s, following Gorbachev's rise to power in the Soviet Union which had rendered East-West relations in general more amiable. The new reporting rules became effective in 1987.[72] A few years later, those reports enabled the Scientific Committee to assert that krill fishery occurred in highly concentrated areas, some of which were close to important growth areas for major predators, thus providing the scientific basis for the recommended precautionary measures on krill that became effective in 1991.[73]

4.4   Constructing a Truth Table

The first step of a truth table construction is already done: the initial specification of the model which structured the presentation of cases here. Entering the codings of those cases into the table is the next step—and frequently, as noted, one that encourages refinement of the model. The ability to use contradictions as case-oriented leads in order to evaluate the causal model is important because QCA, like all comparative analysis, is highly vulnerable to misspecification of the model. Recall that statements about necessary causes highlight those factors which are present or absent in all configurations with a given outcome, whereas sufficiency claims are supported by all causal configurations that are uniquely associated with the given outcome. The basis of both types of claims breaks down in the presence of spuriosity. On one account, the problem of missing variables is less acute in qualitative than in statistical analysis, because the intensive approach of the former ensures a more in-depth familiarity with the cases and thus lesser likelihood that important factors are ignored. On the other hand, statistical representations make allowance for misspecification by means of confidence intervals and more generally by the underlying assumption of probabilistic relationships among variables.[74] The extended, fuzzy-set version of QCA is much closer to statistical approaches in this regard by including a functional equivalent to confidence intervals, "fuzzy adjustment", to allow for imprecise measurement of set membership as well as procedures for significance tests according to specified probability criteria.[75]

The number of cases reviewed above (ten) and the causal conditions modelled (five) would make it difficult indeed to systematically compare these cases in the same narrative mode as they were presented. In the truth table, they show up as one double entry (two cases captured by one configuration of causal condition), four successes and five failures.

Table 5.1. *Ten cases of shaming.*

Advice	Commitment	Shadow of the future	Inconvenience	Reverberation	Success	Cases
1	0	1	1	1	1	Overfishing
1	0	0	1	0	0	Mesh-size 1
1	0	0	1	1	0	Mesh-size 2
0	0	0	1	0	0	Loophole
1	1	1	1	1	1	Compliance
1	1	1	1	0	0	EC unilat.1
1	1	1	0	0	1	EC unilat.2
0	0	0	1	0	0	Krill cap 1
1	0	0	0	0	1	Krill report Krill cap 2

There are no contradictions, which may lend credibility to the model but this also implies that one of the heuristic strengths of the Boolean approach cannot be tried out here, i.e., its ability to support refinement of the model.[76]

From this table it is easy to compute an equation listing the observed configurations associated with a given outcome. Each such configuration is a complex statement about the absence or presence of the modelled conditions in cases with that outcome. For compactness, conditions are represented by initials and upper-casing indicates presence and lower-casing absence:[77]

(A) SUCCESS = A·c·S·I·R + A·C·S·I·R + A·C·S·i·r + A·c·s·i·r

Since two cases display the same configuration, this is already a step forward in descriptive compactness.[78] Depending on the persuasiveness of the causal substantiation, conducted in part within individual cases by marshalling earlier conceptual and substantive research and in part comparatively by constructing and refining the truth table, it is also a statement with explanatory value. A first observation is that in all cases of successful shaming, the management practice in question had violated scientific recommendations. Accordingly, this data set is compatible with the claim that a basis in regime-generated scientific advice is a *necessary* condition for shaming to induce behavioural change. Secondly, with regard to sufficiency the series of configurations in equation A expresses the *diversity* of combinations that are associated with the outcome. As such, QCA sits well with the assumption of mechanism-oriented regime effectiveness research that there is usually more than one causal pathway to a given outcome.

4.5 Analytical Reduction

The purpose of the next step is to condense equation A further to expose more general patterns, and this minimization occurs in three rounds.[80] The first round combines features of the methods of agreement and difference by a complete series of paired comparisons among positive cases which allows removal of redundant factors within each configuration. Identification of such redundant factors is straightforward: if two terms differing in only one causal condition yield the same outcome, the distinguishing factor must be irrelevant.[81] Consider the Norwegian overfishing of Barents Sea cod in the early 1980s and the Russian compliance failure a decade later.[82] The two cases are equal in all (modelled) respects except that the Russians violated a regime commitment whereas the Norwegians did not. Since both are cases of successful shaming, we can conclude that whenever the shared conditions are present, the ability to base shaming in regime commitment is not essential to induce behavioural change. In other words, the causal propositions in the two initial terms are overly restrictive—and by removing the redundant condition a more general statement replaces the two.

A caveat is in place here. While they form part of the basis of QCA, both the method of agreement and the indirect method of difference are unreliable if there is more than one sufficient cause for an outcome—a situation not uncommon in social life and indeed the point of departure for QCA. The reason is that these methods reduce complexity by denying causal status to factors that are either absent in some positive cases (method of agreement) or present in both positive and negative cases (indirect method of difference).[83] None of those denials hold if the assumption of singular causation is relaxed, implying that both methods can be excessively rejective of causal hypotheses. In Boolean minimization, by contrast, the rejection of such a condition is not generalized. The condition is rejected as causally redundant *only* in the specific context defined by the pattern of absence and presence of other conditions included in the paired comparison. Hence, the configurative nature of the Boolean approach permits a more disciplined reduction of causal statements than do the method of agreement and indirect method of difference.

In essence, paired comparison of configurations mimics experimental design by observing the (non)impact of an operative variable while keeping other causal candidates constant. An inductive movement from complexity to generality occurs in a systematic and restrained manner. The product of these paired comparisons is an equation listing the minimized, or least restrictive, set of causal propositions permitted by the cases considered. As in our data set there are only two occurrence of cases agreeing both on the outcome and on all conditions except one, the Boolean exercise provides only a moderate reduction:

(B) SUCCESS = A·S·I·R + A·C·S·i·r + A·c·s·i·r

The next round of minimization removes terms that are contained by others, i.e., form subsets of more general or less-restricted terms. For instance, a statement that commitment combined with non-inconvenience (C·i) is sufficient for shaming to succeed contains a statement including the same requirements and also a third—such as reverberation (C·i·r). Inspection of equation B, however, reveals that no such redundancy exists among the causal statements involved.

The same goes for the third round of simplification, relevant whenever some of the remaining terms are not essential to account for the initial configurations listed in the truth table. Such superfluous terms, which do not uniquely cover any original case representation, should be removed if the goal is to achieve the most parsimonious causal statement compatible with the data set.[84] Note that the term "superfluous" can be misleading and that this final round of simplification may be undesirable for other reasons. Whereas the first and second rounds enhance the generality of causal propositions, the third essentially narrows the range of causal pathways to the outcome that are laid bare in the analysis. In the social world, such "superfluous" pathways could very well be of greater practical interest than those remaining in the most compact statement—perhaps because the conditions involved in those terms turn out to be more accessible for amendment by social actors desiring to affect the outcome.[85]

In our data set, however, partly due to limited diversity, the second and third rounds of minimization yield no improvement in generality. Equation B can be rewritten as:

(C) SUCCESS = I·A·S·R + i· (A·c·s·r + A·C·S· r)

While the causal pattern remains rather messy, this clarifies that whenever the sought-for behavioural adaptation is inconvenient, shaming must be bolstered by not only scientific advice but also the risk of cooperative breakdown and domestic reverberation in order to succeed. In contrast, adaptation that is not inconvenient can be induced without domestic reverberation but only under certain conditions. Specifically, there appears to be two pathways to successful shaming in such situations, the first of which is of greater substantive interest. We see from the first bracketed term that if the target is not committed to the standards that are violated and the issue is not perceived as grave enough to threaten the regime, it would suffice that the shamer can invoke regime-based scientific advice. The second term points to a much more demanding pathway, involving also target commitment and a risk of cooperative breakdown; and since the behavioural change called for is not inconvenient, the success of this particular causal configuration seems over-determined.

So far, therefore, Boolean analysis of the ten cases has exposed science-basis as an important factor for shaming efforts to succeed—this data set even suggests that it may be a necessary condition. A second observation is that violation of regime conservation measures—a factor usually given much attention in analyses of regime effectiveness—does not stand out as a salient cause in this data set. This may be because commitment was conceived to include non-binding instances as well. Thirdly, equation C brings out that the more inconvenient the sought-for behavioural change, the more "pull conditions" must be present for shaming to succeed.[86]

4.6   Pursuing Generality: Assessing Simplifying Assumptions

With a view to reaching less restrictive causal statements, QCA allows reasoned introduction of assumptions about the non-existing combinations of the modelled conditions. The most effective version would be to code positively, and thus add to the equation, only those non-existent combinations that would allow further simplification by pairwise comparison.[87] While this avenue to greater generality may seem arbitrary or even dubious, in important respects it differs favorably from that taken in statistical analysis. This is because simplifying assumptions are not made at the outset, as in statistical packages which often make strong assumption about homogeneity, additivity, and linearity—in QCA they may or may not be introduced depending on the purpose of the investigation. Moreover, when such assumptions are introduced, the researcher is able to *specify* them in substantive terms and thus evaluate their plausibility.

The limitations on diversity in the present data is considerable, but hardly greater than in most narratively structured comparison: it can be expressed as 23 missing cases out of 32 logical combinations.[88] When assuming that the non-existing configurations yield the outcome that would most *radically* minimize restrictions on the causal statement, the solution is:

(D) $SUCCESS^{Minimizing} = A \cdot i + A \cdot S \cdot R$

A procedural note is in order here. When assumptions are made about non-existing configurations, Boolean minimization may eliminate also causal conditions that would pass the necessity test. This is why it is important to test for necessity before sufficiency and ensure that any necessary conditions are retained in solutions that harbour simplifying assumptions.[89]

Equation D is considerably more compact. Science basis stands out as a necessary condition for successful shaming in this data-set and if the behavioural adaptation sought for is not inconvenient, such basis is also sufficient. If on the other hand the target perceives accommodation of shamers' demands as inconvenient, two additional conditions must be present: the perception that the contested issue is grave enough to threaten the cooperation and a strong domestic constituency that reverberates the criticism. QCA warns us, however, that the price of reaching such a potent causal statement is to accept the plausibility of all of the following assumptions:

(E) $ASSUMED\ SUCCESS^{Minimizing} = A \cdot (C \cdot s \cdot i \cdot r + c \cdot S \cdot i \cdot r + c \cdot s \cdot i \cdot R + C \cdot s \cdot i \cdot R + c \cdot S \cdot i \cdot R + c \cdot S \cdot i \cdot R + C \cdot s \cdot i \cdot R)$

None of those assumptions run counter to the reasoning behind the model nor to the empirical observations of successful and failed shaming. Specifically, all assumptions are loyal to the finding that scientific basis is a necessary condition for success, none of them are contradicted by any of the cases represented in the data set, and none of them involve inconvenience, the model's only "push" factor.[90] In other data sets, however, radically minimizing assumptions may be less substantively plausible and even here their multitude and diversity calls for some hesitance. Fortunately, QCA permits more selective introduction of simplifying assumptions on non-existing configurations. We may at this stage, for instance, be unconvinced that the regime commitment condition is of such minor importance to the success of shaming efforts. A more prudent approach would then be to remove those simplifying assumptions that harbour the claim that success is possible without commitments—that is, three of the terms in equation E. The minimized equation would read as follows:

(F) $SUCCESS^{Selective} = A \cdot (C \cdot i + s \cdot i \cdot r + S \cdot I \cdot R)$

This more prudent set of simplifying assumptions permits causal statements that are somewhat more restricted than equation D but still rather general. As before, science basis is a necessary ingredient of successful shaming. If the behavioural change called for is not inconvenient, success would in addition require either commitment or the *absence* of two factors which are generally supportive of shaming efforts, threat to the cooperation and domestic reverberation. Whenever the behavioural change is inconvenient, however, successful shaming would require the support of three of the four pull factors: science, the shadow of the future and domestic reverberation. The main point to make here, however, is that as far as usage of simplifying assumptions is concerned, QCA compares favourably with both narratively structured qualitative analysis and statistical approaches. Narrative comparativists would never be able to conduct thought experiments of the type shown here with the same level of accuracy and transparency. In much statistical analyses, the assumptions imposed in order to reach simpler representations are explicit but much less available for substantive evaluation—partly because they are hardwired into the procedure and partly because the substantive plausibility of abstract assumptions such as homogeneity and linearity is more difficult to pin down.[91]

4.7 Vulnerability to Miscodings

Conceiving causal relationships deterministically, as the Boolean version of QCA does, makes strong assumptions on the accuracy of the data.[91] The threat to validity posed by sloppy or opportunistic coding is enhanced further by the fact that modelled variables must be coded dichotomously, even when cut-off points can be hard to define in terms that would settle each case unequivocally.[92] In a strong statement of this, Goldthorpe argues that the dichotomous-variable requirement in the QCA version used here disables the analyst to cope with border cases, i.e., those which are not clearly captured by either of the categories of a dichotomous variable.[93] As we have seen, this criticism of QCA is now largely obsolete because the fuzzy-set version permits partial membership in categories and procedures for addressing measurement error.

Even for the Boolean version, however, it is a very simple matter to assess the sensitivity of the findings to the coding of specific cases—by rerunning the minimization with the conditions correspondingly recoded. Consider the successful attempt to shame opponents of krill regulations into accepting first fine-scaled reporting and then an ecosystem-based quota in 1991. Upon reflection, characterizing the latter as not inconvenient is not entirely beyond dispute. The reasons for coding them as such were that the quota was set higher than the preceding year's harvest and that several user states were scaling down their operations in the region for other reasons. On the other hand, this coding would presuppose that the user states had no worries about future implications of accepting a symbolic quota. Once in place, however, such conservation measures have had a tendency in CCAMLR practice to be sharpened over time and the Eastern European effort reductions could after all be temporary. Recoding the cases as inconvenient yields no contradictions; and with the same selective assumption as above, the minimized equation would be:

(G) SUCCESS = A·(C·i + s·i·r + S·I·R)

This statement is identical with E, and the introduction of radically minimizing assumptioins yields a statement equivalent with D. This means that the results are not vulnerable to the coding of the two krill cases. The more general point to make is that by this simple exercise we are able to assess the robustness of the results to the coding of cases that are hard to pin down on one or several conditions. Had the impacts of such recoding been greater, this would have been a strong inducement to go back to the relevant Southern Ocean cases and seek more evidence on whether or not the krill reporting and quota measures were actually perceived by the fishing states as inconvenient.

4.8 Analysis of Negative Cases

So far, only limited use has been made of the cases featuring failed efforts to pressure governments to improve their management practice by means of shaming. These negative cases were indirectly used when attending to possible contradictions in the process of specifying the model, i.e., by ensuring that the configurations included in the sufficiency analysis are only present in positive cases. The failed shaming efforts also played a role during the minimization of the initial sufficiency statement by diminishing the problem of limited diversity in the data set.

It can be of interest to make more direct use of the negative cases. The following statement expresses the conditions, as far as our model and cases are concerned, for shaming efforts to *fail*:

(H) success = A·c·s·I·r + A·c·s·I·R + a·c·s·I·r + A·C·S·I·r + a·c·s·I·r

We note immediately that this equation is compatible with the hypothesis that inconvenience is a necessary condition for shaming to fail. In order to examine what other ingredients are required to *guarantee* failure, equation H can be minimized according to the same procedures as those applied on positive cases. With radically minimizing assumptions, the result would be as follows:

(I) success = s·I + I·r

Depending on the plausibility of the assumptions underlying equation I, it would seem to support the earlier finding that commitment is peripheral to the effectiveness of shaming efforts. We also note that although a basis in authoritative scientific advice was identified above as a necessary condition for successful shaming, at least under radically minimizing assumptions this factor is not a part of sufficiency statements on failure. Again, a strength of the QCA procedure is that it supports substantive evaluation of the assumptions that are made about missing configurations in order to reach statements as general as equations D and I.

5. CONCLUSIONS

The underlying research strategy proposed here is highly disaggregative. Effectiveness studies are rendered comparable by focusing not on international regimes as complex social realities but on specific *mechanisms*—simple explanatory capsules connecting the regime and some problem-relevant behaviour. This chapter has narrowed in on one such mechanism, shaming.[94] As would be expected, shaming was not always successful in inducing behavioural change. The problem-related activities sometimes affected, however, mapped onto key turning points or long-standing disputes in the histories of the regimes involved: sharpening of international rules, national implementing regulations, and compliance control practices. The explanatory model constructed around the shaming mechanism is specific to it; examination of significantly different mechanisms, such as learning and obligation, or of more general versions of the incentive-alteration mechanism will require different models and separate analyses.

While this forms a necessary background, the core of this chapter has turned on whether a particular comparative technique, Qualitative Comparative Analysis, is a *promising* tool for improving comparison across detailed case-studies of international regimes. The answer flowing from the application in this chapter is affirmative. The reason is basically that QCA permits analytical reduction, or simplification, of the data without ceding on the view that comparison must proceed configuratively—even when the number of cases is fairly low.

In the *model development stage*, QCA and variable-oriented competitors like structured and focused comparison and statistical inference all rely upon received theoretical and substantive knowledge. If an important difference exists, it would be that the QCA procedure explicitly compels the researcher to re-examine the model in the process of *constituting cases*. Thus, in the Boolean version of QCA the non-acceptance of contradictory cases—cases displaying the same value on the causal conditions yet disagreeing on the outcome—may provide clues for model refinement that are more likely to escape non-formalized narratives and probabilistically oriented studies. On the other hand, the random element of social reality suggests that in any case such clues must be used with caution. The notion of a "contradictory" case is also less significant in the fuzzy-set version of QCA, since partial membership in outcome and causal categories will redefine many crisp-set contradictions to fuzzy-set discordances.[95] Beyond this, QCA joins variable-oriented methods in encouraging strategic variation in the causal conditions specified. One difference is that QCA's ability to encompass reasoned assumptions to cope with limited diversity is likely to make users less worried about the degree-of-freedom issue and thus more prone to rest satisfied with the cases they know well and are unlikely to misrepresent. This upholds one of the presumed edges of qualitative over quantitative approaches.

It is during the stage of *data analysis*, however, that the distinction between variable-oriented analyses and QCA is the sharpest. The ability of the latter to capture causal conjunctions, even in small-to-intermediate-N situations, is an important edge over statistical inference. This is achieved primarily by the fact that simplifying assumptions can be introduced in a way that maintains a clear connection to the underlying cases—thus allowing substantive evaluation of their plausibility. The upshot of this is that justifiable counterfactual arguments can be systematically combined with existing data in order to tease out simpler, or more general, causal accounts than are available without simplifying assumptions. At the same time, the set-theoretic algebra found at the core of QCA protects it from the simplistic rejection of causal conditions threatening narrative application of Mill's logical methods in the presence of multiple and conjunctural causation.

Worth restating here is that two severe limitations of Boolean QCA, i.e. that variables must be dichotomous and that the analysis makes no allowance for measurement error and non-modelled causality, are lifted in the fuzzy-set version of QCA. So far, too few comparative studies have applied the fuzzy-set version to determine whether it will strengthen QCA's claim to the methodological middle ground between qualitative and quantitative analysis—but the potential is clearly there. Multiple-value variables permit more refined case characterization and may render QCA analysis more attractive to scholars inclined to in-depth narrative studies of one or a few cases. At the same time, introduction of probability reduces the contrast between QCA and quantitative approaches to causal inference.

NOTES

[1] Broadly speaking, a regime is effective if it contributes substantially to solving the problem it was set up to address; see the chapters by Underdal and Young in this book. I would like to thank Steinar Andresen, Thomas Bernauer, Gary Goerz, Alf Håkon Hoel, Jon Hovi, Charles Ragin, Jon Birger Skjærseth, Duncan Snidal, Arild Underdal, Albert Weale, Oran Young, Michael Zürn, and participants at a research seminar at Swiss Federal Institute of Technology (ETH), November 2002, for very helpful comments.

[2] See respectively, Ragin, 1987, and Ragin, 2000. Unlike crisp sets, fuzzy sets permit partial membership in a category—implying that both causal and outcome variables can be multichotomous. Software for both versions are available at (www.u.arizona.edu/~cragin/QCA.htm), but the fuzzy-set programme is not yet fully functional. It is nevertheless already in use by comparativists. A bibliography of QCA studies and some working papers applying the fuzzy-set version are downloadable at (http://smalln.spri.ucl.ac.be/).

[3] See Haas, Keohane and Levy (eds.), 1993; Andresen and Wettestad, 1995; Stokke and Vidas (eds.), 1996; and Young (ed.), 1999. For an overview of approaches and performances in the last decade's regime effectiveness research, see the chapter by Underdal.

[4] See, however, Miles, Underdal et al., 2002, which combines case-studies with a series of analytical procedures, including simple statistical analysis and QCA. The number of observations that go into this analysis is in the lower thirties.

[5] Related to this is the problem of multicolinearity, i.e., that findings become sensitive to intercorrelations among independent variables.

[6] King et al., 1994, p. 129. Responding to criticism, they have later softened this statement by conceding that such selection can indeed be sensible and efficient if it complements earlier investigations of the same causal relationship; see King et al., 1995, p. 477. See also Ragin, 2000, p. 68

[7] Ragin, 1987, p. 51.
[8] Mill, 1904/1843; see section 3 below.
[9] See for instance Little, 1995.
[10] See for instance Ragin, 1997, pp. 36–7. Of course, variation-oriented research also frequently addresses multiple conjunctural causation. Statistical interaction models rapidly exhaust the degrees of freedom in low- to intermediate-N situations, however, and even when the number of observations is high, multicolinearity tends to make findings indeterminate; see Smith, 1990, p. 785.
[11] On this approach, see George, 1979, and George and McKeown, 1985; see also Andresen and Wettestad in this book.
[12] This is true in particular of Haas, Keohane and Levy (eds.) 1993; Stokke and Vidas (eds.), 1996; and Young (ed.)1999.
[13] Young and Levy, 1999, p. 21.
[14] Keohane, Haas and Levy, p. 19.
[15] Stokke and Vidas, p. 18; italics added.
[16] This is less striking, but still true, of Young (ed.), 1999; see in particular pp. 19–22 and the short appendix, "Notes on Methodology".
[17] The notion of "mechanism" has been in use longer in the physical and biological than in the social sciences; see Hedström and Swedberg, 1996. The emphasis below is on human agency mechanisms; see also the chapter by Hovi in this book.
[18] Stinchcombe, 1991, p. 367.
[19] Elster, 1983, p. 24.
[20] Little, 1991, p. 15.
[21] Hedström and Swedberg, 1996, pp. 298–9.
[22] Stinchcombe, 1991, pp. 367, 371–3; also Little, 1995, p. 35–6; and Elster, 1983, p. 23.
[23] Simon, 1976/1945.
[24] Haydu, 1998.
[25] Stinchcombe, 1991, p. 367.
[26] Ibid, pp. 368–9, 383–4; also Hedström and Swedberg, p. 303, fn. 18. On unrealistic assumptions more generally, see Hovi, 1998.
[27] Stinchcombe, 1991, pp. 370, 385.
[28] Elster, 1998, pp. 49.
[29] Haas, Keohane and Levy, 1993; also Young and Levy, 1999.
[30] Eckstein, 1973.
[31] Sartori, 1991.
[32] Mill, 1904/1843.
[33] Ibid, Ch. VIII, and the discussion in Ragin, 1987, pp. 36–42.
[34] Mill, 1904/1843, pp. 256–8.
[35] For this reason, the indirect method is also coined the joint method of agreement and difference; ibid., p. 256–8.
[36] Ibid, p. 259; to Mill, the primacy of the artificial experiment is exactly its ability "...to produce the precise *sort* of variation which we are in want of for discovering the law of the phenomenon—a service which nature, being constructed on a quite different scheme from that of facilitating our studies, is seldom so friendly as to bestow upon us". (pp. 249–50). More contemporary textbooks on methodology typically concur with this view see for instance Kidder, 1983, who notes on p. 38 that "No experimenter can be 100 percent sure that "this" experimental treatment was the cause of "that" effect, but experimenters can be surer than most other researchers". She adds, however, that in social research this greater

internal validity comes at the price of poor representation of natural processes and thus questionable external validity.

37 Ragin, 2000.

38 Section 4.4 shows such a truth table for the cases coded in this chapter. On non-observed combinations, see below.

39 Frequency thresholds could be placed on such tests requiring, e.g., three or more instances before a configuration is deemed sufficient. Furthermore, probabilistic procedures can be introduced: a causal configuration can be "almost always" or "usually" necessary or sufficient for a given outcome. Such quasi-necessity or quasi-sufficiency statements would permit, depending on the frequency distribution, the number of cases, and the probability criterion chosen, one or more cases that deviate from the patterns described above.

40 As we shall see, this is very much an issue in the truth table developed in section 4.4.

41 See the discussion of this in the case-studies below.

42 Ragin, 1987, p. 109.

43 See the discussion below of simplifying assumptions. For a broad treatment of counterfactual analysis, see and Tetlock and Belkin (eds.), 1996. If the set of cases does cover those actually existing, the statement on non-existing cases may shed some light on the institutional or evolutionary constraints which explain why those configurations are not to be found in the real world. In a social background study of U.S. presidents, for instance, it could support an exploration into why there are no females or blacks in the universe of cases; see Ragin, 1987, pp. 104–5. On evolutionary, or filtering explanations see Little, 1995, pp. 40–1.

44 On the Barents Sea cases see Stokke, 2001, Stokke et al., 1999; on the CCAMLR cases, see Stokke, 1996; and on the Nortwest Atlantic cases, see Joyner, 1998, Stokke, 2000, and Gezelius, 1998.

45 On phases as cases in the study of international regimes see Underdal, 2002, p. 57.

46 none of the cases of shaming reviewed display any unclarity as to whether the target engage in the behaviour that is criticized. Other cases may differ in this regard, implying that the role of the regime in enhancing (or failing to enhance) transparency regarding management practices should appear as a variable—and not as a parameter as in this chapter.

47 On the moratorium on commercial whaling in the context of regime effectiveness, see Andresen, 2002.

48 A theory of shaming in international relations is yet to be developed; two building-blocks which have informed this section are the study of reputation in international relations (e.g. Mercer 1996) and the socio-psychological study of embarrassment (see for instance Sueda and Wiseman, 1992).

49 This is important also because external criticism can sometimes have an effect that is contrary to the intended, i.e., to strengthen domestic support of the policies that are criticized. On the notion of reverberation in the international-domestic interphase, see Putnam, 1988.

50 See the discussion by Andresen and Wettestad in this book.

51 See for instance Ragin, 1994, chapter 4.

52 Galtung, 1969, p. 464, refers to this as giving the model "validity from above" to contrast it with the empirical confirmation it may receive "from below".

53 On the significance for causal analysis of adequate variation in the dependent variable, see King et al., 1994, pp. 128–39, 141–2; recall however the qualification expressed in King et al., 1995. The matter is even less straightforward if one searches for necessary rather than sufficient conditions; see Dion, 1998.

54 See the cases on high-seas fisheries in section 4.3 below.
55 Stokke et al., 1999.
56 For readability, this coding is represented verbally here by indicating the presence of a condition by upper-case letters and absence in lower-case ones; a mid-level dot signifies logical AND, i.e. the intersection of the causal conditions before and after: ADVICE ··commitment · SHADOW · INCONVENIENCE · REVERBERATION = SUCCESS.
57 The binary coding for this case would be ADVICE · commitment · shadow · INCONVENIENCE · reverberation = success.
58 Nikitina and Pierce1992.
59 This case is identical to the previous one except that here the fisheries bureaucracy was credibly challenged by conservation-oriented domestic actors: ADVICE · commitment · shadow · INCONVENIENCE · REVERBERATION = success.
60 That is, in the Russian zone and in the Grey Zone. The latter, established to allow inspections in a disputed part of the Barents Sea, includes large areas of undisputed Norwegian and Russian waters; see Stokke et al., 1999. Russian inspection vessels have been few in numbers; in 1989, Norwegian inspections in the area counted some 1200, whereas the Soviet figure was 118—none of which revealed violations of any kind.
61 In binary terms, this case can be summarized as ADVICE · COMMITMENT · SHADOW · INCONVENIENCE · REVERBERATION = SUCCESS.
62 Stokke, 2001.
63 On the historic role of Iceland in furthering coastal states rights versus those of distant-water fishing nations, see Robinson, 1996.
64 In short: advice · commitment · shadow · INCONVENIENCE · reverberation = success. The travelling capacity (see Sartori, 1991) of that particular combination of causal configuration and outcome appears to be high: very similar stories, and with equivalent Boolean coding, could be told about United States and Russian efforts to shame Japanese and other vessels out of the Doughnut Hole in the Central Bering Sea in the late 1980s—and Russian attempts of the same in the Sea of Okhotsk Peanut Hole; see, respectively, Balton, 2001 and Oude Elferink, 2001.
65 For a detailed discussion, see Gezelius, 1998.
66 In other words: ADVICE · COMMITMENT · SHADOW · INCONVENIENCE · reverberation = success.
67 Or as Boole would have put it, ADVICE · COMMITMENT · SHADOW · inconvenience · reverberation = SUCCESS. As another species, Greenland Halibut, proved targetable on a large-scale, relations soon froze again; see Joyner, 2001, and Stokke, 2000.
68 Stokke, 1996.
69 The fact that non-harvesting states outnumber user states sets CCAMLR and the International Whaling Commission aside from most living resource management regimes.
70 In other words, there was no shadow of the future associated with ignoring shamers; see the truth table in section 4.4. On the Japanese approach to CCAMLR, see Stokke, 1991.
71 In binary terms, this case would be expressed as advice · commitment · shadow · INCONVENIENCE · reverberation = success.
72 In binary terms: ADVICE · commitment · shadow · inconvenience · reverberation = SUCCESS.
73 In short: ADVICE · commitment · inconvenience · shadow · reverberation = SUCCESS.
74 Smith, 1990, p. 786; Goldthorpe, 1997, pp. 6–7; Coppedge, 1995, Ragin, 2000, p. 108.
75 Ragin, 2000, pp. 109–16, 227–9. Probabilistic criteria can be introduced in crisp-set QCA as well but their feasibility is much higher in the fuzzy-set version since the number of cases included in assessments of causal conditions is usually higher. This is so because

more cases are likely to have partial membership in a fuzzy-outcome category than full membership in a crisp one; see p. 227.

[76] That there are no contradictory cases here may also be related to the fact of relatively few observations, considering that the logical maximum is thirty-two (2^5); see the discussion of limited diversity above and the application below.

[77] Mid-level dot signifies logical AND (the intersection of sets) and "+" signifies logical OR (the union of sets).

[78] Frequency distribution may be ascribed to those configurations, but this is not essential to subsequent operations.

[79] While this minimization can be done by hand even in large sets, a version of the QCA computer programmes facilitates the operation considerably.

[80] Ragin, 1987, p. 93.

[81] The first and the second terms on the right-hand side of equation (A); or see the truth table above.

[82] Mill, 1904/1843, pp. 255–9.

[83] Ragin, 1994, p. 127.

[84] For a somewhat different argument but compatible conclusion, see Ragin, 1987, p. 98. On the policy implications of causal analysis of manipulable conditions, see Ragin, 2000, p. 203–4.

[85] The conditions that pull in the direction of behavioural change are the presence of, respectively, Advice, Commitment, Shadow, and Reverberation.

[86] Ragin, 1987, pp. 110–3. A simple algorithm helps identify which codings of the various non-existent combinations would minimize the equation.

[87] Recall the two instances of one of the existing nine combinations.

[88] In contrast to a pull factor, a push factor makes behavioural adaptation less attractive to the target of shaming. On the impermissibility of introducing assumptions in counterfactual arguments that are incompatible with those underlying the analysis of existing data, see for instance Fearon, 1991.

[89] Ragin, 2000, pp. 105, 254.

[90] Ragin, 1987.

[91] Ragin 2000 prefers the term "veristic", presumably to avoid the negative connotation of "determinism". The meaning is the same, however: the outcome was produced by the modelled conditions, as measured in the study, and no others.

[92] A specific coding is opportunistic if the decision is done with a side-glance to whether or not it will support the prior hypothesis. As noted, a newer version of the program, still under development, introduces probability and multiple-value variables.

[93] Goldthorpe, 1997, p. 7.

[94] Because of this emphasis on the comparative technique, only limited effort has been invested in substantiating that the regime was vital in triggering this mechanism.

[95] See Ragin, 2000, chapter 7.

REFERENCES

Andresen, S. (2002) The International Whaling Commission (IWC): More Failure Than Success, in E. L. Miles, A. Underdal et al., *Environmental Regime Effectiveness: Confronting Theory with Evidence*, MIT Press, Cambridge, MA, 379–403.

Andresen, S. and Wettestad, J. (1995) International Problem-Solving Effectiveness: The Oslo Project Story so Far, *International Environmental Affairs* 7, 2: 127–149.

Balton, D. A. (2001) The Bering Sea Doughnut Hole Convention: Regional Solution, Global Implications, in O. S. Stokke (ed.) *Governing High Seas Fisheries: The Interplay of Global and Regional Regimes,* Oxford University Press, 143–177.

Chayes, A. and Handler Chayes, A. (1993) On Compliance, *International Organization* 47, 2: 175–205.

Collier, D. and Mahoney, J. (1996) Insights and Pitfalls: Selection Bias in Qualitative Research, *World Politics* 49: 56–91.

Coppedge, M. (1999) Thickening Thin Concepts and Theories: Combining Large N and Small in Comparative Politics, *Comparative Politics* 31: 465–475.

Dion, D. (1998) Evidence and Inference in the Comparative Case Study, *Comparative Politics* 30: 127–145.

Eckstein, H. (1973) Authority Patterns: A Structural Basis for Political Inquiry, *American Political Science Review* 67/December: 1142–1161.

Elster, J. (1983) *Explaining Technical Change: A Case Study in the Philosophy of Science,* Cambridge University Press.

Elster, J. (1998) A Plea for Mechanisms, in P. Hedström and R. Swedberg (eds.) *Social Mechanisms: An Analytical Approach to Social Theory,* Cambridge University Press, 45–73.

Franck, T. M. (1990) *The Power of Legitimacy Among Nations,* Oxford University Press, New York.

Galtung, J. (1969) *Theory and Methods of Social Research,* Universitetsforlaget, Oslo.

George, A. L. (1979) Case Studies and Theory Development: The Method of Structured, Focused Comparison, in P.G. Lauren (ed.) *Diplomacy: New Approaches in History, Theory, and Policy,* The Free Press, New York, 43–68.

George, A. L. and McKeown, T. J. (1985) Case Studies and Theories of Organizational Decision Making, *Advances in Information Processing in Organizations* 2: 21–58.

Gezelius, S. S. (1999) Limits to Externalisation: The EU NAFO Policy 1979–97, *Marine Policy* 23, 2: 147–159.

Goldthorpe, J. H. (1997) Current Issues in Comparative Macrosociology: A Debate on Methodological Issues, *Comparative Social Research* 16: 1–26.

Haas, P. M., Keohane, R. O. and Levy, M. A., (eds.) (1993) *Institutions for the Earth: Sources of Effective International Environmental Protection,* MIT Press, Cambridge, MA.

Haydu, J. (1998) Making Use of the Past: Time Periods as Cases to Compare and as Sequences of Problem Solving, *American Journal of Sociology* 104, 2: 339–371.

Hedström, P. and Swedberg, R. (1996) Social Mechanisms, *Acta Sociologica* 39: 281–308.

Hovi, J. (1998) The Relevance of Unrealistic Models for Empirical Political Science, *Homo Oeconomicus* 15, 1: 45–59.

Joyner, C. C. (2001) On the Borderline? Canadian activism in the Grand Banks, in O. S. Stokke, (ed.) *Governing High Seas Fisheries: The Interplay of Global and Regional Regimes,* Oxford University Press, 207–233.

Keohane, R. O., Haas, P. M. and Levy, M. A. (1993) The Effectiveness of International Environmental Institutions, in P.M. Haas, M.A. Levy and R.O. Keohane (eds.) *Institutions for the Earth: Sources of Effective International Environmental Protection,* MIT University Press, Cambridge, MA, 3–26.

Kidder, L. H. (1981) *Selltiz Wrightsman & Cooks Research Methods in Social Relations,* Hold, Rinehart and Winston, New York, 4th edition; 1st edition 1951.

King, G., Keohane, R. O. and Verba, S. (1994) *Designing Social Inquiry: Scientific Inference in Qualitative Research,* Princeton University Press.
King, G., Keohane, R. O. and Verba, S. (1995) The Importance of Research Design in Political Science, *American Political Science Review* (Review Symposium: The Qualitative–Quantitative Disputation, 454–81) 89, 2: 475–481.
Little, D. (1991) *Varieties of Social Explanation: An Introduction to the Philosophy of Social Science,* Westview Press, Boulder, CO.
Little, D. (1995) Causal Explanation in the Social Sciences, *The Southern Journal of Philosophy* 34/Supplement: 31–56.
Mercer, J. (1992) *Reputation in International Politics,* Cornell University Press, Ithaca, New York.
Miles, E. L., Underdal, A., Andresen, S., Wettestad, J., Birger Skjærseth, J. and Carlin, E. M. (2002) *Environmental Regime Effectiveness: Confronting Theory with Evidence,* MIT Press, Cambridge, MA.
Mill, J. S. (1904) *A System of Logic: Ratiocinative and Inductive,* Longmans, London, 8th edition; 1st edition 1843.
Nikitina, E. N. and Pearse, P. H. () Conservation of Marine Resources in the Former Soviet Union: An Environmental Perspective. *Ocean Development and International Law* 23: 369–382.
Oude Elferink, A. G. (2001) The Sea of Okhotsk Peanut Hole: De Facto Extension of Coastal State Control, in O. S. Stokke (ed.) *Governing High Seas Fisheries: The Interplay of Global and Regional Regimes,* Oxford University Press, 179–205.
Putnam, R. (1988) Diplomacy and Domestic Politics: The Logic of Two–Level Games, *International Organization* 42, 3: 427–460.
Ragin, C. C. (1987) *The Comparative Method: Moving Beyond Qualitative and Quantitative Strategies,* University of California Press.
Ragin, C. C. (1997) Turning the Tables: How Case-Oriented Research Challenges Variable-Oriented Research, *Comparative Social Research* 16: 27–42.
Ragin, C. C. (2000) *Fuzzy-Set Social Science,* University of Chicago Press.
Sartori, G. (1991) Comparing and Miscomparing, *Journal of Theoretical Politics* 3, 3: 243–257.
Simon, H. A. (1976) *Administrative Behavior: A Study of Decision-Making Processes in Administrative Organizations,* The Free Press, New York (3rd edition, new introduction; first edition 1945).
Smith, H. L. (1990) The Comparative Method: Moving Beyond Qualitative and Quantitative Analysis (Charles C. Ragin), in book review, *Population and Development Review* 16, 4: 784–7.
Stinchcombe, A. (1991) The Conditions of Fruitfulness of Theorizing about Mechanisms in Social Science, *Philosophy of the Social Sciences* 21, 3: 367–388.
Stokke, O. S. (1991) Transnational Fishing: Japan's Changing Strategy, *Marine Policy* 15, 231–243.
Stokke, O. S. (1996) The Effectiveness of CCAMLR, in O.S. Stokke and D. Vidas (ed.) *Governing the Antarctic: The Effectiveness and Legitimacy of the Antarctic Treaty System,* Cambridge University Press, 120–151.
Stokke, O. S. (1997) Regimes as Governance Systems, in O.R. Young (ed.) *Global Governance: Drawing Insights from the Environmental Experience,* MIT Press, Cambridge, MA, 27–63.
Stokke, O. S. (2001) Managing Fisheries in the Barents Sea Loophole: Interplay with the UN Fish Stocks Agreement, *Ocean Development and International Law* 32, 3: 241–262.

Stokke, O. S. (2001) Managing Straddling Stocks: The Interplay of Global and Regional Regimes, *Journal of Ocean and Coastal Management* 43: 205–234.

Stokke, O. S. and Vidas, D. (1996) The Effectiveness and Legitimacy of International Regimes, in O.S. Stokke and D. Vidas (eds.) *Governing the Antarctic: The Effectiveness and Legitimacy of the Antarctic Treaty System,* Cambridge University Press, 13–31.

Sueda, K. and Wiseman, R. L. (1992) Embarrassment Remediation in Japan and the United States, *International Journal of Intercultural Relations* 16: 159–173.

Tetlock, P. E. and Belkin, A. (1996) *Counterfactual Thought Experiments in World Politics: Logical, Methodological, and Psychological Perspectives,* Princeton University Press.

Underdal, A. (2002) Methods of Analysis, in E. L. Miles, A. Underdal et al, *Environmental Regime Effectiveness: Confronting Theory with Evidence,* MIT Press, Cambridge, MA, 47–59.

Young, O. R. and Levy, M. A. (with Osherenko, G.), (1999) The Effectiveness of International Regimes, in O. R. Young (ed.) *The Effectiveness of International Environmental Regimes*: *Causal Connections and Behavioral Mechanisms*, MIT Press, Cambridge, MA.

Chapter 6

A QUANTITATIVE APPROACH TO EVALUATING INTERNATIONAL ENVIRONMENTAL REGIMES

RONALD B. MITCHELL
University of Oregon

1. INTRODUCTION

To date, analysts of international environmental regimes have largely eschewed quantitative methods.[1] Yet, applying statistical procedures to large sets of quantified data offers rich opportunities to address questions central to this research program. Quantitative analysis can shed light on questions that either cannot be or usually are not answered by qualitative methods while also allowing reexamination of questions already addressed by such methods. Careful modeling and analysis of appropriate data could identify which features of a regime are responsible for a regime's success and which are superfluous, how much of a contribution regimes can make to resolving environmental problems, and the extent to which the effectiveness of a particular type of regime depends on factors such as the type of problem or international context. Thus, quantitative analysis offers a valuable complement to qualitative techniques in evaluating regime effects and effectiveness.

Consider some questions regarding regime effectiveness. Are sanctions always more effective at inducing behavioral change than rewards and, if not, under what conditions are rewards more effective?[2] Are pollution problems, on average, more difficult or easier to resolve than wildlife preservation problems? Do demands for new behaviors generally work better or worse than bans on existing behavior?[3] Such questions are difficult to answer convincingly with case studies of single regimes because most regimes do not employ both sanctions and rewards, address both pollution and wildlife problems, or ban some behaviors while requiring others. We certainly want to analyze those rare regimes that exhibit such variation, since they convincingly control many other variables. Yet, case studies face inherent problems of generalizability. Even commendable recent efforts to draw conclusions across multiple regimes, each analyzed by a different scholar, face difficulties in ensuring convincing comparability across regimes.[4] The findings of carefully designed case studies often fit the case studied well but cannot be convincingly extended to many, and sometimes to any, other cases.[5]

Quantitative analysis involves the opposite trade-off, generating propositions that hold reasonably well across many cases but that cannot explain any particular case well.[6] It can identify what "tends to happen" in regimes in general or in regimes of particular types. It can tell us whether the influence of regimes on behavior is generally larger or smaller than other influences. It can help "fill in the blanks" left by qualitative analysis, using patterns *across regimes* to clarify why certain types of regimes address certain types of problems better than others, or why regimes in one issue area work better than otherwise-similar regimes in a different issue area. Such comparisons across regimes can move us beyond case study insights that a particular type of regime *can* produce a desired outcome to the often more useful claim that such a design *is likely to* produce such an outcome in some other context, moving us from possibility to probability. Large-N comparisons allow us to refine claims of qualitative research, such as, evaluating the general claim that country capacity influences compliance by examining whether the lack of a particular capacity inhibits compliance with some types of regimes but not others.[7] Quantitative techniques offer the promise of replacing claims that "this strategy worked in this historical case" with more convincing policy-relevant and contingent prescriptions of which strategy is likely to work best to address a given problem under given conditions. Although a variety of quantitative techniques could be used to investigate regime consequences, in this chapter I delineate one quantitative approach, that of using regression analysis on panel data.[8]

2. DEFINITIONS

Recent work on qualitative methodology in general and counterfactuals in particular reminds us that any attempt to make causal claims requires comparing at least two cases.[9] Here I clarify some terms useful for discussing quantitative study design, generally avoiding the term "case" because of its multiple, often widely divergent, meanings.[10] *Units of analysis* are the entities or phenomena about which the researcher collects data.[11] Units of analysis, often called cases, are a sample from a population or class of all conceptually-similar units that could have been studied. *Variables* are the dimensions, characteristics, or parameters of these units of analysis, with any variable having two or more possible *values*. Quantitative studies examine covariation between the values of two variables in a database in hopes of distinguishing underlying causal relationships among those variables in the world. Dependent variables (DVs) are those whose variation we seek to explain. Explanatory or independent variables (IVs) are those whose variation we look to as possible explanations of the variation in the DV, based on theoretical claims regarding their causal influence on that DV. Control variables (CVs) are IVs believed to influence the DV that are included in an analysis in order to separate their influence on the DV from that of the primary IV of interest. To avoid confusion, I distinguish between a unit of analysis and an observation. An *observation* is one set (or vector) of the observed values of all variables (IVs, CVs, and DV) for a given unit of analysis. These definitions allow us to speak of multiple observations of a single unit of analysis, as when we observe a regime (the unit of analysis) at several points in time. In a spreadsheet analogy, each column corresponds to a different variable (IV, CV, or DV); each row corresponds to a single observation; each cell contains the value of a given variable for a given observation; the first column contains a name (or other identifier) for each observation; and the dataset could contain rows corresponding to multiple observations from each unit of analysis as well as observations from multiple units of analysis. A quantitative study of regime consequences requires defining some potential consequent of regimes as a dependent variable, the presence or absence of a regime or some regime characteristic as the independent variable of interest, and some set of other factors predicted to affect the dependent variable as control variables. The analyst would then seek out regimes (units of analysis) that allow relatively comparable observations across these IVs, CVs, and DVs.

Given these definitions, qualitative research is best distinguished from quantitative research by the fact that the former examines relatively few units of analysis while the latter examines many. The benefit of a qualitative approach stems from the fact that the study of one or two units of analysis holds many variables constant across however many observations are analyzed (since many variables are constant across all observations of a given unit of analysis). This eliminates those variables as potential explanations of variation in the DV and thereby improves the ability to evaluate the influence on the DV of the remaining IVs that do vary. The benefit of a quantitative approach lies in capturing evidence from a sufficient number of different units of analysis that one can determine whether the influence of one or two IVs on the DV holds across a wide range of values for the many variables that are likely to vary across these units of analysis. Beyond this definitional distinction, in practice quantitative analysis usually examines not only more units of analysis but also more observations and more independent and control variables.

Finally, although recognizing the value of a broader definition, I use regime here to refer to the governance structures surrounding international conventions and treaties, including the norms, rules, principles, and decision-making procedures as well as the numerous actors who bring those components to life.[12]

3. MODELING FOR QUANTITATIVE ANALYSIS OF REGIME EFFECTS

A long list of regimes now exists which case studies have shown to have been effective.[13] As much of the literature and other chapters in the present volume clarify, regime effectiveness has multiple possible meanings.[14] A quantitative approach has the advantage of addressing questions central to this literature while separating the identification of regime effects from the judgment of regime effectiveness. A regime's effects are those changes in some DV of interest to the analyst that are best explained by the regime and cannot be explained by other variables. Indeed, most regimes have both intended and unintended, direct and indirect, and desirable and undesirable effects.[15] Although effectiveness can be used as a synonym for direct and intended effects, more often a regime's effectiveness involves the additional step of deciding whether a change in the DV of interest that can be attributed to the regime was either sufficiently far from the no-regime counterfactual or sufficiently close to some identified goal (of the regime or the analyst) to meet the analyst's criteria for categorizing a regime as effective. Although the following discussion focuses on intended and direct effects, for expository purposes, similar procedures could be used to analyze any of the intended or unintended effects of regimes, such as a regime's effects on equity, economic growth, or the development of other regimes.

Existing studies of regime effects and effectiveness have identified a range of factors that explain how they altered state and nonstate behavior relative to some period prior to the regime's creation, relative to some behavioral arena outside the regime, or relative to a hypothetical no-regime counterfactual. Quantitative analysis allows us to build on this work by asking questions that require cross-regime comparisons such as whether these findings hold across a range of conditions, whether regime influences are large or small relative to other determinants of behavior, and what features of regimes explain why one induces significantly more behavior change than another?

Accurately answering these and other cross-regime questions requires efforts to model the wide range of variables that can cause change in environmental behaviors, including regime-related factors among them. Even if regimes are the IV of primary interest, modeling the sources of environmental behaviors (i.e., including a range of non-regime IVs hypothesized as influencing environmental behaviors) rather than the effects of environmental regimes has several advantages, even for those exclusively interested in the latter question. First, non-regime IVs can serve as *control variables*, making any argument that a regime caused observed changes in behavior more convincing by demonstrating that the covariation of regimes and behaviors exists even when these other factors have been controlled for. Second, non-regime IVs can serve as *comparators*, providing a basis for declaring a regime's influence as "large" or "small." Thus, assessing the magnitude of economic and technological influences on behavior provides a way to know whether regimes have the potential to contribute significantly to resolving an environmental problem or not. Third, non-regime IVs can serve as *interaction terms*, clarifying the influence of regime-related IVs by demonstrating whether and how their influence depends on the values of non-regime IVs.[16] In what follows, I demonstrate methods for modeling a single regime and for comparing multiple regimes and then delineate methods for conducting empirical analyses using these models.

3.1 Modeling a Single Regime

As both a valuable exercise in its own right and a foundation for a model that can compare regime effects, I start by developing a model for quantitative analysis of a single regime's effects. Developing such a model requires identifying an appropriate dependent variable, identifying a set of corresponding independent variables, and interpreting the findings of the resulting model. I use the 1985 Sulfur Protocol of the European Convention on Long-Range Transboundary Air Pollution's (LRTAP) as an initial example.

Given the definition of regime effects noted above, the first step of modeling requires choosing an appropriate behavior or environmental indicator as a DV. One can, of course, evaluate how a regime effects any variable of interest. But both theoretical and empirical reasons exist for thinking that regime effects are likely to be concentrated in behaviors that the regime sought to influence. Therefore, it seems preferable, at least initially, to employ DVs that correspond to the goals identified in the agreements that form the legal basis for the regime. In choosing a DV, although environmental quality is, ultimately, the variable of concern, using behavior has three distinct advantages. First, showing that a regime affected a relevant behavior is a necessary, even if not sufficient, condition for showing that the regime affected environmental quality. Second, behaviors constitute easier variables to model accurately because, while they may be subject to the influence of many variables, they are subject to both fewer and generally more systematic and well-understood influences then are environmental quality indicators. Third, despite its problems, behavioral data is usually more available, more comprehensive, and of better quality than environmental quality data. These points are made not to argue that modeling behavior is easy but simply that modeling environmental quality is even more difficult. Although considerable early work focused on compliance,[17] more recent work has argued for behavior change and environmental progress as more appropriate metrics, contending that such an approach captures the important variation evident in regime-induced behavioral change that falls short of or exceeds legal compliance.[18] In seeking a DV for the 1985 LRTAP sulfur protocol, consider that the agreement required a thirty percent reduction from 1980 levels by 1993. Rather than assessing whether each country complied with this standard in 1993, a focus on behavior change gains more insight into regime effects by examining each country's SOx emissions from 1985 through the present. Such an approach accords more closely with a view that regimes work by initiating processes of behavior change, processes the evidence of which is likely to be visible long before and long after a compliance deadline.[19]

After selecting a particular behavior as a DV, we need a model of the factors that cause variation in that behavior to identify the influence, if any, of the regime. One approach involves evaluating covariation of the DV with membership in the regime (the IV of interest). Conceptually, this assumes that only members are influenced by a regime, an assumption that I relax below. To avoid misestimating the effects of regime membership on behavior, we need to include those additional IVs that correlate with both membership and emissions to serve as control variables. Bringing in all IVs alleged to drive the behavior (whether or not they correlate with membership), however, permits estimating the magnitude of their effects, thereby providing comparators that give some leverage on the question of whether membership had a large or small effect relative to other factors. Adding more variables, although requiring more resources, also avoids excluding IVs that *appear* unlikely to covary with membership but actually do. Variables likely to influence environmental behaviors include a variety of economic, technological, social, and political variables. Those investigating "environmental Kuznets curves" have developed models to predict national pollution levels that identify useful indicators of economic growth, population, trade, inequality, technology, and other factors.[20] As a preliminary model to estimate national sulfur emissions for the LRTAP case, then, we might specify a model as follows:

(A) EMISS = α + β_1*MEMBER + β_2*INCOME + β_3*POP + β_4*COAL + β_5* EFFIC + ... + β_N*OTHER + ε

where EMISS is annual emissions of sulfur dioxide and MEMBER is coded as 0 in years of nonmembership and 1 in years of membership. Following the Kuznets curve literature, this illustrative model includes generic drivers of emissions of most pollutants such as per capita income (INCOME) and population (POP) although others could certainly be added. It also includes emission-specific drivers such as the fraction of the country's power plants using coal (COAL) and the average efficiency of those power plants (EFFIC) since sulfur emissions stem in large measure from coal burning. Since this is an illustrative model, I use OTHER to note the need to include other variables based on more detailed knowledge of the drivers of sulfur emissions.

What would the results of such a model, or similar models for other regimes, tell us? β_1 represents the expected difference in emissions that (if we have modeled emissions correctly) would arise from a country becoming a regime member, holding all other variables constant. We would predict this number to be negative, on the assumption that membership in a pollution control regime leads states to reduce their emissions. This coefficient corresponds to a counterfactual in qualitative analyses. Counterfactual emissions for a member state in a given year, i.e., its emissions had it not been a member, can be roughly estimated as its actual emissions for that year minus β_1.[21] Using the model in this way could supplement qualitative efforts to generate counterfactuals in indices of regime influence.[22] The coefficients of the other IVs, β_2 through β_N, correspond to the estimated increase in emissions that would arise from a one unit increase in that IV.

The t-statistic on β_1 allows evaluation of the likelihood that the difference in emissions estimated as due to membership could have occurred by chance. Although good qualitative analysis also assesses the likelihood that the observed outcome could have occurred by chance, quantitative analysis encourages prior establishment of a criterion (by convention, a probability of 5%) of whether to interpret an observed covariation of an IV with the DV as random or as resulting from a systematic, and presumably causal, effect of the IV on the DV.[23] For IVs with "statistically significant" t-statistics (and for which independent theoretical support exists for making causal claims), the β can be interpreted as the average magnitude of the "effect" the IV has on the DV, having controlled for all other IVs.[24] It is important to distinguish the *statistical significance* of the t-statistic from the meaningfulness or what we might call *policy significance* of that IV. Thus, a study might convincingly show that the lower emissions of members relative to nonmembers cannot be readily explained by factors other than their membership in the regime but that the difference was so small as to be environmentally meaningless. A t-statistic provides some insight into whether the covariation of IV and DV was "real" (more precisely, whether it was likely to have occurred by chance) while the β can, under certain conditions, be evaluated in comparison to other βs or as a fraction of emission levels to assess whether the covariation of the IV and DV was "large."[25]

The R^2 of the model equation as a whole represents the proportion of the variation in the DV, in this case EMISS, around its mean explained by the variation in all the IVs taken together. Thus, the R^2 provides an estimate of how well the analyst has captured the factors that influence the DV, or how completely the analyst has modeled the DV.[26]

3.2 Modeling to Compare Regimes

Building on this single regime model, how do we devise a model that allows us to combine data from several regimes to address the comparative questions raised at the beginning of this chapter? Such a model helps estimate the average effect of regimes across a range of conditions rather than the effects of a single regime under that regime's particular conditions. It also allows us to ask which features of regimes best explain the variation in regime effects. We can model three types of regime influence: membership, features, and membership-feature interactions. The most obvious element involves using membership (as above) as the primary independent variable of regime influence, with membership varying by country, year, and regime. Intuitively, this corresponds to (and allows us to evaluate) a theory that holds that regimes only influence member state behavior. Regime influence is estimated by comparing a country's behavior while a member to its behavior while a nonmember (eliminating cross-country effects) and to nonmember behavior during the same time period (eliminating cross-time effects). Regimes may, however, create or reinforce norms and other social pressures that also influence nonmembers, albeit less so than members. This suggests including indicators of regime features that vary by regime (and over time if they are added or dropped subsequent to regime creation) but whose values are the same for observations of both member and nonmember countries. Lastly, regime features may influence both members and nonmembers, but to different degrees. This requires including membership-feature interaction terms if we are to assess how regime features influence members, how they influence nonmembers, and whether the influence differs across the groups.

As an example, how might we assess an initially simple version of the "enforcement" school's claim that sanctions are necessary for a regime to significantly influence behavior?[27] Since assessing that model requires combining data from regimes with and without sanctions, an appropriate model requires a DV that is comparable across regimes. Consider the following model:

(B) $\text{CRB} = \alpha + \beta_1 * \text{MEMBER} + \beta_2 * \text{SANCTION} + \beta_3 * \text{MEM-SANCT} + \beta_4 * \text{CINCOME} + \beta_5 * \text{CPOP} + \ldots + \beta_N * \text{OTHER} + \varepsilon$

where CRB is some annual measure of Change in Regulated Behavior under various regimes, MEMBER is again coded as 1 in years during which a state is a member and 0 otherwise, SANCTION is coded as 1 for years in which a regime containing sanctions was in force and 0 otherwise (in other analyses, other types of regime features could be substituted), and MEM-SANCT is coded as 1 in years for which a sanction-based rule is in effect for a particular state and 0 otherwise. Building on the logic in the prior model, CINCOME is the annual change in per capita income, CPOP is the annual change in population, and OTHER represents a range of other factors believed to drive variation with CRB. Assuming that the operationalization of CRB under various regimes rules allows comparison across regimes (see below) and that omitted determinants of behaviors do not correlate with the included IVs, such a regression could shed considerable light on how crucial sanctions are to regime influence. The value of β_1 and its t-statistic would document how much membership tends to influence behavior, holding "type" of treaty (defined as sanctions or not) constant.[28] The coefficient of SANCTION, β_2, appears to represent an estimate of the influence of sanctions on state behavior. And it does.[29] But, it estimates the average change in the behaviors of both members *and nonmembers* of regimes that employ sanctions compared to regimes that do not. That is, it reflects how all states in the sample (whether members or not) differ with respect to behaviors regulated by sanction-based regimes and behaviors regulated by other types of regimes. Thus, perhaps surprisingly, β_2 tests whether sanctions alter behavior through a norm-based process in which all states (even nonmembers who are not subject to official sanction) respond to new sanction-based regimes emerging in the international system. As an example, consider the influence of the non-proliferation regime on the nuclear programs of states that are not party to it.

Yet, this coefficient seems likely to underestimate the effect of sanctions since we have theoretical reasons to believe that sanctions influence member states more than nonmembers, a view that can be evaluated by including the interaction term MEM-SANCT. The coefficient on MEM-SANCT, β_3, represents the additional change in behavior (CRB) induced among *members* of sanction-based regimes. Thus, β_1 estimates the influence of becoming a member of a non-sanction regime, and $\beta_1 + \beta_3$ estimates the influence of becoming a member of a sanction regime. Simply constructing this model helps clarify theoretical claims. Interpretations of the range of results that could emerge include, inter alia, that a) regimes have no effects (if β_1, β_2, and β_3 are not statistically significant), b) only regimes with sanctions have effects and they effect member and nonmember states equally (if β_2 is statistically significant and β_1 and β_3 are not); c) regimes only effect members and do so with or without sanctions (if β_1 is statistically significant and β_2 and β_3 are not); or d) regimes only effect members and do so only if they have sanctions (if β_3 is statistically significant and β_1 and β_2 are not).

Before being confident in our interpretation of such results as regime effects rather than mere correlation, we need to ensure we have excluded other possible explanations of the variation in environmentally-harmful behaviors. The most important benefit that including variables such as income and population provides is to increase our confidence that our estimates of the influence of membership and sanctions (i.e., β_1, β_2, and β_3) accurately reflect their real correlation with CRB rather than a spurious correlation driven by omitted variables. But the coefficients on these variables also provide insight into the influence of major drivers of environmentally-harmful behaviors (contributing to the environmental Kuznets curve literature) and allow us to assess whether the influence of regime membership or sanctions is large relative to estimates of the influence of non-regime variables (e.g., β_4 and β_5). Again, if interpreted cautiously, they provide a means of going beyond whether regimes have an influence to assess how large that influence is.

Such a model could be extended to evaluate the extent to which regime effects depend on contextual factors. For example, Brown Weiss and Jacobson contend that international conferences and reports (e.g., the 1972 UN Conference on the Human Environment; the 1987 report of the World Commission on Environment and Development; and the 1992 UN Conference on Environment and Development) raise the salience of environmental issues for a few years and thereby lead to "improved implementation and compliance."[30] We might operationalize this claim by supplementing the model above with a conference variable CONF that, for example, has the value of 1 in the year of a major conference and in the two subsequent years and 0 otherwise and an interaction term MEM-CONF coded as 1 in those same years for member states and 0 otherwise. The coefficient on CONF would identify whether conferences and reports improve environmental behavior by all countries, while the coefficient on MEM-CONF would identify whether they have a more significant influence on countries that are members of regimes. If the coefficient on MEM-CONF were statistically significant, this would suggest that the influence of regimes on member states is contingent (partially if MEMBER is also statistically significant and wholly if it is not) on the salience contributed by large international conferences and reports.

This discussion illustrates how we might begin to evaluate the long list of extant claims regarding the types of regimes that are most influential and the conditions under which they are. Claims regarding sanctions and international conferences are only two on that list but the discussion demonstrates a more general model that could be used to examine how regime features and the conditions in which regimes operate influence regime effects.

3.3 Refining a Dependent Variable

This section further develops a dependent variable that would allow comparison across regimes, believing there is value in engaging some of the theoretical difficulties involved in such an endeavor so that the process of engaging the obvious empirical obstacles can begin. Between the first and second models above, the dependent variable was switched from emissions to change in regulated behaviors. This reflected the need for a common dependent variable in order to analyze two or more regimes or subregimes that address different behaviors. Other scholars have also begun addressing this problem of making comparisons. Sprinz and Helm have proposed measuring effectiveness as the amount of progress (expressed as a percent) induced by a regime toward that regime's "collective optimum" from a no-regime counterfactual.[31] Their strategy requires estimating both the no-regime counterfactual and the collective optimum using game theory, optimization, or interviews of experts.[32] Miles and Underdal attack the same problem by using qualitative case studies to assess effectiveness on different scales (ranging from 0 to 4 for behavioral change and 1 to 3 for environmental improvement) and then normalizing them to a range from 0 to 1.[33] Both approaches produce a common metric of effectiveness ranging from no improvement relative to the no-regime outcome to full achievement of the collective optimum. These metrics hold considerable value for comparing effectiveness across regimes. They cannot serve as dependent variables in a regression model of effectiveness, however, because both are qualitative assessments *of* effectiveness and effectiveness is precisely what we seek to derive from the regression analysis. A regression estimates both the magnitude (β) and likelihood (t-statistic) of regime effects as the degree of covariation between some behavioral DV and some regime-related IV. Thus, using either metric as a DV would involve regressing a qualitative assessment of regime effect on some regime characteristic to see if the regime had an effect. Although this makes little sense, other research programs have made such errors.[34] Although neither set of authors has suggested using their metric to quantitatively analyze regime effectiveness, the temptation for others to do so should be avoided.

For a dependent variable to be useful in making relative judgments about disparate regimes, it must be denominated in *comparable* not just *common* units. Because environmental problems vary significantly in their resistance to remedy, the metric must capture both the amount of change a regime induced *and* how hard that amount of change was to induce.[35] Consider comparing the climate change and ozone protection regimes. Assume, hypothetically, that careful analysis demonstrated that the climate regime was responsible for slowing the growth of greenhouse gas emissions by five percent whereas the ozone protection regime was responsible for actually reducing the production of ozone depleting substances (ODSs) by ninety percent, both estimated after controlling for other factors. Both regimes were "somewhat" effective, since they altered behavior. Judging which was more effective proves more challenging. On the one hand, given that the climate regime sought to stabilize greenhouse gas emissions and the ozone regime sought to eliminate ODSs, the ozone regime appears to have had a greater effect since it came closer to achieving its goal. On the other hand, changing energy consumption patterns is so much more difficult and costly than altering ODS consumption patterns that a good case can be made that even a five percent reduction would constitute a major success. Whether ultimately one would decide in favor of the climate or ozone regime, the example illustrates that we want a metric that captures both the amount of behavior change and the difficulty of inducing such change.

Assessing the relative effectiveness across regimes, as opposed to the absolute effectiveness of a regime relative to the counterfactual, requires assessing both the *amount of change* and the *per unit effort* needed to make such change. Consider these components in turn. First, we want a metric that is comparable across units of analysis. We cannot enter data on numbers of whales killed, acres of deforestation, and tons of pollutants emitted in a single regression, even though all can be expressed numerically. How should we address this problem? Regime goals differ too much to expect to create a single metric that allows convincing comparisons across *all* regime types. Developing a few categories of regimes based upon such criteria may allow us to make meaningful comparisons among regimes *within* a category. Thus, we might imagine a "pollution" category for regimes addressing acid precipitation, ozone loss, climate change, and various river and ocean pollutants; a "wildlife" category for regimes addressing protection or management of endangered species, whaling, polar bears, fur seals, and various fish species; and a "habitat" category for regimes covering wetlands, world heritage sites, and desertification. One can imagine devising indicators that would allow comparison within but not across these categories: for pollutant regimes, levels of emissions; for wildlife regimes, numbers of animals killed or changes in species population; and for habitat regimes, relevant acreage.

Even when indicators can be expressed in similar units (for example, sulfur dioxide, nitrogen oxide, volatile organic compounds, ODSs, and CO2 emissions can all be expressed in tons emitted), differences in their levels make a regression using absolute levels (raw data) inappropriate. To compare across regimes, or even across countries within a regime, requires normalizing data. Often, analysts address this by using indexing (measuring relative to a given year's level that is set as 100) or first differences (annual changes in absolute levels). To facilitate comparison across regimes, countries, and time, however, suggests normalizing absolute levels into annual percentage change scores (APCs). Like indexing, using APCs removes variance due to regime-based and country-based differences in initial levels of an activity but additionally recalibrates (and thus allows comparison across) every year. Tables 6.1 and 6.2 provide illustrative examples relevant to the first two protocols of the LRTAP regime dealing with sulfur and nitrogen oxides.

Table 6.1. *Dependent variable as absolute metric.*

Example: Sulfur and nitrogen oxide emissions (000s of tonnes)

Subregime	Country	1988	1989	1990	1991	1992
Sulfur	Belgium	354	325	372	334	318
Sulfur	Iceland	18	17	24	23	24
Nitrogen	Belgium	345	357	339	335	343
Nitrogen	Iceland	25	25	26	27	28

Table 6.2. *Dependent variable as annual percentage change (APC).*

Example: Sulfur and Nitrogen Oxide Emissions (% change from prior year)

Subregime	Country	1988	1989	1990	1991	1992
Sulfur	Belgium	-3.5%	-8.2%	14.5%	-10.2%	-4.8%
Sulfur	Iceland	12.5%	-5.6%	41.2%	-4.2%	4.3%
Nitrogen	Belgium	2.1%	3.5%	-5.0%	-1.2%	2.4%
Nitrogen	Iceland	4.2%	0.0%	4.0%	3.8%	3.7%

The second component needed to compare regime effects in a meaningful way is per unit effort (PUE). As the ozone-climate example makes clear, simply comparing the behavioral change induced by two regimes (whether in APC or other terms) fails to account for differences in the difficulty of inducing such change.[36] The challenge is to capture such differences in a way that allows comparison across regimes, countries, and time. If we accept APC as part of our DV, then it makes sense to define PUE as the difficulty of achieving a 1% change in the relevant behavior, be it emissions reduced, animals not killed, or acres protected. In pollution regimes, this corresponds to the abatement costs of a 1% emission change; in wildlife regimes, perhaps to the benefits foregone by not killing 1% of a given species or the costs of protecting an additional 1% of the population; and in habitat regimes, perhaps to the cost of protecting an additional 1% of the existing acreage. Calculating PUEs as a fixed monetary amount for a given percentage change has the virtue of avoiding the need to calculate different PUEs for different levels of the activity while still capturing the increasing marginal cost of environmental protection.[37]

The product of these PUE and APC constructs creates a total effort score that has several virtues as a DV for comparing regime effects. Essentially, it represents the effort made at environmental protection in "regime effort units" or REUs. Regressing REUs on a set of IVs that include at least one regime-related variable, would allow us to use the β on any regime-related variable as a metric of regime effects that would, if used cautiously, be comparable across analytic units. Thus, a well-specified regression model of environmental effort (in REUs) that produced a significant t-statistic on a membership variable would allow interpretation of β as the change in environmental effort induced by membership, with βs being comparable across regimes. REUs also have the advantage of keeping efficiency and effects separate. Consider a regime that induced one state (with a PUE of $20 million) to spend $40 million to reduce its sulfur emissions by 2% and an equally wealthy state (but which had a PUE of $5 million) to spend $10 million to reduce its sulfur emissions by 2%. The difference in REUs ($40 vs. $5 million) appropriately reflects the common-sense view that the regime had more effect on the former state (it induced a more costly change in behavior) but that the latter state was more efficient in undertaking its commitments.

The argument for using REUs as DVs to allow comparison across regimes will remain largely theoretical, however, unless we can convincingly identify PUE scores for different regimes. Using REUs to compare countries within a regime requires only estimating how the costs of making a 1% change *on a given environmental problem* vary by country.[38] Comparing the effects of different regimes or the responses of individual countries across regimes requires comparing the costs of making a 1% change *on two different environmental problems*. How do we assess whether the costs of inducing a 1% reduction in sulfur emissions into the atmosphere are greater or less (both on average and for specific countries) than those of inducing a 1% reduction in mercury discharges into a river? Though difficult, the problem may not be unresolvable. One approach involves limiting comparisons to regimes with relatively similar types of costs. Thus, we may feel confident comparing abatement costs for sulfur and nitrogen oxide emissions but less confident comparing them with mercury and cadmium discharges. Initial efforts may need to compare similar regimes and address more challenging comparisons after developing experience and methodologies for identifying PUE in different contexts. Despite these difficulties, when PUEs are available, REUs based on them may offer opportunities to make more meaningful cross-regime comparisons than are possible by using metrics that only capture behavioral change (e.g., APCs).

3.4 Refining the Set of Independent Variables

If we can establish a dependent variable that allows meaningful comparison across regimes (whether defined in terms of REUs, APCs, or some superior metric), analysis requires refinement of our choices of regime-related and other independent variables beyond that in the models above. On the regime-related variables side, the success of the research approach recommended here depends on scholars creating categories of regime features that simultaneously allow the testing of existing theories (e.g., realist, institutionalist, and constructivist) about how regimes influence behavior but facilitate reliable coding of real regimes into those categories. This may prove quite difficult. To take but one example, consider a project seeking to compare the effects of sanctions and rewards: how should it categorize a regime that provides financial aid but terminates that aid to countries that violate its terms? Initial research will need to start with crude dummy variables, refining them in the light of theoretical and empirical improvements.

Undertaking the analyses proposed here also requires careful thinking about non-regime IVs. For a model to produce interpretable explanations of changes in environmental effort, the analyst must identify a set of IVs that are sufficiently generic and generalizable that they apply to a broad range of regimes while retaining explanatory power across those regimes. Developing a good model involves the art of balancing explanatory power with generalizability, sacrificing model specificity up to a point at which doing so requires "too big" a loss in explanatory power. In part, resolving this problem requires an iterative process of selecting a set of regimes for study, attempting to apply potential IVs across those regimes, and either excluding regimes or devising a more general IV until a balance that satisfies the analyst is found.

An optimal approach to model specification may involve a generic model that includes "core" IVs that could be applied to a dataset of most regimes, a set of several intermediate models that all use these core IVs but each of which couples them with IVs that apply relatively well to their particular subset of regimes, and many regime-specific models that add additional IVs that have little applicability outside of a particular regime. The generic model could include a set of "usual suspect" IVs, such as indicators of income, economic growth, levels of economic and technological development, type of government, population, and level of environmental concern. Indeed, the environmental Kuznets curve literature provides an initial source of such variables and their indicators. Developing a list of such variables may operate best as a collective activity in which these core IVs are evaluated, critiqued, and improved as proxies that are more explanatory, more generalizable, or both are identified. Among intermediate models, one might imagine a specification for pollution treaties that added variables for development, technology, and intensity of resource use while a specification for wildlife treaties added, instead, demand for the species as exhibited by price, stock recruitment rates, and number of countries having access to the species. Further research could identify more useful distinctions, including modeling regimes that address, say, overappropriation separately from those that address underprovision problems, with indicators of administrative capacity playing a central role in the first and indicators of financial capacity playing a central role in the second.[39]

4. CONDUCTING THE EMPIRICAL ANALYSIS

Operationalizing the models suggested here engages empirical questions of sample size and the appropriate unit of analysis, the type and availability of relevant data, and the analytic techniques to be used on that data. Before proceeding, however, a few caveats deserve mention. As already noted, quantitative analysis trades off accuracy for generalizability: including more units of analysis and more observations means doing so with less knowledge and detail. We rightly place more confidence in a researcher's assessment of the Atlantic tuna regime's effects if she studied only that regime than if she studied it as one of ten fisheries regimes. However, we also rightly are more cautious in generalizing from an explanation of regime effects derived solely from the Atlantic tuna regime than from one derived from a larger set of regimes. If variables and models are carefully specified, quantitative methods can capture the presence or absence, strength, or quality of even quite subjective institutional and contextual variables. But, resource constraints and the need to abstract and simplify case-specific features to a sufficiently high level that they apply to a range of regimes often means that attempts to map findings to any given regime become less compelling. And, indeed, even those claims of quantitative analyses that are convincing may be too probabilistic or vague for many purposes.

4.1 Choosing Sample Size and the Unit of Analysis

Quantitative analysis of environmental regimes has been eschewed to date, at least in part, because of the assumption that there are so few environmental regimes and that they are sufficiently heterogeneous that they cannot be readily combined into a dataset susceptible to such analysis. Overcoming this apparent obstacle requires thinking carefully about the unit of analysis and sample size. Most statistical techniques require at least as many observations (remember the definitions above) as independent and control variables. Many more observations are needed to distinguish real effects from random covariation of the IV and DV, with at least 5 (and preferably 20) times as many observations as IVs usually recommended.[40] Even higher ratios are recommended when the IV of interest is expected to have only a small effect on the DV or if the measurement of variables is imprecise, two problems that seem particularly likely in the study of regimes.[41] If we assume that a reasonable regression model of any DV of interest requires 5 to 10 IVs, this suggests that we need data sets of at least 50 and preferably a few hundred observations.[42]

If we conceive of our units of analysis as involving regimes or their absence, than the heterogeneity of regimes makes it likely that we cannot construct a database of sufficient size and comparability to run regression analyses. Of the several hundred extant multilateral environmental treaties, most have little reliable data on any conceivable dependent variable and fewer still have comparable data for the period prior to regime formation.[43] Indeed, reliable data collection often only starts upon regime formation! Quantitative analysis become possible and appropriate, however, if we consider one of three ways to increase the number of observations: examining "subregimes" rather than regimes, observing multiple years rather than one year before and one year after regime formation, and observing individual countries rather than all states as a group.

First, theoretical considerations recommend viewing regimes as composed of distinct sub-units. Evaluating the "regulatory effects of regimes" seems as valuable as evaluating "the regulatory effects of governments." Questions like "do governments induce compliance with their regulations" or "do citizens comply with laws" entail such high levels of aggregation that they are unlikely to identify particularly compelling relationships. Assessing whether hiring more police officers "reduces traffic violations," for example, requires either mindlessly aggregating running red lights with exceeding the speed limit or using one of these metrics in lieu of both. Yet, it is precisely the variance in speeding vs. traffic light violations that provide insight into the conditions under which people comply with traffic laws. Likewise with regimes. Most regimes involve multiple "subregimes," i.e., analytically distinct components such as different proscriptions and prescriptions or different compliance strategies. For example, the stratospheric ozone regime can be viewed as consisting of three subregimes: one related to the ozone depleting substances (ODSs) phaseout commitments of developed states, one related to the ODS phaseout commitments of developing states, and one related to the commitments of developed states to finance the ODS phaseout of developing states. Since the effects of these subregimes are likely to vary, it makes sense to treat these as separate units of analysis so long as each has a separate indicator of its effect. Comparing the behaviors targeted by different subregimes has the additional virtue of holding many variables constant across that subset of observations derived from the same regime.

Second, because regimes do not bind equally on all states, it makes sense to use countries rather than regimes as the unit of analysis. Because some states never join certain regimes and those that do, do so at different times, we can compare the behavior of states for whom an international rule is binding to their own behavior before the rule became binding as well as to that of states who are not legally bound.

Third, whatever the dependent variable, making a convincing argument requires comparing observations of member state behavior under the regime to some pre-regime period, to their behavior in similar contexts without a regime, to corresponding counterfactual thought experiments, or to the behavior of comparable nonmembers. In all of these instances, each regime-year can be considered to be a separate observation. Data on many air, land, and water pollutants as well as catch and trade statistics for various species are often available for ranges of years that span entry into force of the corresponding regimes. There is no reason to simply average data for the five years before a regime enters into force and compare it to the average for five years thereafter, when non-aggregated annual data provides greater analytic leverage.[44]

Taken together, these points suggest the value of defining units of analysis at the subregime-country level and recording data on all appropriate variables for all relevant years. That is, each observation would be identified in terms of subregime, country, and year.

4.2 Availability of Data

Do enough regimes with enough data exist to make quantitative analysis possible? The answer is a resounding yes, at least for some regimes. First, several data sets exist that can provide the foundation for calculating APC figures. Extensive country-year data exists on pollutants regulated under various LRTAP protocols, under the ozone regime, and under various marine and river pollution treaties. In several of these cases, data is available for ten to twenty years and for scores of countries, providing hundreds of observations for a single regime or subregime. Similarly extensive data sets exist for whaling, polar bears, various marine mammals, and many fisheries that have been regulated by international regimes. Less detailed data are available on catch, and in some instances populations (such as annual bird counts), relevant to many agreements on bird and land animal preservation. Careful coordinated research could extend this list by identifying extant datasets that contain data relevant to evaluating the effects of particular regimes or by piecing together such datasets from subsets of data developed for various scientific, rather than social scientific, purposes.

Grounds for guarded optimism also exist regarding PUE figures. Most fisheries regimes have historical catch per unit effort information.[45] Researchers at IIASA have estimated abatement costs based on different scenarios for a range of countries and years that could serve as PUE estimates for European and North American acid precipitant regimes.[46] Sprinz and Vaahtoranta generated country-specific abatement costs for the ozone and acid rain regimes.[47] Estimates comparing the costs of environmental control across pollutants or across countries could be used to develop datasets that could serve as at least rudimentary PUE estimates for other regimes. The success of these analysts at estimating abatement costs using both sophisticated modeling and more crude proxy variables suggests that such efforts are likely to bear at least some fruit.

On the IV side, data on treaty entry into force and country membership are readily available for all treaties. Several analysts have already coded particular regime features for a range of environmental regimes, including data on institutional structure, monitoring, and enforcement, data that could easily be further enhanced through more systematic coding of environmental treaties.[48] Country-year data are also available on a wide variety of political and economic variables that are central to any model of environmental behavior, including various permutations of GNP, population, energy use, type of government, and level of development, with most available in electronic format.

Undoubtedly, many regimes we would want to evaluate will have data for only a few years or a few countries, have data of such poor quality that it would make little sense to use it, or have no data at all. The obvious strategy in such cases is to recognize the inability to analyze such regimes in the short term and attempt to establish data collection systems that will allow such analysis in the future. An alternative possibility, however, involves a more careful and iterative search for data by identifying indicators relevant to the effectiveness of a given subregime and determining whether they are available and, reciprocally, identifying available data sets and determining to which subregimes they might be relevant. Such a process may uncover nonobvious variables that are both relevant and available to support the use of quantitative analysis to evaluate regimes. As most case study scholars know, extensive relevant data turns up for many regimes if sufficient research time is invested. A systematic attempt to work with such scholars could take advantage of their knowledge of individual data sets to create a meta-database of environmental indicators for analysis. Indeed, the belief that relevant data sets do not exist may owe more to the assumption that quantitative analysis is not possible than to the real unavailability of such data.

4.3 Using Panel Data

To take advantage of the model of regime influence, choice of units of analysis, and data resources described to this point, we must also choose appropriate analytic techniques. Defining observations in terms of subregime, country, and year allows use of panel or pooled time-series data. Although mathematically complex, the analytic techniques used to analyze panel data are conceptually easy to follow. Their major advantage lies in their ability to "take into account unobserved heterogeneity across individuals and/or through time."[49] Panel data can identify the extent to which the dependent variable covaries with the regime-related independent variables after controlling both for differences across countries and for variation over time.

Conceptualized visually, the values of the DV fit in a matrix of rows of country-subregimes, columns of years, and cells of data, as shown in Tables 6.1 and 6.2 above. The values of IVs can be fit in corresponding matrices. If those matrices are stacked vertically, each observation would consist of drilling a single "core" through these matrices, picking up the value of the DV and the corresponding regime and other IVs for a subregime-country-year. Many IVs, for example, membership or annual percentage change in GNP, are what are called "individual time-varying variables"[50] that vary by both country and year (both columns and rows differ). Other "individual time-invariant variables" vary by country but only slowly by year, such as administrative capacity or level of development, and are captured in matrices in which the value for a given country is the same for all years but those values vary across countries (rows differ but columns do not). "Period individual-invariant variables" involve time-specific differences that affect all countries equally, such as changes in regime features and changes in world oil and coal prices, and can be captured in matrices in which all countries have the same values for a given year but values vary across years (columns differ but rows do not). Tables 6.3 through 6.6 provide examples of these variables.

Table 6.3. *Independent variable of interest that is individual, time-varying*

Example: "Membership" based on entry into force

Subregime	Country	1988	1989	1990	1991	1992
Sulfur	Belgium	0	1	1	1	1
Sulfur	Iceland	0	0	0	0	0
Nitrogen	Belgium	0	0	0	1	1
Nitrogen	Iceland	0	0	0	0	0

Table 6.4. *Control variables that are individual time-invariant*

Example: Land Area (000s of sq. kilometers)

Subregime	Country	1988	1989	1990	1991	1992
All	Belgium	30.5	30.5	30.5	30.5	30.5
All	Iceland	103.0	103.0	103.0	103.0	103.0

Table 6.5. *Control variables that are period, individual-invariant*

Example: World Oil Price Index ($/bbl)

Subregime	Country	1988	1989	1990	1991	1992
All	Belgium	81.2	107.7	123.5	120.7	131.3
All	Iceland	81.2	107.7	123.5	120.7	131.3

Table 6.6. *Control variables that are individual, time-varying*

Example: GNP per capita (000s of constant 1995$)

Subregime	Country	1988	1989	1990	1991	1992
All	Belgium	24.3	25.1	25.7	26.1	26.4
All	Iceland	25.5	25.5	25.6	25.7	24.7

What advantages does analysis of such panel data have for evaluating the effects of regimes? Consider efforts to estimate how membership influences state behavior. Any analysis of the influence of regimes on state behavior must address an inherent problem of endogeneity: agreements are signed only when states, and by those states that, are ready to limit environmental harm. Therefore, by definition but for reasons unrelated to IEAs, the activities of member states will differ both from their prior behavior and from that of nonmember states. Cases where different treaty provisions correlate with behaviors or environmental quality may be mere reflections of underlying differences in the problem being addressed or other factors. Addressing these obstacles that require careful theorizing and the use of analytic techniques that are available but are only beginning to be applied to the task.

Cross-section data (looking at a range of countries in a given year) would estimate the effect of membership by comparing member behavior to nonmember behavior, failing to address the likelihood that member countries differ in systematic ways from nonmembers. Such data makes it difficult to decipher whether "better" behavior by members reflects the influence of membership or the fact that those most willing and able to alter their behavior become members. Even with proxies for such willingness or ability included in the model, the possibility remains that member and nonmembers differ in some systematic but unobserved way. In contrast, time-series data estimates the membership effect by comparing the behavior of states as members to their behavior as nonmembers, controlling for other factors. This approach ignores the possibility that other influences that occur contemporaneously with becoming a member (for example, the end of the

Cold War in the LRTAP sulfur case) explain the change in behavior. Regression using time-series data cannot distinguish whether membership or other coincidental factors are responsible for behavioral differences.

Panel data begins to address the endogeneity problem by taking advantage of both types of variation simultaneously. Panel data uses changes in nonmember behavior over time to estimate how time-varying factors would have effected member behavior, thereby avoiding erroneously attributing those effects to membership. Panel data controls for country-specific factors by using changes in behavior during the period in which a country was not a regime member to estimate how its behavior would have been driven by non-regime factors when it was a member, thereby avoiding erroneously attributing those effects to membership. Thus, panel data improves our estimate of regime effects by more effectively separating regime effects from those due to time or country variables.[51] Panel data analysis also has advantages in deriving causal inferences, assessing measurement errors in variables, correcting for autocorrelation, evaluating the model specification, and addressing data heteroskedasticity.[52] Even more progress can be made in this regard by employing statistical methods explicitly designed to address endogeneity problems, e.g., two-stage least squares models.[53]

5. CONCLUSION

Quantitative analysis offers opportunities to investigate certain aspects of regime effects for which qualitative techniques are less well-suited. Although factor analysis, contingency tables, and other techniques are certainly possible and should be explored, the present chapter has investigated the contribution that regression analysis using panel data could make to determining whether, which type of, and under what conditions, regimes wield influence. Studies that collect data on a range of regimes provide valuable means for identifying general trends across regimes, evaluating whether some regimes are more effective than others, and determining how non-regime factors condition the effects of a particular type of regime.

Stating that quantitative techniques can complement qualitative analyses and contribute to the regime consequences research project does not mean, however, that undertaking such analyses will be easy. Indeed, the foregoing argument has sought to identify and clarify the numerous theoretical and empirical obstacles to using quantitative analysis to answer questions central to research on regime effects. Devising a dependent variable that would allow meaningful comparison across regimes requires careful attention to creating a comparable metric of behavioral change and a comparable metric of the difficulty of inducing behavioral change. Likewise, representing regime influence in the model requires careful specification if we are to determine how regimes influence members, how they influence nonmembers, and how their influences differ across the two. Comparing across regimes also requires careful attention to specification of non-regime control variables. A model designed to apply to all regimes is likely to produce weak and perhaps uninterpretable estimates of regime effects; one designed to apply well to a single regime precludes comparison across regimes. Intermediate models specified to explain the variation in the dependent variable across a set of regimes that are selected for similarity in their predicted impacts may reach the right balance between these too-generic and too-specific extremes. Applying such a model to panel data using subregime-country-years as our observations allows us to control for variables in ways that more aggregated analyses cannot. Such data appears to be available, at least for enough regimes to make the enterprise worth pursuing. A well-specified model and corresponding data would allow us to evaluate whether regimes influence states, whether they do so in ways that would be unlikely to have occurred by chance, which ones do so better than others, and a variety of other as yet unidentified but important questions.

ACKNOWLEDGEMENTS

An earlier version of this chapter appeared as Ronald B. Mitchell, 'A Quantitative Approach to Evaluating International Environmental Regime', *Global Environmental Politics*, 2:4 (November 2002), pp. 58-83. © by the Massachusetts Institute of Technology. The chapter has benefited greatly from comments from Arild Underdal, Oran Young, Detlef Sprinz, and participants in a conference on "Regime Consequences: Methodological Challenges and Research Strategies" hosted by the Centre for Advanced Study of the Norwegian Academy of Science and Letters in June 2000. This chapter was completed with the generous support of a Sabbatical Fellowship in the Humanities and Social Sciences from the American Philosophical Society and a 2002 Summer Research Award from the University of Oregon.

NOTES

[1] For some exceptions, see Meyer et al. 1997; Downs et al. 1998; and Miles et al. 2001. Several scholars have put together data sets that code a variety of parameters for a range of environmental treaty regimes. The International Regimes Database (IRD) has begun pulling together an extensive set of data on thirty different treaties which, once completed, will constitute a significant advance in the data that will be available to the policy and scholarly community. Haas and Sundgren examined trends in environmental treaty making (Haas and Sundgren 1993). Dmitris Stevis has collected data on membership and characteristics of international environmental institutions (Stevis 1999).

[2] Downs et al. 1996.

[3] Princen 1996.

[4] Brown Weiss and Jacobson collected extensive information on compliance and its determinants for ten countries and five different treaties (Brown Weiss and Jacobson 1998). Miles et al. have developed a database of 44 cases involving regime phases or components (Miles et al. 2001).

[5] Mitchell and Bernauer 1998.

[6] Thus, the convincing, if contested, quantitative finding that democratic states rarely go to war against each other proves unsatisfactory in explaining why any particular war occurs.

[7] Haas et al. 1993; Brown Weiss and Jacobson 1998; and Victor et al. 1998.

[8] For an initial application of this approach, see Mitchell 2003a.

[9] King et al. 1994; Fearon 1991; and Biersteker 1993.

[10] See Ragin and Becker 1992; Galtung 1967; King et al. 1994; Yin 1994.

[11] King et al. 1994, 52.

[12] Krasner 1983.

[13] Haas et al. 1993; Mitchell, 1994; Brown Weiss and Jacobson 1998; Victor et al. 1998, Young 1997; Young 1999a; Miles et al. 2001.

[14] See Young 1999a; Helm and Sprinz 2000; Miles et al. 2001.

[15] Underdal and Young this volume; see also Young 2002.

[16] Thus, as a hypothetical example, a study that used the end of the Cold War as a control for the contextual variable "polarity" might identify that the regimes in the study sample had only a "small" average effect when polarity was controlled for. Including a polarity-regime interaction term, however, might demonstrate that this "small" effect was the average of a quite large effect of regimes in the post-Cold War uni-polar world and no effect in the Cold War bi-polar world.

[17] Mitchell 1994; Mitchell 1996; Chayes and Chayes 1993; Brown Weiss and Jacobson 1998.

[18] Young 1999a; Young 1999b; Victor et al. 1998; Miles et al. 2001; Stokke 1997; Wettestad 1999.

[19] Levy 1993; Levy 1995; Sprinz 1998.

[20] For a review of this literature, see Harbaugh et al. 2001.

[21] A more refined counterfactual might subtract $\beta 1$ from emissions forecast by the model using each states' actual values for all the IVs. The impact of regime membership for that state would then consist of the difference between its actual emissions and the emissions forecast by this method.

[22] Helm and Sprinz 2000; Sprinz and Helm 1999.

[23] The criteria usually viewed as necessary to infer a causal relationship between A and B are demonstrating "relationship" (co-variation of the values of A with the values of B), "time precedence" (changes in A precede changes in B), and "nonspuriousness" (the ability to rule out other possible causal variables) (Asher 1976, 11; Kenny 1979, 3-5).

[24] Of course, a fully accurate interpretation of the β in this way requires that the analyst have paid careful attention to multi-collinearity, heteroskedasticity, omitted variable bias, and a variety of additional statistical concerns.

[25] Meaningful comparison of the magnitude of coefficients requires, inter alia, careful attention to the order in which variables enter the regression equation, as noted in any standard statistics textbook.

[26] The adjusted R^2 is conceptually identical but corrects this estimate to reflect the fact that adding more IVs to a regression equation can increase the R^2 even if the additional IVs do not have any significant correlation with the DV.

[27] Chayes and Chayes 1995; Downs et al. 1996. A more accurate depiction of the theoretical claims made by Downs et al. would need, at a minimum, to reflect their view that the importance of sanctions depends on the ambitiousness of the regime goals which they refer to as "depth of cooperation."

[28] $\beta 1$ represents the change in behavior induced in members of a regime, controlling for type of regime (i.e., comparing members of sanction-based regimes to nonmembers of those regimes, and members of non-sanction-based regimes to nonmembers of those regimes).

[29] $\beta 2$ represents the change in behavior that correlates with variation in whether a regime has sanctions or not, controlling for membership (i.e., comparing members of sanction-based regimes to members of other regimes, and nonmembers of sanction-based regimes to nonmembers of other regimes).

[30] Brown Weiss and Jacobson 1998, 528-530.

[31] Sprinz and Helm 1999; Helm and Sprinz 2000.

[32] Sprinz and Helm 1999, 365.

[33] Underdal 2001, 4.

[34] Indeed, the seminal quantitative work on economic sanctions made precisely this mistake, regressing a DV that included "the contribution made by sanctions to a positive outcome" on whether sanctions were imposed or not to determine whether sanctions influence state behavior (Hufbauer et al. 1990).

[35] Miles et al. 2001; Young 1999b; Wettestad 1999.

[36] The notion of differences in the difficulty of inducing behavioral change has many similarities to Miles et al. (2001) notion of problem "malignity."

[37] A pollution PUE of $500 implies that inducing a country to reduce its pollution from 10,000 units to 9,900 units (100 units or 1%) will cost a regime $500 but inducing a country to reduce its pollution from 1,000 units to 900 units (100 units but 10%) will cost the regime $5,000 ($500 * 10%).

[38] Indeed, the assumption that abatement costs, and by implication PUE scores, vary by country underlies the flexibility mechanisms designed into the Climate Change Convention.

[39] Ostrom 1990; Mitchell 1999.

[40] Tabachnick and Fidell 1989, 129.

[41] Tabachnick and Fidell 1989, 129.

[42] Statistical power analysis confirms these general rules of thumb, suggesting that a regression model using 8 independent variables, a statistical significance test (i.e., α) of .05, and a power criterion of .80 would need a sample of 107 to detect a "medium" effect size and a sample of over 700 to detect a "small" effect size (Cohen 1992, 155-159).

[43] Mitchell 2003b.

[44] Murdoch et al. 1997.

[45] Peterson 1993.

[46] Alcamo et al. 1990.

[47] Sprinz and Vaahtoranta 1994.
[48] For example, databases created by Peter Haas, Dimitris Stevis, Edith Brown Weiss and Harold Jacobson, and the International Regimes Database all have systematic codings of several variables for various environmental treaties. See Haas and Sundgren 1993, 401-429; Brown Weiss and Jacobson 1998; Victor et al. 1998; and Stevis 1999.
[49] Hamerle and Ronning 1995.
[50] Hamerle and Ronning 1995; Finkel 1995.
[51] Finkel 1995.
[52] Finkel 1995.
[53] Mitchell 2003a.

REFERENCES

Alcamo, J., Shaw, R. and Hordijk, L. (eds.) (1990) *The RAINS Model of Acidification: Science and Strategies in Europe,* Kluwer Academic Publishers, Dordrecht.

Asher, H. B. (1976) *Causal Modeling.* Sage Publications, CA.

Biersteker, T. (1993) Constructing Historical Counterfactuals to Assess the Consequences of International Regimes: The Global Debt Regime and the Course of the Debt Crisis of the 1980s, in *Regime Theory and International Relations,* edited by V. Rittberger, Oxford University Press, New York, 315–338.

Brown Weiss, E. and Jacobson, H. K. (eds.) (1998) *Engaging Countries: Strengthening Compliance with International Environmental Accords,* MIT Press, Cambridge, MA.

Chayes, A. and Chayes, A. H. (1993) On Compliance, *International Organization* 47: 175–205.

Chayes, A. and Chayes, A. H. (1995) *The New Sovereignty: Compliance with International Regulatory Agreements,* Harvard University Press, Cambridge, MA.

Cohen J. (1992) A Power Primer, *Psychological Bulletin* 112: 155–9.

Downs, G. W., Rocke, D. M. and Barsoom, P. N. (1996) Is the Good News about Compliance Good News about Cooperation? *International Organization* 50: 379–406.

Downs, G. W., Rocke, D. M. and Barsoom, P. N. (1998) Managing the Evolution of Cooperation, *International Organization* 52: 397–419.

Eckstein, H. (1975) Case Study and Theory in Political Science, in F. Greenstein and N. Polsby (eds.) *Handbook of Political Science, Vol. 7, Strategies of Inquiry,* Addison-Wesley Press, Reading, MA, 79–137.

Fearon, J. D. (1991) Counterfactuals and Hypothesis Testing in Political Science, *World Politics* 43: 169–195.

Finkel, S. E. (1995) *Causal Analysis with Panel Data,* Sage Publications, CA.

Galtung, J. (1967) *Theory and Methods of Social Research,* Columbia University Press, New York.

Haas, P. M., and Sundgren, J. (1993) Evolving International Environmental Law: Changing Practices of National Sovereignty, in N. Choucri (ed.) *Global Accord: Environmental Challenges and International Responses,* MIT Press, Cambridge, MA, 401–429.

Haas, P. M., Keohane, R. O. and Levy, M. A. (eds.) (1993) *Institutions for The Earth: Sources of Effective International Environmental Protection,* MIT Press, Cambridge, MA.

Hamerle, A., and Ronning, G. (1995) Panel Analysis for Qualitative Variables, in G. Arminger, C. C. Clogg, M. E. Sobel, (eds.) *Handbook of Statistical Modeling for the Social and Behavioral Sciences,* Plenum Press, New York, 401–451.

Harbaugh, W., Levinson, A. and Wilson, D. (2000) *Re-examining the Empirical Evidence for an Environmental Kuznets Curve*, National Bureau of Economic Research, Cambridge, MA.

Helm, C. and Sprinz, D. (2000) Measuring the Effectiveness of International Environmental Regimes, *Journal of Conflict Resolution* 44: 630–652.

Hufbauer, G. C., Schott, J. J. and Elliott, K. A. (1990) *Economic Sanctions Reconsidered: History and Current Policy,* Institute for International Economics, Washington, DC.

Kenny, D. A. (1979) *Correlation and Causality,* John Wiley and Sons, New York.

King, G., Keohane, R. O. and Verba., S. (1994) *Designing Social Inquiry: Scientific Inference in Qualitative Research,* Princeton University Press.

Krasner, S. (1983) *International Regimes,* Cornell University Press, Ithaca, New York.

Levy, M. A. (1995) International Cooperation to Combat Acid Rain, in H. O. Bergesen and G. Parmann (eds.) *Green Globe Yearbook: An Independent Publication on Environment and Development,* Oxford University Press, NC, 59–68.

Levy, M. A. (1993) European Acid Rain: The Power of Tote-Board Diplomacy, in P. Haas, R. O. Keohane, and M. Levy (eds.) *Institutions for the Earth: Sources of Effective International Environmental Protection,* MIT Press, Cambridge, MA, 75–132.

Meyer, J. W., Frank, D. J., A. Hironaka, A. , Schofer, E. and Tuma, N. B. (1997) The Structuring of a World Environmental Regime, 1870 – 1990, *International Organization* 51: 623–629.

Miles, E. L., Underdal, A., Andresen, S., Wettestad, J., Skjaerseth, J. B. and Carlin, E. M. (eds.) 2001, *Environmental Regime Effectiveness: Confronting Theory with Evidence,* MIT Press, Cambridge, MA.

Mitchell, R. B. and Bernauer, and T. (1998) Empirical Research on International Environmental Policy: Designing Qualitative Case Studies, *Journal of Environment and Development* 7: 4–31.

Mitchell, R. B. (1996) Compliance Theory: An Overview, in J. Cameron, J. Werksman and P. Roderick (eds.) *Improving Compliance with International Environmental Law,* Earthscan, London, 3–28.

Mitchell, R. B. (1994) *Intentional Oil Pollution at Sea: Environmental Policy and Treaty Compliance,* MIT Press, Cambridge, MA.

Mitchell, R. B. (1999) International Environmental Common Pool Resources: More Common than Domestic but More Difficult to Manage, in J. S. Barkin and G. Shambaugh (eds.) *Anarchy and the Environment: The International Relations of Common Pool Resources,* SUNY Press, Albany, NY.

Mitchell, R. B. (2003a) *The Relative Effects of Environmental Regimes: A Quantitative Comparison of Four Acid Rain Protocols*, paper presented at the International Studies Association Conference, Portland, OR.

Mitchell, R. B. (2003b) International Environmental Agreements: A Survey of Their Features, Formation, and Effects, *Annual Review of Environment and Resources* 28.

Murdoch, J. C., Sandler, T. and Sargent, K. (1997) A Tale of Two Collectives: Sulphur Versus Nitrogen Oxides Emission Reduction in Europe, *Economica* 64: 281–301.

Ostrom, E. (1990) *Governing the Commons: The Evolution of Institutions for Collective Action,* Cambridge University Press.

Peterson, M. J. (1993) International Fisheries Management, in P. Haas, R. O. Keohane and M. Levy, *Institutions For The Earth: Sources of Effective International Environmental Protection,* MIT Press, Cambridge, MA, 249–308.

Princen, T. (1996) The Zero Option and Ecological Rationality in International Environmental Politics, *International Environmental Affairs* 8: 147–176.

Ragin, C. C. and Becker, H. S. (1992) *What is a Case? Exploring the Foundations of Social Inquiry,* Cambridge University Press.
Sprinz, D. and Helm, C. (1999) The Effect of Global Environmental Regimes: A Measurement Concept, *International Political Science Review* 20: 359–369.
Sprinz, D. and Vaahtoranta, T. (1994) The Interest-Based Explanation of International Environmental Policy, *International Organization* 48: 77–105.
Sprinz, D. (1998) Domestic Politics and European Acid Rain Regulation, in A. Underdal (ed.) *The Politics of International Environmental Management,* Kluwer Academic Publishers, Dordrecht, 41–66.
Stevis, D. (1999) Email communication.
Stokke, O. S. (1997) Regimes as Governance Systems, in O. R. Young (ed) *Global Governance: Drawing Insights from the Environmental Experience,* MIT Press, Cambridge, MA, 27–63.
Tabachnick, B. G. and Fidell, L. S. (1989) *Using Multivariate Statistics,* HarperCollins, New York.
Underdal, A. (2001) Conclusions: Patterns of Regime Effectiveness, in E. L. Miles et al (eds.) *Environmental Regime Effectiveness: Confronting Theory with Evidence,* MIT Press, Cambridge, MA.
Underdal, A. and Young, O. R. (eds.) (forthcoming) *Regime Consequences: Methodological Challenges and Research Strategies,* Kluwer Academic Publishers, Dordrecht.
Victor, D. G., Raustiala, K. and Skolnikoff, E. B. (eds.) (1998) *The Implementation and Effectiveness of International Environmental Commitments,* MIT Press, Cambridge, MA.
Wettestad, J. (1999) *Designing Effective Environmental Regimes: The Key Conditions,* Edward Elgar, Cheltenham, UK.
Yin, R. (1994) *Case Study Research: Design and Methods,* 2nd ed., Sage Publications, CA.
Young, O. R. (ed.) (1997) *Global Governance: Drawing Insights from the Environmental Experience,* MIT Press, *Cambridge*, MA.
Young, O. R., (ed.) (1999a) *Effectiveness of International Environmental Regimes: Causal Connections and Behavioral Mechanisms,* MIT Press, Cambridge, MA.
Young, O. R., (1999b) *Governance in World Affairs,* Cornell University Press, Ithaca, New York.
Young, O. R. (2002) The Institutional Dimensions of Environmental Change: Fit, Interplay, and Scale, MIT Press, Cambridge, MA.

Chapter 7

FORMAL THEORY AND REGIME EFFECTIVENESS: RATIONAL PLAYERS, IRRATIONAL REGIMES

HUGH WARD, GRANK GRUNDIG and ETHAN ZORICK
Department of Government, University of Essex

1. INTRODUCTION

Global and regional environmental problems are frequently conceptualised as collective action failures. Environmental quality is a public good. If it is provided, it can be enjoyed whether or not an individual or a nation has made sacrifices to maintain it. So it may well be rational to free-ride on others' contributions to the solution of the problem, unless there are strong nation-specific benefits from cooperating.[1] This often leads to the failure to maintain global environmental quality. Starting with Keohane (1984), international regimes have been seen as encouraging nations rationally pursuing their various interests to co-operate to a greater extent than would otherwise be the case, so long as others do so as well. This argument partly derives from game-theoretic models of collective action. Despite the important contribution game-theory has made, many scholars believe that it has definite limitations. Regimes can raise awareness of issues, change perceptions of problems and nations' interests in their solution, or act as a locus for institutionally-based learning about possible policy responses. Furthermore, they can act as the sites where normative discourses about what is proper to do and who should pay the price contend for dominance. Some doubt whether these processes can adequately be understood within a rational-choice framework based on actors choosing efficient means to given ends.

Rather than go over the general problems with the application of rational choice to international relations (IR) (e.g. Hollis and Smith, 1990; Walt, 1999), we try to put the approach to work to conceptualize and to explain regime effectiveness, raising specific issues as we go. First we discuss whether regime effectiveness can adequately be characterized as an *economically efficient* response to a collective action failure. Then we discuss a range of games in which rational players (not exclusively nations) pursue their interests in a process that leads to partial and inefficient responses to collective action failures in the international system. We avoid full technical specifications, concentrating on the key intuition, with references back to the formal literature for the more technically minded. These games are mechanisms in Bunge' s (1997) sense—processes capable of bringing about a change in a system. As they are partly based on interests, they are what Young and Levy (1999) call utilitarian mechanisms. However, we will show that interests interact with information transmission, learning, expectations shaping, and norms. Games might seem to be reductionist mechanisms, accounting for the complex phenomena of regimes in terms of "component parts," such as states, at a lower level of analysis (Stinchcombe, 1991; cf. Hovi, 2000). However, we argue that there is an ineradicably social component to game-theory, linked to common beliefs and related to issues about learning and social norms.

In the first section we sketch the game-theoretic approach. In the next section we refine the question we are seeking to answer. Rather than attempting to explain collective action failure over the global environment *per-se*, the issue is why *responses to collective action failure,* in the form of regimes, may not be as effective as desirable. We present a view of regime effectiveness that is consonant with this position and then discuss some of its problems. We loosely group mechanisms under three headings: inefficiencies due to the bargaining process; failures consequent on the articulation of power; and failures to achieve effective outcomes due to inefficient learning. This places the mechanisms broadly within the three-fold division of regime theory along neo-institutionalist, realist, and knowledge/discourse-theoretic lines. We limit ourselves to mechanisms that seem to us to be potentially empirically significant and to raise issues either about: 1) how effectiveness should be conceptualised; 2) whether rational choice explanations of ineffectiveness are satisfactory; or 3) the empirical problems of testing hypotheses about effectiveness. Our overall argument is that rational choice raises significant issues about regime effectiveness but does not constitute a free-standing approach. Rather it works best in conjunction with a range of other approaches.

2. RATIONAL CHOICE

Rational-choice theory encompasses any approach that assumes that faced with alternatives actors generally choose to do things that they believe will bring about relatively desirable consequences. For the moment we focus on game-theory, but the bounded rationality variant will be discussed below in section 4.ii. A game-theoretical model comprises: 1) a specification of the players of the game; 2) a specification of the contingencies at which players can make moves and the moves that they can make in those contingencies, [2] 3) a specification of what players know in contingencies when they can make moves; 4) and a payoff function that assigns a payoff to each player at each possible endpoint of the game, where an endpoint is such that no player can make a further move. The rules specify elements 1) through to 4), generating what is called the extensive form of the game. Players choose a strategy that tells them how to play in all contingencies in which they have to make a move. The payoff function induces a preference ordering over strategies, conditional on the strategies chosen by the other players. Players are assumed to be rational in the sense that they choose strategies that generate the highest payoff given what other players are doing i.e. they choose best replies. It is assumed to be common knowledge among the players that all of them are rational. Here common knowledge means that, for instance, players 1 and 2 are rational; know each other are rational; know that each knows the other is rational; and so on indefinitely. Without this assumption it is not possible to predict rational play (cf. Bicchieri, 1993).

Game theory uses the idea of strategy-equilibrium in order to predict rational play. A Nash equilibrium, the simplest version of this idea, is a set of strategies, one for each player, such that no player can strictly increase its payoff by switching strategy. For any set of strategies that do not form an equilibrium, at least one player has an incentive to switch strategies, because it is not choosing a best reply. If each expects the other to adopt their strategy corresponding to the equilibrium, their expectations are fulfilled. Most games with significant application to regime effectiveness have more than one equilibrium, even after obviously implausible equilibria have been rejected. This gives rise to a coordination problem: in order to play rationally, players have to have shared expectations about which equilibrium will eventuate. This common conjecture is assumed to be common knowledge, in the sense just discussed in relation to rationality. Without such a conjecture, there is no guarantee that what you are doing is a best reply to what the other side is doing, because they may not attend to the same equilibrium. Game theory does not reduce explanation down to properties of individual players, because common knowledge is a *system* of beliefs. It cannot be defined in terms of what A and B believe, considered separately, but only in terms of what each believes about what the other believes, and so on indefinitely up a chain of higher-order beliefs about beliefs.

To date the most significant game-theoretic model for regime theory has been the Prisoners' Dilemma Supergame. Because there is a time dimension to interactions among states there may be possibilities of inter-state cooperation, even in the absence of hegemons coercing others to cooperate (Keohane, 1984). Freeriders can be punished by others using conditional strategies like tit-for-tat, under which they react to non-cooperation by switching to non-cooperation themselves in the following round. So long as the game never ends, the threat of this deters freeriding, if players care enough about the future and stand to lose enough from the collapse of cooperation (Hardin, 1982; Axelrod 1984; Taylor 1987). Otherwise the game is analogous to the Prisoners' Dilemma played just once, where it is best not to cooperate no matter what the other side is doing.

Regimes function in numerous ways to increase the possibilities of conditional cooperation (cf. Keohane, 1984; Axelrod and Keohane, 1985; Oye, 1986; Young, 1989a; Levy, Keohane and Haas, 1993; Susskind, 1993). However, to say that regimes are *potentially* functional does not explain why they come into existence (Keohane, 1984). Most environmental regimes cannot be considered to be institutional hangovers left after the power of the hegemons who forged them in their interests has declined. So there is a second-order collective action problems, because institutions are also public goods (e.g. Sened, 1997). Thus it is not obvious that nations have incentives to cooperate in their construction. We seek to explain why rational play may lead to regimes that are not fully efficient responses to an *underlying* collective action failure. First we need to define what is meant by an ineffective regime. The supergame model is of great help in clarifying the rational choice view. First it conceptually clarifies what regimes do. Then it clarifies what it means for a regime to be efficient, which is a view of effectiveness that serious consideration needs to be given to, although we argue it is ultimately unsatisfying.

3. DEFINING REGIME EFFECTIVENESS

The underlying collective action problem we consider involves playing an infinite number of rounds of a mixed-motive game such as the one shown at the bottom of Figure 7.1.[3] Considering only conditional strategies involving credible threats, if players put enough weight on the future, there typically will be a plethora of equilibria of this underlying supergame.[4] The lowest average payoff a nation need accept is 0, because defection always

FORMAL THEORY & REGIME EFFECTIVENESS 155

yields it at least this much. Figure 7.1 shows payoff pairs for states X and Y. Various versions of the Folk Theorem suggest that, *any* payoff-pair inside the quadrilateral drawn in heavy lines in Figure 7.1 may arise in equilibrium, so long as enough weight is put on future payoffs, and so long as each side gets at least its security level of zero (Fudenberg and Tirole, 1992, 145-203).[5] Beside equilibria in which each side conditionally cooperates all the time, of the sort commonly discussed in regime theory, there will be equilibria in which some players delay the point at which they start to cooperate, or in which their average cooperation level is low (Ward, 1996a).
[6]

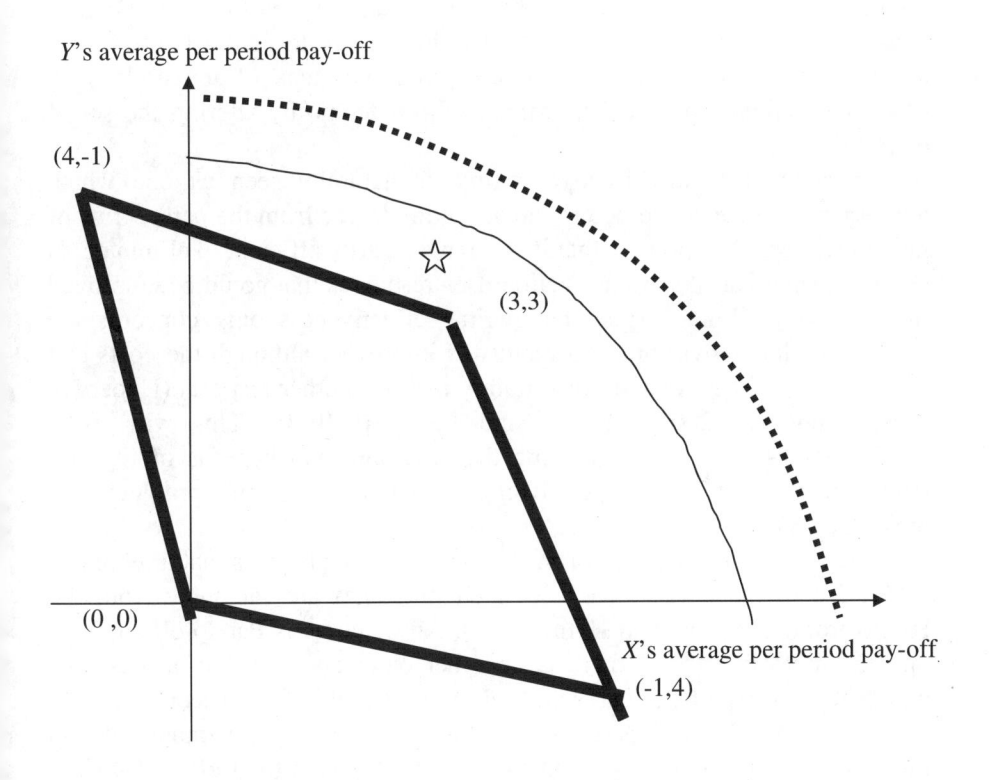

Figure 7.1. *Average payoffs under various rules.*

Payoff matrix for each round of the underlying game: C cooperate; NC not cooperate.

	C	NC
C	3,3	-1,4
NC	4,-1	0,0

We distinguish between norms and institutions in a way often used by game-theorists interested in collective action failure (e.g. Sened, 1997, 54-76; Knight, 1998). This draws on the point that there will often be a multiplicity of equilibria. As we have said this means that rational play is only possible if players have a common conjecture. Then norms (or conventions) are just equilibria which, for whatever reason, have become subject to a common-conjecture (cf. Hardin, 1982). In contrast institutions are a modified set of rules, different from the rules of the underlying collective action game, which structure the outcome by altering the set of equilibria. [7]

For economists an effective regime is naturally seen as one which addresses the issue concerned to the optimum degree from the perspective of human welfare. The point is that it is not necessarily efficient to eliminate all environmental harms, because action uses resources that could be employed in other ways. Some argue that regime effectiveness only concerns the degree to which environmental quality is improved, although the costs and side-benefits of regime activity certainly matter in other respects (Underdal, 1992; Underdal, 2001a; Young and Levy, 1999, 9). This will strike economists as artificially divorcing the environmental benefits of regimes from their opportunity costs, confusing *having an impact* on a problem with making an *effective response*.

A more precise statement of the economist's viewpoint is that a regime is *ineffective* to the extent that associated outcomes are far away from the Pareto frontier (Sprinz and Helm, 1999). An outcome is Pareto efficient, or on the Pareto frontier, if there is no other outcome such that at least one nation (or actor) is better off and none is worse off. If we accept, as most economists do, that interpersonal comparisons of utility are impossible, so there is no sense in talking about maximizing the sum-total off well-being, among the few ways we can proceed is to identify outcomes that are worse-all-round. This is the basic insight behind distinguishing Pareto inefficient and efficient outcomes. For instance the non-cooperative outcome is inefficient because nations only control pollution up to the level that is optimal for them nationally, the spillover effects on other nations' welfare being ignored (e.g. Sandler, 1997).

We relate this view of effectiveness to the supergame model of regimes. In Figure 7.1 the Pareto frontier of the underlying game is the heavy line segment through the points (-1,4), (3,3) and (4,-1). While all points within and on the edges of the heavy quadrilateral are feasible under some pattern of play, any such point to the south-west of the Pareto frontier can be improved on for both sides.[8] First regimes change the rules of the game in ways that make forms of conditional-cooperation possible that give rise to payoffs nearer this Pareto-frontier. For example regimes may: 1) provide operational definitions of freeriding and cooperation and generate shared, low-cost information about compliance, allowing freeriding to be punished; 3) dispel distrust through diplomatic activity. Secondly, regimes may move the Pareto frontier of the underlying game outwards relative to the origin, implying that potentially all sides can do better. For instance they can: 1) reduce transaction costs; 2) share information about how best to turn effort into results; 2) encourage issue-interlinkages increasing the benefits of cooperation relative to freeriding; 4) increase the capacity of nations with weak administrative systems to comply at low cost; 5) increase the premium on building a reputation for being trustworthy by clearly identifying those who break agreements.

To summarize a regime is effective to the extent that: it gives rise to a new Pareto frontier as far as possible outwards from the origin; and it coordinates attention on an equilibrium as near as possible to its Pareto frontier. As processes, regimes are increasingly effective to the extent to which equilibrium moves northeast from the origin. This is illustrated in Figure 7.1. The frontier in heavy dots is that furthest out under *any* regime that can be envisaged, given the underlying structure of the international system. The frontier shown in light dots is that to which some *particular* regime gives rise; and the payoffs generated by the equilibrium the particular regime coordinates expectations on are marked by a star. The particular regime is effective to the extent to which the star is "near" the heavily dotted "ideal-regime" frontier. Call this view *effectiveness as efficiency*.

Rather than just focus on the distance from what could be attained when measuring how effective a particular regime is Underdal (1992) argues that distance from the no-regime counterfactual is also relevant. Sprinz and Helm's index of effectiveness (1999) is the ratio: (welfare at Pareto optimum - welfare under regime)/ (welfare at Pareto optimum - welfare in no-regime counterfactual). This combines information about what is attainable and what would happen without a regime. There is a definitional issue and a substantive issue about the no-regime counterfactual. If the underlying collective action game is an infinitely repeated Prisoners' Dilemma, the origin in Figure 7.1, where neither side ever cooperates, is always at equilibrium, and it is the unique equilibrium if players place low enough weight on the future (e.g. Taylor, 1987). There *may be* just one equilibrium, then. However the underlying collective action game need not be of this form (Ward, 1996a). For instance if it is repeated 2-player Chicken, there are always at least two equilibria no matter what weight is put on the future – both patterns where one side always cooperates and the other side always defects. From what we know of repeated games, it would be *exceptional* for the underlying game to have just one equilibrium. If several equilibria exist and there is a stable outcome, a regime is in operation, as expectations are coordinated (cf. Keohane, 1984). This is true even if there are no rule changes and even if there is little or no cooperation. To construct the counterfactual without a regime we typically have to "imagine away" those properties of the underlying game that give rise to multiple equilibria, which hardly seems sensible. Typically we can only sensibly talk about some *change in* a regime having a positive causal impact on effectiveness compared to a *pre-existing* regime. This is possible when the new equilibrium is further from the origin, either because the rules are changed or expectations are coordinated on some other point, or both.

By relying on expert judgements to operationalise the non-cooperative baseline and relatively reliable data on marginal abatement costs, Helm and Sprinz (1998) make numerical estimates of the degree to which the European sulphur-dioxide and nitrogen-dioxide regimes approach efficiency, compared to the no-regime counterfactual. From their perspective a regime is fully effective if the marginal social benefit, summing benefits across all nations, is equal to the marginal cost of abatement in each country concerned. This is the condition for Pareto-efficiency, given that benefits and costs can be monetised, compared across nations, and added.[9] If marginal social benefits exceed marginal abatement costs, for instance, a country can increase the overall wellbeing of the set of nations involved by stricter regulation. The ability to monetise costs and benefits, to add them up and compare them across nations and individuals may be essential to the solution of some underlying conceptual and measurement problems with effectiveness as efficiency. Going back to Figure 7.1, without a monetary metric, there is no obvious measure of how far an equilibrium is from the "ideal frontier". However, monetisation assumes the comparability of utility that it is the rationale of Pareto efficiency to avoid, so we are on the horns of a methodological dilemma.

Sprinz and Helm (1999; cf. Underdal 1992) consider the technical limits on efficiency but they do not consider constraints on the success of all regimes inscribed in the political and economic structures of the international system. The condition for a full welfare optimum that they employ might well not be attainable under any regime that can be envisaged without major change in such aspects of the system as the power structure, the economic structure, and the hegemonic discourse (if such exists). However, unless we compare the particular regime outcome to the ideal regime counterfactual, we confuse regime effects with system effects. As in the case of all such counterfactuals, deep disagreements about limits due to systems constraints will exist between different theoretical traditions in IR. How constraining is it that the world economic system is capitalist, for example? The fact that it is difficult to answer such questions in no way excuses those interested in regime effectiveness from asking them.

Concerns about the difficulty of measurement inevitably enter the debate about how effectiveness should be conceptualised (e.g. Keohane, Haas, and Levy, 1993, 7).[10] It is often difficult to tell where the Pareto frontier is (Young, 1989b; Sebenius, 1992). One of the reasons is that it is difficult to put a monetary price on the benefits of environmental cleanup. Ultimately measuring effectiveness as efficiency relies on being able to put a price on aspects of environmental quality that are not bought and sold in the marketplace. Examples include benefits people derive from knowledge of the existence of a species. While economists have put considerable effort into developing methodologies for monetising such benefits, as part of environmental cost-benefit analysis, many authors are highly critical (e.g. Sagoff; 1988; Foster (ed.), 1996), and it is not clear how the problems can be overcome.

It is dangerous to adopt a static perspective on effectiveness as the view under discussion does. A regime is robust if nations continue to comply with it despite "shocks" that might make it hard for them to continue to do so. Building capacity to monitor compliance and to implement pledges is also important, allowing the Pareto frontier to be reached with higher probability in future. Environmental regimes often move the efficiency frontier because they encourage technical change or economies of scale in producing pollution control devices (e.g. Victor, Raustiala, and Skolnikoff (eds.), 1998). These dynamic considerations are difficult to capture in a static cost-benefit analysis or to build into measures of effectiveness as efficiency.

More than one regime will be Pareto efficient. Regimes that imply the same reductions in harmful activity can be funded in very different ways, because of the possibility of transfer payments between countries to subsidise others' control of pollution. Regimes have distributional impacts, which are ignored from the effectiveness as efficiency viewpoint. A regime, which is efficient in the short term may be perceived as unfair either by some nations or some groups within powerful members of the regime, leading to the regime becoming moribund (Wiegent, 2001). Like other applications of Paretian welfare economics, effectiveness as efficiency ignores distributional issues; but these are an important dimension of regime effectiveness.

To monetise benefits economists typically discount future monetary flows of costs and benefit back to their present value, and this is implicit in defining effectiveness as efficiency. However, this gives rise to ethically problematic results. First there are considerable problems in deciding which discount rate to use (Arrow *et al*, 1996). Whichever is chosen, the optimal time-path for exploiting non-renewable resources under standard methods of discounting is generally to start relatively rapidly, gradually reducing the rate of exploitation, leaving nothing left in the very long term (Heal, 1998). To externalise costs and risks onto future generations who may be poorer than us, in such a way that we cannot compensate them for losses, seems unethical (e.g. Goodin, 1982). It conflicts with the "green golden rules" for sustainability that as much use-value should be available for future generations as we enjoy and that core biological processes should be protected (e.g. Daley, 1991). These rules are demanding as a practical basis for international negotiation. However, granted certain technical assumptions, if we both avoid giving no weight to the far future and allowing it dominate our decisions, the optimal plan is still to run down a non-renewable resource, but leaving some left even in the far-future (Chichilnisky, 1996; Heal, 1998). Also the combination of irreversibility and potential for learning suggests efficient plans will involve lower levels of environmental exploitation than standard discounting suggest, because this means we will be less constrained in the future when better information might indicate that upside-risks are high (Chichilnisky and Heal, 1993). Crude discounting of the future is a deeply and contentiously value-laden process, and so effectiveness as efficiency is far from being value-neutral.

In this section we have tried to clarify what effectiveness typically means from a rational choice perspective. We have set out a large number of problems both of a conceptual nature and with operationalising the concept. In the light of these, effectiveness as efficiency may seem profoundly unattractive and impractical. However it raises issues that cannot be ignored about the opportunity costs of cleaning up the global environment and what is ultimately obtainable in the current international system. We think that a resolution of the difficulties requires a distinction between "major" global issues that threaten the future of humanity as a whole and "secondary" issues. It is more crucial over major issues that natural capital is not traded away for current consumption, whereas over secondary issues this is less important, because what is being protected is not so vital to a satisfying life as a human-being grounded in a sustainable, diverse ecology. For major issues effectiveness needs to be linked conceptually with sustainability. A regime is effective to the extent that, within constraints set by the nature of the international system, it: 1) protects the integrity of vital environmental processes directly and indirectly related to variables the regime governs; 2) ensures that as much use-value is available for future generations as we enjoy from our current consumption of the aspect of the environment the regime governs. In addition to inter-generational equity, much of the discourse of sustainability is also linked to ideas of intra-generational justice. An effective regime should achieve a just distribution of current regime costs and benefits. This is important because, with major problems, these often *vitally* effect members of the current generation. Justice probably implies distributing costs and benefits to protect the most vulnerable, because of what is at stake for a satisfactory life. With secondary issues, we find something closer to the conventional economist's view quite appealing: an effective regime pushes the outcome as near as possible to the ideal Pareto frontier; but this frontier should be calculated on the basis of far lower discount rates than are conventional, for reasons of inter-generational equity and to preserve room for changing policy should things go worse than expected. Again we think that intra-generational equity is a consideration, but less so than over major issues, because what is at stake is less important to a satisfying life.

Of course this sketch raises all sorts of questions. Linking effectiveness to things as hard to conceptualise and to measure as sustainability or justice will not seem progress to some! Others will object to the anthropocentrism of our approach. In the remainder of this paper we discuss mechanisms that might limit the effectiveness of regimes conceived in terms of Pareto efficiency. Our aim is to raise issues about what rational choice can add to explanations of effectiveness conceived of in *this* way; but the implication of what we have said in this section is that this may not always be the real issue.

4. MECHANISMS CENTERING ON BARGAINING

Standard bargaining theory from economics provides only limited insight into regime effectiveness. However, from the game-theorist's point of view the methodological issue is whether more realistic models based on bounded rationality amount to anything more than sophisticated description. After raising this issue we discuss models of the domestic/international interface, partly because this enables us to consider questions about individual motivation and about human agency. The general theme of this section – bargaining over regime rules in search of better-all-round solutions than business-as-usual – has been central to neo-institutionalist work on regimes.

4.1 Inefficient Outcomes of Regime Bargaining

Bargaining takes place at various stages of regime development. It can be conceived as occurring over a set of modified rules together with a set of supergame strategies which are in equilibrium under those rules, leading to a self-enforcing agreement (Fearon, 1998). Then there are two forms of inefficiency. First the per-unit-time payoff of at least one party to the deal could be made higher with none being made worse off as a consequence. Second there may be delay in striking a deal that is efficient in the first sense, generating a period in which players' payoffs are lower than need be, with negotiation breakdown a special case.

In Figure 7.1 we drew the Pareto frontier generated by the "ideal regime" concave to the origin.[11] The payoff vector that results from each side choosing never to cooperate can be seen as defining players' payoffs in the event that there is a negotiation breakdown. Assume that each side knows each other's preferences and the two nations take turns to make offers. As soon as one side accepts the other's offer, bargaining terminates; but it can go on indefinitely if a deal is not struck. Of the approaches to bargaining applicable to this situation, by far the most well-known is that first axiomatised by Nash (1953) and given a game-theoretic rationale by Rubenstein (1982).[12] The prediction is that the outcome will maximise the product of the two sides' payoffs, measured as increments from the payoff they get if bargaining breaks down. This implies settlement will be on the Pareto frontier. Models like this have been applied in insightful ways to international environmental problems. For example Chen (1997) uses the Nash bargaining model to show that the climate-change regime will give a better deal to nations with relatively high payoffs along the business-as-usual path [13] and that more populous countries will do worse. [14] In most models of this sort players settle immediately, because under equilibrium strategies they will never get a better offer. [15] However, there may be ways to explain inefficient delay: 1) Compte and Jehiel (1997) assume that players can call in an arbitrator who will split the difference between the bids in the last round, giving an incentive to make "unrealistic" bids earlier on; 2) nations that do increasingly well in relative terms along a business-as-usual trajectory may delay settlement in order to exploit enhanced bargaining power in a war of attrition (Fearon 1998). However, as long as it is assumed that players have perfect information and unbounded rational capacity, it is difficult to explain why they would settle inside the Pareto-frontier, because this amounts to throwing away payoffs.

4.2 Bargaining with Incomplete Information and Bounded Rationality

Bargaining over regimes is often described as a process of trading concessions across different dimensions (e.g. Sebenius, 1983) or "lubricating" progress by making side-payments (e.g. Chen, 1997). Efficiency Limit Theorems for trading games with incomplete information suggest that negotiators are unable to exhaust the gains from trade when they have incomplete information about each other's preferences and there is some positive probability that there are no such gains (e.g. Fudenberg and Tirole 1991, 274-288). However, problems may go well beyond imperfect knowledge of others' preferences.

According to the theory of bounded rationality, actors make reasonably well-founded attempts to bring about desirable consequences in the situation in which they find themselves, but they may well not maximise their payoffs (Simon, 1985). A strong case can be made for applying this approach to collective action phenomena (Ostrom, 1997). A number of themes relating to bargaining under bounded rationality can be identified in the literature. Negotiators do not necessarily know which agreements are on the Pareto frontier. Much bargaining is *integrative*, seeking to discover deals that are better-all-round. *Distributive bargaining* along the Pareto frontier, where there is direct conflict of interest, is far less significant (Young, 1989b; cf. Sebenius, 1992). Strategic misrepresentation of information may be a considerable problem (Sebenius, 1992). Negotiators may ignore information that fails to fit an existing paradigm (Gross-Stein, 1988), so for example fruitful institutional innovations may be sidelined. There are cognitive constraints on negotiators' ability to process information, especially under pressure (Holsti, 1989), so negotiators may be satisficers seeking "good enough" solutions (Simon, 1985; Quattrone and Tversky, 1988). This can result in inefficient delays in settlement when they initially expect too much and even settlement within the Pareto frontier when aspirations are too low (Ward, 1979). Rather than maximising expected utility, individuals over-exaggerate some risks, under-exaggerate others and combine information about risks and benefits in ways that differ from those assumed by game theory (Kahneman, Slovic and Tversky, 1982; Farnham (ed.), 1994; Berejikian, 1997). Hence ineffective regimes may result from the failure of negotiators to take what are "objectively reasonable" gambles. Negotiators operating in groups embedded within bureaucracies may activate inappropriate standard-operating-procedures or be subject to group dynamics leading to irrational choices (Janis and Mann, 1977).

Regimes may come about as a result of tacit bargaining (Schelling, 1970) without formal negotiation e.g. rival national fishing fleets, sometimes helped by their navies, have often fought to a tacit *modus-vivendi*, unbacked by international law or formal institutions. As a norm is in operation, such coordination is still a regime, even if there are no rule changes. It is an example of what Hardin (1982, 155-72) calls a contract by convention. Studies of domestic politics suggest that highly unstructured regimes will generally be less effective (Ostrom, 1990; Ostrom Gardener and Walker, 1994). If regimes are understood in the way that we suggest, empirical studies of international regime effectiveness should include the widest possible spectrum, whereas existing small-n comparative studies are biased towards those with a formal structure arrived at after direct negotiation (e.g. Haas, Keohane and Levy (eds.), 1993; Young and Levy, 1999). The danger is of sampling on the dependent variable – specifically choosing regimes that are likely to be more effective – giving rise to biased estimates of causal effects (King, Keohane and Verba, 1995, 129).

No doubt bounded rationality will play an important role in accounting for ineffective regimes. We require a theory of outcomes under full rationality to tell how much they matter, of course. Moreover, issues arise about the nature of explanation. Game theorists and many IR theorists seek law-like generalisations, backed by a theory of their limits of applicability that also accounts for the observed pattern. Attracted to positivist philosophies of science and strongly influenced by what they take to be the methods of the natural sciences, their focus is on prediction, not understanding human action from the point of view of the agent. Some are unconcerned about whether theory is "realistic" if it makes accurate predictions (e.g. Friedman, 1953). Even though the way that actors make choices may not be well-described by standard rational choice models, they often make similar predictions to those based on bounded rationality and have the additional virtue of parsimony (Friedman, 1953). For instance negotiators may act "as if" they are fully rational or cease to play, where there is competition over who should occupy their role (cf. Cross, 1996). From this perspective the theory of bounded rationality is little more than sophisticated description. The component parts do not form a coherent theory allowing testable hypotheses to be framed about how far outcomes will depart from those of fully rational play or from efficiency.

Loosely formulated verbal models abound in the literature on international negotiation. They are unsatisfying because they lack the transparency of assumptions, rigorous derivation of conclusions, and clear statements of when conclusions apply that come when intuitions are formalised (Powell, 1999, 3-39). However, bounded rationality can be formalised using standard mathematical tools and modelling approaches from economics, leading to logically coherent models with testable implications (e.g. Rubinstein, 1998). This step needs to be taken in relation to regime bargaining, and it will require ruthlessly focusing on certain aspects of bounded rationality. Even then models will probably be complex compared to the standard models in the Nash tradition. This may not be a bad thing in itself, though.

In criticising game theory Walt (1999) says formal theories are useless if they are empirically false or based on questionable core assumptions. Things are not this simple. Models – including purely verbal and informal models – necessarily simplify reality. As they always include false assumptions, it must be possible to derive empirically false conclusions from them. However, this is not always an argument in favour of parsimonious, highly unrealistic models. All depends on "leverage"—roughly the ratio between what can satisfactorily be explained about the object of research at hand and model complexity (King, Keohane and Verba, 1994, 29-31). The challenge is to increase the leverage of our theories of regime bargaining, both over relatively parsimonious game-theoretic models in the Nash tradition and over loosely formulated verbal models in the bounded rationality tradition.

4.3 The Domestic/International Interface: Rent-Seeking in Two-Level Games

First-generation game theoretic models in international relations typically treated the state as a unitary rational actor, but this is not inherent in the approach. Drawing on Putnam's two-level game analysis (1988), and more formal development of the perspective (reviewed in Sprinz and Weiss, 2001), negotiators look for deals that will neither be subject to veto by other nations nor by important domestic constituencies. The implication of Olson's work on domestic collective action (1965) and Buchanan and others' work on rent-seeking (e.g. Buchanan, Tollison and Tullock (eds.), 1980) is that numerically small groups whose members have an intense interest in the outcome are more likely than large groups with a diffuse interest to overcome the collective action problem of organising to lobby government. This means that the overall pattern of domestic constraints on international negotiators is unlikely to lead to efficiency. For instance in the issue-area of trade the outcome will be biased in favour of socially inefficient forms of protectionism (Nelson, 1988; Hillman, 1989; Riezman and Wilson, 1995; Krugman, 1997), and protection can take the form of reducing production costs by avoiding environmental regulation. Similarly, because of their importance to the re-election chances of politicians, through their ability to control investment and jobs and to fund campaigns, the "carbon lobby" will have inordinate influence over the US position on global climate change (Newell and Paterson, 1998). Ineffective regimes may also be the consequence of organised interests interfering with the domestic implementation of international treaties, an important mechanism, which raises similar methodological issues to those discussed in this section. Things may be worse in authoritarian systems in which leaders focus on providing private goods to a small political elite in order to retain power, under-providing public goods such as environmental quality (Sandler, 1997; Bueno de Mesquita *et al*, 1999). As with any externality that is not properly costed, there is an economically inefficient level of activity.[16]

This mechanism seems to us to be of prime importance in accounting for many obviously ineffective regimes. The domestic-international interface has been relatively undertheorised in influential accounts of environmental regime effectiveness (e.g. Miles and Underdal *et al*, 2001). Although it relates to how "malign" the underlying collective action dilemma is, detailed modelling will be required to say exactly how and why. Having made one methodological point, we use the domestic international interface to illustrate a common objection to rational choice -- that it has the wrong model of human motivation and individual agency.

Attempts to apply collective action theory to the green movement suggest that the view deriving from Olson's work is over simplistic, because it cannot account for what activists do (e.g. Dalton, 1994; Jordan and Malone, 1997; Opp, 1999): 1) they over-estimate the chances that their contribution will help achieve success; 2) they are not motivated by material selective incentives, but are motivated by a range of non-material selective incentives, including expressive motivations surrounding their conception of their political identity; 3) leaders' use of resources is constrained not only by the political opportunity structure but also by their personal ideological beliefs about legitimate forms of action. A sceptic could argue that this does not matter much to the account of regime effectiveness under discussion, because the green movement demonstrably fails to mobilise the latent environmental sentiment expressed by large majorities of respondents, a fact for which Olsonian collective action theory provides a plausible explanation. But this is to ignore the role environmental NGOs may yet play in influencing mass public opinion in ways that unfreeze domestic constraints that prevent progress on issues like climate change.

While game theory can start from any model of motivation so long as it gives rise to well-defined preference orderings over endstates, some claim it risks becoming unfalsifiable once a range of non material motives, including altruistic motives, are allowed in (Green and Shapiro, 1994; cf. Friedman (ed.), 1996). No matter how apparently irrational behaviour is, some combination of non-material and material benefits can be cooked up *post-hoc* to "explain" it. Then the theory amounts to the vacuous tautology that people do what they prefer, as we know from the preferences revealed by their actions. This can be avoided by specifying in advance which motives count and how much. Then in the event of observed behaviour not fitting predictions, we should even-handedly consider dropping the rationality assumption rather than just modifying our assumptions about motives (Ward, 1996b). However, there remains the question of whether activists do things because they regard them as inherently right, not because they have consequences that increase their payoffs, however broadly construed. The methodological issue of whether human action is always consequentialist, as rational choice claims, resurfaces in the debate about bureaucratic politics within IR theory. Do individuals blindly play bureaucratic roles or bring their own interests and interpretations to bear, stretching the role within institutional constraints (Hollis and Smith, 1990)? The latter view is the more plausible, but it does suggest there is more to human action than efficient goal pursuit.

5. MECHANISMS CENTERING ON POWER

While neoliberal analysis usually points to the mutual gains from cooperation in mixed motive games (Keohane, 1984; Martin, 1992; Snidal, 1985,1986, 1991; Stein 1982, Oye 1986; Axelrod and Keohane 1985), for realists cooperation should not be observed except as a by-product of the struggle for power. Regimes reflect powerful actors' interests and have no independent influence. Realists argue that states must concern themselves with relative, as well as with absolute payoffs, because relative payoffs influence relative military capabilities. The implication is that there will be less cooperation than models based on the Prisoners' Dilemma supergame suggest (Grieco 1988a, 1988b, 1990, 1993). A key counter-argument highlights the flexibility of choice states have: relative losses are typically small compared to the size of any nation's economy; and so resulting security concerns are easily overcome by choosing slightly more "guns" and slightly less "butter" (Powell 1991, Powell 1993).[18] We assume here that security concerns do not predominate but that states do use their power to get regimes that suit their interests, as Krasner argues (1991). Whereas Krasner simply assumes an efficient regime, we discuss two ways in which inefficiency could arise.

5.1 The Power Structure and Ineffective Regimes

According to hegemonic stability theory (Kindleberger 1986; Snidal 1985; Gowa 1989, Lake 1993), regimes are public goods "supplied" by the hegemon, with "small" states exploiting the hegemon because it has a "large" interest in the outcome. Although provision will be sub-optimal, the efficiency gap will be smaller to the extent that the power distribution is unipolar and the hegemon has an incentive to act. This account of leadership has strongly influenced comparative studies of environmental regime formation (e.g. Miles and Underdal *st al*, 2001), but things may not be this simple.

A decisive coalition is one with the power to impose any regime to which all its members assent. Building decisive coalitions is at the heart of regime bargaining in the numerous contexts in which no single nation predominates. For instance it is of the essence when regimes are built within the overall architecture of EU environmental policy, where winning coalitions must include not only member states but, increasingly, majorities in the EU Parliament and among the EU Commissioners (Weale *et al*, 2000, 123-32). Ineffective regimes result when decisive coalitions cannot be built to bring about functional changes in rules. Explaining ineffectiveness often requires looking at the interaction between the power distribution and the preference distribution, considering all players, not just at the most powerful actor.

When decisive coalitions set new rules for collective action games yielding more favourable equilibria for their members, those outside the coalition may suffer (Sened, 1997). If utility was fully transferable and information complete, there would never be an incentive for a decisive coalition to design and impose rules that prevented an *efficient* result, although the outcome could be highly inequitable. Through making transfer payments, the benefits of moving to the Pareto frontier could be split in such a way that all gain. However, without transferability, it may pay members of a decisive coalition to impose rules which, while ineffective, yield them higher benefits (North, 1990). Transferability of gains can sometimes be brought about through issue-linkage (Sebenius, 1983). Leadership certainly is important to fostering such deals (Martin, 1992b). [19] But they can also be blocked by the combination of power and interests. This is significant in relation to climate change where it is difficult to share the North's gains from a tighter regime with the South, given the US is prone to block linked concessions on trade and development and the EU is sceptical about emissions trading and other flexibility measures.

In regime bargaining it is generally the case that a number of veto players exist that can block any proposed regime they dislike compared to the status-quo. Depending on context, vetoes may be states, powerful transnational industries, or even powerful domestic institutions that can veto treaties negotiated by their administration. Leaders frequently compete in making sidepayments to vetoes, either to get them to accept change or to block it. The leader wanting the least progress has a considerable advantage, even if it superficially appears to have much lower capabilities to make side payments (Ward, Grundig and Zorick, 2001). It can block proposals more progressive than it wants merely by inducing one veto to exert itself in suitable ways. Far smaller amounts of resources are typically required to do this than to persuade *all* vetoes to accept a more progressive proposal. This leads to a considerable status-quo bias in regime bargaining when leadership competition exists. Patterns are much more complex than those expected when a single leader distributes side-payments.

In the light of the complexities we have sketched it is hardly surprising that the degree of concentration of capability is only weakly related to regime effectiveness (Underdal, 2001b). Our methodological point is that the relationship between the distribution of capabilities and regime effectiveness is complex, with the initial distribution of preferences, the degree of transferability of gains, and the degree of leadership competition intervening.

5.2 Commitment Tactics, Reputational Effects, and Inefficiency

As we have seen in repeated collective action games there are typically multiple equilibria over which players interests diverge. Ward (1996a) argues that this generates incentives to pre-commit to doing little or nothing, so as to bring about a regime-equilibrium favouring your interests. An ineffective regime may arise because several nations pre-commit in ways that are effectively irreversible, triggering retaliation by others and possibly regime breakdown, a situation analogous to the collision outcome in a Chicken game (Ward, 1996a; Schelling, 1970). A nation may refuse to make concessions on particular issues for fear that it will lose its reputation for toughness in future negotiations over other issues.[20] States that bluff about how tough they will be in bargaining may be forced out of regimes by reputational considerations when others use strategies which periodically call possible bluffs (Schneider and Cederman 1994; cf. Alt *et al*, 1988). This, too, could reduce regime effectiveness.

Different regimes cannot be treated as independent cases if they are tightly interconnected by considerations of reputation, or by issue-interlinkage. Specifically the unit-homogeneity assumption necessary for satisfactory causal inference (King, Keohane, and Verba, 1994, 91-4) is likely to be violated. The impact of independent variables on regime effectiveness will differ across cases when, for example, a major actor decides that having backed down on one issue, it has to play tough on another to maintain reputation. Explicit statistical modelling of effects like this is possible in data with a time dimension, but cross-sectional estimates of effects will be biased. Small-n comparative methods of the sort that are generally preferred in regime theory suffer from exactly the same potential problems. Any solution will be dependent on a theory of reputation.

6. MECHANISMS CENTERING ON INFORMATION AND DISCOURSE

So far the models we draw on have nothing to say about where issues or preferences derive from, a problem with game theory that many critics coming from knowledge-based perspectives on regimes identify (e.g. Adler and Haas, 1992; Hasenclever, Mayer and Rittberger, 1997, 136-210). We tackle the issues head-on by exploring what game theory says about transfer of information, the central theme of the epistemic communities literature (e.g. Haas 1990a; Haas,1992). For those who think that discourses constitute the very nature of the international system, "anarchy is what states make of it" (Wendt, 1992) and the problems regimes deal with are "social constructs" (Hisschemoller and Gupta, 1999). Short-shrift is given to game theory. In contrast we illustrate the way in which game theory can add to our understanding of how normative discourses contend in regime bargaining.

6.1 Inefficient Information Transfer and Regime Effectiveness

True game theory assumes actors have fixed *underlying* preferences. They prefer greater wealth, a cleaner environment, being re-elected, etc. Without some such postulate there is no foundation on which to build a model. But the central developments in game theory over the last thirty years concern games of incomplete information in which actors' *second-order* preferences about how to achieve those goals and in what proportion may shift during the course of the game (e.g. Morrow, 1994a, 219-57). In games where information is asymmetrically distributed, some players have information that others do not. Moves where explicit attempts to convey information are made occur in some models, but information transfer may also be tacit, by inference from behaviour. As the game progresses, as a result of inferences drawn from observing others' moves and comparing them with prior beliefs, actors may come to know more about the trade-offs between their underlying goals, the uncertainties they face, and what their best strategies are. A variety of refinements to the basic notion of Nash equilibrium have been suggested, but generally at each stage actors' strategies must remain best responses in the light of what they have come to believe, and current beliefs must be rationally updated from prior beliefs.

Largely on the basis of induction from a relatively small set of cases the epistemic communities literature claims that scientists' influence will be greatest when: the problem is complex and uncertainty is high; there is a perception of crisis and politicians are looking for new solutions, not advisors who will legitimate old solutions; the internal consensus in the community is great and its members are highly regarded within their professions; and members of the community come to occupy important bureaucratic roles within states, particularly states with considerable influence (Haas, 1990b, 352-53; Haas, 1992; Adler and Haas, 1992, 379-81). No theoretical account is given of the limits of application of these generalisations (Sebenius, 1992) and they look far from credible in some contexts, including climate change (cf. Haas, 1990b, 358-60). Empirical studies suggest that a significant minority of regimes exist where the regime has failed to serve as an arena for learning (Underdal 2001b). What might the theory of games of incomplete information add?

First when "talk is cheap", in that there are no sanctions on people caught lying, it is difficult to convey information – even the truth – when others put a high probability on your interests varying from their own (Austen-Smith 1990, 1992; Morrow, 1994b). In brief, they see risks in believing you, because you have incentives to lie. A government deciding whether to listen to an epistemic community faces a trade-off: the pooling of information among experts "averages out" random judgmental errors. However, experts have their own interests. The consensus within the community depends on the positions of scientists from another nation whose preferences you are in a much poorer position to judge and who are more likely than "home-grown" experts to have interests at variance to your own. From a game-theoretic perspective, information is especially likely to be ignored when there are questions about the motives of its providers, distributional issues loom large *and* it is costly to make mistakes on the basis of false information. The observation that expensive advice will be more likely to be ignored is commonplace in the epistemic community literature (e.g. Adler and Haas, 1992, 383), but the interaction between conflict of interest, message credibility, and the costs of action goes unrecognised.

Second, where there are credible independent sources of information against which claims can be checked, information from others is more likely to be influential, even if they are believed to have conflicting interests ((Krehbiel, 1991, 61-103; Lupia and McCubbins, 1998). Even if cross-checking is not always carried out, the threat may be enough to deter, where reputations matter. From this perspective there are dangers in the degree of the monopoly over the validation of knowledge claims and closure of debate against counter-arguments exhibited as some epistemic communities drive towards consensus. The relationship between consensus and knowledge transmission may be non-monotonic. Although dissensus does allow politicians to make convenient choices of experts to legitimate pre-existing positions (e.g. Haas, 1992, 11), it facilitates cross checking.

Whereas the epistemic community literature relies on the assumption that nations' interests are often ill-defined, leaving room for scientists to insert their viewpoints, we believe that politicians' prior beliefs and existing second-order preferences condition when advice will be heeded. This point is essential to any plausible theory of the failure to transmit information in regimes, because the minds of those seeking advice are not *tabula rasa*. Whatever the plausibility of the mechanism we sketch it is enough to convey our main methodological points: 1) it is a misunderstanding to argue that game theory assumes fixed preferences and cannot deal with learning; 2) the regimes literature lacks an adequate theory of information transmission and games of incomplete information may be of help. [21]

6.2   Ineffective Regimes and the Contention of Discourses

Supergames characteristically have many equilibria, as we have shown. [22] All may stand to lose unless there is coordination of behaviour on an equilibrium exhibiting some degree of conditional cooperation. Above we suggested that coordination could arise through bargaining. This is not the only plausible possibility, for there is an alternative cognitivist account of coordination (Hardin, 1982, 164). Some equilibria may be focal points -- arrangements that are "prominent" solutions, with the ability to create a common conjecture (Schelling, 1970). A number of authors have pointed to the importance of focal points to environmental regime bargaining, and some have argued that, because interests are often ill-defined, they may be crucial determinants of outcomes (e.g. Young, 1989b). The most plausible ideas about focal points for regime theory do not come from "within" game-theory. [23] Indeed normative considerations often focus attention in regime bargaining (Barrett, 1992).

Game theory can help in conceptual analysis of issues around justice and equity. However, with respect to concrete problems like regime bargaining it is more useful to see these ideas as deriving from discourses – structured ways of viewing the world, embedded in language, that allow information to be put together into more or less coherent packages. For example there are numerous discourses about environmental problems and each gives rise to distinctive views about key terms of debate such as sustainability, justice between nations, and justice across generations (e.g. Dobson, 1998). Negotiations are in part a search for common standards of justice (Zartman, Druckman, Jensen, Pruitt, and Young, 1996). Discourses are lenses through which the world is viewed and partly constitute what players see as in their interests (Stokke, 1998); but players also use discourses as tools to get what they want.

Where environmental regimes are being constructed discourses "contend", because the game is not one of pure coordination where all equilibria have the same payoffs. For example, radically different accounts are given of what a fair distribution of the cost burden would be in relation to global climate change including: 1) arrangements where those standing to gain most make the biggest sacrifices; 2) mathematically symmetrical arrangements like equal cuts all round or equal per-capita emissions; 3) arrangements where those historically responsible bear higher costs; 4) "grandfathering", where rights to pollute are assigned in direct proportion to national levels of activity historically (e.g. Paterson, 2001; Weigent, 2001).[24] Each conception relates to some notion of justice or equity and is losely associated with a certain set of possible regime outcomes. Nations actively attempt to steer attention towards one or more of these conceptions. They are not just mediums through which discourses "speak", though (cf. Hollis and Smith, 1990). Rather discourses are one set of background factors conditioning the rules of the game, in the sense that they give nations "rhetorical moves". By using "rhetorical moves" nations push conceptions that they think will give rise to regimes serving their interests – as currently conceived given the discourses that shape their view of the international power structure and their underlying interests (cf Paterson, 1992; Young, 1994, 48-50). This does not mean that they have complete room for manoeuvre, because existing discourses put limits on what can be construed as just and there are costs to obviously cynical appeals to principle. In short, discourses both constrain and enable states' actions (cf. Stokke, 1998).

As regards regime effectiveness, this implies as subtle modification to the view that the international power structure can give rise to ineffective regimes, discussed above. In short, there is an ideological dimension to the notion of dominant coalitions: 1) part of the reason why such coalitions are dominant is that the play of discourse at the international level makes for others accepting the deals they strike (Cox, 1983; Stokke, 1998, 139-40); 2) and ineffective regimes arise when dominant coalitions view the world in ways that turn out to be counterproductive. As regards methodology, our discussion illustrates the point that rational choice theory cannot bootstrap its way to a complete explanation of the social. It is inherently limited in its ability to explain the rules of the game. Nevertheless it can play a major role in explaining how rules evolve from *existing* rules, as part of a structuration approach (Ward, 1995).

7. CONCLUSION

No doubt it is broadly right to explain regime effectiveness in terms of how "malign" the underlying game is and how much capacity exists to solve the problem (e.g. Underdal, 1992; Miles and Underdal *et al*, 2001). However, in this paper we draw attention to problems with conceptualising effectiveness in terms of the degree to which the environment is cleaned up. Although we are critical of using Pareto efficiency as a way of conceptualising and measuring effectiveness, we think that effective responses do balance environmental benefits against opportunity costs, though things ought to come out differently on major than they do on minor issues. We draw attention to some of the complexities in the relationship between institutional capacity and effectiveness, particularly in relation to the international and domestic power distributions and information transmission. We argue that testing hypotheses about regime effectiveness is far from straightforward because the cases are often not independent, and that methodological problems require further modelling of issues like reputation.

Rational choice has methodological and empirical problems that we have tried to expose in an open and honest manner. We doubt whether they are qualitatively worse than other approaches, but this was not the place to make the comparison. We agree that bounded rationality is a problem, but we see considerable advantages in going beyond loose formulations to formal modelling. Certainly rational choice can gain from other approaches, as we have illustrated in relation to what might be regarded as the most difficult potential case – discourse theory (cf. Stokke, 1998). However, writing this paper shortly after the collapse of the negotiations at the Hague where the climate change regime foundered on the rock of embedded national interest and domestic politics in the US, we would warn against neglecting rational choice in favour of the idealist view that we can always talk our way out of social traps if only we attend to good advice, build institutional capacity and re-think interstate relationships.

NOTES

[1] Actually complex packages of public, semi-public and private benefits are typically supplied when nations contribute towards the resolution of a regional or global environmental problem (e.g. Sandler, 1997). Common-pool problems where non-renewable and renewable resources are potentially divisible but it is impossible to exclude anyone from the pool, are often distinguished from relatively pure public good problems. Institutional arrangments to deal with common pool problems, such as the definition of property rights,

FORMAL THEORY & REGIME EFFECTIVENESS

are public goods in themselves, as are institutional arrangements to provide pure public goods. In the remainder of this chapter we will talk in terms of public goods.

[2] The contingencies are called information sets. These can be thought of as situations that could arise in the game which are distinguishable from each other by a player, given the information it has at that point in time. The idea is that players may not have the information to distinguish between what are, in fact, distinct situations.

[3] This happens to be a Prisoners' Dilemma but the argument generalizes to most other mixed motive games commonly used to characterize collective action, including games with different levels of cooperation (Ward, 1996a). Zürn (1992) argues that how difficult the underlying game is to deal with using an institutional solution depends on whether it is a Prisoners' Dilemma, Assurance, Coordination Game, Chicken game etc. Certainly Assurance and games of *pure* coordination are easier, but in supergame form the others generate qualitatively similar sets of dilemmas and it is not obvious, with equal weight on the future, one is easier to solve than another (Ward, 1996a).

[4] Tit-for-tat does not embody a credible threat, since activating the threat leads to a pattern of play worse for those using it than ignoring a defection. However, subgame-perfect equilibria where threats are credible can be found. Barrett (1999) has argued that in relation to climate change we should further restrict attention to "renegotiation proof" equilibria in which, if some player deviates from the cooperative equilibrium path, players should have no incentive to renegotiate towards an alternative equilibrium avoiding the inefficiencies of the punishment phase.

[5] For this to be possible players must be able to adopt mixed strategies dependent on a random device which both can observe, allowing for correlation between randomizations carried out by players.

[6] Taylor (1987) shows that in infinitely repeated Prisoners Dilemmas with more than two players there are often asymmetric equilibria in which some group of player conditionally cooperate while others always defect—a possible model for regimes that fail to bring in all relevant nations.

[7] Cf. Krasner (1982),Young (1989, 12 – 13), List and Rittberger (1991, 89 – 90). The key definitional issue is whether institutions are "just" rules of the game. From the perspective of neo-institutionalist critics of rational choice (e.g. March and Olson, 1989), human action is made *meaningful* to individuals only by some logic of appropriateness and interpretability that is built into social and discursive structures, an argument with significant implications for IR theory (Hollis and Smith, 1990, 143 – 71).

[8] Whether a pattern is an equilibrium depends on the weighting of the future of course.

[9] Sprinz and Helm (1999) suggest that environmental damages should be discounted by nation-specific political weightings when measuring effectiveness, but there is still an assumption that *weighted* dollar damages can be compared and summed.

[10] E.g. while construing effectiveness as compliance with the letter of treaty obligations is problematic because the rules of the regime may be very weak or even dysfunctional (Downs, Rocke, and Barsoom, 1995), to understand effectiveness in terms of impact on the targeted problem (Young and Levy, 1999, 9) raises more difficult measurement issues than the lawyers' emphasis on compliance.

[11] So the set of possible payoffs is convex and bounded.

[12] Even if players cannot sign binding contracts, as Nash originally assumed, the Nash solution is the limit as the period between offers goes to zero of the equilibrium of the bargaining game where both players have equal discount rates (Rubinstein, 1982). A generalised version of the Nash solution applies when discount rates are not equal, with more patient bargainers doing better (Binmore and Dasgupta, 1987).

[13] Because they can walk away from the table and still do reasonably well.

[14] Because it is less costly to "bribe" a less populous country into agreement through making transfer payments, so such a country can take a *tougher* bargaining stand.

[15] The game is stationary i.e. its strategic structure is the same looking ahead from any point in time when it is one side's turn to make an offer. Given this, it is intuitively obvious and can be rigorously proven, that in equilibrium players make the same offer each time it is their turn. Delayed settlement can occur when disagreement payoffs are not fixed but result from strategic choices, although there typically are other fully-efficient equilibria (Busch and Wen, 1995; Muthoo 1999, 158 – 70).

[16] According to the Coase Theorem (Coase 1960) as long as property rights are well-defined, bargaining between polluters and those who suffer will generate efficient outcomes no matter who has the property rights. However this argument relies on zero transaction costs, which are rarely approximated in practice (e.g. North, 1990).

[17] Snidal (1991) shows that Grieco's argument is a special case with significant application only to superpower interaction in a bipolar system (Snidal 1991). Grundig (2000) counters that Snidal makes assumptions about third parties from the benefits of bilateral cooperation that do not apply to global environmental issues, among others.

[18] The literature on legislative logrolls to protect the interests of geographically localized industries (e.g. Marshall and Weingast 1988, Shepsle and Weingast 1994) should remind us that trades can also harm third parties, resulting in social inefficiencies, as well as spreading benefits.

[19] As there are short-term costs to maintaining such a reputation, in any finite series of interactions in which players' information about each other is complete, it is irrational to maintain it: in the last interaction, there are no future loses from backing down; given that you will back down in the last interaction, the future is foreclosed, so you may as well back down in the penultimate interaction; and so on. However, Kreps and Wilson (1982) show that if others are uncertain about your preferences, such that you may play tough regardless of apparent short-term incentives, it may pay to maintain a tough reputation until near the end of the sequence.

[20] We concede that this approach has significant methodological problems. Some argue that the Bayesian updating of prior beliefs assumed is empirically implausible in IR (e.g. Walt, 1999). Beliefs about events that occur off the equilibrium path of the game (i.e. events that are unexpected if players stick to the equilibrium) are important because they condition whether it is worth playing in the way the equilibrium requires. However different authors rely on different restrictions to rule out "irrational" beliefs, none of which seems to be justified in terms of some fundamental conception of epistemic rationality (Bicchieri, 1993, 103 – 11). These games use a technical trick to convert them into ones in which the rules are common-knowledge. This involves a notional probabilistic move by nature that chooses some players' types e.g. whether their interests conflict. In games of asymmetric information some players observe what "nature does" and others do not. The problem is that the game remains unsolvable unless the probability with which nature chooses is common knowledge. This common-priors assumption is plausible where relative frequencies of types can be calculated from a large class of similar interactions, but often this does not hold in IR (Sebenius, 1992, 349 – 50).

[21] The same is true for "cheap talk" games where, alongside equilibria where information is transmitted there are typically "babbling equilibrium" in which neither side conditions its move on what others have previously said, so players can say anything in equilibrium.

[22] The most common suggestion is that Pareto-efficient equilibria are particularly plausible focal equilibria. But as we have already said in supergames many arrangements are likely to be Pareto-efficient, so this does not help much (cf. Taylor, 1987).

[23] Arrangements similar to those thought to have worked for analogous problems in the past are often focal points and this often generates forms of path-dependence that lead to inefficient economic institutions (North, 1990).

REFERENCES

Adler, E. and Haas, P.M. (1992) Conclusion: Epistemic Communities, World Order, and the Creation of a Reflective Research Programme, *International Organisation* 46, 1: 367–90.

Alt, J. E. et al (1988) Reputation and Hegemonic Stability: A Game-Theoretic Analysis, *American Political Science Review* 82, 2: 445–66.

Arrow, K. J., Cline, W.R., Mäler, K. G., Munasinghe, M., Squitieri, R. and Stiglitz, J.E. (1996) Intertemporal Equity, Discounting, and Economic Efficiency, in J. P. Bruce, H. Lee and E. F. Haites (eds.) *Climate Change 1995: Economic and Social Dimensions of Climate Change*, Cambridge University Press.

Austen-Smith, D. (1990) Information Transmission in Debate, *American Journal of Political Science* 34, 1:124–52.

Austen-Smith, D. (1992) Strategic Models of Talk in Political Decision Making, *International Political Science Review* 13, 1: 45–58.

Axelrod, R. (1984) *The Evolution of Cooperation*, Basic Books, New York.

Axelrod, R. and Keohane, R. O. (1985) Achieving Cooperation Under Anarchy: Strategies and Institutions, *World Politics* 38, 2: 226–54.

Barret, S. (1992) "Acceptable" Allocation of Tradable Carbon Emission Entitlements in a Global Warming Treaty, in *Tradeable Endowments for Carbon Emission Abatement*, Geneva: UNCTAD.

Barret, S. (1999) A Theory of Full International Co-operation, *Journal of Theoretical Politics* 11, 4: 519–41.

Berejekian, J. (1997) The Gains Debate: Framing State Choice, *American Political Science Review* 91, 4: 789–805.

Bicchieri, C. (1993) *Rationality and Coordination*, Cambridge University Press.

Binmore, K. and Dasgupta, P. (1987) *The Economics of Bargaining*, Blackwell, Oxford.

Buchanan, J. M., Tollison, R. D. and Tullock, G. (eds.) (1980) *Towards a Theory of the Rent Seeking Society*, A and M Press, Texas.

Bueno de Mesquita, B. et al (1999) Policy Failure and Political survival – The Contribution of Political Institutions, *Journal of Conflict Resolution* 43, 2: 147–161.

Bunge, M. A. (1997) Mechanism and Explanation, *Philosophy of the Social Sciences* 27, 4: 410–65.

Chen, Z. (1997) Negotiating an Agreement on Global Warming: A Theoretical Analysis, *Journal of Environmental Economics and Management* 32, 1: 170–188.

Chichilnisky, G. (1996) An Axiomatic Approach to Sustainable Development, *Social Choice and Development* 13, 2: 231–57.

Chichilnisky, G. and Heal, G. (1993) Global Environmental Risks, *Journal of Economic Perspectives* 7, 4: 65–86.

Coase, R. (1960) The Problem of Social Cost, *Journal of Law and Economics* 3, 1: 1–44.

Compte, O. and Jehiel, P. (1997) International Negotiations and Dispute Resolution Mechanisms: The Case of Environmental Negotiations, in Carraro, C. (ed.) *International Environmental Negotiations: Strategic Policy Issues,* Edward Elgar, Cheltenham, 56–71.

Cox, R. W. (1983) Gramsci, Hegemony and International Relations: An Essay in Method, *Millenium* 12, 2: 162–75.

Cross, J. G. (1996) Negotiation as Adaptive Learning, *International Negotiation* 1, 1: 153–78.

Daley, H. E. (1991) *Steady State Economics: Second Edition With New Essays,* Earth Island, Washington DC.

Dalton, R. J. (1994) *The Green Rainbow: Environmental Groups in Western Europe,* Yale University Press, New Haven, CT.

Dobson, A. (1998) *Justice and the Environment: Conceptions of Environmental Sustainability and Dimensions of Social Justice,* Oxford University Press.

Downs, G. W., Rocke, D. M. and Barsoom, P. N. (1995) Is Good News About Compliance Good News About Cooperation? *International Organization* 50, 3: 379–408.

Farnham, B. (ed.) (1994) *Avoiding Losses/Taking Risks: Prospect Theory and International Conflict,* University of Michigan Press, Ann Arbor.

Fearon, J. D. (1998) Bargaining, Enforcement and International Co–operation, *International Organization* 52, 2: 269–305.

Foster, J. (ed.) (1996) *Valuing Nature?: Ethics Economics and the Environment,* Routledge, London.

Friedman, J. (ed.) (1996) *The Rational Choice Controversy,* Yale University Press, New Haven, CT.

Friedman, M. (1953) The Methodology of Positive Economics, in his *The Methodology of Positive Economics,* University of Chicago Press, Chicago.

Fudenberg, D. and Tirole, J. (1991) *Game Theory,* MIT Press, Cambridge, MA.

Goodin, R. E. (1982) Discounting Discounting, *Journal of Public Policy* 2, 1: 53–72.

Gowa, J. (1989) Rational Hegemons, Excludable Goods, and Small Groups: An Epitaph for Hegemonic Stability Theory? *World Politics* 41: 307–324.

Green, D. P. and Shapiro, I. (1994) *Pathologies of Rational Choice Theory: A Critique of Applications in Political Science,* Yale University Press, New Haven, CT.

Grieco, J. (1993) Understanding the Problem of International Cooperation: The Limits of Neoliberal Institutionalism and the Future of Realist Theory, in D. A. Baldwin (ed.) *Neorealism and Neoliberalism,* Columbia University Press, New York, 301–338.

Grieco, J. (1988a) Anarchy and the Limits of Cooperation, *International Organisation* 42: 485–507.

Grieco, J. (1988b) Realist Theory and the Problem of International Cooperation, *Journal of Politics* 50: 600–624.

Gross-Stein, J. (1988) International Negotiation a Multi-Disciplinary Perspective, *Negotiation Journal,* July, 221–31.

Grundig, F. (2002) Relative Gains and International Climate Negotiations, *Essex Papers in Politics and Government,* forthcoming.

Grundig, F., Ward, H. and Zorick, E. (2000) Marching at the Pace of the Slowest: A Model of International Negotiations over Global Climate Change, *Essex Papers in Politics and Government,* 142.

Grundig, F., Ward, H. and Zorick, E. (2001) Formal Approaches to Global Climate Change, in Sprinz, D. F. and Luterbcher, U. (eds.) *International Relations and Global Climate Change,* MIT Press, Cambridge, MA.

Haas, P. M. (1990a) *Saving the Mediterranean: The Politics of International Environmental Cooperation,* Columbia University Press, New York.

Haas, P. M. (1992) Introduction: Epistemic Communities and International Policy Coordination, *International Organisation* 46, 1: 1–35.

Haas, P. M. (1990b) Obtaining International Environmental Protection through Epistemic Consensus, *Millenium* 19, 3: 347–63.

Hardin, R. (1982) *Collective Action,* Johns Hopkins University Press, Baltimore.

Hasenclever, A., Mayer, P. and Rittberger, V. (1997) *Theories of International Regimes,* Cambridge University Press.

Heal, G. M. (1998) Interpreting Sustainability, in G. Chichilnisky, G. M. Heal and A. Vercelli (eds.) *Sustainability: Dynamics and Uncertainty,* Kluwer, Amsterdam.

Helm, C. and Sprinz, D. F. (1999) Measuring the Effectiveness of International Environmental Regimes, Potsdam Institute for Climate Impact Research, working paper 52.

Hisschemoller, M. and Gupta, J. (1999) Problem Solving Through International Environmental Agreements: The Issue of Regime Effectiveness, *International Political Science Review* 20, 2: 151–74.

Hollis, M. and Smith, S. (1990) *Explaining and Understanding International Relations,* Oxford University Press.

Holsti, Ole (1989) Crisis Decision Making, in P. E. Tetlock (ed.) *Behaviour, Society and Nuclear War Vol.1,* Oxford University Press.

Hovi, J. (1999) Causal Mechanisms and the Study of International Regimes, paper presented at workshop on "The Study of Regime Consequences: Methodological Challenges and Research Strategies", November, Oslo, 19–20

Janis, I. L. and Mann, L. (1977) *Decision Making: A Psychological Analysis of Conflict, Choice and Commitment,* Free Press, New York.

Jordan, A. G. and Maloney, W. A. (1997) *The Protest Business: Mobilising Campaign Groups,* Manchester University Press.

Kahneman, D., Slovic, P. and Tversky, A. (1982) *Judgement Under Uncertainty: Heuristics and Biases,* Cambridge University Press.

Keohane, R. O. (1984) *After Hegemony,* Princeton University Press.

King, G., Keohane, R. O. and Verba, S. (1995) *Designing Social Enquiry: Scientific Inference in Qualitative Research,* Princeton University Press.

Krehbiel, K. (1992) *Information and Legislative Organization,* University of Michigan Press, Ann Arbor.

Kreps, D. and Wilson, R. (1982) Reputation and Imperfect Information, *Journal of Economic Theory* 27, 2: 253–279.

Knight, J. (1998) Models, Interpretations, and Theories: Constructing Explanations of Institutional Emergence and Change, in J. Knight and I. Sened (eds.) *Explaining Social Institutions,* University of Michigan Press, Ann Arbor.

Krasner, S. D. (1982) Structural Causes and Regime Consequences: Regimes as an Intervening Variable, *International Organisation* 36, 2: 185–205.

Krasner, S. D. (1991) Global Communications and National Power: Life on the Pareto Frontier, *World Politics* 43, 3: 336–66.

Lake, D. (1993) Leadership, Hegemony and the International Economy – Naked Emperor or Tattered Monarch with Potential, *International Studies Quarterly* 37, 4: 459–89.

Levy, M. A., Keohane, R. O. and Haas, P. M. (1993) Improving the Effectiveness of International Environmental Institutions, in P. M. Haas, R. Keohane and M. A. Levy (eds.) *Institutions for the Earth: Sources of Effective International Environmental Protection,* MIT Press, Cambridge, MA, 397–426.

List, M. and Rittberger, V. (1991) Regime Theory and International Environmental Management, in A. Hurrell and B.Kingsbury, *The International Politics of the Environment*, Oxford University Press, 85–109.

Lohmann, S. (1997) Linkage Politics, *Journal of Conflict Resolution* 41, 1: 38–67.

Lupia, A. and McCubbins, M. D. (1998) *The Democratic Dilemma: Can Citizens Learn What They Need to Know?* Cambridge University Press.

March, J. G. and Olsen, J. P. (1989) *Rediscovering Institutions: The Organisational Basis of Politics*, Free Press, New York.

Marshall, W. and Weingast, B. (1988) The Industrial Organization of Congress, *Journal of Political Economy* 96, 1: 132–63.

Martin, L. (1992a) *Coercive Cooperation*, Princeton University Press.

Martin, L. (1992b) Institutions and Cooperation, *International Security* 16, 4: 25–50.

Miles, E. L, Underdal, A., Andresen, S., Wettestad, J., Skjaerseth, J. B., Carlin, E. M. (2001) *Environmental Regime Effectiveness: Confronting Theory With Evidence*, MIT Press, Cambridge, MA.

Morrow, J. D. (1994a) *Game Theory for Political Scientists*, Princeton University Press.

Morrow, J. D. (1994b) Modelling the Forms of International Cooperation: Distribution Versus Information, *International Organization* 48, 3: 387–423.

Muthoo, A. (1999) *Bargaining Theory with Application*, Cambridge University Press.

Nash, J. F. (1953) The Bargaining Problem, *Econometrica* 21, 2: 128–40.

Newell, P. and Paterson, M. (1998) A Climate for Business: Global Warming, the State and Capital, *Review of International Political Economy* 5, 4:679–703.

North, D. (1990) *Institutions, Institutional Change and Economic Performance*, Cambridge University Press.

Olson, M. (1965) *The Logic of Collective Action: Public Goods and the Theory of Groups*, Harvard University Press, Cambridge, MA.

Ostrom, E. (1990) *Governing the Commons: The Evolution of Institutions for Collective Action*, Cambridge University Press.

Ostrom, E. (1997) A Behavioural Approach to the Rational Choice Theory of Collective Action, *American Political Science Review* 92, 1: 1–22.

Ostrom, E., Gardner, R., and Walker, J. (1994) *Rules Games and Common – Pool Resources*, Michigan University Press, Ann Arbor.

Oye, K. (1986) Explaining Cooperation Under Anarchy: Hypotheses and Strategies, in K. Oye (ed.) *Cooperation under Anarchy*, Princeton University Press, 1–24.

Opp, K. (1999) Contending Conceptions of the Theory of Rational Action, *Journal of Theoretical Politics* 11, 2: 171–202.

Paterson, M. (1992) Global Warming: The Great Equaliser? *Journal für Entwicklungspolitik* 8, 3: 217–228.

Paterson, M. (2001) Principles of Justice in the Context of Global Climate Change, in D. F. Sprinz and U. Luterbacher (ed.) *International Relations and Global Climate Change*, MIT Press, Cambridge, MA.

Powell, R. (1991) Absolute and Relative Gains in International Relations Theory, *American Political Science Review* 85, 4: 1303–1320.

Powell, R. (1993) Guns, Butter and Anarchy, *American Political Science Review* 87, 1: 115–132.

Powell, R. (1999) *In the Shadow of Power: States and Strategies in International Politics*, Princeton University Press.

Putnam, R. (1988) Diplomacy and Domestic Politics: The Logic of Two Level Games, *International Organisation* 42, 3: 427–60.

Quattrone, G. A. and Tversky, A. (1988) Contrasting Rational and Psychological Analyses of Political Choice, *American Political Science Review* 82, 4: 719–736.

Riezman, R. and Wilson, J. D. (1995) Politics and Trade Policy, in J. S. Banks and E. A. Hanushek (eds.) *Modern Political Economy*, Cambridge University Press.

Rubinstein, A. (1982) Perfect Equilibrium in a Bargaining Model, *Econometrica* 50, 2: 97–109.

Rubinstein, A. (1998) *Modelling Bounded Rationality*, MIT Press, Cambridge, MA.

Sagoff, M.(1988) *The Economy of the Earth*, Cambridge University Press.

Sandler, T. (1997) *Global Challenges: An Approach to Environmental, Political, and Economic Problems*, Cambridge University Press.

Schelling, T. C. (1970) *Strategy of Conflict*, Oxford University Press.

Schneider, G. and Cederman, L. (1994) The Change of Tide in Political Cooperation: A Limited Information Model of European Integration, *International Organisation* 48, 4: 633–62.

Sebenius, J. K. (1983) Negotiation Arithmetic: Adding and Subtracting Issues and Parties, *International Organisation* 37, 1: 33–52.

Sebenius, J. K. (1992) Challenging Conventional Explanations of International Cooperation: Negotiation Analysis and the Case of Epistemic Communities, *International Organisation* 46, 1: 323–65.

Sened, I. (1997) *The Political Institution of Private Property*, Cambridge University Press.

Shepsle, K. and Weingast, B. (1994) Positive Theories of Congressional Institutions, *Legislative Studies Quarterly* 19, 2: 149–79.

Simon, H. A. (1985) Human Nature in Politics: The Dialogue of Psychology With Political Science, *American Political Science Review* 79, 2: 293–304.

Snidal, D. (1985) The Limits of Hegemonic Stability Theory, *International Organization* 39, 4: 579–614.

Snidal, D. (1985) Coordination vs. Prisoner's Dilemma, *American Political Science Review* 79, 4: 923–942.

Snidal, D. (1986) The Game *Theory* of International Politics, in K. Oye (ed.) *Cooperation under Anarchy*, Princeton University Press, 24–57.

Snidal, D. (1991) Relative Gains and the Patterns of International Cooperation, *American Political Science Review* 85, 3: 701–726.

Sprinz, D. F. and Helm, C. (1999) The Effect of Global Environmental Regimes: A Measurement Concept, *International Political Science Review* 20, 4: 359–69.

Sprinz, D. F. and Weiß, M. (2001) Domestic Politics and Global Climate Policy, in D. F. Sprinz and U. Luterbacher, *International Relations and Global Climate Change*, MIT Press, Cambridge, MA.

Stein, A. (1982) Coordination and Collaboration: Regimes in an Anarchic World, *International Organisation* 36, 3: 294–324.

Stinchcombe, A. (1991) The Conditions for Fruitfulness of Theorising about Mechanisms in Social Science, *Philosophy of the Social Sciences* 21, 2: 367–88.

Stokke, O. S. (1998) Understanding the Formation of International Environmental Regimes: The Discursive Challenge, in A. Underdal (ed.) *The Politics of International Environmental Management*, Kluwer, Dordrecht.

Susskind, L. E. (1993) *Environmental Diplomacy: Negotiating More Effective Environmental Agreements*, Oxford University Press.

Taylor, M. J. (1992) *The Possibility of Cooperation*, Cambridge University Press.

Underdal, A. (1992) The Concept of Regime "Effectiveness", *Cooperation and Conflict* 27, 3: 227–40.

Underdal, A. (2001a) One Question, Two Answers, in E. L. Miles, A. Underdal, S. Andresen, J. Wettestad, J. Birger. Skjaerseth, E. M. Carlin, *Environmental Regime Effectiveness: Confronting Theory With Evidence*, MIT Press, Cambridge, MA.

Underdal, A. (2001b) Conclusions: Patterns of Regime Effectiveness, in E. L. Miles, A. Underdal, S. Andresen, J. Wettestad, J. Birger Skjaerseth, E. M. Carlin, E. L. Miles and A. Underdal (eds.) *Environmental Regime Effectiveness: Confronting Theory With Evidence* MIT Press, edited: Cambridge, MA.

Victor, D. G., K. Raustiala, K. and Skolnikoff, E. B. (eds.) (1998) *The Implementation and Effectiveness of International Environmental Commitments*: Theory and Practice, MIT Press, Cambridge, MA.

Walt, S. M. (1999) Rigor or Rigor Mortis? Rational Choice and Security Studies, *International Security* 23, 4: 5–48.

Ward, Hugh (1979) A Behavioural Model of Bargaining, *British Journal of Political Science* 9, 2: 201–18.

Ward, H. (1996a) Game Theory and the Politics of Global Warming: the State of Play and Beyond, *Political Studies* 44, 5: 850–871.

Ward, H. (1996b) The Fetishisation of Falsification: The Debate on Rational Choice, *New Political Economy* 1, 4: 283–96.

Ward, H. (1995) Rational Choice Theory, in D. Marsh and G. Stoker (eds.) *Theories and Methods in Political Science*, Macmillan, London.

Ward, H., Grundig, F., and Zorick, E. (2001) Marching at the Pace of the Slowest: A Model of International Negotiations over Global Climate Change, *Political Studies* 49, 3: 438–461.

Weale, A., Pridham, G., Cini, M., Konstadakopulos, D., Porter, M. and Flynn, B. (2003) *Environmental Governance in Europe*, Oxford University Press.

Wendt, A. (1992) Anarchy Is What States Make of It: The Social Construction of Power Politics, *International Organisation* 46, 1: 391–425.

Wiegandt, E. (2001) Climate Change, Equity, and International Negotiations, in D. Sprinz and U. Luterbcher (eds.) International Relations and Global Climate Change, MIT Press, Cambridge, MA.

Young, O. R. (1989a) *International Cooperation: Building Regimes for Natural Resources and the Environment*, Cornell University Press, Ithaca, New York.

Young, O. R. (1989b) The Politics of International Regime Formation: Managing Natural Resources and the Environment, *International Organisation* 43, 2: 349–76.

Young, O. R. (1994) *International Governance: Protecting the Environment in a Stateless Society*, Cornell University Press, Ithaca, New York.

Young, O. R. and M. A. Levy (1999) The Effectiveness of International Environmental Regimes, in O. R. Young (ed.) *The Effectiveness of International Environmental Regimes: Causal Connections and Behavioural Mechanisms*, MIT Press, Cambridge, MA, 1–32.

Zartman, I. W., Druckman, D., Jensen, L., Pruitt, D. G. and Young, H. P. (1996) Negotiation as a Search For Justice, *International Negotiation* 1, 1: 79–98.

Zürn, M. (1992) Interessen und Institutionen in der Internationalen Politik, Leske + Budrich, Opladen.

Chapter 8

DOES REGIME ROBUSTNESS REQUIRE A FAIR DISTRIBUTION OF THE GAINS FROM COOPERATION?

An Essay on the Methodology of Necessary Conditions as Applied to a Substantive Hypothesis Concerning the "Staying Power" of International Regimes

ANDREAS HASENCLEVER[1], PETER MAYER[2], and VOLKER RITTBERGER[3]

Peace Research Institute, Frankfurt[1]; University of Bremen[2]; University of Tübingen[3]

1. INTRODUCTION

According to an ancient tradition in the Christian world, peace is a consequence of justice: *pax opus iustitiae*[1]. The notion that peace cannot be obtained without justice is shared in one way or another by numerous contemporary philosophers and social scientists. John Rawls (1993: 38f), for instance, argues that a well-ordered and stable society presupposes an "overlapping consensus" of its citizens regarding fundamental conceptions of social justice. Without such a consensus, social relations would amount to a brittle *modus vivendi* at best. Similarly, Ernst-Otto Czempiel (1981: 33; 1986: 113f) conceives of peace as a process of declining violence and increasing distributive justice. Peace without justice is impossible because an unfair allocation of wealth and power in a given society cannot be upheld except by violent means. According to Andrew Hurrell (1993: 68f), "justice needs to be seen as intrinsic to the process by which order is produced." Again, coercion alone is considered insufficient for the purpose of constructing durable and peaceful relations among political actors. This view is shared by Oran Young (1994: 134), who argues in regard to international institutions that "it is virtually impossible to achieve high levels of implementation and compliance over time through coercion" and that, therefore, "even great powers have a stake in the development of international institutions that meet reasonable standards of equity." Finally, William Zartman (1995: 592) holds that successful international negotiations—understood as an alternative to war—are guided by some understanding shared by the participants as to what a just outcome would look like.

In the following we will be concerned with the proposition, implied by these views, that distributive justice is a necessary condition for a high level of regime robustness. This hypothesis, which we shall refer to as the *justice hypothesis*, is equivalent to the proposition that inequity in the allocation of benefits and burdens among regime members guarantees a low degree of institutional "staying power" in the face of exogenous shocks. A robust (or resilient) regime is one that masters threats to its existence or effectiveness emanating from its social environment. A distributively just regime is one that meets standards of fairness that its members accept as valid. The justice hypothesis exemplifies a distinctive form of scientific reasoning, which crops up time and again in the literature on regimes and other social phenomena, but is seldom analyzed or applied with some degree of rigor. This *necessary conditions approach* focuses on conditions that must be present for some outcome of interest to occur (Braumoeller and Goertz 2000). In the next section, we explore the meaning of hypotheses referring to such conditions and contrast them with more familiar types of hypothesis. We also discuss ways of evaluating necessary condition hypotheses. In the third section, we shift from matters of form to matters of substance, analyzing the two concepts that enter into our particular hypothesis: regime robustness and distributive justice. It will become obvious that the operationalization of these concepts is fraught with considerable difficulties. Although we are unable to present a definitive test of the justice hypothesis in this chapter, in the fourth section we illustrate and follow up the main results of our methodological and conceptual discussion by looking at an important security institution, the nuclear nonproliferation regime. We suggest that this regime poses a serious challenge to the justice hypothesis, which, in principle, can be falsified by a single unambiguous counter-example.

2. METHODOLOGY: THE NATURE OF NECESSARY CONDITION HYPOTHESES

The justice hypothesis is a proposition that depicts a certain state of affairs as necessary for some phenomenon to occur. Hypotheses of this kind may be called *necessary condition hypotheses*. Understanding and evaluating the justice hypothesis therefore requires clarity about the structure of necessary condition hypotheses. In this section we comment on three questions: (1) What is the meaning of necessary condition hypotheses and how do they differ from other types of hypothesis? (2) What is the potential use of a necessary condition hypothesis? And (3) How can necessary condition hypotheses be tested?

2.1 The Meaning of Necessary Condition Hypotheses

A familiar type of general hypothesis in the social sciences states a relationship of covariance between two variables, which may or may not be interpreted as a causal relationship. For example, the level of income of a person may be hypothesized to increase with the number of years he or she has spent at school or other institutions of formal education. This hypothesis is a causal one if it is assumed that there is a causal mechanism or pathway that links the level of education with the level of income later in life (Little 1991: 25). If the hypothesis is interpreted causally, the variable specifying the cause is called the "independent variable," and the variable specifying the effect the "dependent variable." In view of their characteristic form, such hypotheses—whether or not they are given a causal interpretation—may be called *correlational hypotheses*. Correlational hypotheses state (or imply) that the greater the value of some variable A, the greater (or alternatively, the smaller) the value of some other variable B.[2] Hence, the variables that enter into a correlational hypothesis must be measured at the ordinal-scale level or higher. Correlational hypotheses may be deterministic or probabilistic. If the hypothesis is deterministic, it is assumed that, for any units x and y within the range of application of the hypothesis, the truth of the proposition that x has a greater value on A than y guarantees the truth of the proposition that x has a higher value of B than y. By contrast, a probabilistic correlational hypothesis is consistent with a (usually unspecified) number of deviations from this pattern.

The justice hypothesis as presented in the first section of this chapter is not a correlational hypothesis. It does not relate varying degrees of justice that might be realized in a regime to varying degrees of robustness certain or likely to be displayed by this regime. As a necessary condition hypothesis, it states that some phenomenon (here, a high level of robustness) will not occur or be in existence *unless* some other phenomenon (here, a just distribution of gains and burdens in the regime) is present. Necessary condition hypotheses take the form: B only if A. Every necessary condition hypothesis is logically equivalent to a corresponding hypothesis that states a sufficient condition: "B only if A" is true if and only if "if non-A, then non-B" is true. Thus, the proposition that distributive justice is necessary for a high degree of regime robustness entails (and is entailed by) the proposition that if a regime is unjust then it is moderately robust at best, or more simply: that unjust regimes fall short of a high level of robustness. Since logicians refer to if-then statements as "conditionals", we may call hypotheses of this kind *conditional hypotheses*[3] (e.g., Quine 1982: 21). Conditional hypotheses may be rarer than correlational ones in contemporary social sciences, but this does not mean that they are absent or generally uninteresting (Dessler 1992: 3, n. 4). A case in point is the much debated democratic-peace hypothesis, whose proponents hold that shared democratic institutions are a sufficient condition for a dyad of states to refrain from using military force against one another (or, to put it differently, that for any two states to fight each other in war it is necessary that at least one of them is not a democracy) (Brown, Lynn-Jones, and Miller 1996).

In principle, conditional hypotheses lend themselves to a probabilistic interpretation just as well as correlational ones (Little 1991: 27). Thus, one might render the intended meaning of the justice hypothesis as follows: Unjust regimes are extremely likely to display a low-to-medium level of robustness. However, understanding necessary condition hypotheses in this way seems to miss the pragmatic point of such formulations. Scholars identifying some phenomenon as a necessary condition for some other phenomenon are deliberately making a bold claim, which, in our view, is unduly watered down if interpreted in probabilistic terms right from the start. *Consequently, we will understand and examine the justice hypothesis as a deterministic proposition, according to which injustice in a regime strictly precludes a high level of robustness.*[4]

2.2 The Practical Value of Necessary Condition Hypotheses

General causal hypotheses, if corroborated, may serve at least three practical purposes. They can be used to *explain* events or regularities, to *predict* the outcomes of processes, and to *alter* aspects of reality. These practical goals are to a certain extent interdependent: Often we are able to explain a given event most persuasively if we could have predicted this event had we been informed about the causally relevant factual attributes of the situation. Similarly, the ability to deliberately change some aspect of the world requires the ability to predict the outcomes of at least one of our behavioral options. Because of this partial interdependence, hypotheses that are useful for one purpose tend to be useful for the other two purposes as well and *vice versa*.[5] At first sight, it might seem that necessary condition hypotheses do not score well on this count because they do not satisfy the requirements of a standard model of scientific explanation, which—owing to these interdependencies—is relevant to the purposes of predicting and manipulating outcomes as well. In the following, we try to show that this criticism is at best only partially justified and that necessary condition hypotheses can be valuable for explaining, forecasting, and intervening in social processes.

The model we are referring to is Carl Hempel's (1965) famous "deductive-nomological model of scientific explanation."[6] According to Hempel's analysis, explanation is a deductive argument, where a statement describing the event to be explained (the *explanandum*) follows logically from two sets of premises (the *explanans*): one composed of statements describing the causally relevant aspects of the situation (initial conditions) and one composed of one or more (empirically corroborated) universal hypotheses.

THE DEDUCTIVE-NOMOLOGICAL MODEL OF EXPLANATION

Fa	initial condition (a is an F)
$(x)(Fx \rightarrow Gx)$	universal hypothesis (every F is a G)
------------------	*logically entails*
Ga	Explanandum (a is a G)

Figure 8.1. *The Deductive-Nomological Model of Explanation*

Although necessary condition hypotheses of the form *B only if A* are universal hypotheses, they do not seem to fit this model. The reason is that the complex statement [(*B* only if *A*) and *A*] does *not* entail *B*. Suppose we know, or accept the hypothesis, that only just regimes are robust and we also have reliable evidence of the fact that the food aid regime is a just regime—then this does not suffice to warrant the conclusion that the food aid regime is robust. Both premises might be true and yet the conclusion false.

Nevertheless, hypotheses stating a necessary condition for some phenomenon of interest *can* be used for explanatory purposes even if explaining is construed along the lines of the deductive-nomological model. This is because, as we have seen earlier, every necessary condition statement

B only if A is equivalent to (or synonymous with) a statement expressing a sufficient condition: viz. if non-A then non-B. As a result, although the law-like statement that B only if A does not help to explain the occurrence of B, it may well help to explain why, in a given situation, B *failed* to occur. If, for example, we wish to account for the low robustness of some commodity cartel, we could—if we have reasons to believe that the justice hypothesis is true—rightly point to the skewed distribution of benefits from cooperation that this regime has institutionalized.[7] Obviously, we could also use the justice hypothesis to *predict* that a given unjust regime will not prove robust when exposed to exogenous shocks. The predictive power of the hypothesis is of particular *practical importance*, because it has implications for the appropriate design of international institutions. Not only do states have intrinsic (moral) reasons for basing their cooperative arrangements on just principles; they also have compelling instrumental reasons for doing so, provided that they are interested in a stable international order underpinned by, and composed of, stable international regimes.

Up to this point, we have assumed that the deductive-nomological model is an exhaustive account of explanation. If we relax this—hardly tenable—assumption and take into account more recent developments in the philosophy of science, we can strengthen the case for the explanatory power of necessary condition hypotheses by showing that hypotheses of the form B only if A may not only be useful in accounting for non-B, *but for B as well*. Hempel (1965: ch. 12) was well aware that all genuine explanation in science cannot be analyzed in terms of the deductive-nomological model. He therefore proposed a second model—the "inductive-statistical model"—which is appropriate when events are explained on the basis of probabilistic generalizations rather than strictly universal (deterministic) laws. The basic structure of inductive-statistical explanations is similar to that of deductive-nomological ones except that the relation between the *explanans* and the *explanandum* is no longer one of logical entailment. Rather, if the explanation is supposed to be persuasive, the probabilistic generalizations together with the initial conditions make it *very likely* for the *explanandum* to occur.

Hempel's postulate that statistical explanations are only valid when the premises make the occurrence of the *explanandum* very likely (i.e., when the conditional probability of the *explanandum* given the *explanans* is close to 1) has provoked much controversy. This so-called "high-probability criterion" was introduced to rule out the possibility that both the occurrence and the non-occurrence of the *explanandum* might be explained with reference to the same hypothesis. For example, the statistical hypothesis that 60 % of all heavy smokers contract lung cancer might be used to explain both that Jones, a chain-smoker, became ill and that Smith, who smokes just as heavily as Jones, did not. After all, it was not unlikely that Smith would be spared by the disease. The high-probability criterion has been criticized by philosophers such as Patrick Suppes (1970) and Wesley Salmon (1984) on the grounds that it is at odds with the use of the term "causal explanation" in ordinary language. For we often accept explanations that rely on a statistical hypothesis that attributes a much lower probability to the event we wish to explain. Thus, even if only 6 out of 10 heavy smokers eventually contract lung cancer, the fact that Jones has long been a heavy smoker provides us with a perfectly adequate explanation of his disease (Haussmann 1991: 36f). What is critical is not the (conditional) probability of the *explanandum* as such but the *increase* in this probability that comes with the presence of the supposed causal agent. Under certain conditions, it is enough for heavy smoking to *make it more likely* that a lung cancer develops in order for this fact to support a statistical explanation of a person's illness. In philosophical terminology: It may be enough that heavy smoking have "positive statistical relevance" for the occurrence of cancer.[8]

THE INDUCTIVE-STATISTICAL MODEL OF EXPLANATION

Fa	initial condition (a is an F)
$p(G*F)$ near 1	probabilistic hypothesis (nearly all F are G)
=======	*makes very likely*
Ga	Explanandum (a is a G)

Figure 8.2. *The Inductive-Statistical Model of Explanation.*
Note: $p(G|F)$ stands for "the conditional probability of G given F"

This theory has important consequences for our discussion of the explanatory value of necessary condition hypotheses. This is because necessary condition hypotheses, although they are most naturally interpreted as specifying a deterministic relationship, have *probabilistic implications*. Certainly, the statement "*B* only if *A*" does *not* imply that $p(B|A)$ is high (let alone close to 1) and therefore cannot support an inductive-statistical explanation of the occurrence of *B* as modelled by Hempel. It does imply, however, that $p(B|A)$ is higher than $p(B)$ (assuming that *A* is a "true" condition, i.e., one is not universally met in the population).[9] Consequently, since they entail that *A has a positive statistical relevance for B*, hypotheses of this type can be used in explanations not only of non-*B*, but of *B* as well. Salmon's (1984: 31f) own example refers to a nervous disease called paresis. It is held that this disease, the most famous victim of which was Nietzsche, affects only persons who suffer from an advanced form of untreated syphilis—which is, of course, a necessary condition hypothesis—, although only a small fraction of these persons actually contract paresis. Under these circumstances, it would be perfectly appropriate to explain the fact that Nietzsche came to suffer from paresis with reference to his advanced untreated syphilis, even though at no time it was "very likely" that he would develop this disease (Haussmann 1991: 43f).[10]

2.3   Testing Necessary Condition Hypotheses

Falsificationists such as Karl Popper (1968) argue that scientific progress is a process of trial and error in which our body of knowledge is gradually cleared from false beliefs. Science involves formulating empirically falsifiable theories and subjecting them to hard tests. These tests do not aim at verifying or validating these theories but at refuting them. Theories that have proven false are eliminated, and new conjectures are put to the test. This meta-scientific perspective builds on the insight that there is a fundamental asymmetry between the verification and the falsification of universal generalizations including scientific theories. This asymmetry consists in the fact that falsification of a universal hypothesis in the light of empirical evidence is, in principle, possible, whereas verification is not. A single black swan can show that the hypothesis that all swans are white is false, whereas any number of white swans cannot show that the hypothesis is true, if only for the fact that we have no way of knowing what future swans will look like. Popper proceeds to argue that positive, theory-confirming evidence (the observation of a white swan) is less valuable than negative, theory-infirming evidence (the observation of a swan that is not white), for only the latter contributes to scientific progress in the sense just described.

This latter view has recently been criticized as inadequate for the social sciences (King, Keohane, and Verba 1994: 100 – 105; Van Evera 1997: 43f). These critics point out that both positive and negative evidence is informative and alters our state of knowledge. Whatever the merits of this criticism with regard to the evaluation of social scientific hypotheses in general, however, *in the case of (deterministically interpreted) necessary condition hypotheses, searching for counter-examples rather than trying to amass supportive evidence seems to be the strategy of choice*. As will become obvious, this strategy is less destructive and less insensitive to confirming evidence than it may seem at first sight and is indeed capable of providing a hypothesis with some measure of positive support. The falsificationist strategy involves two steps. First, potential falsifiers are derived from the hypothesis. A potential falsifier is a singular (non-general) and verifiable statement that is inconsistent with the hypothesis under scrutiny (e.g., "There is, at some specific time and place, a non-white swan."). Hence, if a potential falsifier is verified, the hypothesis from which it has been derived is falsified. Second, the truth or falsity of the potential falsifiers is established by empirical observation. If one of the potential falsifiers turns out to be true, the hypothesis (at least in its present form) is refuted; if none of the potential falsifiers derived proves to be an actual one, one starts all over again; that is new potential falsifiers are derived and confronted with the facts. The process only stops when the attempt to falsify the hypothesis has met with success. As long as it continues, though, positive support for the hypothesis accumulates, if only as a side-effect of an activity that is directed at disconfirming it. Thus, the corroboration of the hypothesis *is* a possible outcome of the falsificationist strategy (Opp 1995: 190 – 192).[11]

A necessary condition hypothesis *B* only if *A* states only one thing: there are no *B*s that are also non-*A*s. To say that distributive justice is necessary for a high level of regime robustness is tantamount to saying that there are no highly robust unjust regimes. Thus, every statement of the form "*X* is a highly robust unjust regime" is a potential falsifier of the justice hypothesis. Testing this hypothesis involves completing this sentence schema with names ("the international trade regime," "the ozone regime," etc.) and confronting the resulting statements ("The international trade regime is a highly robust unjust regime," etc.) with the empirical data. As soon as we come across a true statement of this form, we may reject the hypothesis, provided we can assert the truth of the falsifying statement with a sufficient degree of certainty.

But how do we select the names to enter into the schema, that is, *which cases do we look at?* With regard to any given general hypothesis, we can distinguish three kinds of singular (particular) statements: statements that (if true) falsify the hypothesis, statements that (if true) instantiate the hypothesis (without verifying it), and statements that (if true) are irrelevant to the truth or falsity of the hypothesis. An instantiating statement is one that is not just consistent with the hypothesis in the sense that it does not contradict the hypothesis. Rather, it provides an "example" for the hypothesis or another general statement that is implied by the hypothesis. Only (true) instantiating statements provide support for the hypothesis, whereas other statements consistent with the hypothesis are simply irrelevant. Since the justice hypothesis entails (indeed, is equivalent to) the universal generalizations "Unjust regimes are at best moderately robust" and "Highly robust regimes are just," both regimes that are unjust and brittle and regimes that are just and very robust instantiate or confirm the hypothesis. By contrast, observations of just regimes that are not robust neither confirm nor disconfirm the justice hypothesis.

Table 8.1. *The justice hypothesis: falsifying, instantiating, and irrelevant cases.*

Regime cases	Not very robust	Highly robust
Unjust	Instantiating	Falsifying
Just	Irrelevant	Instantiating

Both distributive justice and robustness are complex concepts that require careful analysis and operationalization, before any meaningful test of the justice hypothesis can come off (see section 3 below). Moreover, even after a valid operationalization has been established, measurement of the two variables is likely to be difficult, costly, and uncertain. This fact makes it highly probable that few (if any) regimes are readily allotted to one of the four cells of the above matrix. At the same time, the very difficulty and costliness of the measurement exercise requires that we employ our resources efficiently and follow a research strategy that makes use of our prior, unsystematic knowledge of the justice and robustness of individual regimes.[12]

Since we attempt to refute the hypothesis, we do not select regimes that we believe to be just; for just regimes are either irrelevant to, or instances of, our hypothesis. Neither do we choose regimes that, given our present state of knowledge, are likely to prove both unjust and brittle. What we aim to do is to identify *plausible* potential falsifiers (Opp 1995: 194f).[13] *The cases of prime interest are apparently unjust regimes that seem to be nonetheless highly robust.* If no such cases are available, we turn our attention to seemingly unjust regimes that are not manifestly brittle and to apparently robust regimes which show no clear signs of satisfying criteria of distributive justice.[14] If none of these potential falsifiers turns out to be true, we move on to other regimes. Now regimes will be given priority that, even though less likely to be both unjust and highly robust, still hold (in the light of our present knowledge) a reasonable chance of displaying these attributes. The process does not and cannot produce a definite confirmation of the hypothesis. *With every potential falsifier that is refuted, however, the degree of corroboration increases and we are justified in placing more confidence in the hypothesis.* Note also that, since, ideally, we proceed from more to less plausible potential falsifiers, the testing procedure approaches its saturation point at maximum speed, as it were (although it is impossible to provide hard criteria for deciding whether or not this point is reached in a concrete situation).[15]

Of course, at any time a potential falsifier may be confirmed by the case study. Even then we need not immediately drop the hypothesis, though. This is true for two reasons. First, we cannot rule out that the failure of the hypothesis in this case is due to measurement error. Consequently, we lay this case aside as an "anomaly" with a view toward redoing the case study, once improved measures are available. This decision is the more legitimate the later the anomaly occurs in the testing sequence. Second, while the first option leaves the hypothesis intact for the time being, the second involves its modification. Here we regard the failure of the hypothesis as an indication that we may have overstated its range of applicability (cf. Dion 1998: 137; King, Keohane, and Verba 1994: 101, 103f). For example, if the justice hypothesis is falsified by a security regime, we may hypothesize that the relationship it specifies holds for low but not for high politics. Subsequently, we shift our attention to economic and environmental regimes, seeking as before to identify institutions that are both unjust and highly robust.[16]

3. THE JUSTICE HYPOTHESIS: PROBLEMS OF CONCEPTUALIZATION AND OPERATIONALIZATION

From the logical point of view, testing a (deterministic) necessary condition hypothesis is a fairly straightforward undertaking. Such a hypothesis specifies a logically possible (internally consistent) state of affairs—B and non-A—as empirically impossible, and the task of testing amounts to trying to show that, contrary to the hypothesis, this state of affairs does exist in empirical reality, that there *are* non-As that are Bs. Problems of representativeness and selection bias do not arise. Insufficient degrees of freedom, multicollinearity, and the omission of variables are not an issue. In case of the justice hypothesis, however, these methodological advantages are coupled with quite substantial problems of measurement, which affect both variables—robustness and distributive justice—and are apt quickly to dissolve the initial impression that the hypothesis is easy to evaluate empirically.

3.1 Regime Robustness

Robustness (in our usage) is a property of international regimes that is similar to but more specific than regime stability. While stability may be defined rather broadly as the tendency of a regime to endure (whatever the causes of this tendency), robustness (or resilience) is defined more narrowly as the capacity of a regime to absorb exogenous shocks or to withstand exogenous challenges (Hasenclever, Mayer, and Rittberger 1996: 4 – 11).[17] Robustness is related internally to the notion of an event that threatens the existence or the effectiveness of the regime from outside. *A regime that is resilient does not lose the loyalty or the support of its members when, due to some process or event in the physical or social environment of the regime, the prospects for cooperation deteriorate and incentives for deviant (non-cooperative) behavior increase.* This notion can be further developed in the light of the most common definition of international regimes, which depicts regimes as institutions composed of four types of components:

> Regimes can be defined as sets of implicit or explicit principles, norms, rules, and decision-making procedures around which actors' expectations converge in a given area of international relations. Principles are beliefs of fact, causation, and rectitude. Norms are standards of behavior defined in terms of rights and obligations. Rules are specific prescriptions or proscriptions for action. Decision-making procedures are prevailing practices for making and implementing collective choice. (Krasner 1983: 2)

With this definition in mind, we may explicate the concept of regime robustness as follows: Given an exogenous challenge, the member states demonstrate their continual allegiance to the regime concerned by maintaining its principles and norms and by continuing to comply with its provisions (some of which may have been adapted to the new situation). Changes *within* the regime (i.e., changes only in rules and procedures) in response to an exogenous shock do not indicate cracks in a regime's robustness provided that the altered injunctions are complied with as before; changes *of* the regime (i.e., changes in principles and norms), however, normally do, especially when these changes cannot be accounted for in terms of the explicit purpose of the regime, but merely reflect changes in the underlying power structure (cf. Krasner 1983: 3f). Still, a regime that is continued and complied with, even after drastic revisions in its normative substance have been implemented, has proven more robust than one that (in response to a similar shock) is dismantled altogether.

Several *methodologically relevant consequences* emerge from this definition of the term "regime robustness." To begin with, robustness is a *dispositional concept* describing a property that shows (or fails to show) *only when* certain conditions are met (i.e., only when an exogenous shock has occurred). As a result, it is impossible to rank all regimes by their degree of robustness owing to a lack of commensurability. Regime P, which has survived a serious exogenous shock, cannot be said to be more (or less or equally) robust than regime Q, which, so far, has sailed in fine weather. Regime X, which has faced and mastered two serious exogenous challenges, has not proven more (or less or equally) robust than regime Y, which has confronted—and survived—only one such challenge etc. Subsets of regimes are comparable, though, and partial orderings can be constructed. Two issues here require closer examination: (1) By what criteria do we decide which (if any) of two commensurable regimes is more robust? (2) When are two regimes commensurable?

As to the first issue, we have already outlined the answer. *Differences in the robustness of commensurable regimes* emerge from their memberships' responses to the exogenous challenges. These responses have two dimensions: continuity/change in the level of compliance with the regime; possible normative regime change. A regime is most robust (relative to the strength of the shock it faced) if the level of compliance does not go down after the shock and no changes are made to the normative core of the regime. A regime is least robust if it breaks down in response to the shock. All regimes in a given class of commensurables fall somewhere on the continuum that is marked by these two poles. Table 8.2 represents an ordinal scale that emerges naturally from these considerations.[18]

Table 8.2. *Scale of the variable "regime robustness."*

Membership's response to the shock	Value of variable "regime robustness"
No change of the regime and level of compliance not reduced	High degree of robustness
Either change of the regime or lower level of compliance (but not both)	Medium degree of robustness
Change of the regime and lower level of compliance	Low degree of robustness
Breakdown of regime-based cooperation	Not robust (brittle)

As to the issue of *commensurability*, two regimes are comparable with respect to robustness if they encountered similar or equivalent (i.e., similarly strong) exogenous shocks. Moreover, for two regimes to fall into the same class of commensurables, the number of similar shocks they have confronted should not vary too much. It would not be plausible to attribute the same level of robustness to two regimes, when one of them has survived, say, four shocks (of a given strength) before it collapsed in the wake of the fifth, whereas the other did not even survive the first one. Having undergone a similar number of similar shocks is sufficient for two regimes to be comparable with regard to robustness. It is not necessary, though. Obviously, a regime that survives a severe exogenous shock has proven more robust than a regime that collapses in the wake of a less serious challenge. In addition, to avoid perverse attributions, we stipulate that regimes that are ineffective in the sense that their injunctions are generally ignored ("dead-letter regimes") are brittle by definition. Similarly, regimes that break down in the absence of any external stimulus are defined as being not robust.[19]

Another methodologically relevant consequence flowing from our definition of the term "robustness" is that we have to be clear about what we mean by an *exogenous shock* and how we measure the strength of an exogenous challenge. We have already noted that an exogenous shock is an event that occurs in the environment of a regime and tends to reduce the willingness or ability of the regime members to cooperate in the issue area governed by the regime. A robust regime prevents this tendency from prevailing. Since shocks of identical strength may be absorbed by one regime and cause the breakdown of another (reflecting the fact that some regimes are more robust than others), shocks must be defined independently of the outcome of the situation that they are predicated of. To do so, two (not mutually exclusive) approaches suggest themselves: an inductive one and a deductive one.

The *inductive approach* searches for events that seem to have put historical regimes under considerable strain—events that appear to have weakened given regimes if not prompting their collapse—and then generalizes on these observations. The result is a (possibly hierarchically ordered) list including such events as a sudden deterioration of the overall political relationship of central regime members, a sharp recession, a dramatic change in the identity of the actors in the issue area, or similar.

By contrast, the *deductive approach* draws on theories of international cooperation and regimes, specifying—at an abstract level—the kinds of events that, according to these models, tend to destabilize an ongoing cooperation among states. Subsequently, these abstract event types are interpreted in terms of more concrete real-world phenomena. Perhaps most useful in this regard is a substream of the regimes literature that has been labeled the "situation-structural approach" (Zürn 1992). *Situation-structuralists* use simple models from the theory of strategic choice—such as the Prisoner's Dilemma or the Battle of the Sexes—in order to depict and analyze the constellations of interests (payoff structures) that characterize given issue-areas in international relations (Hasenclever, Mayer, and Rittberger 1997: 44 – 59). Drawing on results from game-theoretical research, they use these models (together with other situational variables) to study such problems as the determinants of regime formation or the variation in regime form. Most important from our point of view are the theorems that pertain to the stability of cooperation and the variables that affect it. Thus, situation-structuralists make a fundamental distinction between two types of regimes: coordination regimes and collaboration regimes (Stein 1983).

A COORDINATION GAME: BATTLE OF THE SEXES

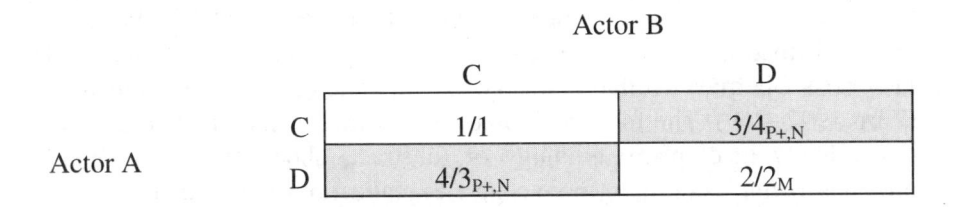

		Actor B	
		C	D
Actor A	C	1/1	$3/4_{P+,N}$
	D	$4/3_{P+,N}$	$2/2_M$

A COLLABORATION GAME: PRISONER'S DILEMMA

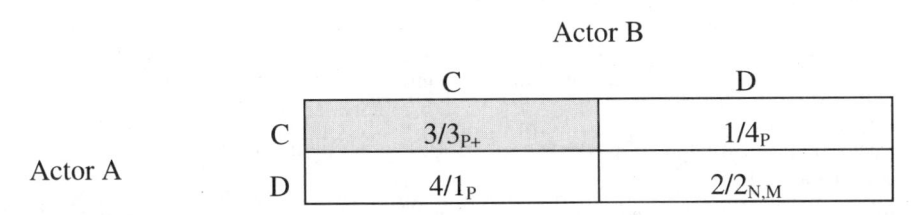

		Actor B	
		C	D
Actor A	C	$3/3_{P+}$	$1/4_P$
	D	$4/1_P$	$2/2_{N,M}$

Figure 8.3. *Situational Structural Approaches.*

Legend: C = cooperative option; D = non-cooperative option (defect); M = maximin solution; N = Nash equilibrium; P = Pareto-optimum; P+ (hatched cells) = qualified Pareto-optimum/cooperative outcome/outcome possibly institutionalized by regime (i.e., solution that is both Pareto-efficient and superior to the "natural outcome" resulting from independent decisionmaking); 4 = individually most desired outcome; 1 = individually least desired outcome

Coordination regimes arise in situations such as the Battle of the Sexes; collaboration regimes are responses to situations resembling the Prisoner's Dilemma. This basic variable (regime type) affects the modal stability of the regime: Institutionalizing solutions to coordination problems, *coordination regimes* direct their members to adopt behavioral patterns that represent Nash equilibria of the game. As a consequence, no actor has an incentive to withdraw from the convention, once it is established, so long as noone else defects. This property should make coordination regimes inherently stable. By contrast, cooperation in a Prisoner's Dilemma is not a Nash equilibrium and members have an incentive to cheat on their partners. This fact makes much greater demands on an institution designed to secure cooperation among sovereign states and is likely to result in *collaboration regimes* exhibiting a lower average degree of stability than coordination regimes.

Situation-structural analyses also provide clues as to what kind of events (changes in the structure of the game) are exogenous shocks to a regime. For each type of situation (Battle, PD, etc.), several factors are hypothesized to play an important role in facilitating or inhibiting processes of regime formation. We can therefore define a *shock* as any event external to the regime that causes, or involves, the dissolution of a facilitating factor or the emergence of an inhibiting one.[20] The factors that facilitate and inhibit regime formation in coordination situations and in situations resembling the Prisoner's Dilemma overlap to a large extent, although they are not identical (Zürn 1992: 219). The following table derives from some of these factors a (most likely incomplete) typology of (abstract) shocks to a regime and provides examples of their (more concrete) realizations in world politics.

Table 8.3. *Types of exogenous challenges to international regimes.*

Type of exogenous shock	Paradigmatic realization/example
Shrinking shadow of the future: a. rapidly increasing discount rate b. growing doubts as to the continuation of the game	a. sharp recession in member states (for environmental regimes) b. rapidly declining fishery
Change in the distribution of power (e.g. hegemonic decline)	U.S. in the 1960s and 1970s
Breakdown of mutual trust/increased sensitivity for relative gains	Events that led to the second Cold War
Emergence of new relevant actors unfamiliar with or unwilling to play by the rules of the game	Disintegration of the Soviet Union
Substantial changes in preference orderings or utilities in major actors	End of the Cold War (for North-South relations or for NATO)

It is best to regard the two approaches to defining exogenous shocks to international regimes not as mutually exclusive but as complementary. The deductive approach has the virtue of being more systematic than the inductive one. It offers the prospect of a *theory* of exogenous shocks that defines the most important categories of shocks and possibly also includes propositions about the relative weights of the various types of shock. At present, this theory is still in its early stages, however. Moreover, even if all the types and weights were specified, there would still be the problem of relating these abstract concepts to empirical phenomena, and in this translation process unsystematic, intuitive, and inductively acquired knowledge about exogenous challenges is likely to play an indispensible role. Conversely, a purely inductive approach is plagued by problems of causal attribution and therefore is likely to remain unsatisfactory as long as the supposed challenges are not understood theoretically and analyzed with the aid of categories derived from a general model of international cooperation. Unfortunately, neither of the two approaches—whether used singly or in combination—is likely soon to come up with a compelling solution to the problem of how to assess the relative strength of given exogenous shocks. In the meantime, it seems reasonable to treat the five types of shocks derived from the situation-structural theory of regimes as equivalent. Since these types are not mutually exclusive, the challenge posed by a given event (say, the end of the Cold War) is the more serious the more types of shock it exemplifies simultaneously.

Fortunately, not all of the above mentioned problems need to be solved in order to devise a meaningful test of the justice hypothesis. In particular, it is not necessary to order all (or a large sample of) regimes by their level of robustness.[21] A reasonable *procedure* is to begin by looking for cases that are highly robust by the measures specified in this section (i.e., regimes that have undergone several shocks or confronted a challenge simultaneously exemplifying several types of shock *and* have done so without either significant normative change or a reduction in the compliance following suit). Subsequently the regimes thus identified are examined with respect to their degree of distributive justice as defined in the next section. Any of these highly robust regimes that clearly fails to meet the criteria of distributive justice constitutes a counter-example to the justice hypothesis, which must be regarded as a serious anomaly if not an actual falsifier of this hypothesis. In our empirical illustration in the fourth section of this chapter, we shall proceed this way.

3.2   Distributive Justice in International Regimes

Most students of international regimes agree that states create regimes in order to reap gains from cooperation. Depending on the substance of the principles, norms, rules, and procedures that constitute the regime and on the character of the issue area, the nature, size, and allocation of these gains vary considerably across the range of actual and hypothetical institutions. The members of any given regime may benefit more or less equally, or some may do better than others, possibly even to the extent that some participants would have been better off without the regime. *Distributive justice* is a standard of evaluation that applies to the way institutions—whether domestic or international—allot benefits and burdens to the actors who participate in them. According to the justice hypothesis, only regimes that conform to this standard are highly robust. To test the hypothesis, it is therefore necessary to clarify what is meant by "distributively just" in this context.[22]

In order to specify the defining features of a just regime, we have the choice between two approaches that might be labeled "externalist" and "internalist," respectively. *Externalists* define "distributive justice" by an allocation principle (or a set of such principles) that is not necessarily identical with what the actors themselves regard as just. The term "distributive justice" is either nominalistically defined ("I henceforth use the word 'distributive justice' to mean such and such") or interpreted in terms of some (supposedly) objective conception of justice. It is usually regarded as the task of moral philosophy to provide us with a conclusive answer to the question of what is objectively just (whether or not this answer is congruent with the actors' moral beliefs).[23] Externalists therefore often rely on philosophical accounts of justice such as Rawls's (1971) theory of justice as fairness with its famous two principles when conceptualizing the variable distributive justice for regimes (e.g., Zürn 1987). The external approach may be perfectly and perhaps singly adequate for purposes of normative evaluation, that is when we wish to know whether a given regime is morally desirable and therefore deserves our support. However, it is *not* the best choice for the purpose of testing the justice hypothesis, which is not a normative statement but an *essentially analytical proposition about a causal relationship in the social world*. Although using some external standard as an operational definition of distributive justice and testing the hypothesis on that basis might produce an interesting empirical result in itself, the *validity* of the operationalization remains in doubt as long as it cannot be ruled out that this externally defined variable called "distributive justice" is uncorrelated with the normative beliefs and perceptions of justice entertained by the actors themselves. To put it differently, distributive justice (in this context) should be defined with a view to the actors' subjective conception of justice, because *otherwise we have no reason to expect the causal mechanism underpinning the justice hypothesis—viz. the justice motive—to operate in the first place*. Obviously, people's sense of injustice is aroused only by what *they* regard as unjust.

Any definition of the term "distributive justice" as employed in the justice hypothesis, therefore, should be based on an internal standard of evaluation, that is on a distributive principle or on a combination of such principles that is considered valid and pertinent by the actors themselves. *Internalists* need not assume that conceptions of justice vary from person to person (each having his own ideas about what is just) or that these understandings themselves are perfectly variable (any conceivable distributional pattern qualifying as a potentially just distribution). On the contrary, although there is often disagreement on what is just in a given situation, important aspects of the idea of distributive justice are not controversial. Consequently, there is no need to begin with a *tabula rasa* when trying to identify the conceptions of justice that are accepted in a given community. Most fundamental, it is not in dispute that distributive justice is based on a principle of equality demanding that like cases be treated alike

(Hart 1961: ch. 7). This formal dimension of distributive justice might also be stated in the following terms: only a *rule-governed* allocation of benefits and burdens is a just allocation (Bull 1977: 76). Obviously, *formal justice* is not sufficient to settle conflicts about the fair distribution of goods and bads, as any two persons are at the same time similar in countless regards and dissimilar in countless others. Formal justice therefore needs to be supplemented by an understanding of which similarities and dissimilarities, respectively, are morally relevant. In common morality, we find a small number of *precepts of justice* that go some way toward filling this gap (Perelman 1990; Rawls 1971: sec. 47). These precepts are of two types: One precept requires institutions to conform to parity; the others demand some form of proportionality (H. P. Young 1994). *Parity* means that the shares that the parties receive are equal in size or equivalent in value; *proportionality* means that each receives in proportion to some morally significant variable. The most important proportionality precepts are the contribution principle ("To each according to his or her input") and the need principle ("To each according to his or her needs"). Social-psychologists describe these precepts and their variations in detail and use experimental designs to investigate the conditions under which individuals and groups tend to select one of these precepts rather than another (Deutsch 1975; Elster 1995; Hegtvedt 1992).

Recent work by Cecilia Albin, Zartman, and others exemplifies the internalist approach to distributive justice in regimes (Albin 1993, Zartman 1995; Zartman *et al.* 1996). These studies are concerned with international negotiation but their results have important implications for regime analysis, since regimes for the most part emerge from a process of "institutional bargaining" in which agreement is reached on the constitutional contract of the regime (Young 1989, 1991). Zartman and his collaborators might be seen as meeting a challenge that Hurrell (1993: 68f) had posed several years ago, when he called on students of regimes to begin to view "notions of justice ... as intrinsic to the process by which order is produced." They argue that notions of justice play an integral and irreducible part in states' attempts to settle or reduce their conflicts by way of negotiation. Most provocative is their claim that, in "the process of negotiating the exchange or division of the items contested between them, negotiators come to an agreement on the notion of justice which will govern this disposition; if they do not, negotiations will not be able to proceed to a conclusion" (Zartman *et al.* 1996: 80). In some cases, a ready-made principle of justice—usually some variant of parity—works as a "salient solution" or "focal point" (Schelling 1960) coordinating the expectations and the concession-making of the parties (Albin 1993: 230f). In other cases, the shared notion of justice that forms the basis of the agreement is the product of the negotiations themselves. Here, negotiation is a "search for justice," the result of which is expressed in what Zartman calls a "formula," although the actors are selfish and power is not absent from the negotiating table (Zartman 1995: 892, 897f).[24]

This perspective invites the criticism that, by foregoing an external standard of justice, there is a danger of ending up with a definition of justice according to which just is whatever negotiators accept—in which case justice cannot explain acceptance and is redundant as an analytical category. Zartman and his collaborators, however, seem to avert this danger by advancing a (falsifiable) empirical hypothesis about the content of just (and therefore acceptable) formulas. They suggest that the formulas that are accepted are either issue-specific interpretations of one of a small list of precepts of justice (similar to the one above) or combine one or more of these precepts in a sort of compromise ("compound justice") (Zartman *et al.* 1996: 84). This specification of the range of possible negotiation outcomes is still fairly broad and inclusive; however, it appears to be sufficient to save the central claim these authors make—the claim that only formulas perceived as just are accepted—from tautology.

In the specific context of this chapter, however, their argument is problematic in yet another respect. According to Zartman and his collaborators, negotiations do not succeed and hence regimes are not created unless the actors select or form a common notion of justice that serves as the keystone of the regime ("territory for security", "unequal cuts in forces so as to restore parity," "embedded liberalism," etc.) The problem is that this is another necessary condition hypothesis, which seems to *entail* the justice hypothesis. To see this, consider the following: The hypothesis put forward by Zartman and his collaborators seems to imply that all regimes are just (from an internalist perspective), because only just formulas are endorsed and worked out in the first place. However, if all regimes are just, then all robust regimes must be just as well, which is another way of saying that only just regimes are robust (the justice hypothesis). Therefore, if Zartman and his collaborators are right, then the justice hypothesis is true *but it is also trivial*—given that we already know that regimes are fair as such.

However, we need not accept the conclusion that the justice hypothesis is trivial, even if we stick to the internalist approach to defining distributive justice. Once more, we have *two options*: One is to reject Zartman's claim, the other is to show that the conclusion does not follow. We look at the two options in turn. The contention that all successful negotiations involve the acceptance by the parties of a just formula is likely to provoke grave doubts even in the minds of many internalists. Critics might point out that the internalism of Zartman and his collaborators is too narrowly focused on the issue area to which the negotiations pertain. The relevant internal standards of justice, it might be argued, are those of the international community as a whole (although, in some cases, regional communities may have further developed these principles or added new ones). As a consequence, principles of international distributive justice do not operate at the level of specific issue areas (such a ozone depletion, conventional arms control in Europe, etc.) but at the level of what Robert Keohane (1989: 4) calls the fundamental "conventions" of international society or what Zartman (1995: 895, 899) himself refers to as "generalized formulas." Only principles that exist independently of the issues under negotiation have the *critical* potential that is implicit in the idea of justice and in morality more generally. Although these general principles of distributive justice influence the choice of the issue-specific formulas, the latter cannot be expected *generally* to reflect international justice conventions faithfully because of the intervention of power asymmetries and perhaps of other considerations besides justice, such as efficiency. Therefore, the contingent outcomes of international negotiations are unreliable signposts when it comes to establishing the internal (i.e., community) standards of regime justice.

This argument, however, can be challenged on the grounds that it implicitly assumes that the states system is what Rawls (1971: 4f) calls a "well-ordered society." By this he means a society "effectively regulated by a public conception of justice" in which "everyone accepts and knows that the others accept the same principles of justice" and "the basic social institutions satisfy and are generally known to satisfy these principles." This assumption is a strong one, which is likely to recruit very sparse support in most quarters of the community of International Relations scholars. Stanley Hoffmann (1981: 164) may be exaggerating somewhat when he remarks that in "the international milieu, there is a cacophony of standards," but he is more likely to be correct than those international communitarians who perceive a broad and substantial "overlapping consensus" on principles of international justice. Thus, it is questionable whether the concept of an international justice convention has any real-world referents or, if it has, as to whether these ideas form a coherent whole. Keohane (1989: 4) himself mentions only one international convention that seems to qualify as a principle of distributive justice: reciprocity. Reciprocity, however, seems too vague and flexible a criterion to underpin a distinction between just and unjust regimes.[25] Zartman (1995: 895, 899) mentions several "generalized formulas," but these are fairly heterogeneous and incoherent and will therefore often conflict in concrete cases ("first come, first served," "polluter pays," "self-determination only through referendum," etc.). Since there are no meta-level principles to decide which of these formulas trumps in conflict, it is again up to the negotiators to apply, to concretize, or to ignore these overarching principles as they see fit.

If the first option we have when trying to avoid the conclusion that the justice hypothesis is trivial drops out, the second one is much more plausible and paves the way toward a workable concretization of the idea that (in the present context of study) the distributive justice of regimes should be understood in internalist terms. Here, the undesirable conclusion is avoided by questioning the logical soundness of the inference (rather than the truth of its premise), and it is indeed possible to accept without inconsistency Zartman's internalism and his hypothesis that agreed formulas reflect common notions of justice *and* to deny that all regimes are just. This is because the agreement on a formula or—in the language of regime theorists (Krasner 1983: 2; Müller 1993: 39 – 42)—on principles and norms is not the end of the process of regime formation. In particular, there is no automatism that determines the shape, precision, and degree of obligatoriness of the rules and decision-making procedures of the emerging regime once a set of principles and norms has been adopted. As a consequence, we can regard the principles and norms of the regime as embodying a common issue-related understanding of justice shared by the members of the regime *without* making a judgment on the fairness of the regime as such. *The regime is distributively just (or fair) to the extent that the specific injunctions it requires its members to observe (i.e,. the concrete rules of the regime) reflect this normative consensus.*[26] Just regimes involve a set of behavioral guidelines that can be described as an unbiased translation of the principles and norms into verifiable obligations. Conversely, a regime in which only one item of the "trade" that produced the formula is represented at the level of the (comparatively) precise and stringent prescriptions and proscriptions is distributively unjust. By implication, this perspective on regime justice, although radically internalist in that it does not look beyond the issue-area in question when defining what is just in the eyes of the actors, does not betray the notion that justice inheres a critical potential. Particular regimes may well be judged unfair—if only by their own standards.[27]

Along the lines of the argument discussed above, it might nevertheless be objected that this perspective dignifies regimes that are the product of power, coercion, and deception more than of a concern with international justice. But this objection rings somewhat hollow as long as there is no sufficiently firm and substantial consensus on what international justice means beyond individual issue areas. Moreover, the role of power and coercion in the creation of regimes must not be overstated. As Young (1989: 362, 368f) has pointed out, structural or at least very common attributes of institutional bargaining, such as the rule of unanimity or the presence of a veil of uncertainty, narrowly circumscribe the influence of those factors. Finally, it should be added that the radically internalist perspective outlined in the previous paragraph has two advantages that make it particularly attractive in the context of a study that is concerned with the requirements of an empirical test of the justice hypothesis.

First, it should not be too difficult to apply this criterion to individual cases and to decide whether a given regime is just. At a minimum, this approach should make it much easier to come to a judgment on the distributive justice of a regime than its alternative, which is burdened with the difficulty of justifying why one particular "justice convention" (or combination of such conventions) is chosen rather than another as a standard of distributive justice for the regime under consideration.

Second, this conception of regime justice is *minimalist* in the sense that a regime that fails to meet this standard is likely to be unjust according to every other reasonable criterion of justice (whether internal or external) as well. In fact, this criterion seems to be implied by two of the most fundamental and least controversial of all moral ideas: the idea that one is obliged to keep one's promises (or *pacta sunt servanda*) and the idea that discrimination (or the selective application of a general rule) is unjust (i.e., the idea of formal justice). The minimalist (non-demanding) nature of our criterion means that we are much more likely to err on the side of justice than on the side of injustice. This fact, however, is of considerable value in the light of the methodological argument we have made above. In the second section of this chapter, we have advocated a falsificationist strategy for evaluating the justice hypothesis. When applied to this hypothesis, this strategy directs us to search for regimes that are both highly robust and *unjust*. Our minimalism with respect to the concept of distributive justice, therefore, has the effect of *reducing* the probability that we have committed a measurement error, should we identify a given regime as a counter-example to, and consequently as a reason to reject, the justice hypothesis.

4. THE NUCLEAR NONPROLIFERATION REGIME—A COUNTEREXAMPLE TO THE JUSTICE HYPOTHESIS?

In this section we argue that the nuclear nonproliferation regime (NPR) deserves the attention of scholars who wish to assess the empirical standing of the justice hypothesis, because this regime seems to combine two properties, which, according to this hypothesis, are mutually exclusive: a high level of robustness and a distribution of benefits and burdens that fails to meet the criterion of justice. Since the following observations are not the product of a thorough study of the NPR and its history, we do not claim to demonstrate conclusively that this regime is inconsistent with the justice hypothesis. Our goal is the more limited one of highlighting some basic and well-known facts about this regime that, in our view, justify its closer examination given that, as we have argued in section two, testing of a necessary condition hypothesis should proceed by identifying and determining the truth value of plausible potential falsifiers of the hypothesis.

The goal of the *nuclear nonproliferation regime* is to prevent or at least to slow down the spread of nuclear weapons. The regime rests on several pillars, the most important of which is the Treaty on the Non-Proliferation of Nuclear Weapons (NPT), which entered into force in 1970. Other sources of principles, norms, rules, and procedures of the regime include the Guidelines of the London Suppliers Club, the Statute of the International Atomic Energy Agency (IAEA), the safeguard rules in INFCIRC/66 and INFCIRC/153, the Comprehensive Test-Ban Treaty (CTBT) of 1996, and the various treaties establishing regional nuclear weapon free zones (Parker 1998: ch. 3). The goals of the NPR are pursued through a set of rights and obligations that differentiate between various categories of states: between states that possess nuclear weapons (nuclear weapon states, NWS)[28] and states that do not (non-nuclear weapon states, NNWS), and between suppliers (only some of which are NWS) and recipients of nuclear technology. NWS have undertaken not to transfer nuclear weapons to NNWS, not to threaten the use of nuclear weapons against such states, and to take steps toward nuclear disarmament. NNWS have pledged not to produce or acquire nuclear weapons and to allow the IAEA to monitor their compliance with this norm. All regime members retain the right to develop peaceful nuclear industries, and technologically advanced states are obligated to assist, and to cooperate with, less advanced states should the latter desire to use atomic energy for civilian purposes. Trade in nuclear technology is therefore admissible and encouraged. Suppliers, however, must not trade with states that have not accepted IAEA controls ("safeguards") on the use of their nuclear material and facilities. The IAEA has the right to report treaty violations to the United Nations Security Council, which may take action if it concludes that the member's noncooperation constitutes a threat to international peace and security.

Highly robust. Throughout its existence, the NPR has been accompanied by doubts about its efficacy and durability. Toward the end of the cold war, however, Joseph Nye (1987: 401) expected the NPR to prove "more durable" than other security regimes, and a few years later John Gerard Ruggie (1992: 563f) counted the regime among those multilateral institutions that had shown to be markedly robust in the face of the dramatic upheavals of the late 1980s and early 1990s. In the course of the thirty years that the regime has been in place, it has passed through several crises. But this is no indication of its low robustness. On the contrary, the challenges, together with the fact that they could not destroy the regime, testify to its staying power. Indeed, a glance at the history of the regime suggests that *it meets the criteria for a high level of robustness (as developed in section 3.1) reasonably well.*

A minimum requirement of robustness is that the rules of the regime are generally *complied* with. This is because when gauging a regime's robustness we compare, *inter alia*, its pre- and post-shock levels of compliance. Without this precondition, regimes that are not respected by their members would be robust almost by definition. Despite some spectacular cases of defection (see below), the NPR seems to meet this requirement. According to Charles Parker (1998: 112f), the regime has proven significant in more than one respect. First, it has achieved an almost universal coverage. Only three states—India, Pakistan, and Israel—have failed to accept NPT- or NPT-equivalent obligations. Second, it seems to have induced change in the behavior of states. The diffusion of nuclear weapons has been much lower than experts had predicted in the 1960s, and there are successful cases of "nuclear roll-back" such as South Africa, Ukraine, and Kazakhstan. Third, compliance with its provisions has been relatively high. Although there have been serious violations, these can be regarded as exceptions given the almost global membership. Over the years, the *substance of the regime* has not been static, but the changes that have occurred are changes *within* the regime rather than changes *of* the regime. The rights and obligations that form the normative core of the regime have been there from the beginning; they have been concretised and elaborated over the years. For example, the nuclear disarmament norm is part of the NPT, although the progress that its addressees have made in this respect has been painfully slow, and the CTBT, which was concluded in 1996 and has been signed by a vast majority of states, has not yet entered into force.

Finally and most importantly, there have been *serious exogenous challenges* and they do not seem to have undermined the loyalty of the vast majority of the regime members. If anything, they have fostered the willingness of the international community to strengthen and defend this important security regime. Thus, although several of such challenges occurred in the first half of the 1990s (the dissolution of the Soviet Union, which temporarily created three more nuclear powers, locked in a severe security dilemma [Schimmelfennig 1994]; the detection of Iraq's secret nuclear armament program; North Korea's announcement to withdraw from the NPT), the other members of the regime did not reduce their commitment in order to regain unilateral leeway, but instead agreed to the NPT's indefinite extension in 1995. Similarly, the Indian and Pakistani nuclear tests in 1998 provoked international responses that evidenced at least as much the strength of the norm against nuclear testing as its weakness (Frank and

Schaper 1999).[29] None of this guarantees that the NPR will not fall into decay sometime in the near future, but for the time being it can be said to have proved remarkably robust by the criteria outlined in the preceding section (see also Parker 1998: 116f).[30]

Even though unjust? It is certainly not impossible to think of a moral defense of the NPR given that it seemed to have worked as an important constraint on the spread of nuclear weapons and thus reduced the danger of immensely devasting nuclear wars. But few have attempted a moral defense of the regime that specifically builds on the idea of distributive justice. Indeed, for Hedley Bull (1984: 10f), the NPR exemplifies the general truth that "[j]ustice is a particular virtue, and sometimes conflicts with other goals; in international relations order, or peace and security, is sometimes regarded as a higher good than justice." This reading of the regime is confirmed in the light of our minimalist criterion of distributive justice.

Use of this criterion involves forgoing the application of an external standard and exempting the formula that the regime is based upon from a critique in terms of justice. In the preceding section, we have identified this formula with the normative superstructure of the regime or its principles and norms. A regime is unjust not because the bargain it has sprung from was unjust but because it has been implemented in a biased and discriminatory fashion. At the beginning of this section, we have already outlined the "nuclear bargain" (Smith 1987: 257) without which there would have been no NPR or at least not the regime that we know. Basically, the NNWS traded their sovereign right to acquire nuclear weapons and to conduct their nuclear activities without outside supervision and interference for the NWS's pledge to give them access to the peaceful use of atomic energy, not to supply other states with nuclear weapons, and to work toward becoming NNWS themselves through the conclusion of nuclear disarmament treaties. This bargain may or may not satisfy a reasonable external standard of distributive justice. What makes the NPR an unjust regime by our criteria, however, is the selective and partial manner in which this bargain was worked out in the subsequent construction of the regime.

The bias that renders the regime unjust becomes manifest when we compare the general and therefore less immediately obligatory and constraining *norms* with the specific and therefore more immediately obligatory and constraining *rules* of the regime (Müller 1989: 283 – 287). *The general pattern that shows is that those components of the bargain that were exclusively or primarily in the interest of the NWS had a much better chance of giving rise to concrete and binding rules than those terms of the bargain that were the main concern of the NWWS.* Thus, while the rules that specify the verification and export control norms have been steadily improved, refined, and hardened, the norms that require cooperation in the development of a civilian nuclear sector and particularly the norms requiring the NWS to engage in a serious process of nuclear disarmament have found very little (if any) concretization. As a result, it is difficult to avoid the conclusion that the NPR, viewed as a whole, is (by its own standards) discriminatory and therefore unjust.[31]

It seems therefore that, at least in the case of the NPR, injustice *has been* compatible with a high degree of robustness. This is not to say that the elements of discrimination and injustice present in the NPR do not act as a strain on the regime and one that may well threaten its success and its existence in the long run. Indeed, the justice issue has been implicated in most of the shocks and crises that have plagued the regime in the last thirty years. Still, it cannot be overlooked that, so far, the regime has mastered these crises despite the double standards it tends to apply when it comes to demanding that its members make their actions suit to the words.

5. CONCLUSION

In this chapter we have looked at the hypothesis that only regimes that secure a fair distribution of the benefits and burdens of cooperation among their members prove highly resilient when confronted with exogenous challenges to their existence and effectiveness. The bulk of the chapter has been concerned with clarifying the methodological issues that are involved in empirically testing such a hypothesis. We have argued that a necessary condition hypothesis such as the justice hypothesis lends itself well to the application of a falsificationist strategy, which involves identifying and examining plausible potential falsifiers of the hypothesis under consideration. Although this methodological choice would seem to make testing the hypothesis a straightforward undertaking, this has turned out not to be the case. What renders the empirical evaluation of this proposition difficult and its results uncertain are the problems that arise when it comes to conceptualizing and operationalizing its variables. Since robustness presupposes the notion of an exogenous shock that puts the regime's survival or effectiveness at risk, it is necessary to specify what processes or events qualify as *prima facie* exogenous challenges to a regime and precisely how a regime reveals its degree of resilience when encountering such a challenge. This raises severe problems of commensurability, although not all of them need to be solved in a test of this kind. As to distributive justice, we have advocated a radically internalist approach to defining outcome fairness in international regimes. This approach seems to be the preferred one given that our purpose has not been one of normative evaluation (which may require an external standard) and that, at present, the international society seems to lack a firm and substantial consensus on general principles of distributive justice. The chapter concludes with a brief examination of a particular regime, the nuclear non-proliferation regime, which we contend is a *plausible potential falsifier* of the justice hypothesis. While our analysis of the regime falls short of the requirements of a potentially falsifying case study, it suggests that the NPR may well be more than that and amount to an *actual falsifier* of the justice hypothesis; at a minimum, it points to an apparent anomaly that proponents of this hypothesis must address successfully if they wish to uphold their proposition without either qualification or modification.

NOTES

1 An earlier version of this chapter was presented at the 41st Annual International Studies Association Convention, Los Angeles, 14 – 18 March 2000. We wish to thank Steinar Andresen, Martin Beck, Andrew Bennett, Gary Goertz, Olav Schram Stokke, and Michael Zürn for helpful comments and discussion. Part of the research done for this paper was supported by a grant from the Deutsche Forschungsgemeinschaft.

2 To avoid unnecessary complication, we concentrate henceforth on directly proportional correlation hypotheses, leaving aside the inversely proportional (the more A, the less B) variant. David Dessler (1992: 3, n. 4) describes correlational hypotheses as "generalizations that relate the variation in some outcome across a population of cases to variation in some independent variable."

3 This terminology is not entirely satisfactory for at least two reasons. First, some authors use "conditional hypothesis" (or "generalization") to refer to relationships that are hypothesized to hold only under certain circumstances. Conditional (or contingent) hypotheses in this sense take the form: if C then H, where "C" denotes a certain set of circumstances and "H" stands for "if A, then B" or some other type of hypothesis. Second and more important, it can be shown that, in the final analysis, correlational hypotheses (as presumably all law-like generalizations [Nagel 1961: 47f]) are if-then statements no less than conditional (i.e., necessary or sufficient condition) hypotheses. For example, the logical structure of ordinal-scale level correlational hypotheses (assuming direct proportionality) may be analyzed as follows: $(x)\ (y)\ ([A(x) < A(y)] \rightarrow [B(x) < B(y)])$, which is another way of saying: for any x and for any y (where x and y are non-identical units belonging to the range of application of the hypothesis), if x takes a smaller value on the variable A than y, then it also takes a smaller value on the variable B. Hence, by "conditional hypotheses" we mean simple if-then statements (if A then B) that allow for no further analysis along such lines. Conditional hypotheses are also referred to as "covering law hypotheses" (Dessler 1992: 1, 3 – 5, Dray 1957: ch. 1; Nagel 1961: 570).

4 Conditional hypotheses should be distinguished from "general factor-claims" (Mill 1988 [1848]). General factor-claims refer to causal tendencies that operate without exception, although, in particular cases, they may be outweighed by other tendencies. For example, justice may invariably work in favor of regime robustness, even though the outcome "high robustness" will sometimes (or even often) not be observable in just regimes owing to the presence of countervailing factors (such as a low degree of institutional success or an inhospitable distribution of power among regime members). By contrast, conditional

hypotheses refer to outcomes rather than unobservable tendencies, for which only indirect evidence can be mustered (Dessler 1992: 6 – 8).

5 The interdependence is not perfect, since there are hypotheses that can be used for explaining but not for predicting (e.g., evolutionary theory). Moreover, prediction but not explanation can rely on non-causal hypotheses, that is propositions simply stating a constant conjunction of certain event-types (e.g., the regular relationship between barometer readings and changes in the weather).

6 For good accounts of the main features of this model, as well as some of the criticisms it has attracted, see, e.g., Haussmann (1991: ch. 1.2.) and Little (1991: 5f).

7 This is, of course, on the assumption that this characterization of the distributional dimension of the regime is accurate and that the particular form of inequality to be found in this regime is indeed unjust. Moreover, the explanation is only satisfactory if the relationship that is specified by the hypothesis is a causal one. That this is the case is most convincingly demonstrated by identifying, and producing evidence of, the causal mechanism that links injustice with low levels of robustness (Little 1991: 24f).

8 F has positive statistical relevance for G if and only if the conditional probability of G given F is greater than the absolute probability of G, formally: $p(G \mid F) > p(G)$."

9 This can be demonstrated as follows: In any population in which "B only if A" is true there are no units which are both B and non-A. Nothing else follows from this statement with respect to the distribution of A and B. So suppose that there are a units which are both A and B, b units which are A and non-B and c units which are non-A and non-B (where a, b, c are natural numbers). In this general population, $p(B) = a/(a+b+c)$ and $p(B \mid A) = a/(a+b)$. Since for any a, b, c: $a/(a+b+c) < a/(a+b)$, it follows that $p(B \mid A) > p(B)$. (Note that if A were not a true condition with respect to this population and hence $c = 0$ it would follow that $p(B \mid A) = p(B)$.)

10 If we have doubts about this explanation, it is not because the statistical generalization that it involves does not meet the high-probability criterion, but rather because we suspect that this might be an instance of "collateral causation," in which two seemingly causally related phenomena are in reality effects of a common cause (Little 1991: 21). Accordingly, Salmon (1984: 22) emphasizes that a complete explanation of a particular fact cannot rely on some set of statistical relevance relations alone, but must include an explanation of these relations "in terms of causal relations."

11 Popper's critics claim that he virtually makes no difference between an untested and a highly corroborated hypothesis (King, Keohane, and Verba 1994: 100 – 103, Van Evera 1997: 43). But this does not well accord with the fact that Popper (1968: para. 82) makes the effort to develop a "positive theory of corroboration." Without this distinction, theoretical knowledge could hardly aid in explaining and predicting events, and using theories for purposes of (social) engineering would be nothing short of irresponsible.

12 The falsificationist strategy as such can be understood as obeying a principle of efficiency. By directing the researcher to focus on potential falsifiers, it calls on him or her not to waste his or her time on experiments and observations that cannot decide the fate of the hypothesis.

13 For convenience, we use the word "falsifier" both to refer to the singular statements that are inconsistent with the hypothesis under consideration and to characterize the objects (here, regimes) these statements describe.

14 Obviously, this case selection strategy does not conform to the methodological rule that cases must not be chosen on the basis of a particular value of the dependent variable (King, Keohane, and Verba 1994: 129 – 132). This rule, however, does not apply when a deterministic conditional hypothesis such as the justice hypothesis is tested, where one

looks for falsifying observations rather than associations between variables (see also Collier 1995: 464 and Dion 1998: 128).

15 At the saturation point of a sequence of tests, further tests will add little to the degree of corroboration (which is mainly a function of the hardness and less so of the number of tests) because the hypothesis has survived virtually every conceivable hard test (cf. Popper 1968: para. 82). At this point the hypothesis may be provisionally accepted as true.

16 If we resort to this "contextualization strategy" (Efinger, Mayer, and Schwarzer 1993, Hasenclever, Mayer, and Rittberger 2000), we should not only continue to try to falsify the now contingent hypothesis. We should also think about why and how, in high-politics regimes (and only there), the causal mechanism connecting a low degree of justice to a low degree of robustness may sometimes be prevented from operating. For example, one might argue that only when the stakes are very high, are powerful actors prepared to use their might to impose and to enforce agreements that maximize their gains at the expense of the legitimate interests of weaker actors.

17 We use the terms "robustness" and "resilience" (or "staying power") interchangeably.

18 It might appear as though we attach too much importance to normative continuity, thus playing robustness off against flexibility, when in fact a measure of flexibility may well be a precondition for robustness. However, in our operationalization of robustness the possibility of learning and adaptation is taken into account by allowing changes within the regime to take place without implying a lack of robustness. Note also that the situations we describe as exogenous shocks create incentives for individual actors to reduce their commitment to the regime. That is, we are not referring to the kind of exogenous shocks that have been discussed in the literature on international environmental cooperation. Shocks of the latter kind (for example, the discovery of the ozone hole) enhance the prospects of cooperation by bringing home to the actors the need to "act" (Young and Osherenko 1993: 234f). While this kind of exogenous shock may well prompt states to consider changes of the present regime as a means of improving (rather than reducing) their cooperation, this is much less likely in the case of the first kind of shock, which is more prone to induce regressive changes of the regime (resulting in lower levels of cooperation) or mere adaptations to a new distribution of power among regime members.

19 The latter stipulation is particularly appropriate in the case that the justice hypothesis is reinterpreted as a general factor claim according to which (imposed or unnoticed) injustice undermines cooperation. If this hypothesis is true, many unjust regimes may not last long enough to experience a serious exogenous challenge. As a consequence, an evaluation of the factor claim would be biased against the hypothesis if these regimes were excluded from the universe of cases.

20 According to institutionalists, many if not all regimes assume a "life of their own" providing them with a measure of independence from the factors that help explain their creation. This proposition is not inconsistent with our definition of shocks, though. After all, robustness is mainly about having acquired such a degree of independence.

21 Precluding a statistical, large-n test, this fact does have important methodological implications for the correlational variant of the justice hypothesis ("The more nearly just a regime, the more it is robust"). Attempts to evaluate this hypothesis empirically, therefore, have to rely on the comparative method (Hasenclever, Mayer, and Rittberger 1996, 1998).

22 Distributive justice is only one of a family of moral ideas that come under the concept of justice. Others include commutative (exchange) justice, procedural justice, and justice as an individual virtue (e.g., Albin 1993, Bull 1977: 75 – 82). Throughout this chapter, when we talk of justice without further qualification, we mean distributive justice.

23 Strictly speaking, this is only true of moral philosophers who, in Michael Walzer's (1987) terminology, proceed by way of either "discovering" or "inventing" moral truths. The third group of philosophers, whom Walzer calls "interpreters" and sides with himself, are internalists who regard ethics as an intellectual activity that essentially takes place within a moral tradition.
24 According to Albin (1993: 229 – 234), the operation of justice principles as focal points is characteristic of distributive negotiations, whereas "negotiated justice" is the hallmark of integrative bargaining. Note that even in the first case the standard of justice is not external. Only those distributive principles can coordinate expectations that are accepted as fair by the actors themselves.
25 Most of the formulas Zartman and his collaborators mention seem to be compatible with the idea of reciprocity. These formulas either correspond to the parity principle or represent a form of compound justice where different proportionality principles are traded so as to achieve a kind of second-order parity (Zartman et al. 1996: 93).
26 Decision-making procedures are irrelevant here, as their immediate implications are for procedural rather than distributive justice.
27 A similar approach to international justice is taken by David Welch (1993), except that he does not distinguish between general and specific provisions in regimes. This is because his interest is different from ours: He is looking for internal criteria for just and unjust behavior or legitimate and illegitimate entitlement claims rather than for just and unjust orders or regimes, and it is in regimes that he finds these criteria.
28 These are the five states that possessed nuclear weapons when the NPT was concluded: the United States, the Soviet Union/Russia, China, Great Britain, and France. Recently, India and Pakistan have unsuccessfully attempted to gain recognition as (official) NWS. This would necessitate a modification of the NPT because of Article IX.3, which defines NWS as those states that have manufactured and exploded a nuclear device before 1 January 1967.
29 Just as we prepare this chapter for publication (October 2002), the NPR faces a renewed challenge from North Korea, which has admitted conducting a secret program to produce nuclear bomb–making material. At present, it is unclear how this instance of "nuclear cheating" in one of the most dangerous regions of the world will affect the regime and its overall effectiveness. The more pessimist scenarios include one in which North Korea develops a nuclear capability; which then prompts Japan and South Korea to follow suit. Other possible outcomes of this crisis are much more favorable to the regime, however. The very fact that North Korea has not denied the program is taken by some observers to indicate its willingness to trade the nuclear option for more economic support and improved relations with its neighbors and the U.S.—suggesting the possibility of a (perhaps tacitly or indirectly negotiated) cooperative solution similar to the one that ended the 1994 crisis.
30 Several of the abstract "types of exogenous shock" we have distinguished in section 3.1 seem to apply in the case of the NPR. The most obvious one, of course, is the "emergence of new relevant actors."
31 Discrimination is not unjust because unequal treatment is unjust per se. Proportionality principles such as the need principle ("To each according to his or her needs") require differential treatment. But this distinction must be justified in terms of some value or goal that is accepted by the community in question. It is not part of the underlying bargain of the regime, however, that power is such a value or that the preservation of the international society as a highly stratisfied social system is one of the shared goals.

REFERENCES

Albin, C. (1993) The Role of Fairness in Negotiations, *Negotiation Journal* 9, 3: 223–44.
Braumoeller, B. F. and Goertz, G. (2000) The Methodology of Necessary Conditions, *American Journal of Political Science* 44, 4: 844–58.
Brown, M. E., Lynn-Jones, S., and Miller, S. E. (eds.) (1996) *Debating the Democratic Peace*, MIT Press, Cambridge, MA.
Bull, H. (1977) *The Anarchical Society: A Study of Order in World Politics*, Macmillan, Basingstoke.
Bull, H. (1984) *Justice in International Relations* (Hagey Lectures), University of Waterloo Press, Waterloo, Ontario.
Collier, D. (1995) Translating Quantitative Methods for Qualitative Researchers: The Case of Selection Bias, *American Political Science Review* 89, 2: 461–66.
Czempiel, E. (1981) *Internationale Politik: Ein Konfliktmodell*, Schöningh, Paderborn.
Czempiel, E. (1986) *Friedensstrategien: Systemwandel durch Internationale Organisationen, Demokratisierung und Wirtschaft*, Schöningh, Paderborn.
Dessler, D. (1992) The Architecture of Causal Analysis, paper presented to the Center for International Affairs, Harvard University (unpub. ms.).
Deutsch, M. (1975) Equity, Equality, and Need: What Determines Which Value Will Be Used as the Basis of Distributive Justice? *Journal of Social Issues* 31, 3: 137–50.
Dion, D. (1998) Evidence and Inference in the Comparative Case Study, *Comparative Politics* 30, 2: 127–45.
Dray, W. H. (1957) *Laws and Explanation in History*, Clarendon Press, Oxford.
Efinger, M., Mayer, P. and Schwarzer, G. (1993) Integrating and Contextualizing Hypotheses: Alternative Paths to Better Explanations of Regime Formation?, in V. Rittberger, (ed.) *Regime Theory and International Relations,* Clarendon Press, Oxford, 252–82.
Elster, J. (1995) The Empirical Study of Justice, in D. Miller, and M. Walzer, (eds.) *Pluralism, Justice and Equality*, Oxford University Press, 81–98.
Frank, K., and Schaper, A. (1999) Das Nichtverbreitungsregime in der Krise? Massenvernichtungswaffen in Indien, Pakistan, Nordkorea und Irak, *Friedensgutachten* 1999, LIT, Münster, 228–37.
Hart, H. L. A. (1961) The Concept of Law, Oxford: Clarendon Press, Oxford.
Hasenclever, A., Mayer, P. and Rittberger, V. (1996) *Justice, Equality, and the Robustness of International Regimes: A Research Design* (Tübinger Arbeitspapiere zur internationalen Politik und Friedensforschung 25), Tübingen. [http://www.uni-tuebingen.de/uni/spi/taps/tap25.htm]
Hasenclever, A., Mayer, P. and Rittberger, V. (1997) *Theories of International Regimes*, Cambridge University Press.
Hasenclever, A., Mayer, P. and Rittberger, V. (1998) *Fair Burden-Sharing and the Robustness of International Regimes: The Case of Food Aid* (Tübinger Arbeitspapiere zur internationalen Politik und Friedensforschung 31), Tübingen. [http://www.uni-tuebingen.de/uni/spi/taps/tap31.htm]
Hasenclever, A., Mayer, P. and Rittberger, V. (2000) Integrating Theories of International Regimes, *Review of International Studies* 26, 1: 3–33.
Haussmann, T. (1991) *Erklären und Verstehen: Zur Theorie und Pragmatik der Geschichtswissenschaft*, Suhrkamp, Frankfurt.
Hegtvedt, K. A. (1992) When Is a Distribution Rule Just? *Rationality and Society* 4, 3: 308–31.

Hempel, C. (1965) *Aspects of Scientific Explanation and Other Essays in the Philosophy of Science,* Free Press, New York.
Hoffmann, S. (1981) *Duties Beyond Borders: On the Limits and Possibilities of Ethical International Politics,* Syracuse University Press.
Hurrell, A. (1993) International Society and the Study of Regimes, in V. Rittberger, (ed.) *Regime Theory and International Relations,* Clarendon Press, Oxford, 49–72.
Keohane, R. O. (1989) Neoliberal Institutionalism: A Perspective on World Politics, *International Institutions and State Power: Essays in International Relations Theory.* Westview Press, Boulder, 1–20.
King, G., Keohane, R. O. and Verba, S. (1994) *Designing Social Inquiry: Scientific Inference in Qualitative Research,* Princeton University Press.
Krasner, S. D. (1983) Structural Causes and Regime Consequences: Regimes as Intervening Variables, in S. D. Krasner (ed.) *International Regimes,* Cornell University Press, New York, 1–21.
Little, D. (1991) Varieties of Social Explanation: An Introduction to the Philosophy of Social Science, Westview Press, Boulder.
Mill, J. S. (1988) [1848] *A System of Logic,* Duckworth, London.
Müller, H. (1989) Regimeanalyse und Sicherheitspolitik: Das Beispiel Nonproliferation, in B. Kohler-Koch (ed.) *Regime in den internationalen Beziehungen,* Nomos, Baden-Baden, 277–313.
Müller, H. (1993) *Die Chance der Kooperation: Regime in den internationalen Beziehungen,* Wissenschaftliche Buchgesellschaft, Darmstadt.
Nagel, E. (1961) *The Structure of Science: Problems in the Logic of Scientific Explanation,* Harcourt, Brace & World, New York.
Nye, J. S., Jr. (1987) Nuclear Learning and U.S.-Soviet Security Regimes, *International Organization* 41, 3: 371–402.
Opp, K. (1995) *Methodologie der Sozialwissenschaften: Einführung in Probleme ihrer Theoriebildung und praktischen Anwendung,* 3rd ed., Westdeutscher Verlag, Opladen.
Parker, C. (1998) *Security Regime Significance in the Post Cold War Context: The Case of the Nuclear Non-Proliferation Regime,* The Swedish Institute of International Affairs, Stockholm.
Perelman, C. (1990) De la Justice, in: *Oeuvres III: Ethique et Droit.* Bruxelles: Editions de l'Université de Bruxelles, 13–86.
Popper, K. R. (1968) *The Logic of Scientific Discovery,* Harper & Row, New York.
Quine, W. V. O. (1982) *Methods of Logic,* 4th ed., Harvard University Press, Cambridge MA.
Rawls, J. (1971) *A Theory of Justice,* Harvard University Press, Cambridge MA.
Rawls, J. (1993) *Political Liberalism,* Columbia University Press, New York.
Ruggie, J. G. (1992) Multilateralism: The Anatomy of an Institution, *International Organization* 46, 3: 561–98.
Salmon, W. C. (1984) *Scientific Explanation and the Causal Structure of the World,* Princeton University Press, Princeton.
Schelling, T. C. (1960) *The Strategy of Conflict,* Harvard University Press, Cambridge.
Schimmelfennig, F. (1994) Arms Control Regimes and the Dissolution of the Soviet Union: Realism, Institutionalism and Regime Robustness, *Cooperation and Conflict* 29, 2, 115–48.
Smith, R. K. (1987) Explaining the Non-Proliferation Regime: Anomalies for Contemporary International Relations Theory, *International Organization* 41, 2: 253–82.

Stein, A. A. (1983) Coordination and Collaboration: Regimes in an Anarchic World, in S. D. Krasner (ed.) *International Regimes*, Cornell University Press, Ithaca, New York, 115–140.

Suppes, P. (1970) *A Probabilistic Theory of Causality*, North-Holland, Amsterdam.

Van Evera, S. (1997) *Guide to Methods for Students of Political Science*, Cornell University Press, Ithaca, New York.

Walzer, M. (1987) *Interpretation and Social Criticism*, Harvard University Press, Cambridge, MA.

Welch, D. A. (1993) *Justice and the Genesis of War*, Cambridge University Press.

Young, H. P. (1994) *Equity in Theory and Practice*, Princeton University Press.

Young, O. R. (1989) The Politics of International Regime Formation: Managing Natural Resources and the Environment, *International Organization* 43, 3: 349–76.

Young, O. R. (1991) Political Leadership and Regime Formation: On the Development of Institutions in International Society, *International Organization* 45, 3: 281–308.

Young, O. R. (1994) *International Governance: Protecting the Environment in a Stateless Society*, Cornell University Press, Ithaca, New York.

Young, O. R. and Osherenko, G. (1993) Testing Theories of Regime Formation: Findings from a Large Collaborative Research Project, in V. Rittberger (ed.) *Regime Theory and International Relations*, Clarendon Press, Oxford, 223–50.

Zartman, I. W. (1995) The Role of Justice in Global Security Negotiations, *American Behavioral Scientist* 38, 6: 889–903.

Zartman, I. W., D. Druckman, Jensen, L., Pruitt, D. G. and Young, H. P. (1996) Negotiation as a Search for Justice, *International Negotiation* 1, 1: 79–98.

Zürn, M. (1987) *Gerechte internationale Regime: Bedingungen und Restriktionen der Entstehung nicht-hegemonialer internationaler Regime untersucht am Beispiel der Weltkommunikationsordnung*, Haag + Herchen, Frankfurt.

Zürn, M. (1992) *Interessen und Institutionen in der internationalen Politik: Grundlegung und Anwendung des situationsstrukturellen Ansatzes*, Leske + Budrich, Opladen.

PART II

BROADER CONSEQUENCES

Chapter 9

METHODOLOGICAL ISSUES IN THE STUDY OF BROADER CONSEQUENCES

THOMAS GEHRING
University of Bamberg

1. INTRODUCTION

The study of the broader effects of international regimes is just beginning. For a long time, regime analysts operated with a two-fold fiction, namely that a regime could be established largely in isolation from other regimes and that its consequences were concentrated to its own domain. In the real world, the international system is increasingly densely populated by international governing institutions. A study elaborated for the Rio Summit of 1992 counted more than 125 important multilateral environmental regimes alone, most of which were institutionalized separately from each other (Sand 1992). Every year, states conclude about five new important environmental agreements (Beisheim et al. 1999: 350 – 51). Against the backdrop of this trend and the sheer number of independently established international regimes, it is difficult to image that interaction among regimes is an irrelevant phenomenon.

Moreover, regime analysts have long established that the effects of international regimes are frequently not limited to adaptations of behavior. Quite often, institutions influence the preferences of relevant actors (Oberthür 1997). It is difficult to believe that these secondary consequences are always entirely limited to a regime's own domain (Levy et al. 1995: 308 – 12). It may well be that an international regime affects the structure of a domestic political system. In addition, modern international regimes include, beyond a set of substantive norms regulating collectively desired behavior, collective decision-making systems (Young 1999a: 24 – 49.) Their proliferation may empower non-state actors or otherwise have an impact on interaction within the international system far beyond the issue-areas regulated by the particular regimes (Princen and Finger 1994).

The study of the broader consequences sets out to question, and replace where necessary, the fiction both of the isolated operation of international regimes and of the limitation of their effects to their own issue-area. Broader consequences research focuses on regime effects that occur beyond a given regime and the issue area governed by it. It is an attempt to expand the study of regime effectiveness to those effects that have been ignored so far. Thus, it deals with an object of inquiry that is located at the margin of classical regime analysis. Moreover, this object is negatively defined. The new field of regime analysis constitutes first and foremost a residual category that collects numerous different side effects and externalities of regime governance.

Having been ignored by classical regime analysis does not imply that the broader effects of international regimes have altogether escaped the attention of international relations scholars. There are several strands of literature on which the study of broader consequences may draw. Within the literature on transnational relations, attention has been drawn to the importance of non-state actors for the establishment and development of international regimes. This is true for environmental nongovernmental organizations (NGOs) (Princen 1994; Clark 1994); human rights NGOs (Price 1998); "epistemic communities" (Haas 1990); or "advocacy networks" (Keck and Sikking 1998). Although is has been observed that transnational actors of this type regularly emerge in the context of international regimes (Risse-Kappen 1995: 28 – 32), the emphasis of systematic inquiry has been on the influence of non-state actors on regime decision making, rather than on the effects of regime establishment on the emergence and development of these actors. Likewise, International Relations has a long tradition in analyzing the impact of the international system on domestic society. This "second image reversed" research (Gourevich 1978) currently explores, for example, the effects of "internationalization" or "globalization" on domestic society (Garrett 1998; Scharpf 1999) and on domestic political systems. Whereas internationalization and globalization are not least consequences of the effectiveness of international institutions, especially of the world trade system (GATT/WTO) (Milner and Keohane 1996: 22 – 24), authors of this strand of literature usually do not distinguish between the broader consequences of one or more international regimes and other sources of internationalization and globalization.

This is also true for the intensive discussion on the changing nature of state sovereignty (Litfin 1997) and the transformation of the originally "Westphalian" nation-state into some "post-Westphalian" entity (Caporaso 1996). However, if this debate is moved into the context of European

METHODOLOGICAL ISSUES OF BROADER CONSEQUENCES 221

integration, it is immediately related to the influence of the European Union, that is an (admittedly quite specific) institution for governance beyond the nation-state. Within the integration literature, it is hotly debated whether the European Union strengthens the state vis-à-vis domestic society (Moravcsik 1994; Grande 1996), or whether it undermines its ability to control internal and external affairs by providing non-state actors with additional opportunities for action (Marks et al. 1996; Stone Sweet and Sandholtz 1997). Similar effects on domestic political systems are also produced by international regimes, albeit at a lower scale (Wolf 1999). The study of the broader regime consequences may thus draw on several existing literatures that address related issues. It promises to contribute to these literatures by adding a particular regime perspective. In remarkable contrast, research on the interaction of international regimes that co-exist within the international system is largely absent.

This chapter addresses a number of methodological issues concerning the study of broader consequences. In the light of the residual nature as well as the novelty of the object of inquiry, it will be difficult, and cannot be the purpose of the present paper, to identify a common methodology or analytical approach that is suited to cover the study of all broader consequences alike. The goal will be more modest. This chapter shall systematize different sub-fields of the study of broader consequences and identify research strategies. Section 2 starts with the brief outline of a conceptual framework for the identification of broader consequences that takes process components duly into account. Section 3 then discusses promising dependent and independent variables in an attempt to systematize the heterogeneous field of study. In its final part, section 4 addresses a number of methodological problems of some priority fields of broader consequences research.

The chapter concludes that the study of the broader consequences of international regimes opens a multifaceted and fascinating new field of research on the effects of international governing institutions.

2. A CONCEPTUAL FRAMEWORK FOR THE STUDY OF BROADER CONSEQUENCES

It has become almost usual in the context of research on the simple effectiveness of international regimes to consider a regime as an instrument established by interested actors to bring about change. In this perspective, a regime consists of a set of norms that define the obligations of member states (see also the "consensus definition", Krasner 1982: 186). "Effects" are then conceptualized as changes in behavior of relevant actors caused by these norms (outcomes) as well as changes in the target of regime-assisted cooperation, for example in trade flows or the quality of the waters of a regional sea (impact). The assessment of simple effectiveness can afford to rely on this simplified model of international regimes (Underdal 1992) unless it inquires into how and why the institution produces these consequences (Young 1999b; Hovi in this volume). In contrast, broader consequences are not always immediately apparent. Frequently they constitute unintended, even unanticipated, effects of intentional action (Martin and Simons 1998) that occur, by definition, beyond the issue areas expressly addressed by relevant regimes. Before we can start to assess and measure them, we will have to identify areas of possible effects. Therefore, the study of broader consequences will need a more complex conception of the operation of an international regime that allows us to identify pathways of their generation.

While cooperation does not necessarily require communication (Axelrod 1984), analysts widely agree to limit regime analysis to international institutions that emerge from negotiations (Keohane 1993; Levy et al. 1995). Only institutions of this type may be used instrumentally to bring about collectively desired change within the international system. What distinguishes them from other types of institution is the *communication* from which norms and behavioral guidelines emerge. The establishment of an international regime enables actors to act (outside its confines) and simultaneously communicate about norms (within these confines), rather than merely communicate by action (Kratochwil and Ruggie 1986). Actors may pollute a regional sea and simultaneously negotiate an arrangement for its collective clean-up. Whereas the role of communication had been largely ignored as long as regime analysis was predominantly based on non-cooperative game theory, negotiations and collective decision making have recently gained a considerably higher priority both theoretically (Young 1989, 1994; Morrow 1994; Fearon 1998) and within the effectiveness debate (Victor et al. 1998). In a process-oriented perspective, international regimes are best understood as decision making systems beyond the nation-state that shape the expectations of relevant actors. They are more or less dynamic (Gehring 1994) and evolve over time as collective decisions are made and practices of governance change.

Whereas non-communicative evolution of cooperation is characterized by its inherent strict limits, negotiations about a cooperative arrangement do not have inherent limits. Significant participation in a trade war requires resources, while communication about trade preferences does (almost) not. Small states and even non-state actors may perfectly well participate in these negotiations. Likewise, there are no inherent limits to the deliberate linkage of issues. Therefore, negotiation situations tend to become over-complex

(Scharpf 1991: 278). All actors interested in cooperation have a common interest in the limitation of a negotiation situation, although they may have differing ideas about the precise nature of the limitation. They are caught in a battle of the sexes – type coordination problem that must be settled in occasionally tough pre-negotiations (Gross Stein 1989) before actual negotiations may start.

If successful, negotiations produce a borderline between actors that are entitled to participate and those that are not, as well as between subjects that are discussed and others that are not. This borderline has no immediate corollary in the outside world and it could have been drawn differently. It does not have any immediate relevance for action beyond the negotiation forum, but it matters for the process of norm-molding by communication. Communicative interventions by some actors are now more relevant than those by others. Demands and proposals on some issues are more easily accommodated within an emerging agreement than others. The borderline determines the constellation of interests within the negotiations (Sebenius 1983, 1991). It matters, for example, whether a cooperation process starts with a limited membership and expands progressively, like the Schengen and ozone layer regimes, or whether it comprises a huge membership from the outset, like the law of the sea and the climate change regimes (Downs et al. 1998). Hence, although it is socially constructed, the borderline does not at all constitute mere fiction. It is a "social fact" (Searle 1995) that influences the output of a negotiation process. Accordingly, in studying broader consequences, we should not bother too much with the fact that the borders of and between regimes could have been drawn differently, nor that they may be changed over time. What matters is that they exist and that they are relevant for collective decision making and norm-molding as long as they exist.

A process-oriented perspective on international regimes and the relevance of institutionally established boundaries suggests that we conceptualize an international regime as a social system that processes information (Gehring 2002). Like all systems, it is constituted along the distinction between the system and its own environment (Luhmann 1984; Willke 1996). The system includes the regime-specific communication process and its own (i.e., regime-specific) criteria for the selection of relevant information as well as its own rules for transforming information into valid norms and other forms of institutional output, such as collectively validated knowledge. Whether scientific information matters for collective decision making depends on how the collective decision process is organized. The system operates entirely according to its own rules, that is, it is operationally closed. Yet, it depends on the *input* of information from its environment, for example through negotiations of the actors involved. If they interact in the form of bargaining, the system is sensitive exclusively to information about state interests. If they also argue (Elster 1994; Gehring 1996; Risse 2000) and feed into the process convincing knowledge, and if this information gains influence on the collective decision process, the system will "observe" other aspects of its environment. The system also produces an *output*. It releases signals into its environment that are relevant to outside actors, for example a cooperative arrangement, a decision on the noncompliance of a member state, or a report on scientific findings. Hence, despite the operative closure of the system, there is a steady exchange of signals across the system/environment boundary.

On this basis we may now distinguish between two different types of consequence of regime governance.

First, the output of a regime may change the environment of addressees. Upon adoption of a cooperative arrangement or an important decision, it releases a signal into its environment. Although the signal is hardly more than the selection of a collectively agreed solution, it may induce a member state to adapt its behavior, if (and only if) it is accompanied by the expectation that other member states will adapt their behavior accordingly, thus promising to bring about cooperation. It may also induce other actors to react. Firms and other economic actors expecting government action or reactions by relevant other economic actors may be motivated to adapt "voluntarily". Political parties and associations may consider a regime decision sufficiently relevant for them to adjust their political action. They may, for example, launch a campaign for, or against, ratification or compliance.

Second, despite its importance for the success of regime governance, output is not the only way in which an international regime may change the environment of other social systems. A second way of considerable importance for the study of broader consequences is related to the input side. The particular way in which an international regime observes its environment determines opportunities for action of different actors within the communication process. Opportunities for action may be limited to states. However, they may extend to non-state actors in control of relevant information if, for example, the scientific or technological foundations of collective action (Haas 1992) or information about implementation gain importance within the institutionalized decision process (Raustiala 1997). Increased sensitivity of a regime toward different aspects of its environment may, therefore, increase the opportunities for action of previously "weak" actors, for example small, relatively powerless, states and non-state actors, within the decision process. Changes of the regime-specific decision process may induce interested actors, for example environmental NGOs or networks of scientists, to develop transnational activities. They may also encourage interested individuals or domestically operating groups to form corporate actors capable of exploiting these transnational opportunities (Risse-Kappen 1995).

To sum up, the interaction-based conception of international regimes as social systems designed to mould norms by communication within a world of other social systems and individuals gives some hints as to where to look for broader effects. Regimes may generate broader (as well as simple) consequences by changing the environment through their generalized expectations, or sets of norms. Effects may also be brought about by the provision of opportunities for communicative action within the process of norm-molding.

3. KEY AREAS OF BROADER CONSEQUENCES RESEARCH

As *consequences* of international regimes necessarily imply causation, studies the broader consequences of international regimes must clarify the variables in the relationships that they intend to study. In this section, I identify some major lines of (actual or possible) inquiry.[1] It should be emphasized that identifying key independent and dependent variables does not exclude the possibility of feedback loops or co-evolution processes in which the direction in the relationship between variables changes. The identification of dependent and independent variables is primarily a heuristic device to structure the extended field of research on broader consequences and a necessary analytic device to explore regime consequences.

Within the context of regime effectiveness, we wish to study the broader consequences of international regimes on some target. This is what distinguishes the regime perspective from other studies focusing, for example, on changes within the international system or domestic effects of international drivers. Accordingly, the independent variable must be related to at least one international regime. However, international regimes may have broader consequences for virtually all sorts of targets. Hence, we may explore effects on an almost unlimited variety of dependent variables. Based on current strands of analysis and existing literature, the following four main areas of research may be identified.

Other Issue Area(s). An international regime may have an impact on one or more issue-areas beyond its own domain. The evaluation of the simple effectiveness of an international regime focuses eventually on its impact on the target problem. If governance is effective, the climate change regime must have an observable impact on the state of the global climate. Currently, the assessment of the effectiveness of an international regime is largely limited to the issue area governed (simple effectiveness). If we intend to estimate the net social benefit of an international regime, we will also have to assess the externalities caused by a given regime beyond its own domain, for example, the effects of the climate change regime on the state of the ozone layer and on air pollution, on agriculture and forestry, and on the economic performance of the global economy or of national economies.

The study of externalities in this understanding, which is hardly beginning to emerge, may appear in one of two alternative designs. First, one may want to explore as far as possible all externalities created by a given regime, or an important component of an existing regime, in order to assess the net social benefit of, say, the regime for the protection of the ozone layer. In this case, the independent variable provides the fixed starting point of research, while the dependent variable may have to be modified over time, as further externalities in additional issue areas become apparent, or anticipated ones prove to be nonexistent. Yet, one may also want to attribute an observed effect to a number of existing regimes. For example, the state of the environment of the North Sea is not merely affected by the relevant regional marine protection regime (OSPARCOM), but also by several global marine protection regimes controlling single sources of marine pollution, and by the LRTAP regime that affects the extend of acid deposition into the North Sea, as well as the regime for the protection of the River Rhine—let alone economic regimes such as GATT/WTO that influence the intensity of maritime transport (Breitmeier 2000: 46). In this type of "backward induction" a researcher attempts to identify suitable independent variables (regimes) that explain an observed aggregate effect (the state of marine pollution) (see Walter and Zürn in this volume). It is still a limited number of clearly identifiable regimes (i.e., a set) to which influence will be attributed. Strictly speaking, assessment of the contribution of the "main" regime governing the observed issue area, in the example OSPARCOM, would fall into the realm of simple effectiveness, while that of more marginal regimes, like LRTAP and the River Rhine regime, might constitute broader consequences. It appears that the distinction between simple effectiveness and broader consequences is not as sharp as may be assumed at first glance. It is only heuristically fruitful.

One may also want to inquire whether international regimes at large contribute to increasing, for example, the life expectancy of the population in given countries or even all over the world (see Hughes in this volume). Studies in this vein also employ a sort of "backward reasoning," starting with a readily observable dependent variable that is to be explained by suitable independent variables. Yet, in this case, the question is not whether, and to which extent, one or more identified regimes contribute to bringing about the observed effect. Rather, it is whether it may be demonstrated that *the universe of unspecified regimes* explains the observed change, or whether it must be attributed to some other explanatory variables not related to international regimes. In this case, the distinction between simple effectiveness and broader consequences diminishes completely.

International Regime(s). The dependent variable may also be one or more international regimes. In recent years, it has been observed that international regimes may influence each other. The most widely discussed case is the interaction between the Word Trade Organization (GATT/WTO) and several international environmental regimes that include trade restrictions, like the Basle Convention on the Transboundary Movement of Hazardous Wastes, the Convention on International Trade in Endangered Species (CITES), or the Montreal Protocol (see Petersmann 1993; Lang 1993; Moltke 1997). At closer inspection, issue areas of international regimes frequently "overlap" (Stokke 1999), especially in international environmental relations (United Nations University 1998, Oberthür 2001). Many subject areas are governed by several institutions with different memberships. Moreover, "regime density" (Young 1996) within the international system grows steadily and may even increase the prospect of interaction between regimes up to the point of eventual "treaty congestion" (Brown Weiss 1993: 679). This strand of research challenges the original fiction that an isolated regime may be established to deal with an isolated international problem. Broader consequences research sets out to replace it with the concept of a regime that is embedded within a population of other regimes.

It should be clear then, what a regime is. Some conceptualize regimes so as to comprise all social norms relevant for action within a given area of international relations, for example *the* human rights regime (Donnelly 1986) or *the* nonproliferation regime (Müller 1993). This overly broad conception involves an important analytical problem. It is based on the delimitation of the related issue area by the external observer. It does not take into account that the actors involved have actually chosen to deal with the subject matter in the form of a number of separate agreements emerging from distinct negotiation processes. Thus, it implicitly assumes that it does not matter how system boundaries are drawn and how collective decision making is organized. Practically, this approach would de-emphasize the relevance of interaction among these institutions. Others follow a very narrow regime concept and conceive of every protocol adopted within the regime on long-range transboundary air pollution (LRTAP) as an independent regime (Sprinz and Vaahtoranta 1994). Some regimes, like LRTAP, develop by a steadily increasing number of protocols, while others, such as the regime for the protection of the ozone layer, do so by successive amendments of an existing one. Yet, neither the London nor the Copenhagen revisions of the Montreal Protocol have been conceptualized as independent regimes so far. The above interaction-based concept suggests that international regimes are temporarily or permanently existing decision-making systems. A regime is then best identified by its system-specific communicative interaction process. Accordingly, the LRTAP regime as well as the regimes on the protection of the ozone layer and on global climate change are best considered as separate regimes, but not the protocols and amendments adopted within their framework. This conception allows us, for example, to distinguish between a global and a regional regime addressing the same substantive problem. Hence, we may examine interaction between the International Whaling Commission and the North Atlantic Marine Mammal Organization (NAMMCO) (Caron 1995), or between the Basle regime on hazardous wastes and the Bamako Convention of the African countries on the same subject (Meinke 1997, 2002).

"Ideally," an interaction situation involves two regimes and a single direction of influence. In this case we may easily identify a source regime (independent variable) and a target regime (dependent variable). Alternatively, the dependent variable and/or the independent variable may also be a component of a regime or a decision adopted within its framework. This will be the case, for example, if we explore the effect of the non-compliance procedure of the Montreal Protocol on the development of implementation control arrangements within the climate change regime or within LRTAP and its protocols. We may also take a limited set of identifiable regimes as either the independent or the dependent variable. For example, we may explore the consequences of a number of environmental regimes with trade restrictions for GATT/WTO. We may also inquire into the influence of the global London dumping convention on a number of regional seas conventions. More complex situations may have to be disaggregated to allow causal analysis (see section 4 and Gehring and Oberthür in this volume).

Hypothetically, we might also want to explore whether the existence of the whole population of international regimes has implications, for example, for the development of a new regime. Yet, this is a systemic research perspective. It asks whether the modern international system with its numerous international regimes and organizations has an impact on the establishment of a new institution. It falls entirely out of the existing literature on regime interaction. Therefore, it is better dealt with it in the context of systemic effects.

Beside the "regular" cases of regime interaction mentioned, there are two specific cases that need some elaboration. The present framework does not exclude the possibility that we can explore the consequences of an important decision or component that is part of a given regime for another decision or component of the same regime. The independent and the dependent variables are then chosen from within the same regime. It is exclusively a matter of definition whether we consider this case still to be covered by the study of broader consequences. Without incurring any *theoretical* problem, we may therefore expand the analytical framework to exploring, for instance, the consequences of the NO_X Protocol on the Second SO_2 Protocol within the framework of the LRTAP regime. In this vein, we might even expand research to the interaction between different instruments (e.g., directives) of the European Union. Of course, causal mechanisms and empirical effects will be influenced by the fact that these cases are embedded in a particular overarching institutional framework within which conflicts may be *collectively* recognized and communicatively settled. But these are empirical, not conceptual differences.

A second specific case that has not yet attracted much attention is the exploration of institutional reactions of a regime to its own broader consequences. For example, the world trade system does not only affect other international regimes (and vice versa). It proscribes discrimination between identical goods according to their modes of production (Stevens 1995; Hudec 1996; Farber and Hudec 1996; Howse 1998). This obligation constrains the member states' opportunities for action especially in the areas of environmental policy making and regulation of labor conditions. These unintended effects generate pressure that might force the institution to expand its regulatory activity in order to address the non-economic consequences of economic regulation (Schoenbaum 1992; Tarasovsky 1997; Esty and Geradin 1998; Charnovitz 1998). In cases like this, the independent and the dependent variables are identical, but the transmission of influence involves externalities that reach beyond the regime's domain. Once again, it is exclusively a matter of definition whether this path is dealt with under the heading of broader consequences.

It should be noted that research on regime interaction significantly overlaps with the exploration of regime externalities. Overlap will occur if the causal pathway by which a source regime influences a target regime involves the creation of externalities. For example, the ozone regime generates (malign) effects on the climate change regime because the promotion of hydrofluorocarbons contributes to destabilizing the global climate. Thus, it reduces the problem-solving capacity of the climate change regime. What distinguishes the two areas of inquiry, therefore, is primarily a diverging research interest. While externalities research is primarily interested in the *impact* of an international regime on issue areas beyond its own domain, whether it causes adaptations within any regime possibly governing the target issue area, the study of regime interaction emphasizes the interplay between social institutions, whether or not channeled through changes in impact of the issue-areas governed.

Domestic political system. The study of broader consequences may also inquire into the influence of international regimes on a domestic political system, or a part of it. Studies of this design adopt a "second image reversed'" perspective (Gourevich 1978) that has a long tradition within international relations research. What distinguishes research on the domestic consequences of international regimes from other "second image reversed" studies is their specific focus on the impact of institutions, rather than aggregate developments at the international level, as a source of influence. Research is still in its very beginnings and a wide range of possible dependent variables might be chosen according to the particular research interests.

It may be expected, however, that an important cluster of dependent variables will relate to the modification of power relations within constellations of actors (e.g., social groups, organized interest groups, state organs). Occasionally, a single regime as important as GATT/WTO may serve as the independent variable. Hence, if an international institution causes significantly increased trade flows, it may be expected to change power relations among interest groups within domestic political systems (Rogowski 1989; Milner 1988). More often, sets of related regimes may constitute the suitable independent variable to assess changes of domestic political systems. For example, the existence of human rights standards tends to empower interest groups claiming compliance over others that do not (Klotz 1995; Forschungsgruppe Menschenrechte 1998; Lutz and Sikking 2000). Or environmental institutions may effectively support particular branches of government (Haas 1990). In yet other cases, the universe of regimes constitutes the appropriate independent variable. It has been observed that both the European Union, which for these purposes may be understood as a particularly well advanced regime, and regular international regimes contribute to shifting power from parliaments to the executive branch of government (Moravcsik 1994; Wolf 1999; Breitmeier in this volume). While the isolated effect caused by any single regime will be insignificant, all regimes contribute to the observed effect in basically the same way and influence is channeled through virtually a single causal pathway.

Another possible research focus is the influence of international regimes on the political status of a domestic political system, or of domestic political systems at large, rather than on the power distribution within it. Hence, one may inquire into the level of democracy and human rights in political systems, or even attitudes of a population toward democracy and human rights, as witnessed by suitable indicators (Hughes in this volume). In this case, the independent variable will almost inevitably be the universe of (unidentified) regimes, rather than any set of precisely identifiable ones.

International system. Finally, international regimes may exert influence on the international system at large. Regimes may contribute to eroding state sovereignty (Litfin 1997). They might have reduced the level of conflict in East-West relations prior to the political turn in the Soviet Union (Rittberger 1990). The emergence and importance of non-state transnational actors, such as non-governmental organizations (Princen and Finger 1994, Price 1998) and "epistemic communities" of scientists (Haas 1992), is attributed to the proliferation of international regimes. Regimes may also foster the relevance of international law and the "juridification" of international relations (Keohane et al. 2000). Research on the broader consequences of international regimes therefore might well contribute to the study of overall change in the international system.

A significant change of international society only rarely will be caused by a single regime. Studies intending to identify measurable systemic effects will usually take a larger set, or even the whole universe of regimes as the independent variable. The aggregate effects of all relevant East-West regimes may have reduced the intensity of conflict between the two military blocs before 1990. Or the aggregate effects of all international regimes and organizations may have contributed to stabilizing peace.

However, occasionally a single regime may serve as the suitable independent variable. Once again, one may think of GATT/WTO as an extraordinarily important international regime that may have significantly empowered multinational corporations, which are a type of internationally operating non-state actors, vis-à-vis the states, which are the traditionally most important actors. A study also may take a single regime as its independent variable and explore a causal pathway by which the international system is affected. For example, Litfin (in this volume) argues that the regime on global climate change forces member states to take into account scientific knowledge when determining their action and in this way changes existing sovereignty patterns.

As we move along from the exploration of regime externalities and interaction to the assessment of regime consequences on domestic society and the international system, the complexity of the dependent variables increases significantly. In order to grasp broader consequences, the independent variables usually also will tend to be more highly aggregated. We may well explore the externalities generated by a single regime, or even by an important component of a regime, that are observable within one or a limited number of issue areas beyond its own domain. Likewise, research on regime interaction will frequently deal with a constellation in which a single regime influences a single target regime. It may also usefully address interaction at the level of components, for example if we study the broader effects on a target of the emissions trading system envisaged within the Kyo-

dep. V indep. V	other issue area(s)	(other) regime(s)	domestic political system	international system
part of regime one regime	externalities	regime interaction		
set of regimes			domestic consequences	systemic effects
universe of regimes				

Figure 9.1. *Priority areas of broader consequences research.*

to Protocol, rather than the effects of the entire climate change regime. In other cases, it will be sets of regimes whose externalities or interaction are explored, but these sets will still be composed of a comparatively small number of readily identifiable regimes. In contrast, we cannot expect to identify some highly aggregated domestic or systemic consequences at the level of the single regime, or even of a limited set of identifiable regimes. Surely, the effects produced by a single regime may be assumed to contribute in one way or another to the broader effect in question, but frequently they will be insignificant in isolation, and they are often difficult to disentangle from parallel effects caused by other regimes. Hence, broader consequences of these types will generally be driven by larger sets of regimes or even by the entire population of international regimes existing within the international system.

The main areas of current and presumably of future research on the broader consequences of international regimes are summarized in Figure 9.1. The rows identify the major independent variables, the columns the major dependent ones. Research on the impact of one or more international regimes beyond their own domains as well as research on the interaction of regimes tend to concentrate on comparatively limited sources of influence. Their main independent variable is a single regime, or a component thereof, or a limited set of readily identifiable regimes. In contrast, studies exploring regime consequences for domestic political systems and for the international system will tend to be based on an independent variable that comprises a larger set, or even the entire universe, of regimes.

4. METHODOLOGICAL PROBLEMS

The study of the broader consequences of international regimes does not seem to require a completely new methodology, or methods entirely unknown to the well-advanced analysis of simple effectiveness and regime analysis at large. Nevertheless, despite the wide array of differing research interests, each of which poses specific analytical problems, broader consequences research differs systematically from the study of simple effectiveness in a number of important respects.

First, the situations bringing about broader consequences are usually significantly more complex than those generating simple effects. While the exploration of simple effectiveness regularly addresses regime effects on a single issue area, the assessment of externalities will frequently deal with a number of different issue areas on which a given regime has an impact. Likewise, an interaction situation may involve a whole set of regimes influencing each other's institutional development and performance. Any assessment of the domestic consequences of international regimes or of their effects on the international system at large obviously must handle highly complex dependent variables. A higher level of complexity renders the isolation of clear-cut causal effects more difficult. Compared to the study of simple effectiveness, the exploration of broader consequences will therefore more often have to rely on the careful disaggregation of independent and dependent variables in order to isolate causal effects.

Second, the broader consequences of one or more international regimes will frequently be more remote than effects within their own domains. After all, international governance institutions are usually established in order to bring about particular effects within their own domains, while their broader consequences constitute more diffuse side effects possibly spread over a number of different targets. Moreover, these targets usually will be affected more directly by other drivers so that any analysis is prone with a possibly high number of intervening variables. The consequences of the ozone regime for the state of the ozone layer may be assumed to be easier to observe than its effects on other issue areas or affected target regimes, let alone its effects on domestic society or the international system, *because* it is a major cause of change within its own domain, while it will merely be one among numerous other drivers of change with respect to other targets. Hence, broader consequences research will have to invest more attention to the careful isolation of comparatively remote and diffuse effects.

Third, broader consequences will be generated by chains of causation that are on average longer than those bringing about simple effects. To be sure, this is not always the case. If intensified regulation beyond the nation-state gradually deprives domestic legislatives of power and thereby tacitly changes domestic political systems (Breitmeier in this volume), the causal pathway is short and readily observable. Yet, broader consequences do not only comprise first-order effects, they may well be caused by second- or higher order effects (e.g., an effect of the climate change regime on international trade that generates effects on air pollution). Externalities of this type are caused in a pathway that may involve a number of different issue areas. Likewise, changes of domestic political systems or even of the international system generated by international regimes are frequently channeled through comparatively long causal chains. The longer a causal chain, the more difficult it is to trace, because an observed outcome is affected by more intervening variables and may be attributed less clearly to the independent variable(s) chosen.

Fourth, a clearly identifiable and limited independent variable—be it a regime, or a component of a regime, or even a set of readily identifiable regimes—allows us to employ the qualitative methods most widely used in regime analysis. Methods for attributing changes of the dependent variable to the independent variable include the construction of counterfactual scenarios (Fearon 1991), the exclusion of alternative explanations (Bernauer 1995: 373; Bierstecker 1993) and, more generally, the search for causal pathways (Hovi in this volume). In contrast, some research on broader consequences deals with independent variables at a comparatively high level of aggregation. Studies of this type will frequently not allow concentration on single regimes and the particular causal pathways that are operative. Instead, they may have to resort to quantitative analysis.

These general problems appear in differing combinations and intensity in research addressing the four main areas of broader consequences research. In the remainder of this section, I will discuss the problems for each of these areas separately.

The evaluation of "externalities," that is of the impact of a regime, a regime component, or a set regimes beyond its own domain, is, like the dominant branch of effectiveness research, in the first regard related to the output side of international regimes. Generally, the evaluation of externalities may not seem to be entirely different from assessing the impact of a given regime within its own domain. Yet, at close inspection it turns out to be prone to two analytic problems. One relates to their empirical mapping of externalities and the other to their scoring into an integrated overall assessment of social benefits (Underdal et al. 2000: 17 – 18).

The problem of complexity of the analytic situation may be readily dealt with by its appropriate disaggregation. If an international regime causes side effects in, say, five other issue areas, these externalities may be assessed one after the other. What makes the assessment of a regime's externalities difficult is the fact that they will usually be less significant than the regime's impact within its own domain. Hence, mapping of externalities is hampered by the possible insignificance of regime-generated change compared to changes caused by other drivers. Moreover, it will be prone to second- or higher order effects that necessarily involve longer chains of causation. The general advice to deal with these problems is to concentrate on immediate rather than remote effects and to keep causal chains as short as possible. Research should start with the most significant and readily traceable externalities and gradually work toward a more comprehensive assessment.

The second analytical problem relates to the integration of the externalities of an international regime and its impact within its own domain into a comprehensive score. It is specific to a particular research design that intends to measure the effects of a social institution, but generates particular analytical difficulties for broader consequences research. The first step will be to distinguish between positive and negative externalities. This is comparatively simple for externalities that occur within the issue areas of other international regimes. In these cases, we know what the regime members collectively (although not necessarily all of them individually) consider as benign or malign. If the climate change regime has a degrading impact on tropical forests, and if regime members intend to protect tropical forests within the biodiversity regime, it will be safe to treat the observed effect as a negative externality. But what if it led to changes in agriculture, such as the replacement the production of rice by grain or the restructurement of farm sizes? Without a yardstick that is collectively agreed upon by the actors concerned, appraisal of the direction of side effects will be difficult. Hence, it may be fruitful to relate the exploration of impact externalities as far as possible to the analysis of interaction between regimes. The other, even thornier issue is the attribution of values to different externalities and a regime's impact within its own domain. It is the question of how much protection of the global climate justifies the degradation of a square mile of tropical forest.

The analysis of regime interaction is heavily process oriented. Interaction may occur through rather different causal pathways, including ones that involve the creation of externalities beyond the domain of a given regime. However, the emphasis is put on the interference of a process of governance by another process of governance. Therefore, interaction always includes an input dimension. The central problem for the analysis of regime interaction is the fact that interaction situations are frequently complex (Gehring and Oberthür in this volume). More often than not influence is not well directed and asymmetrical. It may run back and forth between the regimes involved (Young 1996). For example, the global London dumping convention and the regional Oslo dumping convention co-developed for almost thirty years and may be expected to have exerted multifaceted influence on each other. Other situations include a whole set of regimes that affect each other in different—and usually unknown—ways. In these cases, the regimes involved constitute the dependent and the independent variable at the same time. This constellation precludes any serious causal analysis (see Carlsnaes 1992). Even a situation limited to two regimes will be too complex for causal analysis, if the institutions affect each other reciprocally or if influence is channeled through more than one causal pathway. Therefore, many studies exploring complicated regime interaction situations do not reach far beyond description and are not able to respond to the core question of this strand of research: under which conditions and transmitted by which causal mechanisms do international regimes interact, rather than merely co-exist ?

To allow causal analysis, the variables must not be too highly aggregated. A complex interaction situation may always be disaggregated into a number of cases of interaction that include not more than two regimes and have a clear direction of influence running from the target regime toward the source regime. Accordingly, a set of regimes should be disaggregated into a number of bilateral relations. For example, if we explore the consequences of one source regime on a whole set of target regimes, it will almost always be better to disaggregate the multi-regime interaction into a number of bilateral ones (see Gehring and Oberthür in this volume). We may investigate the influence of the Basle hazardous wastes regime on the development of several regional seas regimes by exploring in depth its effect on each regional seas regime separately. We might then discover that the situation includes additional cases of interaction, for example ones between the regional seas regimes in question, or ones feeding back from these regimes to the original source regime. Thus we may identify quite a number of separate incidents of interaction, each of which is based on a clear causal chain. Likewise, it may be useful to disaggregate interaction patterns between two regimes into more limited incidents, especially if feedback processes occur over time. While the appropriate unit of analysis is a single case of interaction rather than interaction between two or more regimes at large, the interaction pattern of the overall situation will become apparent as soon as the cases are re-aggregated.

Disaggregation of complex situations into a suitable number of clear-cut cases of interaction will usually contribute to isolating causal effects and clarify, albeit probably not shorten, the length of causal chains. Moreover, it allows us to start with an assessment of the most clear-cut cases and the most readily traceable causal pathways and gradually work toward more difficult cases. Thus, disaggregation contributes to mitigating the problems of remoteness of causal influence and of long causal pathways.

The analysis of domestic or systemic effects of international regimes is also highly sensitive to the problem of complexity. Situations may be difficult to examine as to the causality of influence because they involve many regimes and different causal pathways. Studies with a trend-discovering design that are directed at exploring causal pathways rather than measuring aggregate effects (see Breitmeier and Litfin in this volume) may thus be well advised to limit their analysis to either a single regime or a single type of causal pathway at a time. However, more often than not, domestic and systemic effects will hardly be attributable to a single regime. The assessment of regime consequences for domestic society and the international system deals not only with highly complex dependent variables, it will frequently also require a comparatively highly aggregated independent variable. In these cases it may be useful to employ quantitative rather than, or complementary to, qualitative analytical methods. Resort to the statistical assessment of effects and the successive exclusion of alternative explanatory variables opens broader consequences research for the analysis of aggregate effects that are difficult to approach by qualitative methods. For example, Hughes (in this volume) explores whether observed changes in life expectancy and attitudes toward democracy may be attributed to the existence of the universe of regimes.

For the analysis of the broader consequences, this approach poses two major problems, both related to the establishment of causality. First, effects at a high level of aggregation may generally be attributed to a number of independent variables. An important task will be to control as many of these variables as possible sufficiently well to isolate the influence of regimes as the explanatory factor of interest. Otherwise, one will merely identify room for possible influence of the universe of regimes on some highly aggregated social indicators, which may be filled as well by a number of rival explanatory factors. Second, correlation does not yet say anything about the direction of causal influence. Are more favorable attitudes toward democracy caused by the existence of international regimes, or is the emergence of regimes, for example in the area of human rights, better explained by changes in these attitudes? Since the direction of causality is essential for consequences research, it may be necessary to complement statistical analysis with the construction of causal models that may be tested subsequently.

The analysis of systemic effects of international regimes poses another, more specific problem. The international system is not fully independent from its components, including international regimes. It does not need further elaboration that regimes form parts of the institutionalized international system and are thus nested within an even larger international institution (Buzan 1993; Young 1996). There is nothing special about this kind of nesting of institutions. Think of a political party that is part of a national political system. What matters here is that the higher order institution changes automatically with any modification of a lower order institution. The international system is automatically affected by the establishment of an international regime or the adoption of a significant decision within a regime, much as the political system of a nation-state changes more or less profoundly with the foundation of a new political party. If an international regime encourages actors to adopt collective decisions by arguing rather than pure bargaining, it contributes to "rationalizing" collective decision-making within the international system in the Habermasian sense (Habermas 1981). If it opens collective decision processes to non-state actors, it contributes to undermining the predominance of state actors. It is important to recognize that these changes of the international system are mere *aggregate descriptions* of developments occurring elsewhere, rather than separate systemic effects, because the cause and the target variables are not independent of each other. Only if actors behave differently *because there are so many regimes in the international system* that provide opportunities for action to non-state actors, or that rationalize interaction in a Habermasian sense, we will be faced with an originally systemic effect.

Therefore, we should be clear, when analyzing systemic effects, whether we mean effects that occur at a lower level within the system, that is within one or more international regimes, or whether we mean original modifications of the international system beyond the aggregate effects attributable to the individual regimes. If we take the international system as the aggregate of developments taking place at a lower level, then the system will change all the time. Therefore, it is of little interest to state that some effect occurring at the regime level changes the international system. Rather, we will want to discover *trends* of more profound systemic change of which a regime-level effect is a mere indicator. If we are looking for original systemic effects, we must conceptualize the system separately from its components.

The detection of profound trends of systemic change is hampered by the fact that the international system is unique and we lack an immediate comparison that might inform us what a profoundly changing system looks like. Accordingly, we are faced with the problem of anticipating future outcomes on the basis of minor indicators in the present or immediate past (see Walter and Zürn in this volume). In the first step, we may identify an institutionally driven causal mechanism that changes the nature of interaction prevailing within the international system. Does a particular regime favor scientifically based over interest-based interventions? Or is it particularly open to influence of otherwise weak actors (such as NGOs or small states)? This step involves two analytical problems. The identification of changes in the regular interaction requires a standard of what is to be expected "normally." Usually we do not dispose of an empirical standard that would tell us how international actors behave on average. Therefore, we need some model of regular behavior that must be sufficiently realistic to be useful. If we take a crude rational choice standard of unilaterally chosen strategic action, we will see modifications almost everywhere. If we *assume* that actors regularly behave according to norms (logic of appropriateness) (March and Olson 1989) and communicative action (Risse 2000), and that non-state actors are widely recognized as relevant participants (Keck/Sikking 1998), we might not find any significant modification of standard behavior. The second analytical problem is related to the impact of changes in interaction on the output in terms of regulatory decisions or norms. The mere presence of NGOs or scientists in regime negotiations does not necessarily indicate that these actors influence the output significantly. Once again, we need a counterfactual analysis ("how would states have done in the absence of non-state actors") and the exclusion of alternative explanations ("might states have achieved a similar result on their own?")

Changes occurring within a particular regime automatically constitute changes of the international system, but they are normally of limited significance. In order to identify *significant* system-level effects, we must explore whether similar changes occur in other regimes, that is whether international regimes *systematically* modify the international system in the identified way. In the second step, we might thus substitute a particular regime with a larger set of regimes. We may quite confidently assume that East-West regimes generally reduce the level of conflict in comparison with the parallel non-regime situations (Rittberger 1990). But do regimes generally favor science-based over power-based decisions? Are they generally open to significant influence of nongovernmental groups? If not, we may still project an alleged trend into the future: Does the number of regimes with relevant properties grow over-proportionally? May it be expected to increase further so that it must be assumed to become a widespread phenomenon in the future? If we are able to respond to these questions in the affirmative, we may have discovered a system-wide *trend* of change that is still exclusively based on developments taking place at the regime level.

In order to identify original system-level effects, we must push the analysis one step further and ask whether the observed aggregate change leads to consequences beyond the effects that occur at the regime level. Can it be established that the behavior of states involved in the East-West conflict changed significantly *even in non-regime situations* because of the establishment of East-West regimes? This effect could not be attributed to the single regimes any more; it would constitute an additional effect that had to be attributed to the simultaneous existence of many regimes, that is, to the system. If internationally acting nongovernmental organizations could launch an attack on GATT/WTO or lead a campaign for a new regime against landmines (Price 1998), *because* they had acquired their ability to do so in the context of environmental and human rights regimes, we would have detected a new type of actor in the international system whose action had became independent of a particular regime. Only effects of this type are truly located at the system level.

5. CONCLUSION: THE FUTURE STUDY OF BROADER CONSEQUENCES

International regimes produce consequences that reach far beyond their own domains. So far, regime analysis has largely avoided tackling these broader consequences. It operated under the implicit assumption that the most important effects may be found within the issue areas governed by a given regime. However, the broader consequences of single international regimes or of the increasing population of regimes within the international system are far from negligible. In some cases, they may be as important as the simple effects. At the very least, they merit considerably more scholarly attention than they have received in the past.

International regimes may have important effects on very different targets. Their output in the form of material norms (rights and obligations) may affect the action of state-actors, transnational actors, and sub-national actors alike and cause secondary consequences on all levels of human interaction. Depending on their specific input of information, regimes also provide opportunities for action not only for states, but also for transnational and sub-national actors. Hence, the process of generating regulation becomes a factor that gains importance for certain types of consequence. Therefore, it seems advisable not to base research of broader consequences from its very beginning on an under-complex conception of international regimes that might prove to be too narrow to grasp important types of consequence.

Considering the almost unlimited expansion of this new area of research, any serious research program will have to concentrate on a number of important aspects. The present paper identifies four research priorities that either exist within the current literature or have been identified as meriting future attention. These priorities may be expected to constitute the core of dependent variables within the emerging new field of study. The exploration of the *externalities* produced by a regime beyond its "own" issue area constitutes an immediate extension of the existing research on the simple effectiveness of international regimes. A second research priority that has, in light of an increasing number of independently established international regimes, already attracted considerable interest of both scholars and policy makers is devoted to the study of *interaction between regimes*. Another strand of research focuses on regime effects on *domestic political systems*, and a last priority concentrates on exploring changes of the *international system* that may be attributed to international regimes. Whereas the exploration of externalities is closely related to the assessment of the simple effectiveness of international regimes, both the domestic effects of internationalization and globalization and the changing nature of the international system are intensely discussed in the literature. The study of the broader effects of international regimes may draw on these extensive research traditions. It promises to contribute to these literatures in particular by developing the role of regimes as drivers for processes of change, that is by emphasizing an independent variable that has gained comparatively little specific attention so far. Surprisingly, the analysis of regime interaction relies on the least well-developed conceptual foundation of the four research areas.

Generally, the exploration of the broader consequences of international regimes does not seem to require an entirely new methodology or methods that are completely unknown in traditional regime analysis. However, broader consequences research differs in a number of respects from the assessment of simple effectiveness. Situations will tend to be more complex, while effects will tend to be more remote than simple effects and rely on longer chains of causation. If we attempt to attribute broad changes of societies to the universe of regimes, all the analytic problems of quantitative macro-analysis will turn up.

Despite these analytical difficulties, the multifaceted and newly developing research area devoted to the study of the broader consequences of international regimes opens a fascinating and politically highly relevant new perspective on the effects of governance within the international system.

NOTES

1 This section draws on the discussion of the 1999 Oslo Workshop of the Concerted Action Network on the Effectiveness of International Environmental Regimes (Breitmeier 2000).

REFERENCES

Axelrod, R. (1984) *The Evolution of Cooperation*, Basic Books, New York.
Beisheim, M., Dreher, S., Walter, G., Zangl, B. and Zürn, M. (1999) *Im Zeitalter der Globalisierung? Thesen und Daten zur gesellschaftlichen und politischen Denationalisierung*, Baden-Baden.
Bernauer, T. (1995) The Effect of International Environmental Institutions: How We Might Learn More, *International Organization* 49, 2: 351–377.
Bierstecker, T. J. (1993) Constructing Historical Counterfactuals to Assess the Consequences of International Regimes: The Global Dept Regime and the Dept Crisis of the 1980s, in V. Rittberger (ed.) *Regime Theory and International Relations*, Oxford University Press, 315–338.
Breitmeier, H. (2000) Working Group III: "Complex Effectiveness:" Regime Externalities and Interaction, in J. Wettestad, (ed.) *Proceedings of the 1999 Oslo Workshop of the Concerted Action Network on the Effectiveness of International Environmental Regimes*. Oslo, 45–48.
Brown Weiss, E. (1993) International Environmental Issues and the Emergence of a New World Order, *Georgetown Law Journal* 81, 3: 675–710.
Buzan, B. (1993) From International System to International Society: Structural Realism and Regime Theory Meet the English School, *International Organization* 47: 327–352.
Caporaso, J. (1996) The European Union and Forms of State: Westphalian, Regulatory or Post-Modern? *Journal of Common Market Studies* 34: 29–52.
Carlsnaes, W. (1992) The Agent-Structure Problem in Foreign Policy Analysis, *International Studies Quarterly* 36, 3: 245–270.
Caron, D. D. (1995) The International Whaling Commission and the North Atlantic Marine Mammals Commission: The Institutional Risks of Coercion in Consensual Structures, *American Journal of International Law* 89: 154–174.
Charnovitz, S. (1998) The World Trade Organization and the Environment, *Yearbook of International Environmental Law* 8: 98–116.
Clark, M. L. (1994) The Antarctic Environmental Protocol: NGOs in the Protection of Antarctica, in T. Princen and M. Finger, (eds.) *Environmental NGOs in World Politics*, Routledge Press, London, 160–185.
Donelly, J. (1986) International Human Rights: A Regime Analysis, *International Organization* 40: 599–642.
Downs, G. W., Rocke, D. M. and Barsoom, P. N. (1998) Managing the Evolution of Multilateralism, *International Organization* 52, 2: 397–419.
Elster, J. (1994) Argumenter et Négocier dans deux Assemblées Constituantes, *Revue Français de Science Politique* 44, 2: 187–256.
Esty, D. C. and Geradin, D. (1998) Environmental Protection and International Competitiveness, *Journal of World Trade* 32, 3: 5–46.

Farber, D. A. and Hudec, R. E. (1996) GATT Legal Restraints on Domestic Environmental Regulations ? J. Bhawati and Hudec, R. E. (eds.) *Fair Trade and Harmonization: Prerequisites for Free Trade*, Vol. 2: *Legal Analysis*, MIT Press, Cambridge, MA, 59–94.

Fearon, J. D. (1991) Counterfactuals and Hypotheses Testing in Political Science, *World Politics* 43: 169–195.

Fearon, J. D. (1998) Bargaining, Enforcement, and International Cooperation, *International Organization* 52, 2: 269–305.

(Forschungsgruppe Menschenrechte/lead researcher) (1998) Internationale Menschenrechtsnormen, transnationale Netzwerke und politischer Wandel in den Ländern des Südens, *Zeitschrift für Internationale Beziehungen* 5: 5–41.

Garrett, G. (1998) Global Markets and National Politics: Collision Course or Virtuous Circle? *International Organization* 52: 787–824.

Gehring, T. (1994) *Dynamic International Regimes, Institutions for International Environmental Governance*, Frankfurt a. M.

Gehring, T. (1996) Arguing und Bargaining in internationalen Verhandlungen, Überlegungen am Beispiel des Ozonschutzregimes, in V. von Prittwitz, (ed.) *Verhandeln und Argumentieren: Dialog, Interesse und Macht in der Umweltpolitik*, Leske + Budrich, Opladen, 207–238.

Gehring, T. (2002) *Die Europäische Union als komplexe internationale Institution: Wie durch Kommunikation und Entscheidung soziale Ordnung entsteht*, Baden-Baden (Nomos).

Gourevich, P. (1978) The Second Image Reversed: The International Sources of Domestic Politics, *International Organization* 32, 4: 881–912.

Grande, E. (1996) The State and Interest Groups in a Framework of Multi-level Decision-making: The Case of the European Union, *Journal of European Public Policy* 3: 318–38.

Gross Stein, J. (1989) Getting to the Table: The Triggers, Stages, Functions, and Consequences of Pre-negotiation, *Getting to the Table: The Processes of International Pre-negotiation*, John Hopkins University Press, Baltimore, 239–268.

Haas, P. M. (1990) *Saving the Mediterranean, The Politics of International Environmental Cooperation,* Columbia University Press, New York.

Haas, P. M. (1992) Banning Chlorofluorocarbons: Epistemic Community Efforts to Protect Stratospheric Ozone, *International Organization* 46, 1: 187–224.

Habermas, J. (1981) *Theorie des kommunikativen Handelns*, Vol. 1: *Handlungsrationalität und gesellschaftliche Rationalisierung*, Frankfurt a.M.

Howse, R. (1998) The Turtles Panel, Another Environmental Disaster in Geneva, *Journal of World Trade* 32, 5: 3–100.

Hudec, R. E. (1996) GATT Legal Restraints on the Use of Trade Measures against Foreign Environmental Practices, in J. Bhawati and R. E. Hudec, (eds.) *Fair Trade and Harmonization: Prerequisites for Free Trade*, Vol. 2: *Legal Analysis*, MIT Press, Cambridge, 95–174.

Keck, M. E., and Sikking, K. (1998) *Activists beyond Borders: Advocacy Networks in International Politics,* Cornell University Press, Ithica, New York.

Keohane, R. O. 1993. The Analysis of International Regimes: Towards a European-American Research Programme, in V. Rittberger, (ed.) *Regime Theory and International Relations*. Oxford University Press, 23–45.

Keohane, R. O., Moravcsik, A. and Slaughter, A. M. 2000. Legalized Dispute Resolution: Interstate and Transnational, *International Organization* 54: 421–456.

Klotz, A. (1995) Norms Reconstituting Interests: Global Racial Equality and US Sanctions against South Africa, *International Organization* 49: 451–478.

Krasner, S. (1982) Structural Causes and Regime Consequences, *International Organization* 36, 2: 185–205.
Kratochwil, F. and Ruggie, J. G. (1986) International Organization: A State of the Art on the Art of the State, *International Organization* 40, 4: 753–775.
Lang, W. (1993) International Environmental Agreements and the GATT: The Case of the Montreal Protocol, *Wirtschaftspolitische Blätter* 40: 364–372.
Levy, M. A., Young, O.R. and Zürn, M. (1995) The Study of International Regimes, *European Journal of International Relations* 1: 267–330.
Litfin, K. T. (1997) Sovereignty in World Ecopolitics, *Mershon International Studies Review* 41: 167–204.
Luhmann, N. (1984) *Soziale Systeme: Grundriß einer allgemeinen Theorie,* Frankfurt a.M.
Lutz, E. L, and Sikking, K. (2000) International Human Rights Law and Practice in Latin America, *International Organization* 54: 633–659.
March, J. G., und Olsen, J. P. (1989) *Rediscovering Institutions: The Organizational Basis of Politics,* Free Press, New York.
Marks, G., Hooghe, L. and Blank, K. (1996) European Integration from the 1980s: State Centric v. Multi-level Governance, *Journal of Common Market Studies* 34: 341–78.
Martin, L. L. and Simmons, B. A. (1998) Theories and Empirical Studies of International Institutions, *International Organization* 52: 729–757.
Meinke, B. (1997) Die internationale Kontrolle des grenzüberschreitenden Handels mit gefährlichen Abfällen (Baseler Konvention von 1989), Thomas Gehring and Sebastian Oberthür, (eds.) *Internationale Umweltregime, Umweltschutz durch Verhandlungen und Verträge,* Leske + Budrich, Opladen, 63–80.
Meinke, B. (2002) *Multi-Regime-Regulierung,* Darmstadt, Deutscher Universitäts-Verlag.
Milner, H. E. (1988) *Resisting Protectionism: Global Industries and the Politics of International Trade,* Princeton University Press.
Milner, H. and Keohane, R. O. (1996) Internationalization and Domestic Politics: An Introduction, in R. O. Keohane and H. Milner (eds.) *Internationalization and Domestic Politics,* Cambridge University Press, 3–24.
Moltke, K. von, (1997) Institutional Interactions: the Structure of Regimes for Trade and the Environment, in O. R. Young, (ed.) *Global Governance: Drawing Insights from the Environmental Experience,* MIT Press, Cambridge MA, 247–272.
Moravcsik, A. (1994) *Why the European Community Strengthens the State: Domestic Politics and International Cooperation,* Harvard Working Paper Series 52, Cambridge.
Morrow, D. J. (1994) Modeling the Forms of International Cooperation: Distribution vs. Information, *International Organization* 48, 3: 387–423.
Müller, H. (1993) The Internalization of Principles, Norms, and Rules by Governments: The Case of Security Regimes, in V. Rittberger (ed.) *Regime Theory and International Relations,* Oxford University Press, 361–388.
Oberthür, S. (1997) *Umweltschutz durch internationale Regime: Interessen, Verhandlungsprozesse, Wirkungen,* Leske + Budrich, Opladen.
Oberthür, S. (2001) Linkages Between the Montreal and Kyoto Protocols: Enhancing Synergies between Protecting the Ozone Layer and the Global Climate? International Environmental Agreements, *Politics, Law and Economics* 1, 3: 357–377.
Petersmann, E.-U. (1993) International Trade Law and International Environmental Law, *Journal of World Trade* 27, 1: 43–81.
Price, R. (1998) Reversing the Guns Sights: Transnational Society Targets Land Mines, *International Organization* 52: 613–644.

Princen, T. (1994) The Ivory Trade Ban: NGOs and International Conservation, in T. Princen and M. Finger, (eds.) *Environmental NGOs in World Politics*, Routledge Press, London, 121–159.
Princen, T. and M. Finger, (eds.) (1994) *Environmental NGOs in World Politics*, Routledge Press, London.
Raustiala, K. (1997) States, NGOs, and International Environmental Institutions, *International Studies Quarterly* 41, 4: 719–740.
Risse-Kappen, T. (1995) Bringing Transnational Relations Back In, in T. Risse-Kappen (ed.) *Bringing Transnational Relations Back In: Non-States Actors, Domestic Structures and International Institutions*, Cambridge University Press, 3–33.
Risse, T. (2000) "Let's Argue!": Communicative Action in World Politics. *International Organization* 54: 1–39.
Rittberger, V. (ed.) (1990) *International Regimes in East-West Relations*, Pinter, London
Rogowski, R. (1989) *Commerce and Coalitions. How Trade Affects Domestic Realignments*, Princeton University Press.
Sand, P. H. (ed.) (1992) *The Effectiveness of International Environmental Agreements: A Survey of Existing Legal Instruments*, Grotius, Cambridge.
Scharpf, F. W. (1991) Games Real Actors Could Play: The Challenge of Complexity, *Journal of Theoretical Politics* 3, 3: 277–304.
Scharpf, F. W. (1999) *Governing in Europe: Effective and Democratic?* Oxford University Press.
Schoenbaum, T. J. 1992. Free International Trade and Protection of the Environment: Irreconcilable Conflict? *American Journal of International Law* 86: 700–727.
Searle, R. J. (1995) *The Construction of Social Reality*, Penguin, Harmondsworth.
Sebenius, J. K. (1983) Negotiation Arithmatics: Adding and Subtracting Issues and Parties, *International Organization* 37, 2: 281–316.
Sebenius, J. K. (1991) Designing Negotiations Toward a New Regime: The Case of Global Warming, *International Security* 15, 4: 110–148.
Sprinz, D. and Vaahtoranta, T. (1994) The Interest-based Explanation of International Environmental Policy, *International Organization* 48: 77–105.
Stevens, C. (1995) Trade and Environment: The PPMs Debate, in W. Lang, (ed.) *Sustainable Development and International Law*, Graham & Trotman/Martinus Nijhoff : 239–247.
Stokke, O. S. (1999) Governance of High Seas Fisheries: The Role of Regime Linkages, in D. Vidas, and W. Ostreng, (eds.) *Order for the Oceans at the Turn of the Century*, Kluwer Law International, Haag, 157–172.
Stone Sweet, A. and Sandholtz, W. (1997) European Integration and Supranational Governance, *Journal of European Public Policy* 4: 297–317.
Tarasovsky, R. G. (1997) Ensuring Compatibility between Multilateral Environmental Agreements and GATT/WTO, *Yearbook of International Environmental Law* 7: 52–74.
Underdal, A. (1992) The Concept of Regime Effectiveness, *Cooperation and Conflict* 27, 3: 227–240.
Underdal, A., Andresen, S., Ringius, L. and Wettestad, J. (2000) Evaluating Regime Effectiveness: Developing Valid and Usable Tools, in J. Wettestad (ed.) *Proceedings of the 1999 Oslo Workshop of the Concerted Action Network on the Effectiveness of International Environmental Regimes*, Oslo, 5–30.
United Nations University (1998) Global Climate Governance: A Report on the Inter-Linkages between the Kyoto Protocol and other Multilateral Regimes. 2 Vols., Tokyo.

Victor, D. G., Raustiala, K. and Skolnikoff, E. B. (eds.) (1998) *The Implementation and Effectiveness of International Environmental Commitments: Theory and Practice,* MIT Press, Cambridge, MA.

Willke, H. (1996) *Systemtheorie I: Grundlagen. Eine Einführung in die Grundprobleme der Theorie sozialer Systeme,* _____, Stuttgart, 5th ed.

Wolf, K. D. (1999) The New Raison d'État as a Problem for Democracy in World Politics, *European Journal of International Relations* 5: 333–363.

Young, O. R. (1989) The Politics of Regime Formation: Managing Natural Resources and the Environment. *International Organization* 43, 3: 349–375.

Young, O. R. (1994) *International Governance: Protecting the Environment in a Stateless Society,* Cornell University Press, Ithaca, New York.

Young, O. R. (1996) Institutional Linkages in International Society: Polar Perspectives, *Global Governance* 2: 1–24.

Young, O. R. (1999a) *Governance in World Affairs,* Cornell University Press, Ithaca, New York.

Young, O. R. (ed.) (1999b) *The Effectiveness of International Environmental Regimes: Causal Connections and Behavioral Mechanisms,* MIT Press, Cambridge, MA.

Chapter 10

EXPLORING REGIME INTERACTION
A Framework of Analysis

THOMAS GEHRING AND SEBASTIAN OBERTHÜR
University of Bamberg; University of Bamberg/Ecologic

The international system is populated by a steadily growing number of international institutions. More than two hundred major regimes exist in the field of international environmental protection alone; with five major agreements being adopted per year since the 1980s (Beisheim et al. 1999; see also Sand 1992). While these institutions usually are separately established to respond to particular problems, they increasingly affect each others' development and performance. In some cases, "regime interaction" creates conflict.[1] Whereas the Word Trade Organization (GATT/WTO) promotes free international trade, several international environmental regimes, such as the Basel Convention on the Transboundary Movement of Hazardous Wastes and their Disposal, the Convention on International Trade in Endangered Species of Wild Fauna and Flora (CITES) and the Montreal Protocol for the protection of the ozone layer, establish new trade restrictions (see Petersmann 1993; Lang 1993; Moltke 1997). Likewise, the 1997 Kyoto Protocol to the UN Framework Convention on Climate Change provides incentives for establishing fast-growing mono-cultural tree plantations in order to maximize carbon sequestration from the atmosphere, whereas the Convention on Biological Diversity of 1992 aims at preserving biological diversity of forest ecosystems (see Gillespie 1998; WBGU 1998; Tarasofsky 1999; Pontecorvo 1999). In other cases, interaction creates synergistic effects. The global regime on the transboundary movement of hazardous wastes has been strengthened, for example, upon the establishment of a number of regional regimes addressing the same environmental problem (Meinke 1997).

Traditionally, regime analysts have tended to explore the establishment, development, and effectiveness of international regimes in isolation. The relevance of the growing "regime density" (Young 1996) that may generate a risk of "treaty congestion" (Brown Weiss 1993: 679) has been recognized only recently. Meanwhile, the number of studies investigating specific cases of institutional interaction is steadily growing (see, for example, Zhang 1998; Stokke 1999; Rosendal 2000; Oberthür 2001; Andersen 2002). These contributions focus particularly on environmental regimes because the institutional fragmentation of international environmental politics makes interaction a particularly widespread phenomenon in this field. Most of the research is empirical and descriptive. Despite some attempts to categorize phenomena of institutional interaction (Young 1996, 2002; Stokke 2000; Herr and Chia 1995; King 1997), the conceptual development of the analysis of regime interaction is still at an early stage. Not surprisingly, the influence that regimes may have on each others' development and performance has been repeatedly identified as a key issue for future research (Young et al. 1999; Breitmeier 2000; Young 2002).

This chapter aims at developing a conceptual framework for the analysis of interaction between regimes.[2] It concentrates on situations in which one or more international regimes exert influence on one or more other regimes or on issue areas related to other regimes. It does not address the impact of the growing universe of international institutions on a particular regime, nor the effectiveness-related problem of how to attribute an observed impact to different regimes. International regimes are considered as social systems that comprise, in addition to a catalogue of norms of behavior, a structured and institutionalized process of communication in which norms are molded and collective decisions made. This concept allows for the identification of the boundaries of an international regime on the basis of its specific communication process rather than the substantive problem(s) addressed. Hence, we may find, for example, a regional and a global regime addressing a virtually identical substantive problem, such as dumping of wastes at sea. Without further elaborating this concept here (see Gehring in this volume, Gehring 1994; Levy et al. 1995), we note that it basically reflects the understanding of the term "regime" as most widely used by policy-makers and in empirical research.

Influence between regimes is not limited to cases in which a regime's norms and institutional arrangements are modified upon interaction. It extends to all three levels of a regime's effectiveness: output, outcome, and impact (see Underdal in this volume). A regime will affect another regime's normative *output* if it causes changes of the latter's norms. It will exert influence on another regime's *outcome* if it results in behavioral adaptations that are relevant to the latter's performance. Finally, a regime will affect another regime at the *impact level*, if it directly influences the subject matter governed by the latter (e.g., the state of the environment in the case of environmental regimes). In any case, interaction between regimes is based on a causal link between the source regime(s) and the target regime(s). Therefore, it is a core analytical task of studies addressing regime interaction to demonstrate that a causal connection exists between the regimes involved.

Unfortunately, empirical phenomena of regime interaction are frequently complex. They may include a whole set of regimes that interact with each other, or a co-evolution process in which influence runs back and forth. Under these circumstances, the establishment of clear causal pathways requires the identification of suitable units of analysis (section 1). Moreover, empirical evidence suggests that regime interaction constitutes a rather multifaceted phenomenon. Systematic research should be based upon factors that may be used to distinguish cases of regime interaction according to important criteria. In section 2, we therefore develop a number of conceptual categories of regime interaction that allow a systematic mapping of empirical cases of regime interaction and a more specific distinction of different types of regime interaction. Finally, we address the issue of establishing causality in section 3. It is indispensable for every identified case of regime interaction to demonstrate a causal pathway that clearly links the source regime with the target regime. In the absence of a causal link, regimes would merely co-exist, rather than interact. On the basis of the development of certain types of regime interaction, it may be possible in the longer run to develop generalized causal mechanisms for different patterns of interaction that spell out standard causal pathways and the conditions under which they become applicable.

1. CHOOSING THE APPROPRIATE UNIT OF ANALYSIS

While description of observable social phenomena may be a valuable task on its own (King et al. 1994: 34 – 74), the analysis of regime interaction, like any exploration of regime consequences, is closely related to the examination of causal influence. Causal analysis requires the identification of one or more independent variables that exert influence on one or more dependent variables. It is thus based on the existence of a clear-cut direction of influence between variables. Moreover, it must allow the identification of a causal pathway that generates the observed effect. Accordingly, the causal analysis of regime interaction will generally require (1) the identification of one or more sources from which influence originates (independent variable), (2) the identification of one or more targets that are affected by an interaction process (dependent variable), and (3) a causal pathway connecting the independent variable to the dependent variable in a way that generates the observed effect.

Unfortunately, constellations of interacting regimes are frequently highly complex. A situation involving several source regimes and/or several target regimes connected by varying causal pathways, for example, may be described. In this case, however, the causal influence that drives interaction cannot be analyzed because it is not possible to identify independent and dependent variables. Therefore, such situations do not constitute appropriate units of analysis. Serious causal analysis of interaction phenomena requires that a complex interaction situation is analytically disaggregated into a number of *cases of regime interaction*. Each of these "cases" must fulfill the aforementioned conditions, namely they must allow the identification of a single source regime, a single target regime, and a unidirectional causal pathway connecting the two. While a case of interaction has to be based upon empirical observation, it is an analytical construction that does not exist independently of the analysis.

Disaggregation of complex interaction situations will be particularly useful in three cases: if more than one pathway is operative, if interaction constitutes a feedback (co-evolution) process, or if it involves a whole set of regimes. First, existing international regimes are normally complex. For example, the World Trade Organization (WTO) and the regime for the protection of the Baltic Sea govern broad issue-areas. Even an allegedly single-purpose institution such as the regime for the protection of the ozone layer controls the use of numerous chemicals and promotes a number of different abatement strategies. Moreover, modern international regimes regularly comprise auxiliary arrangements, including funding mechanisms (Keohane and Levy 1996) and systems of implementation review (Victor et al. 1998), that may exert influence on another regime separately from the core arrangements of the source regime. Complex international regimes may interact with each other in more than one way and interaction will then be based on several causal pathways.

For analytical purposes, we should disaggregate a complex interaction situation into a number of suitable cases. We may identify specific components of the source regime that have the potential of affecting the target regime. Consider the case of the international regimes on climate change and for the protection of the ozone layer. One component of the Montreal Protocol for the protection of the ozone layer reinforces international efforts to combat climate change by prescribing the phase-out of chlorofluorocarbons (CFCs) that do not only harm the ozone layer but are also important greenhouse gases. Another component of the ozone regime, namely the promotion of hydrofluorocarbons (HFCs) as substitutes for CFCs, affects the climate change regime adversely, because these substances are powerful greenhouse gases. Yet another component of the Montreal Protocol, its noncompliance procedure, provided a precedent for the elaboration of a similar component of the climate change regime (Oberthür 2001), so that interaction was obviously based on a different causal pathway. Upon closer inspection, we might identify even more different forms of interaction between the two regimes. Interaction between these regimes is thus made up of a number of cases with rather different properties. Influence may be symmetrical or asymmetrical (Young 1996: 7).

The separate study of single cause-effect relationships promises to provide a much clearer picture of the overall interaction pattern than any aggregate analysis could. Obviously, the accuracy of the overall picture will increase with the number of cases explored. Constraints on time and money suggest that research should start with the most important and direct effects and gradually proceed toward cases with a more limited impact on the overall situation or with a less clear cause-effect relationship.

Second, *co-evolution processes* should also be disaggregated into a set of cases of interaction, before they are submitted to causal analysis. As modern international regimes exist over extended periods of time and tend to change more or less profoundly during their lifetime, the analysis of co-evolution of regimes promises important insights into the interaction patterns of regimes. For example, the regional Oslo Dumping Convention and the global London Dumping Convention co-developed for almost thirty years and appear to have been mutually reinforcing (Meinke 2002). If co-evolution involves feedback processes, neither of the regimes in question would exist in its current state without existence of the other. Influence may be bi-directional. We are thus confronted with a problem similar to the co-constitution of agent and structure that has been hotly debated in International Relations (Wendt 1992; Dessler 1989). Unfortunately, collapsing agent into structure and structure into agent (Carlsnaes 1992) renders causal explanation virtually impossible because it makes any invariable starting point for analytical reasoning disappear (see also Hollis and Smith 1991). Similarly, the observation that two or more co-evolving regimes are mutually constitutive does not help explain *how* these regimes exert influence on each other.

Therefore, we should disaggregate the co-evolution process into a suitable number of cases of interaction. The principal strategy is temporalization and phasing (Archer 1985; Carlsnaes 1992). Despite its empirical continuity, we may consider a process of co-evolution as a sequence of separate cases, each of them with a single unidirectional line of influence running from one of the regimes involved to the other. Cases are again best selected according to important decisions, or sets of decisions, that establish components of the source regime with possible effects on the target regime. In doing so, we implicitly assume that a stable situation exists at an appropriate point in time t_0, in which neither of the regimes in question is under pressure to adapt. It may not be possible to identify empirically any such moment within the overall development of an international regime. Nevertheless, *with respect to a particular decision or set of decisions*, such as the decisions to control and phase out CFCs, we will not expect any effect *before* the relevant decisions were adopted (or their adoption was at least anticipated). Accordingly, we may observe at point t_1 an important change within Regime *A*, for example the adoption (or elaboration) of a new set of regulations, with a possible effect on Regime *B*. This effect must inevitably occur later than its cause, at point t_2. The members of Regime *B* may react, for example, by a collective decision adapting regulations to the new situation. Such a response occurs yet another analytical moment later, at point t_3.

If we are able to identify any such influence, it will be clearly directed from the source regime to the target regime. If influence is symmetrical, it will run the other direction in the subsequent phase. Assume that the decision adopted by actors of Regime *B* at point t_3 significantly modifies the environment of Regime *A*. This effect will occur yet another analytical moment later, at point t_4. And it may lead to a further institutional response by actors of Regime *A*, at point t_5. Influence is also clearly directed, but it runs from Regime *B* toward Regime *A*. Hence, we have discovered a feedback loop. The original action of Regime *A* members causes a reaction of Regime *B* actors that feeds back on Regime *A*. "Co-evolution" of the global Basel Convention on the Transboundary Movement of Hazardous Wastes and several related regional regimes may thus be analyzed as a sequence of two phases. In the first analytical phase, the establishment of a moderate control arrangement at the global level may have caused the African countries, and subsequently the countries of other possible target regions, to adopt separate regional regimes prohibiting the import of hazardous wastes. In the second phase, the existence of a number of such regional regimes may have strengthened those favoring a ban of waste exports from OECD countries to non-OECD countries that was eventually agreed under the global regime (Meinke 2002). Once again, the overall interaction pattern is better grasped by the separate exploration of two successive cause-effect relationships than in an aggregate perspective.

Third, *interaction within a whole set of regimes* may be disentangled into a number of bilateral relations of influence. For example, the Baltic Sea is affected by a number of functionally different global environmental regimes addressing, inter alia, oil pollution from ships and dumping of wastes at sea, and by an important regional regime, as well as overall arrangements such as the United Nations Convention on the Law of the Sea (UNCLOS III) with its Exclusive Economic Zones arrangement (Young 1996). It is likely that all these institutions interact with each other—either affecting each others' performance or influencing each others' institutional development. We may well describe the set of institutions involved. We may even try to assess the impact of this set of regimes on the state of the regional common in question (which would constitute an analysis of "simple effectiveness," see Underdal in this volume). However, we would not learn anything about the causal influence between the institutions involved.

Once again, we should distinguish cases of regime interaction on the basis of specific components of the respective source regimes that emerge and develop through collective decision making. At closer inspection, we may discover rather different patterns of causal influence within a set of regimes. For example, a single important decision adopted within a source regime may turn out to exert parallel influence on a number of target regimes. The decision to ban the dumping of certain wastes at sea, adopted under the global London Dumping Convention, might have affected a number of regional seas regimes concurrently, although independently of each other. On the other hand, a single target regime may be affected by different source regimes. We may thus examine separately the influence exerted on the development of the Baltic Sea regime by the London Dumping Convention, by the International Convention for the Prevention of Pollution from Ships (MARPOL 1973/78) and by the UN Convention on the Law of the Sea. The separate exploration of these individual cases promises to reveal a much clearer picture of the interaction pattern than an overall perspective could do.

It is not necessary to elaborate further that these three sources of complexity of an interaction situation may occur simultaneously. In the extreme, we may have to deal with a whole set of highly complex regimes that develop over time. Still, for analytical purposes one may best identify appropriate cases of interaction with a clear direction of influence. The reason is that the separate analysis of interaction cases will reveal different types of interaction and different underlying causal pathways. It may also be discovered that causal pathways change over time. Consequently, analyzing cases of definite inter-regime influence rather than a complex overall situation promises to provide both a better idea of the causal pathways determining the interaction and, by means of re-aggregation of the results, a better picture of the complex overall situation.

2. COPING WITH THE MULTIFACETED NATURE OF REGIME INTERACTION

Regime interaction is a comparatively novel field of research. As is evident from the existing literature, it covers a broad range of cases with rather different properties, but we do not know very much about the core characteristics of these cases. "International regimes" had also once been a concept much criticized for its lack of precision (Strange 1982). Today, we have a fairly clear idea of what an international regime is, what its functions are, of important types of regimes as well as of ways to assess their (simple) effectiveness. This knowledge is a result of more than two decades of conceptually founded regime analysis. It demonstrates how an originally unclear phenomenon may be systematically unfolded through theoretically informed research. The exploration of regime interaction still lacks conceptually founded guidance on how to deal with the multifaceted and empirically complex phenomenon in a similarly systematic way.

First of all, this theoretical gap raises the problem of how to identify cases of regime interaction. A case of regime interaction may be comparatively limited in scope and difficult to recognize. So far, the empirical—and predominantly descriptive—literature on regime interaction tend to focus on areas of eminent interest to policy makers that have been primarily related to conflicts between regimes rather than synergy effects. To be sure, the perceptions of negotiators and stake-holders constitute an important source of information about the existence and nature of a case of regime interaction. However, systematic mapping must be based on conceptually sound criteria in order to minimize the risk that whole categories of interaction or core characteristics of particular cases are not taken into account. In short, researchers must develop their own idea of what constitutes a case of interaction and its core characteristics.

Moreover, there are good reasons to believe that it is not useful, or may even be epistemologically impossible, to simply *describe* a case of interaction without an idea of its central aspects, because description *always* requires distinguishing between important properties (that are worth reporting) and other features (that may be ignored) (King et al. 1994: 42-43). Generally, we generate information about our environment through self-constructed distinctions, internal models, "paradigms," or "theories" that allow us to order individual observations. Hence, we would be unable to identify cars on a motorway without an idea of how cars are to be distinguished from other objects, for example motorcycles. And "cars" remains an amorphous category, unless we introduce further distinctions, for example between vans, limousines, and station wagons. It appears that any systematic study of regime interaction will have to be based on some useful distinctions that help identify cases of interaction by pointing toward their core characteristics.

Distinction alone does not suffice. As cars may be distinguished according to an almost infinite number of aspects, for instance their color, their manufacturer, the size of their steering wheel, we may think of numerous distinctions between cases of regime interaction. What we need are distinctions that presumably tell us something about *important* characteristics, that is those aspects that we believe to be central to cases of interaction. Unless we have an idea of how cases involving few actors differ systematically from those involving many, the number of relevant actors will not be a useful distinction. Likewise, unless we hypothesize that regime interaction in the area of environmental protection differs significantly from interaction in the areas of the economy or security, we cannot expect to gain additional information from this distinction. Hence, useful distinctions are supported by plausible hypotheses about the operation of regime interaction. Generally, this will be true for any distinction that addresses variation of the causal pathways at work because variation of this type promises hints as to *how* interaction operates and *why* it produces the results observed. Distinctions of this sort promise to provide a basis for the inductive development of types of regime interaction. While it is still too early and far beyond the scope of the present paper to put forward a theory of regime interaction, we may well look for categories that have the potential for providing a sound basis for theory development.

The present section first develops a set of generalized distinctions that shed light on a number of key properties of cases of regime interaction. Second, it briefly explores the utility of these categories for empirical analysis. Illustrative reference is made to various cases, particularly in the area of environmental policy. However, the categories introduced are of a general nature and therefore applicable to all policy areas.

2.1 Dimensions of Regime Interaction

Conceptually fruitful criteria for the distinction of cases must address particularly important dimensions of regime interaction. Distinctions based on factors whose variation might have an impact on the causal pathways at work are most likely to be important. In section 1, we have argued that cases of regime interaction always involve action within the source regime. This action will always produce some consequence within the target regime or the issue area governed by it, and may lead to further responses within the source and target regimes. We may thus assume that variation of these factors of regime interaction, namely source regime action and the resulting consequences, matter. However, not every action adopted within an international regime exerts influence on a target institution. A third area of importance pertains to the situation that links the regimes involved. Accordingly, we should look for distinctions related to significant variation of (1) situation-specific aspects, (2) the properties of source regime action, and (3) the type of consequences and responses.

Situation-Specific Causes and Effects. We may expect that some characteristics of a case of regime interaction are specific to the situation, rather than to source regime action or to the consequence generated. Two aspects appear to be particularly relevant in this respect. First, there must be situation-specific drivers that provide a basis for influence between the regimes involved. Second, we need information about the effects of a case on the target regime. We therefore propose two distinctions: one relating to the situation-specific causes and the other to the effects.

The functional interdependence of two or more international regimes and the related issue areas has been established as an important driver for regime interaction (Young et al. 1999: 50). In this case, two issue areas are related by some functional logic. However, in some cases, interacting regimes govern issue-areas with a virtually identical substance. Accordingly, we have to look for a second driver of regime interaction that may replace functional interdependence. We propose that this driver is related to the membership of the regimes involved. Empirically, both the substantive issue areas *and* the memberships of the regimes involved vary across cases. Upon closer inspection, we find that the issue areas governed are in some cases so different that we may expect this variation to be relevant for the causal pathway at work, while in other cases the substance addressed is almost identical and therefore presumably of little explanatory value. Likewise, in some cases we find memberships so clearly distinct from each other that we may expect this variation to influence the causal pathways at work, while this is not true for other cases. Hence, cases may *ideally* be driven either by a functional logic or by a membership-related logic. We derive a distinction between two types of regime interaction, each of which is based on a different logic.

Unless we have an appropriate distinction of the effects generated by a case of regime interaction, we may only observe whether a source regime indeed affects the target regime, but not in which way. Effects can vary to a considerable extent, and we may think of several suitable distinctions. At the most basic level, effects may either reinforce or contradict the "policy direction" (Gehring 1994: 433 – 49) of the target regime. The policy direction indicates the direction of collectively desired change or the objective of maintaining a desired status quo against some collectively undesired change. Hence, we gain a distinction between cases of interaction that produce *synergy* and cases that cause *disruption* from the point of view of the collectivity of target regime actors (although some members may disagree individually). While this distinction is clearly situation-specific, it is *not* immediately related to the causes of interaction. However, it may provide *important* information about the characteristics of cases of regime interaction relevant to whether and how it is responded to (section 2.1.4).

We may, for example, hypothesize that synergistic effects are frequently simply "consumed" without further action because they generate additional benefits "free of charge," while disruption creates conflict and will therefore produce demand for more beneficial solutions. However, *if* synergy leads to institutional adaptation, it may launch a process of dynamic and mutually reinforcing co-development of the regimes involved (see section 1).

By combining these two dimensions of regime interaction, we derive four types of regime interaction depicted in Figure 10.1. In cases that follow a functional logic (left side of Figure 10.1), the memberships of the source regime and the target regime are basically identical. They raise the question of why a group of actors might act within one regime in a way that influences its own governing effort within another issue area. This kind of interference may occur, first, because a serious policy response to the problem addressed within one regime has inevitable consequences for the performance of the other one. This is virtually what Young et al. (1999: 50) call "functional linkage", namely the occurrence of 'facts of life' "in the sense that the operation of one institution directly influences the effectiveness of another through some substantive connection of the activities involved". Second, cases following a functional logic may arise from the fact that governance of distinct issue-areas in separate institutions inevitably separates the related norm-molding processes. Institutional fragmentation diverts attention from externalities generated by these solutions and supports the uncoordinated development of policy solutions.

In the top left box (1.1), we find cases that are driven by a functional logic and produce synergy effects. For example, the phase-out of CFCs agreed upon within the ozone regime automatically supports the objective of the climate change regime because CFCs are also important greenhouse gases (Oberthür 2001). This effect may be explained without reference to the (minor) variation of membership of the two global regimes. Cases of this type are largely unproblematic for the target regime. They enhance its effectiveness without producing additional costs.

In contrast, the bottom left box (1.2) contains cases driven by a functional logic that produce effects running counter to the policy objective of the target regime. For example, WTO/GATT has been established to promote a freer world trade and reduce trade obstacles, whereas several environmental regimes include arrangements that restrict international trade in certain goods, or that use the threat of trade sanctions to enforce environmental obligations like the ozone regime. Accordingly, the largely identical membership of these regimes is faced with a trade-off between their goal of pursuing environmental protection by means of establishing selective trade restrictions, and their goal of freer trade (for some of the rich literature on this subject see Lang 1993, Petersmann 1993, Moltke 1997).

| | effects | |
| | *synergy* | |

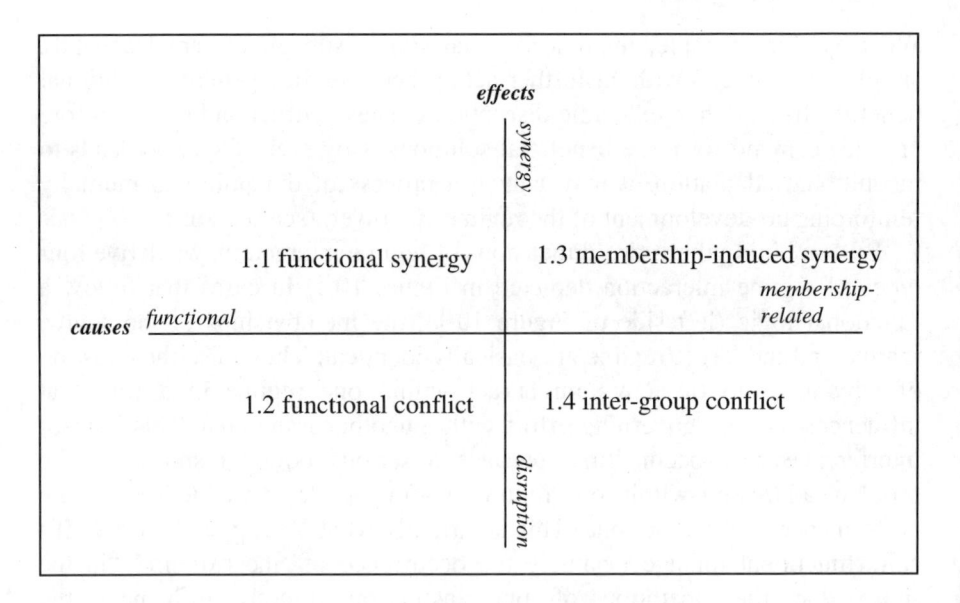

```
                          effects
                            │ synergy
                            │
        1.1 functional synergy  │  1.3 membership-induced synergy
                            │                      membership-
causes  functional          │                         related
        ────────────────────┼──────────────────────────────────
                            │
        1.2 functional conflict │  1.4 inter-group conflict
                            │
                            │ disruption
```

Figure 10.1. *Situation-specific causes and effects of regime interaction.*

Minor differences in membership are not relevant for the causal pathway that links the regimes involved. Cases of this type create demand for response action. They are readily recognizable because they stir conflict between regimes and have been the major focus of academic interest so far.

Located on the right side of Figure 10.1 are cases driven by a logic of membership. Their core characteristic is that different groups of actors operate within the same issue-area. While the functional logic may be based upon some natural law or 'objective' trade-off between different goals, the logic of membership is the exclusive product of the social construction of institutional boundaries. Memberships of the regimes involved may completely overlap, so that a smaller group of actors forms a part of a larger group as in the case of a regional and a global regime operating in the same issue-area. They may also be mutually exclusive as in the case of two regimes addressing the same substantive problem in different regions of the world, or they may partly overlap. In all these cases it is the interplay between the groups of actors involved that constitutes the source of regime interaction.

In the top right box (1.3) we find cases of interaction driven by a logic of membership that generate synergy effects. For example, the rapid development of the global Basel regime on the transboundary movement of hazardous wastes may be attributed to the establishment of several regional arrangements operating within the same issue-area because the number of

EXPLORING REGIME INTERACTION 259

outlets for legal waste exports to the south was significantly reduced and the constellation of interests within the global regime thereby affected (Meinke 2002). Interaction of this type is clearly attributed to the interplay between the groups of actors involved, rather than the (minor) differences of the substantive issue-areas governed by the actual regimes. It may create space for additional action within the original source regime.

Finally, in the bottom right box (1.4) we find cases driven by a logic of membership that creates disruption within the target regime. For example, the interaction between NATO and the Warsaw Pact was dominated by their mutually exclusive membership, while they operated in virtually the same subject area. Disruption will generally create *demand* for suitable response action, although the ability of target regime members to react may be limited. *If* response action takes place within the original target regime, it may well produce its own externalities that affect the original source regime negatively. As a result, we may expect a process of co-evolution.

The distinctions between types of regime interaction according to causes and effects draw attention to the fact that regime interaction may not only be driven by a functional logic that is emphasized by much of the current empirical literature. It may also be driven by a logic of membership that is generated entirely by the human construction of regime boundaries. Moreover, it may not necessarily produce only conflict but also synergy. Moreover, all four situation-specific types of regime interaction can be illustrated by well-known examples and are thus empirically relevant.

2.1.1 Nature of Source Regime Action

Considering the fact that every case of regime interaction is caused by action within the source regime, we may expect that the nature of source regime action sheds light on some other important aspects of an interaction case that are not illuminated by its situation-specific dimensions. Hence, we must identify dimensions in which source regime action varies significantly in ways that provide important information about a case of interaction. Once again, we propose two important distinctions: one relating to the influence of source regime action on the target regime and the other to the motivation of source regime action.

The ability of source regime actors to unilaterally influence the target regime may be expected to have an immediate impact on the causal pathway at work. If this ability is high, source regime action will cause a consequence without consent, or even action, of the target regime actors. In contrast, if the source regime is not able to influence the target regime unilaterally, effective interaction will inevitably depend on consent and action by target regime actors. There are different causal pathways at work, depending on the ability of source regime actors to exert unilateral influence. Hence, we derive an important conceptual distinction between cases that rely on the ability of source regime actors to influence the target regime unilaterally and cases that depend on consent of target regime actors.

Another important aspect is whether the effects on the target regime are intended by source regime actors or not. The actors of the source regime *may* intend to bring about interaction, but in many cases they do not. Intentionality must be kept separate from anticipation. Unintended regime interaction may or may not have been anticipated. If anticipated, unintended regime interaction was not avoided because the costs of doing so were considered higher than the benefits. If unanticipated, effects come about as a surprise, although they might have been possible to anticipate at closer inspection (Martin/Simmons 1998). It does not seem to matter immediately for the causal pathway leading from source regime action to the effect, whether externalities were intended or not. However, if we assume that the intentionality of source regime action may be relevant for the kind of response, this distinction will be important. We may hypothesize, for example, that unintended interaction will more easily become subject to inter-regime coordination than intended action, because source regime actors will be prepared to search for a common solution. On the other hand, it will be easier to identify reliable solutions for intended cases of interaction, because they tend to depend exclusively on human action.

By combining the dimensions of intentionality and ability to exert unilateral influence, we again derive four types of regime interaction (see Figure 10.2). In the top left box (2.1) we find cases in which the members of a source regime intend to affect another regime and are able to do so. For example, a number of European countries agreed in 1990 to abolish police checks at their internal borders. The members of this so-called Schengen regime intended to influence the related policy of the European Communities that had been in stalemate for several years, and they were able to do so successfully (Gehring 1998). In cases of this type, the members of the source regime control the interaction situation almost entirely. They employ the source regime as an *instrument* to influence the target regime. They will have little reason to negotiate with target regime actors about changes of their policy.

The bottom left box (2.2) contains cases in which the actors are capable of unilaterally producing effects on the target regime while not intending to do so. A case in point is the interaction between GATT/WTO and environmental regimes that comprise trade restrictions. The actors negotiating the Montreal Protocol were able to decide unilaterally that trade sanctions be imposed on non-compliant countries. They created tension within the trade regime, but they did not do so *in order* to influence GATT.

EXPLORING REGIME INTERACTION

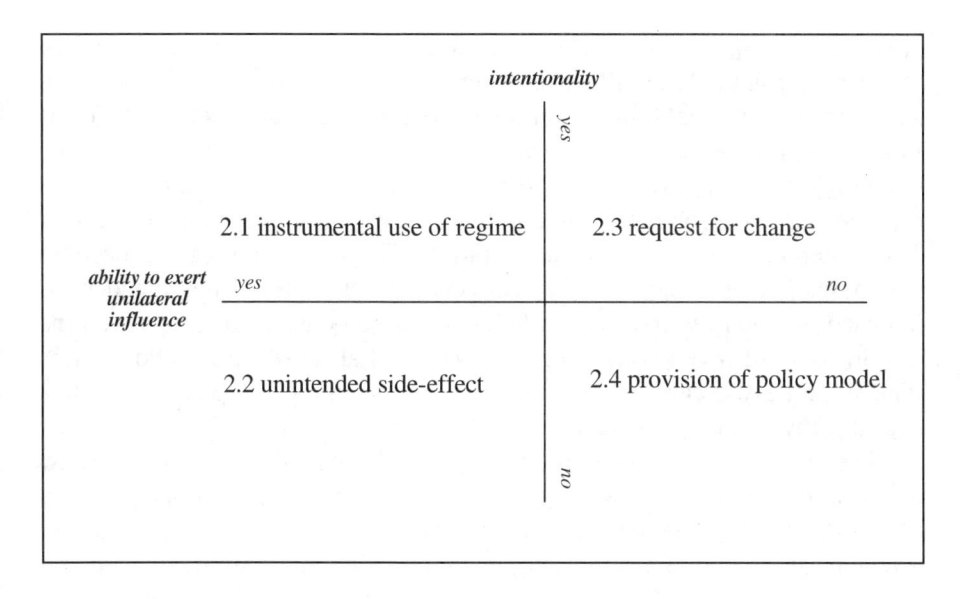

	intentionality	
	yes	
	2.1 instrumental use of regime	2.3 request for change
ability to exert unilateral influence — *yes*		*no*
	2.2 unintended side-effect	2.4 provision of policy model
	no	

Figure 10.2. *Nature of source regime action.*

In these cases, interaction depends exclusively on source regime action. In contrast to the instrumental use of regimes, source regime actors do not entirely control the situation because the generation of externalities occurs involuntarily. We may expect a greater preparedness to negotiate with target regime actors, but also difficulties to actually resolve the issue to the satisfaction of both sides.

Cases at the right side of Figure 10.2 are characterized by a low ability or even inability of source regime actors to unilaterally influence the target regime. In the top right box (2.3) we find cases in which source regime actors nevertheless clearly intend to influence the target regime by requesting the latter to change. For example, the ozone regime's Montreal Protocol requires close control of trade in ozone-depleting substances and products containing these substances. Control is executed predominantly by customs officials. Members of the ozone regime desired to modify the Harmonized System of customs codes of the World Customs Organization (WCO) according to their needs. As they intended to change the customs codes, but could not impose modifications, they had to ask WCO to adapt (Oberthür 2001). Note that *interaction* requires that the request for change is reacted to in some way by the members of the target regime. Arising intentionally, this type of interaction is characterized by action within both the target regime and the source regime. It is based on communication, most probably negotiations, between the two memberships involved.

The bottom right box (2.4) contains cases in which the source regime members are not able to influence the target regime, nor do they intend to do so. Even under these circumstances, a regime may unintentionally exert influence by *providing an innovative policy model* that the actors of the target regime take over voluntarily. A widely discussed example is the diffusion of the Montreal Protocol's non-compliance procedure to several other international environmental regimes. This non-compliance procedure was neither invented *in order to* influence other regimes, nor could it be imposed on other regimes. Nevertheless, it had a considerable impact on the development of several other regimes (Victor et al. 1998). Interaction of this type is entirely controlled by the target regime. It takes place through a causal pathway that is frequently called 'learning' or 'policy diffusion'.

The distinctions related to the nature of source regime action draw attention to the fact that regime interaction is not necessarily a phenomenon of unintended externalities, as emphasized by the majority of the current literature on regime interaction. Regime interaction may well be intended by source regime actors. Even more noteworthy, interaction may occur also in cases in which source regime action alone is not able to generate influence. Hence, these distinctions uncover 'soft' types of interaction that depend on positive reaction from within the target regime to become effective and frequently remain altogether unnoticed.

2.1.2 Consequences

Source regime action will always have some consequence in the target regime or within the issue-area governed by it. Without a consequence, there would be no influence and, thus, no regime interaction. Differences in consequences have so far attracted remarkably little attention within the literature on regime interaction. The few typologies of consequences existing in the literature on regime interaction (see King 1997: 18) have not allowed for the formulation of hypotheses because they do not refer to causal pathways.

First of all, it does not need further explication that information about the nature of the *consequences* caused by a case of interaction will be highly useful. Consequences will always occur either within the target regime or within the issue-area governed by it. However, they may come about in two distinct forms which are immediately related to different causal pathways. In some cases, consequences occur at the outcome level through behavioral changes of relevant actors that affect the target regime's performance. If source regime action causes relevant actors to adapt their behavior individually, the consequence arises outside the institutional framework of the target regime (extra-institutional adaptation). In contrast, the consequence of an interaction may also occur within the target regime itself, i.e. at the output level. (intra-institutional adaptation). In these cases, source regime action causes the members of the target regime to modify *the institution*, usually by amending its norms (see Figure 10.3).

```
    extra-institutional                          intra-institutional
       adaptation                                   adaptation
```

Figure 10.3. *Consequences.*

This distinction is immediately related to the causal pathways at work. In the first case, adaptation involves unilateral action of relevant states and non-state actors outside the regime itself, while in the second case it is channeled through an institutionalized communication process. If consequences occur in the form of intra-institutional adaptation, interaction is dependent on the consent of the target regime actors. Although source regime action may change the decision situation of target regime actors, interaction cannot come about against the will of these actors. It may thus be hypothesized that interaction of this sort will not be highly disruptive. In contrast, extra-institutional adaptation located at the outcome level occurs 'behind the back' of the target regime members without their consent. It is thus not only less visible and may even go unnoticed by both practitioners and scientific observers. It may also easily generate disruptive effects on the performance of the target regime that may be difficult to thwart by action of the target regime itself.

For example, the Montreal Protocol to protect the ozone layer affects the behavior of states and non-state actors related to the production and use of ozone-depleting substances, including CFCs. As CFCs are also greenhouse gases, the Protocol simultaneously affects behavior of state and non-state actors that is relevant to the performance of the climate change regime. This effect occurs without a modification of the rules of, or any other action within, the target regime. Similarly, the Kyoto Protocol provides incentives to maximize carbon sequestration by forests, thus endangering the achievement of the objectives of sustainable forest management pursued under the Convention on Biological Diversity. The consequence of the interaction in the target regime again consists in extra-institutional behavioral adaptations by relevant actors (e.g. investments in mono-cultural tree plantations).

In contrast, if the parties to the Montreal Protocol request that the World Customs Organization adapt its system of customs codes to the needs of the ozone regime, interaction does not result in relevant extra-institutional behavioral adaptations. Instead, it requires intra-institutional adaptation by the World Customs Organization itself through modification of the latter's customs codes. Likewise, the influence of the Montreal Protocol's non-compliance procedure on the Kyoto Protocol manifested itself in the rules of the latter's compliance system. It did not require a modification of the behavior of any state or non-state actor outside the institutional framework of the climate change regime.

The distinction between two different forms of consequences is important for distinguishing two fundamentally different causal pathways leading from the source to the target regime. First, interaction may lead to behavioral changes of relevant actors within the issue-area governed by the target regime but outside its institutional framework. Such extra-institutional adaptation may occur independently from members of the target regime. In contrast, intra-institutional adaptation requires a collective decision taken within the institutional framework of the target regime and therefore depends on the consent of members of the target regime.

2.1.3 Responses to Interaction

Frequently, actors relevant to the operation of either the source or the target regime, or both, respond to an interaction in order to mitigate adverse, or to enhance synergistic, effects. It is important to clearly distinguish response action from the original consequences of a case of interaction. Whereas the original consequences constitute an essential element of every case of regime interaction, subsequent response action does not. It is only present in some, but not in all cases, and it is always intended to modify the original consequence.

In many cases of interaction, there is no response action at all. We may expect that this is particularly true for cases in which the original consequence of an interaction is beneficial for the target regime. In these cases, actors may tend simply to consume this additional benefit without engaging in further efforts to respond actively. For example, the benefits to the climate change regime of the phasing out of CFCs under the Montreal Protocol did not require any further action. While actors might respond to an interaction in order to enhance existing synergies, avoidance or mitigation of disruptive effects may be expected to figure more prominently since they disturb actors.

If response action occurs, it may take different forms. Response action may rely upon collective decision-making within one of the institutions involved or it may take place beyond their confines. If individual actors respond unilaterally to the consequences of an interaction, response will take place outside of any of the institutions involved. If the original consequences of an interaction motivate the members of the target or the source regime to modify the institution, for example by amending regime norms, the response involves collective decision-making within the regimes. This distinction is important because it establishes two forms of response action that display fundamentally different conditions. In one case, response action involves unilateral decisions by individual states and non-state actors, while in the other it is a collective decision resulting from an institutionalized communication process.

Another distinction refers to the relevance of coordination between the regimes involved. Generally, response may be based upon isolated action occurring within one of the regimes or one of the issue-areas governed by them, or it may rely on explicit coordination *between* the two regimes involved. In the former case, an overarching communication process does not exist. In the latter case, however, the response includes an additional communication process that overarches the two regimes, e.g. in the form of an exchange of the relevant secretariats, negotiations between the two groups of actors or even court decision-making. In this case, we have what Young et al. (1999: 50) call a "political linkage" that arises "when actors decide to consider two or more arrangements as parts of a larger institutional complex".

By combining these two distinctions, we derive another two-dimensional matrix distinguishing types of response action (Figure 10.4). At the left side we find cases without explicit coordination between regimes. The bottom left box (4.2) contains cases in which the response does not involve any collective decision-making within either of the regimes involved, or in the form of coordination between the source and the target regime. In these cases, relevant state and non-state actors respond individually. Interested states and, subsequently, non-state actors may be inclined to respond independently, for example to mitigate disruptive effects of desired policies, especially in cases in which collective response action is lacking. Thus, countries may enact domestic regulation on the use of ozone-friendly HFCs promoted under the Montreal Protocol because of the detrimental effect of these substances on the global climate.

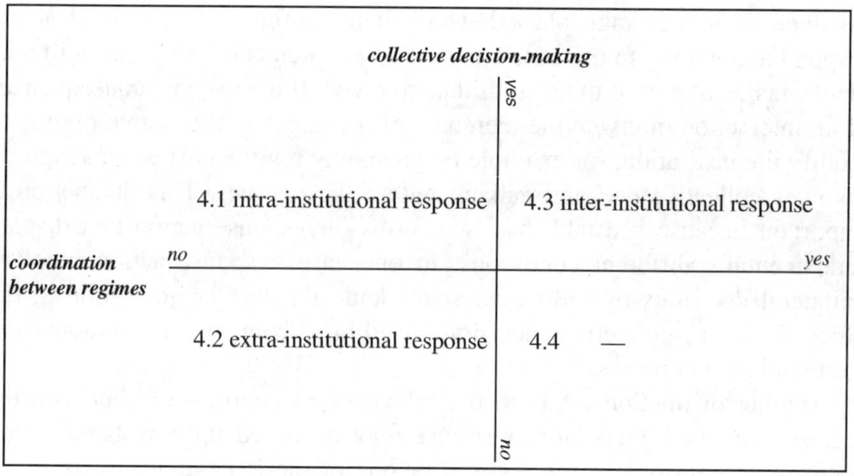

	collective decision-making	
	yes	
coordination between regimes no	4.1 intra-institutional response	4.3 inter-institutional response
yes	4.2 extra-institutional response	4.4 —
	no	

Figure 10.4. *Nature of response action.*

The top left box (4.1) contains cases in which responses occur through uncoordinated collective decision-making within either of the regimes. Such intra-institutional responses require sufficient agreement between regime members and appropriate procedures and institutional structures for collective decision-making that are usually available in modern international regimes. Thus, this form of response action may be assumed to be relatively wide-spread. Target regime members have a particularly strong incentive to act either to avoid disruption or to enhance synergy. However, the source regime will frequently be more capable of acting because it triggered the original consequence in the first place. Especially in situations in which side-effects occur unintentionally, source regime actors may be inclined to act. For example, rules are currently developed under the Kyoto Protocol to counter its potentially disruptive effect on sustainable forest management promoted by the Convention on Biological Diversity.

The right side of Figure 10.4 addresses cases of interaction in which responses are coordinated between the regimes involved. Such inter-institutional coordination is the most demanding form of responses as it requires some overarching institutional framework in which collective decisions can be taken. Accordingly, cases will concentrate in the top right box (4.3), while the bottom right box (4.4) remains empty because coordinated responses always require collective decision-making. Inter-institutional responses are comparatively rare. They will be particularly relevant in situations involving regimes that are 'nested' within a broader institution (on the notion of nested institutions see Young 1996: 2-3). For example, interaction between the various protocols to the 1979 Geneva

UNECE Convention on Long-Range Transboundary Air Pollution may be made subject to collective decisions of the regime members in the responsible 'Executive Body'. Within the European Community conflicts of obligations may be solved by an authoritative decision of the European Court of Justice. However, inter-institutional coordination can also occur between regimes that are not nested. In some cases, regimes coordinate their responses in the form of inter-institutional agreements, memoranda of understanding, or other forms of contractual agreement. For example, the climate change regime and the Global Environment Facility agreed on the terms according to which the latter operates the financial mechanism for the former (see Fairman 1996; Werksman 1996). More frequently, institutions coordinate their activity in less binding ways, in particular by establishing mechanisms for the exchange of information. For example, the original request of the Montreal Protocol to the World Customs Organization to adapt the system of customs codes with respect to ozone-depleting substances has resulted, in addition to a number of relevant decisions in both forums, in a lively exchange of information between the two regimes (see Oberthür 2001). Likewise, the Convention on Trade in Endangered Species (CITES) has established extensive exchanges of information with a number of regimes for the conservation of nature as well as with the World Customs Organization and Interpol (CITES 1999).

The two distinctions introduced here provide a starting point for evaluating the responses to regime interaction more systematically. Whether or not such responses involve collective decision-making or even coordination between the source and the target regime is important since collective decision-making and coordination between regimes open up particular capacities to mitigate conflict or enhance synergy between regimes. At the same time, achieving collective decision-making and coordination places special demands on the members of the regimes involved and may not always produce significant benefits. Whether these forms of response action become relevant will thus depend on the particular circumstances of the case.

2.2 Toward Inductive Analysis of Regime Interaction

While we have argued in Section 1 that complex interaction situations should be disaggregated into a number of limited *cases*, it turns out now that even these cases are highly complex social phenomena. According to the distinctions identified in the previous sub-section, every single case of interaction has different properties relating to its situation-specific causes and effects, to the nature of source regime action and to the consequences and responses. Evidently, these distinctions are not the only ones worth exploring and others may be added in the future. However, we submit that they embody critical factors because they are relevant to the causal pathways that drive regime interaction. They may thus be taken as a sound starting point for advancing research on regime interaction in a systematic manner. The set of distinctions provides instruments for two sorts of research, namely the empirical mapping of cases and the inductive generation of classes of regime interaction.

First of all, the distinctions introduced here may be employed as a checklist when investigating cases of regime interaction. They point to a number of important dimensions of each case and provide criteria for the generation of case "profiles". It has to be noted, however, that each of the distinctions confronts two mutually exclusive ideal types. Real world cases will frequently be of a hybrid nature. For example, interaction between the river Rhine regime and the regime for the protection of the North Sea might be driven by a functional logic as these institutions govern clearly different subject areas that are, nevertheless, substantively linked. However, their memberships also differ significantly, suggesting a logic of membership. Similarly, it may not always be easy to decide whether a source regime was able to influence the target regime unilaterally, since this may be a matter of degree. A researcher intending to merely *classify* empirical cases according to the dimensions developed above may thus decide to turn the bi-polar distinctions into continua. Accordingly, interaction may be located somewhere in the middle between the extremes in mixed cases. However, before pragmatic solutions of this sort are pursued, researchers should check whether disaggregating further the interaction phenomenon in question would resolve the issue (see Section 2).

Second, the distinctions developed may be employed as an instrument for the exploration of dominant patterns of regime interaction. By combining some dimensions of regime interaction, we have made the first step towards a multidimensional typology of cases. Altogether, the distinctions establish numerous possible classes of regime interaction. We may expect that several of these classes will be virtually unpopulated, while cases will concentrate in others. For example, one might hypothesize that cases driven by a functional logic are strongly correlated with unintended source state action. But is this true for functional synergy too? Furthermore, do cases driven by a functional logic lead more often than cases driven by a logic of membership to inter-institutional coordination, and does intentionality systematically influence this variation? Questions of this type will eventually enable us to develop dominant types of regime interaction with similar properties. If complex situations are sufficiently disaggregated and the number of cases is high enough, even systematic application of quantitative methods may become possible. As categories are designed so as to indicate different causal pathways at work, inductively derived patterns of cases of interaction might serve as a basis for hypothesizing about causal connections between the different dimensions distinguished, and for elaborating theoretically well-founded causal mechanisms (see Section 3.2).

3. ADVANCING CAUSAL ANALYSIS OF REGIME INTERACTION

Detection and mapping of possible cases of regime interaction is an important step in the process of evaluating the interaction pattern of a given situation. However, a case may only be established by demonstrating causality through the identification of causal pathways (3.1). This may provide the basis for developing generalized causal mechanisms in the future. Going beyond the standardization of causal pathways, such mechanisms would spell out the conditions under which they become operational (3.2).

3.1 Establishing Causality

The core task of an empirical analysis of regime interaction is to identify, separately for every case, the existence of an actual chain of influence between the regimes involved. Since quantitative or statistical methods for causal analysis of interaction situations seem to be largely out of reach at the present state of knowledge, cases of interaction need to be treated basically as single events that are independent of each other. Establishing causality then involves addressing at least two issues, namely the selection of the appropriate empirical methods based on a clear understanding of the underlying concept of agency and the identification of a causal pathway.

First, researchers aiming at establishing causality in cases of regime interaction may employ a number of well-known *empirical methods*. One important method is the tracing of negotiation and decision processes (see George/McKeown 1985). It will be particularly relevant for analyzing cases that operate at the output level and thus result in consequences within the target regime itself (see Section 2.1.3). In this case, process tracing can reveal important information about whether or not the decision of target regime actors to modify their institution was motivated by the source regime. Frequently, however, it will prove difficult to establish on this basis that decision-making in the target regime was not driven by other factors, such as technical progress. Therefore, process tracing is best complemented by other methods, that may also be employed for establishing causality in cases of interaction that operate at the outcome level and generate consequences in the form of extra-institutional adaptation (see Section 2.1.3). An important and well-known method for establishing causality is the construction of counterfactual scenarios (Tetlock/Belkin 1996, Biersteker 1993, Fearon 1991). This method addresses the hypothetical question of how the target regime and the issue-area governed by it would have developed in the absence of the source regime. A reliable counterfactual scenario disclosing major differences to the actual development will firmly establish causal influence. However, the construction of a *reliable* counterfactual scenario frequently proves impossible because of the many intervening factors that have to be taken into consideration. This will be especially true if the scenario stretches over a longer period of time. Therefore, this method may be complemented by the exclusion of alternative explanations (Bernauer 1995), i.e by exploring the question of whether factors other than the source regime might convincingly explain the observed change in, or effect on, the target institution. These methods are so widely applied in the well-advanced research on the simple effectiveness of international regimes (Underdal in this volume) that they need no further elaboration here.

Thought experiments and counterfactual scenarios model actors' behavior in virtual situations and depend, therefore, on assumptions about how actors might behave in general. Due to the complexity of the real world, researchers will also have to distinguish between actors that are deemed relevant for a particular pathway and those that are not. They will have to draw a line between relevant action to be taken into account and less relevant action that might be ignored. In addition, empirical data required for a plausible explanation will frequently be inaccessible or lacking and must be substituted or complemented with conceptually plausible speculation. In short, causal analysis requires – at least implicitly – a theory of action.

Rational utility maximization is probably the concept most widely employed in empirical studies that explore causal pathways – even though empirical work does usually not make this assumption explicit. The analytical power of the rational actor model stems from the fact that it provides a useful theoretical foundation for exploring the behavior of actors in undetermined situations. This is most important in situations of change in which more than one viable option exists. Consider a situation in which the African countries endeavor to close their continent for waste exports. We may want to employ a theoretically informed thought experiment to investigate how waste producing industries and waste brokers might react. Will they stop waste exports? Doing so would cause high investment for industries and drive brokers out of business. Or will they try to side-step the African ban? They may attempt to do so depending on the ability of the African countries to implement their regional regime. Or will they attempt to find alternative outlets for their waste? If successful, it might be the cheapest and least complicated option. Engaging in this type of reasoning, researchers implicitly ask: Which of a number of available options will best serve the interests of these actors and may thus be expected to be chosen by them? Asking this question is based upon the assumption that the actors intend to maximize their utility, that is, choose the option that ranks highest in their order of preferences. Causal analysis cannot avoid engaging in thought experiments of this type.

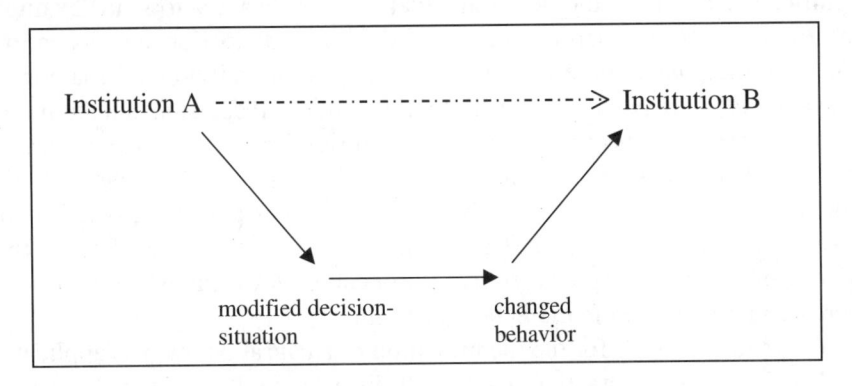

```
Institution A  ------------------>  Institution B
            \                      /
             \                    /
              v                  /
        modified decision-  →  changed
            situation          behavior
```

Figure 10.5. *Model of a Causal Pathway*

Second, causation will be difficult to establish without the *identification of the causal pathway* that is capable of bringing about an observed change. The empirical phenomenon of regime interaction is located at the collective ("system") level. We endeavor to identify cases in which one social institution influences another social institution. However, an international regime is not an actor (at least not in the traditional sense), and it is definitely not capable of affecting the target regime directly. If a source regime affects a target regime, influence will always be channeled through some causal pathway that involves action by non-institutional actors located at some lower ("unit") level. Accordingly, establishing causality means to link occurrences located at the institutional (aggregate) level with developments located at the actors' level (see Hovi in this volume). The basic model of causal explanation of social (aggregate level) events is illustrated in Figure 10.5.

Explanation by causal pathways combines a logic of the situation with a theory of action and a logic of aggregation of actors' behavior (see Coleman 1990: 1-23). Accordingly, identification of a causal pathway that links a source regime with a target regime comprises three major steps. First, we have to establish how an important component of the source regime (or its anticipation) may affect the decision situation of relevant actors. Second, we must prove that the modification of the decision situation results in a change of their individual behavior. And third, we must demonstrate that these behavioral changes produce the effect observed within the target regime (see Esser 1993: 39-63). For example, we may want to establish that the Schengen regime on the abolition of border controls for persons interacted with, i.e. causally influenced, the European Union's related policy. In this case, we will have to demonstrate that the establishment of the regime significantly modified the decision situation of relevant actors, for example because it forced non-parties to choose between participation and abstention. We will then have to establish that changes in individual behavior of relevant actors may be attributed to the modified decision situation, for example that some originally hesitant countries joined the regime because they disliked isolation. Finally, we will have to demonstrate that the aggregate consequences of these behavioral changes paved the way for the development of the Union's Third Pillar (justice and home affairs), that opposition against a largely identical European policy diminished because of increased participation in the Schengen regime.

While this strategy for the identification of a causal pathway is applicable to all instances of interaction, cases will differ as to the actual pathways of influence at work over the whole causal chain. Pathways may involve different types of actors and behavior. Effects observed within the target regime will frequently be attributable to changes in the behavior of key states. However, other types of actors may play an important role in a causal pathway. For example, *waste producing industries and waste brokers* will play a major part in the explanation of influence of the ban of imports of hazardous wastes to Africa on the emergence of other regional waste import regimes. The actual – or even anticipated – change in behavior of non-state actors will modify the decision situation of potentially affected countries in other regions if they realize the emergence or aggravation of an environmental problem that did not require action so far. It may induce them to establish their own regional protection regime. Non-governmental organizations and institutional actors such as secretariats of international institutions may also constitute important actors. Given the diversity of possible cases of interaction, the relevance of varying types of actors will largely depend on the circumstances of the individual case. In most cases, research is best initiated with a focus on key states (or groups of states) because these actors are frequently most influential in bringing about changes within the target regime. Sub-state and non-state actors may be added to the analysis depending on the particular case at hand. They may be given more prominent status in the case of interaction involving 'transnational regimes' (Haufler 1993).

EXPLORING REGIME INTERACTION

Finally, it should be noted that actors generally 'behave' in two distinct forms. They act *outside* the institutional framework of the regimes involved, for example shipping waste from one country to another or allowing their fishermen to catch whales. They may also act *within* an institutional framework, for example by modifying a negotiation position or instigating dispute settlement proceedings, if available. Depending on the particular case of interaction and on the specific causal pathway at work, research may have to focus on the domestic level or on the institutionalized international process. For instance, if a request for change from the side of the source regime leads to intra-institutional adaptation, and possibly to intra- or inter-institutional responses, most of the analysis will concentrate on the international institutional level. In contrast, if source regime action leads to disruptive effects at the level of domestic implementation and does not trigger collective policy responses, most of the analysis will have to address the national level.

3.2   Generalized Causal Mechanisms

Eventually we may want to reach beyond the empirical assessment of cases of regime interaction and the causal explanation of empirically observed pathways of influence. We require generalized knowledge if we intend to generate hypotheses as to what kind of interaction is to be expected in a given situation, or under which conditions a particular type of interaction is probable, or which policy responses may prove particularly effective under given circumstances. If we are not satisfied by the correlation between different types of situation and their effects, but want to know *why* an observed effect comes about in a particular situation, we must identify generalized causal mechanisms. A *generalized* causal mechanism combines a causal chain that brings about an effect in the target regime with the identification of conditions under which this causal chain becomes effective or is likely to become effective. While it reaches beyond an empirically established causal pathway, it may well be based on inductively generated patterns of regime interaction (see Section 2.2) that may provide a starting point for hypothesizing about causal connections between the different dimensions of regime interaction. The development of generalized causal mechanisms may eventually provide a kit of standard forms of interaction (Schelling 1978, Hovi in this volume) that might serve as analytical tools, much like the familiar standard game theoretic situations help analyze problems of cooperation under anarchy.

There has been some endeavor to develop a generalized causal mechanism for one particular type of regime interaction, namely the instrumental use of a "minilateral" regime by a comparatively small number of interested actors to influence or replace a larger multilateral regime governing the same issue-area. Genschel and Plümper (1997) explored why the establishment of a minilateral regime generates a dynamic that gradually affects the existing larger regime in some cases but not in others. Their general answer is that such a dynamic is likely to occur if (a) the group of initiators is able to cooperate without participation of other actors (otherwise the process could not be expected to start), and (b) the incentive for a free rider to abstain from cooperation *decreases* with every additional cooperator. In this case, the advantage of abstaining (and free riding) diminishes gradually and may eventually even turn into a disadvantage. Situations of this type have the potential for self-sustained growth. For example, joining the Schengen regime on the abolition of police controls at the internal borders in Europe became more attractive with every additional member (Gehring 1998). The Schengen regime thus heavily influenced the related EU policy. In contrast, if the advantage of abstaining and taking a free ride for a non-cooperating actor *increases* with every additional cooperator, the growth of the minilateral regime is likely to stop at a rather early stage, and it is therefore unlikely to replace the larger regime.

The formulation of such generalized causal mechanisms may be expected to advance our understanding of regime interaction considerably. It is still too early to outline a research program that would allow the development of generalized causal mechanisms - not least because of the low level of systematic empirical knowledge about types and patterns of interaction between regimes (see Section 2.2). However, such a program would be directed at inquiring into the systematic modification of incentive structures inducing relevant actors to adjust their behavior. A (moderate) rational actors' perspective (see Section 3.1) seems to be particularly well suited for this task. Advancing theoretical research in this direction might enable us one day to make general statements about the dynamics of functional conflict, or the conditions under which voluntary adoption of institutional arrangements from another regime becomes possible, or the prerequisites under which interaction is responded to by collective decision-making or inter-institutional coordination. Knowledge of this type would be of considerable value for the development of institutional designs that might prevent undesirable, and enhance desirable, interaction.

4. CONCLUSION

International regimes do not exist in isolation from one another. They co-exist within the international system and increasingly exert influence on each other's development and performance. In light of the growing number of formally independent international regimes, *interaction between regimes* has already attracted considerable interest of both scholars and policy-makers. Much of the research on regime interaction has been motivated by concern about the detrimental impact of such interaction on the effectiveness of the regimes involved, in particular in the field of environmental protection. In this respect, it constitutes an offspring of the policy-relevant research focus on regime effectiveness that flourished in the past decade. However, research on regime interaction has not yet been based on an elaborate conceptual foundation, and it is not yet guided by theoretical ambition.

This paper aims to contribute to the filling of this conceptual gap. It develops a systematic framework for the analysis of regime interaction that may become the core of a structured research program. The framework avoids limiting attention to particular (kinds of) cases of interaction or specific pathways of influence. Instead, it is intended to facilitate the exploration and mapping of cases of interaction. Empirical knowledge gained on this basis promises to provide a basis for identifying particular patterns of regime interaction and developing a typology of cases of interaction, which would constitute the first step towards identifying causal mechanisms and a theory of regime interaction.

In investigating regime interaction, researchers are faced with situations that are characterized by high degrees of complexity. Frequently, a situation involves two regimes that are themselves sufficiently complex to interact in more than a single way, or it comprises a co-evolution process that develops over time, or it entails interaction among a whole set of regimes. Under these conditions, interaction may appear to go forth and back between the regimes involved without a clear direction of influence, or it may rely on different causal pathways. In order to gain analytical rigor and reach beyond the mere description of a complex situation, we propose to take as the units of analysis *cases of interaction* that are characterized by a clear direction of influence running from a single source regime toward a single target regime. Disaggregating complex overall situations into an appropriate number of cases allows us to examine the causal pathways at work and to identify the particular features of a case. It thus promises to generate a clearer picture of the situation as a whole than an overall analysis.

Furthermore, an important task at the present stage of research is the systematic analysis and mapping of cases. While overall interaction situations may be readily identifiable, cases of interaction will frequently be hidden if they do not stir open conflict between regimes or require action by the policy-makers involved. Therefore, researchers must have a preconceived idea of possible types of interaction and their appearance. The present framework of analysis introduces seven important dimensions of regime interaction. It draws the attention of the empirical researcher to the broadness of the field of regime interaction and allows him to capture even cases of interaction which policy-makers may be unaware of. Based on a systematic empirical mapping of cases, it may be possible to derive inductively a more sophisticated typology of cases (and possibly of different causal pathways) that could provide the basis for the elaboration of conceptually more demanding causal mechanisms.

Finally, regime interaction is limited to cases of actual (and anticipated) influence between regimes. Therefore, causality has to be demonstrated. The application of variation-finding or statistical methods does not seem to be appropriate at the present stage of knowledge. Therefore, demonstration of causality will have to rely on the application of qualitative methods of causal inference and the establishment of causal pathways that plausibly link source regimes with target regimes and their issue-areas. The exploration of a causal pathway will always refer to the behavior of relevant actors at a lower level. The systematic search for causal pathways related to different types of regime interaction promises to provide the necessary basis for the future development of generalized causal mechanisms. Beyond specifying particular patterns of regime interaction, such generalized mechanisms would indicate under which conditions they occur. They would thus offer a tool-kit for the analysis of interaction situations much like the standard game theoretical situations do for the exploration of collective action problems.

Theoretical and conceptually well-founded knowledge about the causes and consequences of regime interaction will be highly relevant to policy-making. It promises to assist the development of policies that help prevent conflict and enhance synergy between regimes. It generates insights into particularly effective political responses and enhances our understanding of the conditions under which linkages between regimes and their issue-areas may be employed to effectively pursue political objectives. Thus, research based on the framework of analysis laid out here not only promises to advance our theoretical understanding of regime interaction, but will also help design effective institutional arrangements.

NOTES

[1] A diversity of terms can be found in the literature to describe the phenomena dealt with here, for example interplay, linkage, inter-linkage, overlap, and interconnection. Throughout this paper, we will use the term regime interaction.

[2] The paper also constitutes a contribution to the EU collaborative research project on "Institutional Interaction – How to Prevent Conflicts and Enhance Synergies between International and EU Environmental Institutions", funded under the EU research and technological development program "Energy, Environment and Sustainable Development" (Contract No. EVK2-CT2000-00079). The authors are solely responsible for the contents

of the paper that does not represent the opinion of the European Community. We thank the project members, the editors of the book and, especially, Olav Schram Stokke for their valuable comments.

REFERENCES

Andersen, R. (2002) The Time Dimension in International Regime Interplay, Global Environmental Politics 2, 3: 98–117.

Archer, M. S. (1985) Structuration versus Morphogenesis, in S.N. Eisenstadt and H.J. Helle, (eds.) Macro-Sociological Theory: Perspectives on Sociological Theory, Vol. 1, Sage, London, 58–88.

Beisheim, M., Dreher, S., Walter, G., Zangl, B. and Zürn, M. (1999) Im Zeitalter der Globalisierung? Thesen und Daten zur gesellschaftlichen und politischen Denationalisierung, Baden-Baden.

Bernauer, T. (1995) The Effect of International Environmental Institutions: How We Might Learn More, International Organization 49, 2: 351–377.

Biersteker, T. J. (1993) Constructing Historical Counterfactuals to Assess the Consequences of International Regimes: The Global Dept Regime and the Dept Crisis of the 1980s, in V. Rittberger, (ed.) Regime Theory and International Relations, Oxford University Press, 315–338.

Breitmeier, H. (2000) Working Group III: Complex Effectiveness: Regime Externalities and Interaction, in J. Wettestad (ed.) Proceedings of the 1999 Oslo Workshop of the Concerted Action Network on the Effectiveness of International Environmental Regimes, Oslo, 45–48.

Brown Weiss, E. (1993) International Environmental Issues and the Emergence of a New World Order, Georgetown Law Journal 81, 3: 675–710.

Carlsnaes, W. 1(992) The Agent-Structure Problem in Foreign Policy Analysis, International Studies Quarterly 36, 3: 245–270.

CITES, (1999) Synergy between the Biodiversity-Related Conventions and Relations with other Organizations, Standing Committee Doc. SC.42.17, Convention on International Trade in Endangered Species of Wild Fauna and Flora, 42nd Meeting of the Standing Committee, Lisbon (Portugal), 28 September – 1 October, 1999.

Coleman, J. S. (1990) Foundations of Social Theory, MIT Press, Cambridge MA.

Dessler, D. (1989) What's at Stake in the Agent-Structure Debate? International Organization 43, 3: 441–473.

Esser, H. (1993) Soziologie, Allgemeine Grundlagen, Frankfurt/M.

Fairman, D. (1996) The Global Environment Facility: Haunted by the Shadow of the Future, in R. O. Keohane and M. A. Levy, (eds.) Institutions for Environmental Aid: Pitfalls and Promise, MIT Press, Cambridge, 55–87.

Fearon, J. D. (1991) Counterfactuals and Hypotheses Testing in Political Science, World Politics 43: 169–195.

Gehring, T. (1994) Dynamic International Regimes: Institutions for International Environmental Governance, Frankfurt/M.

Gehring, T. (1998) Die Politik des koordinierten Alleingangs: Schengen und die Abschaffung der Personenkontrollen an den Binnengrenzen der Europäischen Union, Zeitschrift für Internationale Beziehungen 5, 1: 43–78.

Genschel, P. und Plümper, T. (1997) Regulatory Competition and international Cooperation, Journal of European Public Policy 4, 4: 626–652.

George, A. L. and McKeown, T. J. (1985) Case Studies and Theories of Organizational Decision Making, Advances in Information Processing in Organizations 2: 21–58.
Gillespie, A. (1998) Sinks, Biodiversity & Forests: The Implications of the Kyoto Protocol Upon the Other Primary UNCED Instruments, in Bradnee W. Chambers, (ed.) Global Climate Governance: Inter-linkages between the Kyoto Protocol and other Multilateral Regimes, United Nations University, Institute of Advanced Studies, 117–139.
Haufler, V. (1993) Crossing the Boundary between Public and Private: International Regimes and Non-State Actors, in Rittberger, Volker, (eds.) Regime Theory and International Relations, Oxford University Press, 94–111.
Herr, R. A. and Chia, E. (1995) The Concept of Regime Overlap: Toward Identification and Assessment, in B. Davis (ed.) Overlapping Maritime Regimes: An Initial Reconnaissance, Antarctic CRC and Institute of Antarctic and Southern Ocean Studies.
Hollis, M. and Smith, S. (1991) Beware of Gurus: Structure and Action in International Relations, Review of International Studies 17, 4: 393–410.
Keohane, R. O. and Levy, M. A. (eds.) (1996) Institutions for Environmental Aid: Pitfalls and Promises, MIT Press, Cambridge, MA/London.
King, G., Keohane, R. O. and Verba, S. (1994) Designing Social Inquiry: Scientific Inference in Qualitative Research, Princeton University Press.
King, L. A. (1997) Institutional Interplay – Research Questions, paper commissioned by Institutional Dimensions of Global Change and International Human Dimensions Programme on Global Environmental Change: Environmental Studies Programme, School of Natural Resources, University of Vermont.
Lang, W. (1993) International Environmental Agreements and the GATT: The Case of the Montreal Protocol, Wirtschaftspolitische Blätter 40: 364–372.
Levy, M. A., Young, O. R. and Zürn, M. (1995) The Study of International Regimes: European Journal of International Relations 1: 267–330.
Martin, L. L. and Simmons, B. A. (1998) Theories and Empirical Studies of International Institutions, International Organization 52: 729–757.
Meinke, B. (1997) Die internationale Kontrolle des grenzüberschreitenden Handels mit gefährlichen Abfällen (Baseler Konvention von 1989), in T. Gehring and S. Oberthür, (eds.) Internationale Umweltregime, Umweltschutz durch Verhandlungen und Verträge, Leske + Budrich, Opladen, 63–80.
Meinke, B. (2002) Multi-Regime-Regulierung, Darmstadt: Deutscher Universitäts-Verlag.
Moltke, K. von (1997) Institutional Interactions: The Structure of Regimes for Trade and the Environment, in Young, O. R. (ed.) Global Governance: Drawing Insights from the Environmental Experience, MIT Press, Cambridge, MA, 247–272.
Oberthür, S. (2001) Linkages between the Montreal and Kyoto Protocols: Enhancing Synergies between Protecting the Ozone Layer and the Global Climate, International Environmental Agreements: Politics, Law and Economics 1, 3: 357–377.
Petersmann, E.-U. (1993) International Trade Law and International Environmental Law, Journal of World Trade 27, 1: 43–81.
Pontecorvo, C. M. (1999) Interdependence between Global Environmental Regimes: The Kyoto Protocol on Climate Change and Forest Protection, Zeitschrift für ausländisches öffentliches Recht und Völkerrecht 59, 3: 709–749.
Rosendal, G. K. (2000) The Convention on Biological Diversity and Developing Countries, Kluwer Academic, Dordrecht.
Sand, P. (ed.) (1992) The Effectiveness of International Environmental Agreements: A Survey of Existing Legal Instruments, Grotius, Cambridge.
Schelling, T. C. (1978) Micromotives and Macrobehavior, W. W. Norton, New York.

Stokke, O. S. (1999) Governance of High Seas Fisheries: The Role of Regime Linkages, in D. Vidas and W. Ostreng, (eds.) Order for the Oceans at the Turn of the Century, Kluwer Law International, Den Haag, 157–172.

Stokke, O. S. (2000) Managing Straddling Stocks: The Interplay of Global and Regional Regimes, Ocean and Coastal Management 43, 2-3: 205–234.

Strange, S. (1982) Cave! Hic Dragones: A Critique of Regime Analysis, International Organization 36, 2: 479–494.

Tarasofsky, R. G. (ed.) (1999) Assessing the International Forest Regime, IUCN Environmental Policy and Law Paper 37, IUCN, Gland.

Tetlock, P. E. and Belkin, A. (eds.) (1996) Counterfactual Thought Experiments in World Politics: Logical, Methodological, and Psychological Perspectives, Princeton University Press.

Victor, D. G., Raustiala, K. and Skolnikoff, E. B. (eds.) (1998) The Implementation and Effectiveness of International Environmental Commitments: Theory and Practice, MIT Press, Cambridge, MA.

Werksman, J. (1996) Consolidating Governance of the Global Commons: Insights from the Global Environment Facility, Yearbook of International Environmental Law 6: 27–63.

WBGU (1998) Die Anrechnung biologischer Quellen und Senken im Kyoto-Protokoll: Fortschritt oder Rückschlag für den globalen Umweltschutz? Sondergutachten 1998, Bremerhaven.

Young, O. R. (1996) Institutional Linkages in International Society: Polar Perspectives, Global Governance 2: 1–24.

Young, O. R., Aggarval, A., King, L. A., Sand, P.H., Underdal, A. and Wasson, M. (1999) Institutional Dimensions of Global Environmental Change (IDGEC), Science Plan, Bonn.

Young, O. R. (2002) The Institutional Dimensions of Environmental Change: Fit, Interplay, and Scale, MIT Press, Cambridge, MA.

Zhang, Z. X. (1998) Greenhouse Gas Emissions and the World Trading System, Journal of World Trade 32, 5: 219–239.

Chapter 11

INTERNATIONAL REGIMES AND DEMOCRACY
Consequences on Domestic and Transnational Level

HELMUT BREITMEIER
Institute for Political Science (Darmstadt University of Technology)

1. INTRODUCTION

We live in an era of denationalization where social interactions increasingly transcend territorial boundaries and where states have lost their ability to manage political issues independently of other states (Zürn 1998: 73)[1]. International governance conceived of as the establishment and operation of social institutions consisting of sets of rules, decision-making procedures, and programmatic activities that define social practices and guide interactions of those participating in these practices can partly re-establish the problem-solving capacities of states and thereby enhance *output-oriented legitimacy* of governance that has been undermined by denationalization in the last decades (Young 1997: 4). *Output-oriented* legitimacy of government (*"government for the people"*) implies that collective decisions should serve the common interest of the constituency. It justifies obedience of the people because the powers of government are utilized for the purpose of the management of problems that members of a collectivity cannot solve individually or in absence of governmental authority.

Government derives legitimacy not only from its capacity for problem-solving but also from the ability of the people to participate in political decision-making. *Input-oriented legitimacy* (*"government of the people"*) can be understood as "self-government" as it implies that decisions that are binding for a collectivity should reflect the preferences and originate from participation of the constituency in political decisionmaking (Scharpf 1998: 2).

Democratic theorists increasingly have put attention on the possible de-democratizing effects of international governance systems on national democracies. Robert A. Dahl (1994: 28) diagnosed that increasing output-oriented legitimacy achieved through the extension of governance beyond the nation-state coincides with a decrease in the ability of the people to influence policy making in a democratic polity. In a similar way, David Held (1997: 261), as another proponent of the de-democratization thesis, argued that although national political systems will further persist, the evolution of, *interalia*, a transnational economy and of new organizational, administrative, or legal structures connected with denationalization would inevitably create new political spaces beyond the nationstate which, if they are not recaptured by the political process, can circumvent the democratic state and thereby reduce the possibility of a collectivity to participate in political decisionmaking. However, democratic theorists seem to have been much less interested in analyzing consequences produced by international governance systems that can also lead to the fostering or stabilization of national or transnational democratic political processes.

Against this background, I will map the consequences of international governance on the democratic process from a broader perspective by dealing with effects that not only constrain the ability of citizens or democratic institutions to influence policymaking in a democratic polity, but which can also result in democratization of authoritarian political systems and therefore impact on the democratic process in a more positive way. I will identify these effects on two different levels of analysis. From a state-centric view, I will describe the consequences of international governance on the level of territorially delimited national democracy. A second level of analysis will focus on consequences occurring on the transnational level of emerging global civil society. In the following I will first describe the dependent variable of the "democratic process". Modern democratic theory developed a number of approaches that differ especially with respect to the normative foundations considered as a prerequisite for democracy (Abromeit 2002; Schmidt 1995). Against this background, I will explain why the concept of deliberative democracy is particularly well suited to describe both national and transnational democratic processes. In a second step, I will investigate the consequences of international regimes on the democratic process from a broader perspective. In this context, I will identify which data exist that can illustrate the assumed regime consequences and which methods have been applied to study these consequences. I will further discuss which other variables are relevant for explaining variances concerning the impacts of international governance on the democratic process. Particular attention will be given to the role that nongovernmental actors can play for improving *input-oriented* legitimacy of international governance on both national and transnational levels of democracy.

2. DELIBERATIVE DEMOCRACY: A CONCEPT FOR BOTH LEVELS OF ANALYSIS

What is deliberative democracy? Why is the concept particularly well suited to study the effects of international governance on the democratic process on both domestic and transnational levels? Can we distinguish certain arenas of the democratic process on which international governance can be assumed to impact? The concept of deliberative democracy can be broadly defined as comprising a family of views "according to which the public deliberation of free and equal citizens is the core of legitimate political decision-making and self-government" (Bohman 1998: 401). Proponents of the concept argue that deliberative democracy is superior to representative democracy because it is the goal of the process of deliberation to reach consensus in a society rather than to outvote the minority. Such an understanding ties the conditions for *input-oriented* legitimacy no longer exclusively to the principle of democratic representation established by general elections or to the execution of political will-formation within traditional democratic decision-making procedures, but emphasizes the importance of a functioning public that guarantees free and equal access of the individual to public deliberation. Jürgen Habermas (1998: 166) argues that the deliberative concept does not consider traditional democratic institutions as unnecessary, but that a functioning public, the quality of deliberation, access to public deliberation, and the discursive structure of opinion- and will-formation are further conditions for democratic legitimacy. In a similar way, Joshua Cohen (1997: 412f) conceptualizes deliberative democracy as a framework of social and institutional conditions within which favorable conditions for participation, association, and expression will be provided to facilitate free discussion among equal citizens. The authorization to exercise power as well as the exercise of power itself will be tied to such discussion and the responsiveness and accountability of political power will be achieved within a framework of regular competitive elections, conditions of publicity, or legislative oversight.

The model of "reflexive democracy" put forward by Rainer Schmalz-Bruns (1995: 163 – 165) takes increasing complexity of collective action problems as a starting point. The model tries to overcome the dilemma that a strengthening of democratic participation will damage the effectiveness of policy making. It assumes that the demand of the state for information on how to cope with complex problems will result in a strengthening of civil society that could act as a supplier of expertise to the political process and thereby further enhance the effectiveness of governmental policies. Against the background of horizontal diffusion of the effects produced by decisions of political systems, the model pleads for more flexibility in respect of participation rights or competencies in decision making for civil society. It further suggests how to realize these rights and competenc es in such a way that they make variable forms of political organization possible. The model aims at a transformation of political institutions by democratizing parties, associations, and institutions through the extension of participation rights, by improving the process of the shaping of public opinion through the establishment of advisory bodies or deliberative policy forums, and by coupling the different levels of political decision making. From this perspective, institutions are conceived of as a means of civic self-qualification (Schmalz-Bruns 1995: 189).

The concept of deliberative democracy hardly corresponds to current reality of democratic politics, and some of the normative claims involved with deliberative democracy bear the character of utopia. Jack Knight and James Johnson (1994: 287 – 289) point to three difficulties that must be taken into account when putting the concept into practice. First, consensual procedures must not lead inevitably to increased legitimacy of political decision making immediately. Deliberative procedures may also first lead to increased political conflict because interest groups will realize their own preferences and can be tempted to follow their own self-interest rather than the common good. Therefore, the concept will require that individuals and groups participating in the political process share a common standard of "reasonableness" necessary to sustain the ideal (Knight and Johnson 1994: 288). The authors further maintain that other normative claims that are incompatible with the deliberative ideal can provide a further difficulty for realizing the concept. However, the rise of competing normative claims involves a problem which is not only limited to the deliberative ideal, but that such claims can affect the functioning of other conceptions of democracy equally. The third difficulty arises from the normative claim involved with the concept for free and equal access of individuals or groups to relevant deliberative arenas. When previously unheard constituencies will be included only late in a deliberative procedure, it will be likely that existing consensus will have to be renegotiated. A possible re-framing of a problem in an issue area very likely will entail the inclusion of new constituencies in public deliberation.

Of course, it is difficult to implement the ideal of deliberative democracy. However, the concept broadens the view for analytic questions that are not simply limited to consequences of international governance on democratic polity. Building the study of the consequences of international governance on the concept of deliberative democracy directs analysis on the effects of international governance on representative institutions (e.g., on parliaments, on the relationship between the legislative and the executive, or on democratic institutions on subnational levels) as well as on the political process impacting on these institutions. Deliberative democracy is particularly well suited for studying the consequences of international governance on the evolving "post-national" democracy on the transnational level, because it directs our view on analyzing the character of discursive processes occurring in the context of international governance systems (Habermas 1998).

For several reasons, representative democracy is hardly a concept that could be used to realize democracy on the level of transnational democracy at the moment. First, representative democracy relies on a majoritarian mode of democratic decision making that is currently not realized in international policy-making systems. Although the European Parliament consists of nationally elected representatives, the EU policy-making process is much too strongly dominated by national governments and the European Commission (Abromeit 1998: 4). Therefore, the European Union still takes on the character of a semi-democratic polity rather than of a fully developed representative democracy on the supra-national level. Second, a majoritarian mode of democratic decision making requires the existence of normative foundations that assure that the minority of the people defeated in the democratic process will give in the will of the majority. These cohesive forces of democracy or the establishment of a "we-identity" in a community of fate which are the result of historical experiences, common values, cultural attributes, or common language have not yet sufficiently evolved on a transnational sectoral level (Scharpf 1998: 5 – 6). Finally, the functional differentiation of world politics establishes a political context within which it is nearly impossible that a territorially delimited demos that clearly separates members from non-members could evolve. Therefore, even if the cohesive forces that hold together the demos of functional transnational systems would exist, the special context of international governance prevents a majoritarian and representative mode of transnational democracy from being realized beyond the nation-state in the near future (Wolf 2000: 168).

3. EXPLORING REGIME CONSEQUENCES ON THE DEMOCRATIC PROCESS FROM A BROADER PERSPECTIVE

With the use of a deliberative conception of democracy, two realms become relevant for the study of the effects of international governance on the democratic process: domestic democratic institutions and public spheres on both domestic and transnational levels. Democratic theory has so far mainly produced generalized assumptions about the possible impacts of international governance on the democratic process. Moreover, these impacts were only one-dimensionally conceived of under the heading of de-democratization. The other dimension concerning whether international regimes could impact on the democratic process in a more positive way, was not addressed sufficiently, nor did an understanding evolve concerning whether the possible de-democratizing impacts produced by international regimes arise for any democracy equally. Possible variances with respect to the susceptibility of democratic polities may also depend on factors located within polities. In the following pages, I will deal first with the consequences of international human rights norms on the democratic process. Section 3.1. will support the argument that in many states international governance triggered democratization of authoritarian political systems and that international governance at least stabilized the conditions for the functioning of many existing democracies. In sections 3.2 and 3.3, attention will be given to possible de-democratization. Both sections will analyze regime consequences that can affect input-oriented legitimacy in a more negative way and will examine empirically the problematique of the democratic deficit involved with international governance. In a first step, attention will focus on de-parliamentarization as a possible effect of international governance. In a second step, impacts of state-dominated forms of international policy making on transnational or domestic public spheres will be described.

3.1 Global Juridification and Domestic Internalization of Human Rights

In many instances, international governance represents a response of national governments to the demands of civil society for international cooperation. Since the nineteenth century, civil society increasingly collaborated across national borders and demanded that national governments enhance international cooperation on humanitarian issues or issues related to impacts of modern warfare on populations (Chatfield 1997; Keck and Sikkink 1998). Such demands were motivated by the belief that internationally agreed upon principles, norms, and rules could improve the collective well-being of society or the rights of individuals and of the collectivity vis-à-vis the state. When the international peace movement began to lobby for the replacement of war by the pacific settlement of international disputes in the late nineteenth century, it was motivated by the fear of new firearms technologies, the consequences of the use of dynamite for land warfare, and the massive armament of armies made possible through rapid population growth in Europe and North America (Tuchman 1969: 276 – 86). Non-state actors called for the creation of regimes and for the strengthening of international norms or participated in designing and implementing international programs for the management of transboundary problems that were launched under the authority of international institutions.

The democratic problematique involved with international governance took on a new dimension only in the second half of the twentieth century when the number of international treaties concluded in single issue-areas grew significantly. For example, between 1900 and 1945, the average yearly number of newly founded international environmental treaties was fewer than one, but from 1960 onward it significantly increased to around nine (Frank, Hironaka, and Schofer 2000: 100). Similar developments of international juridification also occurred in other issue-areas. The evolution of international norms for the protection of the individual against inhuman treatment by states or private actors began with the formation of global prohibition regimes against piracy and privateering, slavery and slave trade, and against "white slavery" consisting of government-licensed female prostitution in Europe and in the United States, or of the recruitement to prostitution by force or fraud (Nadelman 1990). These international norms, which evolved as a result of transnational entrepreneurs, were primarily established to protect individuals or groups against arbitrary acts of state authorities or private actors. They represent the beginning of an historical development of international norm production for the protection of human rights which, after the end of World War II, first culminated in the creation of the 1948 Universal Declaration of Human Rights.

The second half of the twentieth century was characterized by a broadening of the functional scope of international human rights documented by the numerical growth of international legal agreements on both global and regional levels as well as by increasing density and specificity of international rules governing human rights issues. Although these norms and rules sometimes represent only minimum standards and often lack implementation, the existence and further development of these norms and rules encouraged people living under undemocratic rule to demand compliance with these norms or realization of democratic rights guaranteed by international agreements that a state refused to sign, ratify or give to the people although it had formally acceeded to.

In the same period, the third wave of democratization took place on domestic levels involving the transformation of many authoritarian political systems toward democratic rule (Huntington 1991). Can we draw a simple correlation between global juridification of human rights and increasing democratization of authoritarian political systems? Did the growth of international human rights norms affect democratization of authoritarian political systems? Such a correlation would suggest that global juridification could explain the new dimension of democratization processes that evolved in many states. Manfred G. Schmidt (1995: 184) argues, however, that although the proportion of world population living under democratic rule increased until the early 1990s, the majority of world population still lives under authoritarian rule. At the same time, some democracies also experienced regressions to less democratic standards. Therefore, drawing a simple correlation would produce misleading results about the impacts of international juridification on domestic democratization processes, since the correlation will not explain variances between states occurring in this period with respect to the transformation from authoritarian to democratic rule nor will such a correlation take into account reverse developments of regressions of democracies.

From a methodological view, the wave of constructivist studies poses new challenges for researching regime consequences on domestic levels, since such studies will require an understanding of the causal mechanisms by which international norms affect social identities. The case studies included in a volume edited by Thomas Risse, Stephen C. Ropp, and Kathryn Sikkink (1999) take social constructivism as a point of theoretical departure, arguing that struggles between governments, domestic society, and transnational human rights networks about the implementation of international human rights norms almost always involve the social identities of actors. In dealing with the consequences of international human rights norms on domestic levels of eleven states located in Africa, Asia, Eastern Europe, and Latin-America, the case studies included in the volume go beyond simply correlating the increase of international norms with observed domestic behavior. Such correlations could at best reveal *that* international norms matter. Rather, the project aims at explaining *how* or by which mechanisms a few human rights norms (which represent a central core of rights established within important global human rights agreements) were internalized and implemented domestically. The findings of the collaborative project illuminate, and also offer ways out of, some of the methodological problems involved with the study of the consequences of international norms on the domestic level. They describe how international governance can trigger the establishment of fundamental human rights and stimulate democratization in authoritarian states.

Empirical Method and Causal Mechanisms. Comparative case study research seems to be the appropriate and also the most feasible methodological tool that can be applied in studying the consequences of international norms on domestic levels. The findings of the collaborative project on the domestic internalization of international human rights norms, however, rely on a small part of the variety of international human rights regimes. Complexity with respect to the manifold variety of human rights regimes to be dealt with and the number of states that must be considered as objects of investigation represents a constraint for the quantitative study of the consequences of international norms on the democratic process. Since correlations between macro-data involving the number of democratic states and the number and quality of human rights norms established and ratified by states seem to produce misleading results, the comparative method must put special attention on identifying causal mechanisms between international norm development and domestic norm internalization. The research carried out to verify such causal mechanisms and to test alternative causal pathways involves significant investment costs with respect to the gathering of empirical data. Under the circumstances, a comparative study of domestic internalization of international norms must rely on a relative small set of cases.

The empirical case studies presented by Risse, Ropp, and Sikkin(1999) establish a causal mechanism by which international human rights norms are internalized into domestic practices. Nongovernmental actors are ascribed a crucial role in this process of norm internalization since they act as carriers and translators of these norms. These actors politicize normviolation, or demand adoption of, and compliance with, norms from governbents. Since nongovernmental actors in an authoritarian state lack possiblities on the domestic level to influence their government toward achieving improvements of the human rights situation, they bypass their state and link with allies on the transnational level. This "boomerang effect" makes it possible for transnational human rights networks to put pressure from the global human rights polity on a norm-violating state (Keck and Sikkink 1998:12 – 13). Three modes of social interaction tested by the project regarding how far they can explain the broader socialization process by which an international society of states transmits norms to members (Risse and Sikkink 1999: 12 – 17). *Instrumental adaptation and strategic bargaining*, the first mode of social interaction (involving, for example, the release of political prisoners to overcome political sanctions) is relevant only in the early stages of the process but does not account for the shift from normviolation toward internalization of, and compliance with, international norms. *Argumentative discourses*, the second mode of social interaction, describes socialization of international human rights norms as a result of communication, argumentation, and persuasion. Even if actors accept the validity of human rights norms in their discursive practises, argumentative discourses will be necessary to clarify whether participants in the discourse understood correctly the information provided about the human rights situation in a state, whether the human rights situation in a single state was defined correctly, or whether the validity of a norm, though globally accepted, will be questioned by competing cultural understandings. The case studies show that the shift of a norm-violating state toward internalization of and compliance with international human rights norms was brought about by argumentative discourses that were established by transgovernmental human rights networks. Though not irreversible, the process of continuing self-entrapment of a state in domestic or transnational discourse became a costly enterprise for governing elites. This entrapment in talks with human rights groups created expectations within civil society that a government should comply with the rules of the dialogue. When a state relapsed into old habits of repression, domestic and transnational groups experienced a further strenghtening of their position vis-à-vis the government, since governmental elites forfeited credibility. *Institutionalization and habitualization,* as a third mode of social interaction (which involves the incorporation of norms in the standard operating procedures of domestic institutions) complements the mode of *argumentative discourses.*

Process-Orientation and Relevance of Other Variables. The findings of the collaborative project establish that only a process-oriented study of the consequences of international norms makes it possible to analyze both increasing and decreasing internalization of international norms in domestic practices. Therefore, a process-oriented study can also cope with the phenomenon of possible regression of states to less democratic standards. In carrying out such process-oriented studies, the investigator traces back the causal mechanisms that finally lead to the outcome of a case. Process-tracing proved to be a method by which these causal mechanisms could be identified. The three modes of social interaction were examined by the project for their relevance in five stages of the political process that make up the so-called "spiral-model" of human rights change (Risse and Sikkink 1999: 20). The early stages of the political process consist of a *repressive situation* (phase I) characterized by oppression of civil society by the state, of *denial* (phase II) when the norm-violating state refuses to accept the validity of human rights norms, and of *tactical concessions* (phase III), when a state increasingly begins to lose control over domestic and transnational politicization of its norm violation by policy networks. During these early stages, states rely on the mode of *instrumental adaptation and strategic bargaining,* and transnational human rights networks make efforts to put norm violations of a state on the international agenda. Arguing becomes more important during phase III and then dominates during the following stage of *prescriptive status* (phase IV), when a state accepts the validity, and regularly refers to the human rights norm. The case studies suggest that the more norm violation by a state is politicized by transnational and domestic pressure groups, the more likely a norm-violating government finally engages in a public dialogue with its critics. In addition, norm-violating governments and the domestic or transnational human rights networks increasingly accept each other as valid interlocutors. Translation of international norms into national legal regulation and domestic compliance can be conceived of as matters of routine and occur in the final stage of the spiral model, where *rule consistent behavior* (phase V) of a state can be observed. In this final stage of norm internalization, the mobilization of human rights networks normally decreases.

Besides the causal role played by nongovernmental actors in translating international human rights norms into domestic practises, one could finally speculate which other conditions could be operating in achieving domestic internalization of international norms. Thomas Risse and Stephen C. Ropp (1999: 267), for example, agree that Great Power pressure frequently has been supportive for achieving a change of the human rights situation in single countries. However, the case studies also demonstrate that this has seldom been crucial and that Great Powers mostly became active only after human rights groups were already blaming a state for norm-violation. In addition, the empirical findings also hardly seem to confirm the thesis put forward by a variant of modernization theory that socio-economic changes, such as the increase of the middle class, could improve conditions on the domestic level for the adoption of international norms. Emprical evidence also does not establish a direct correlation between economic growth and improvements of the human rights situation. Other contextual factors, though unresearched with respect to their contribution to the adoption of international norms on domestic levels, will deserve further attention. For example, one could argue that the existence of specific Western or postmodernist cultural values support the internalization of international human rights norms on the domestic level (Inglehart 1988).

3.2 Regime Consequencs on Democratic Polity: De-parliamentarization

The empirical findings that international governance can also strenghten processes of democratization or protect the democratic process on the domestic level run counter to the de-democratization thesis put forward by democratic theorists. Nevertheless, it will become obvious from the following discussion that the de-democratization thesis must be taken seriously. Democratic theorists will have to weigh both the democratizing and de-democratizing consequences of international governance against each other. The following discussion will use two opposite views on the character of state-society relationships as points of departure for analyzing the changing roles of parliaments and other democratic institutions on the subnational level in the era of denationalizing political processes. I will argue that national parliaments must be considered as particularly vulnerable to the loss of influence in the policy-making process resulting from international governance. De-parliamentarization can be understood as a phenomenon resulting from the internationalization of policy making, where international legal agreements are concluded first before national parliaments finally ratify them. Democratic theorists correlate the growth of international policy-making with de-democratization on the domestic level. However, such a simple conclusion poses a number of problems. Although few comparative case studies have been completed, one can first suspect that variances exist regarding the development of de-parliamentarization between different democracies. Democratic theorists put forward the argument about the de-democratizing effects of the European Union, but the empirical basis that could provide evidence of de-democratization in general or de-parliamentarization in particular for the different EU-member states from a comparative perspective is still weak. Furthermore, empirical case studies comparing both phenomena for the broader set of OECD-countries are lacking likewise. Second, it can also be assumed that the degree of de-parliamentarization is not only determined by the embeddedness of a state in international policy making but that it is also closely connected with the character of national democratic polity itself. Therefore, the main challenge faced by democratic theorists putting forward the thesis of the de-democratizing effects caused by international governance not only consists in developing blueprints for new forms of democracy beyond the nation state (Held 1995; Schmalz-Bruns 1999). Rather, it will also be necessary to study the phenomenon empirically to provide further evidence for the de-democratization thesis. Furthermore, empirical studies should also clarify how far international governance contributes to the phenomenon in comparison with domestic factors.

The first conception of state-society relationships puts special emphasis on state autonomy vis-à-vis societal actors. The concept of the new raison d'état put forward by Klaus Dieter Wolf (1999) understands international governance not only as a mechanism by which congruence between the globalized political space and the political steering capacity of the nation-state can be re-established, but also as a strategy by which the state can increase or uphold its autonomy from domestic society and realize its own preferences independently of societal constraints. The new raison d'état suggests that self-interested governments partially compensate the loss of external autonomy that they suffer from the erosion of national sovereignty by extending state autonomy vis-à-vis domestic society. In a study on the EU-decisionmaking process, Andrew Moravcsik (1997) describes in a similar way how international governance systems strengthen the role of governments vis-à-vis other actors on the domestic level. The establishment of the stabilization program of the European Monetary Union represents an example that illustrates the practices of the new raison d'état. European governments agreed internationally on austere criteria governing membership in the European Monetary system before domestic publics and parliaments could influence international policy making. Most national governments would not have been able to implement austere policies alone as they feared that domestic constituencies would not accept drastic cuts in national social budgets and therefore would vote them out of offices. The theorem of the new raison d'état attends to the new leeway accrued to states in multi-level negotiation systems where states negotiate first before they ask domestic democratic institutions for approval, where governments can blackmail parliaments by pointing out that rejection of the international agreement concluded by the government would endanger the establishment of the international regime as a whole or damage the international reputation and credibility of the state. The theorem further suggests that the autonomy-seeking of the state will constrain other democratic institutions such as city councils, district parliaments, or parliaments on the federal level significantly in their efforts to connect local, regional, or federal levels to processes of international policymaking.

The second conception of the state takes an opposite view regarding the autonomy of the state vis-à-vis civil society. Against the background of increasing embeddedness of the state in international policy making, Fritz W. Scharpf (1991) argued a decade ago that the mode of hierarchical interaction between state and society will be transformed toward horizontal interaction. Domestic factors and international governance were both taken into account by Gunther Teubner (1999) as points of departure for developing a new understanding of state-society relationships. He argues that increasing complexity of political issues, sectoralization, functional differentiation, or increasing self-organization of society, the decreasing ability of the state for autonomous problem-solving, as well as the significant growth of international governance support a historic transition from hierarchy to heterarchy in state-society relationships. The democratic state is conceived of as a "network state" is embedded in national and transnational policy networks for the purpose of improving the outcomes of governmental policies. The transition toward the network state is associated with bargaining gaining relevance as a strategy for political decisionmaking chosen by governments, domestic and transnational interest groups, or international organizations.

Although the two conceptions of the state rest on opposite premises regarding the autonomy of the state vis-à-vis society, they both suggest that de-parliamentarization occurs. However, they imply different conclusions about how one should judge the implications for national democracy involved with de-parliamentarization from a political viewpoint. The concept of the new raison d'etat describes the authoritarian variant of an increasingly de-democratizing political process, where only governments can preserve or increase their influence in the political process. It further implies that representative institutions on subnational levels, such as parliaments, which were established in federal states or regional authorities, suffer in a similar way from autonomy-seeking of the state. In contrast, the concept of the evolution of the network state describes a process of growing self-appropriation of the state by national and transnational civil society. The partial loss of the parliament's role as a center of political decision making will be compensated by new deliberative forms of informal decision making that are established outside the parliamentary sphere and that provide for participation of domestic as well as transnational actors.

Empirical Method and Causal Mechanisms. Both conceptions of the state come to different assessments regarding the causal relevance of international governance for de-parliamentarization. While the approach of the network state considers international governance as only one among other factors accounting for de-parliamentarization, the theorem of the new raison d'état exclusively puts emphasis on the effects produced by international governance for the democratic process. The theorem, however, fails to establish by which mechanisms a state could maximize its own autonomy from civil society in light of the growing need to seek information from nongovernmental experts. Against the background of increasing complexity of policies, one could argue that a trade-off between state and society seems to occur where civil society helps the state to raise output-oriented legitimacy of governance while the state at the same time allocates new forms of political participation, many of which are informal or bear the character of adhoc bodies. The discussion of both conceptions of the state provides a point of departure for measuring de-parliamentarization understood as a phenomenon caused by international governance. The indicators currently referred to describe growing embeddedness of the democratic state in international policy making as a cause for the phenomenon of de-parliamentarization. The internationalization of policymaking is certainly an empirical fact that supports the argument that de-parliamentarization occurs. However, the figures do not establish by which mechanisms de-parliamentarization will be caused on the domestic level nor do they make it possible to detect any variances in the degree to which different democratic polities suffer from de-parliamentarization. Therefore, data describing the growing involvement of single OECD countries in international policy making only provide a first approximate value for de-parliamentarization.

For Germany, an increasing development toward de-parliamentarization resulting from international governance was detected by Klaus von Beyme (1997: 185 – 186), who explored how far 150 law-making initiatives introduced into the German Bundestag between 1949 and 1994 were caused by external stimulus from both the European Union and from international politics. The study comes to the conclusion that the Bundestag suffered a reduction of its de-facto law-making competence, since 13.3 percent of all law-making initiatives were initiated from international governance. While in sum the European Union (6.0 percent) and international politics reaching beyond the EU-level (7.3 percent) both account nearly equally for this development, for more recent periods the figures describe a strong increase in those law-making initiatives introduced into the Bundestag that were caused by regulations of the European Union. They increased from 16.0 percent in the tenth legislation period (1983 – 1987) to 20.9 percent or 20.6 percent in the eleventh and twelfth legislative periods (1987 – 1990 and 1990 – 1994). A more comparative perspective regarding the degree to which the legislation of a number of EC-member states was determined by the European Community's supra-national law-making machinery was taken by the Bremen globalization project. The project shows that, in the early 1960s, a development began where the number of regulations annually passed by the European Community exceeded the number of bills passed in Germany, France, or Italy. Between 1980 and 1990, the number of regulations passed by the European Community was nearly ten times higher than the number of national laws passed in the United Kingdom, more than seven times higher than in Germany, more than six times higher than in France, and nearly three times higher than in Italy (Beisheim et al 1999: 328 – 35).

Although the growing determination of national law by international policy-making takes on a special dimension in the European Union, it is by far not limited to EU member states. First, non-member states that can influence EU policy-making to only a minor extent have to adjust their national legislation to EU regulation in order to comply with the standards valid for trading with the EU. Second, the data produced by the Bremen project also provide empirical evidence for the strong extension of international policy making in the OECD world. The figures produced by the project indicate that participation of Canada, Germany, France, the United Kingdom, Italy, and the United States in international multilateral agreements significantly trended upward between 1945 and 1974. Further figures about the number of bilateral agreements newly concluded by these six states and by Japan and Mexico show that at least Canada, Germany, France, Mexico, and the United States experienced a strong increase in participation in these agreements in the different five-year periods explored between 1945 and 1979. Such correlations may support the argument that de-parliamentarization is caused by international governance and also substantiate why the phenomenon is already highly developed in EU member states for which an era of "post-parliamentary governance" has been predicted (Andersen and Burns 1996: 229). However, correlations do not give an insight in the mechanisms operating within the political system which support the transformation of the political process towards de-parliamentarization.

Process Orientation and Relevance of Other Variables. From the view of the theorem of the new raison d'état, de-parliamentarization must be understood as a phenomenon where the inclusion of parliaments in the policy-making process occurs late rather than where participation could be totally prevented by governments. According to the theorem of the new raison d'état, parliaments will be marginalized and will only take the roles of notaries of outcomes negotiated by and representing the interests of governments. The network-state approach considers that the growing relevance of bargaining with actors located within or beyond its own national borders will occur inevitably at the expense of the role of the parliament, since the real decisionmaking process will migrate to round tables, or informal negotiations between actors relevant for issue-area-specific problem solving. Therefore, the role of the parliament originally understood as the center of political decision making transforms more toward a forum of public debate. The discussion of both approaches suggests that only a process-oriented study will establish how far the phenomenon occurs within single democratic states. Such a conclusion particularly applies when dealing with reactions taken by parliaments or civil society to oppose de-parliamentarization or the erosion of national democratic decision making by international governance. Parliaments made increasing efforts to adapt to the internationalization of policy making. In the last decade, the German Bundestag established new sub-committees dealing with globalization of the UN system. The Bundestag's subcommittee on the United Nations and international organizations could reduce parliament's information deficit and institutionalize interaction between the parliament and the government on international issues (Ehrhart 1998: 134). In comparison with the U.S. Congress, however, the German parliament made much less effort to prevent or initiate the establishment of international regimes or to politicize the efficiency of the UN system (Krause 1999: 552).

The previous discussion suggests that the impacts of international governance on democratic political systems, *inter alia*, can be assumed to depend on the attributes of democratic polities themselves. Originally, the constitution-building of modern democracies was overwhelmingly determined by the necessity to develop a constitutional framework for domestic governance. In the aftermath of modern constitution building, the legislative had to fight for a determining influence on the declaration of war, and it took until the second half of the twentieth century before parliaments realized control of national foreign policy. The balance of power between governments and legislatives has undergone significant changes in the last few decades. In many democracies, it took some decades until the conflict between governments and legislatives about participation of representative institutions in decision making on the waging of war could be resolved. One striking example concerns the adoption the 1972 War Powers Resolution in the United States (Kittel 1993: 15 – 26). In the last few decades, the U.S. Congress re-established its own power vis-à-vis the U.S. government. It introduced new legislation that enhanced the ability of both chambers to control the government and it also strengthened the resources of the members of the U.S. Congress to cope with the complexity of the political process arising from domestic and international policy making. For example, significant differences exist between the U.S. Congress and the German Bundestag regarding the provision of assistants supporting the work of the members of both legislatures. In the 1990s, the U.S. Congress employed about 23,000 assistants, while the German Bundestag could only rely on the working capacities of 4,500 assistants in the same period (Krause 1999: 549). One can further conclude from such differences between the American and the German polity that attributes of the democratic polity itself account for variances occurring in the degree of de-democratization caused by international governance. Arend Lijphart's distinction between majoritarian and consensual democracies might serve as a starting point for an in-depth analysis how of far the attributes of national democratic polities serve in determining the ability of the political system to cope with the challenges for the democratic process that arise from international governance (Lijphart 1989). Such comparison would be driven by the assumption that differences exist between certain types of democracies concerning their ability to sustain the democratic process in the era of internationalizing politics.

As long as states will remain the most important actors for the creation and management of international regimes, a country's size or the issue area specific power resources available to a state for accomplishing its goals vis-à-vis other states in international regimes could also be considered as further conditions that can influence the extent to which democratic decision making can be undermined by the internationalization of policy making. This is especially true for international governance systems in which policy making is shaped by power structural behavior and where the ideals involved with the deliberative concept will be realized to only a minor extent. The less intergovernmental bargaining that takes plance in a mutual search for compromise, the reaching of consensus, and the reaching of equal payoffs with regard to costs and benefits, the more likely will the collectivities of less powerful states suffer from heteronomy of the more powerful. Policies that result from such asymmetric bargaining situations will be perceived as not reflecting the preferences of collectivities living within the borders of weaker or smaller states.

3.3 Regime Consequences on Domestic and Transnational Publics

The concept of deliberative democracy puts special emphasis on the role of the public sphere. While Hannah Arendt conceived of public space within a model of face-to-face interactions, Habermas (1962) took into account that, in the course of the Enlightenment, a public evolved that uncoupled from space and personal face-to-face communication and that communicates via impersonal communication media (Benhabib 1992). Publics can be understood as social spaces established by communication within, or transcending beyond, national borders. International regimes can be understood as crystallization points within and around which the international society of states and global civil society are engaged in continuous discourse about the appropriateness of regime policies or the procedures by which these policies have been agreed upon. The public actors within these social spaces communicate speech acts via national or transnational media to a larger public. The conceptualization of a domestic public involves normative claims that serve to support the implementation of the democratic ideal. Bernhard Peters (1994: 46f) describes three criteria that establish a domestic public. The first criterion of "equality and reciprocity" demands open access to public communication to all individuals or groups prepared and able to give their views on specific issues. It suggests that participants in public communication should be able to change from their roles as listeners to roles as speakers and vice versa and that interactions among participants should be non-hierarchical. The second criterion of "openness" shall guarantee that decisions about the relevance of single issues will be subject to public debate themselves rather than that imposed by supervising authorities. A third element consists of the "discursive structure" of a public. A discourse-theoretical conception of domestic and transnational publics implies that "arguing" is the dominant mode of communication, that participants in communicative action pay respect to each other and that they refrain from sanctioning criticism of other participants in a discourse. We know from the reality of domestic politics that such criteria can hardly be fulfilled. The practical challenge consists in approximating the political process to these claims as far as possible.

Can domestic and transnational publics be treated as identical objects of investigation differ simply with respect to territorial (de-)limitation? Domestic publics naturally differ in many ways from transnational publics. In contrast to domestic publics, which communicate on the basis of common language, transnational publics often require translation from and into different languages to make possible the exchange of information, arguments and counter-arguments within different national, social, cultural, or geographical contexts. The problem of lacking common language is only relevant when a context of direct personal communication predominates. Modern publics operate on the basis of impersonal communication. Seyla Benhabib (1997: 33) conceives of a public as a construction of mutually linked associations, networks, or organizations that all engage in anonymous public conversation. Individuals can participate in public deliberation, for example, via political parties, domestic or transnational social movements, or trade unions. The concept of a public requires that civil society has reached a certain level of viability and independence from the state. While this is self-evident in a national democratic polity, transnational civil society is yet in an evolutionary stage (Breitmeier and Rittberger 2000). Since expanding denationalization will make the further rise of transnational civil society inevitable, the classic antagonism between the state and civil society will remain an important feature determining political processes on the transnational level. Therefore, normative questions concerning the state-society relationship will gain relevance in connection with the study of regime consequences on both levels of analysis.

Empirical Method and Causal Mechanisms. A formerly widespread prejudice that domestic publics would be shaped by mass ignorance concerning international policy-making processes was partly relativized by Max Kaase and Kenneth Newton (1995), who provided data which on the one hand revealed relatively strong support of the people in Europe for the European Union, the United Nations, and NATO; on the other hand, the data revealed that the people in Europe lack knowledge about the polity and politics of these organizations. Against this background, one must conclude that people, although they support international cooperation, are less informed about institutions and political processes relevant in connection with international governance. One structural factor accounting for lacking information on international politics consists in the smallness and variety of international governance systems. The narrow definition of an issue area managed by an international regime can be considered an important causal factor responsible for the difficulties occurring in fulfilling the normative claims described above for many sectoral transnational publics. The general approach of subdividing broader problems, such as the management and conservation of marine species into smaller subproblems taken for the purpose of raising the problem solving capacity of international governance has led to a patchwork of international treaties. For example, a nested system of institutions exists in the field of international fisheries. Any of these regimes can be distinguished from others because of its special focus on the conservation or management of a small range of fisheries species. In addition, regulations between different regimes in the field of fisheries also often overlap. Because of the juxtaposition of bilateral, regional, or global regimes evolving during the last decades, these regimes also differ concerning the scope of law (Petersen 1993; De Yturriaga 1997). The decentralized structuring of global and regional governance on fisheries makes it difficult for transnational public actors to establish a broader public that reaches beyond political processes taking place within the boundaries of single well-known regimes, to keep track of and to participate in relevant political processes occurring in neighboring issue areas, or to bring issue-related problems together and to produce a common framing, although they are managed by different governance systems. The complex structure of international institutions for the management of fisheries impedes the evolution of a more comprehensive discourse on global fisheries and the exchange of information between the scattered public spheres that evolved around regimes and international organizations including, for example, the Food and Agriculture Organization, the European Union and its Common Fisheries Policy, the meta-regime of the Law of the Sea, or the regime secretariats managing dozens of global, regional, or bilateral regimes governing fisheries in the South Pacific, the Barents Sea, the Baltic Sea among others, for the global management and conservation of whales or of straddling fish stocks, of Antarctic marine living resources, of tuna or tuna-like species in the Atlantic or in the Eastern Pacific Ocean, and of Pacific salmon or salmon in the North-Atlantic (Hall 1998; Hyvarinen, Hall, Lutchman, and Indrani 1998; Vidas and Ostreng 1999).

The bundling of issue-related regimes in a more government-like form would establish a central location around which discourses on regime-related issues could be transmitted to a broader transnational public more easily, since public debate initiated within a more centralized forum would not only reach specialists who are involved with regime-related matters due to professional involvement. Furthermore, merging a number of related international regimes could make it easier for transnational actors or for the media to take notice of more complex relationships within the broader issue area and to politicize the inter-linkages existing between regimes. For example, the anchoring of the GATT to the newly created World Trade Organization made it possible to bring a number of partly isolated discourses about international economic issues together in a global forum and to politicize them in a broader context with respect to the inter-linkages between economic and social or environmental regimes.

However, such a restructuring of international regimes or relocation under broader organizational frameworks is not in all cases a desirable option. It is certainly possible to avoid problems that primarily refer to regional or bilateral contexts that would be shifted to the global level. Not every international issue takes on a global dimension. The patchwork of international regimes implies that a fragmentation into different regime-specific smaller publics occurs that produces unneccessary costs for transnational actors when realizing the demand for participation. The current structuring of international governance often requires transnational public actors to invest significant resources and energy in the coordination of political activities in broader issue areas, because too many political processes run parallel in various international fisheries commissions or international organizations that are located at different parts of the world. The diffusion of fisheries regimes reduces the number of participants in sectoral publics, often mainly to experts. The strategy of partitioning broader fields of international politics into smaller issue areas normally governed by only a few issue-specific international legal agreements also affects domestic publics, since single issues are withdrawn from public attention on the domestic level.

In connection with analyzing the democratic problematique involved with international governance, the study of regime inter-linkages and interactions between sectoral publics across the issue-specific boundaries of single regimes is gaining more relevance. It seems that the limitation of the study of regime consequences on domestic or transnational publics to single case studies alone will provide only a fragmentary picture. Comparative case study research based on a larger set of cases will be necessary to describe how far transnational public actors will be able to influence international policy making, particularly in comparison with states and transnational economic actors. Whether international policy making is the result of societal self-determination or of heteronomy arising from the dominance of governments or transnational economic actors can only be established by transcending the traditional methodological approach of case study research towards comparison on a more quantitative basis. The quantitative element of such a methodological orientation of the study of regime consequences involves not only the study of a larger number of regimes and transnational publics and the analysis of a larger set of states and domestic publics, but also of the interactions among single regimes.

Process Orientation and Relevance of Other Variables. In addition, exploring the consequences of international governance on the public sphere again demands that we take a process-oriented perspective. The attributes or resources owned by different types of public actors determine the influence that they can exercise in the different stages of the political process. Scientific experts, in particular, were granted strong influence in international policy-making systems. The scientification of international policy making is a result of a growing complexity involved with global politics. Scientific, legal, and technical experts have been involved increasingly in developing consensual knowledge on the causes and consequences of global issues such as climate change, desertification, or stratospheric ozone depletion, and in designing political measures to preserve the environment (Andresen et al 2000). The involvement of experts in the policy-making process is not limited to global environmental politics alone; the demand for input by experts generally exists in all areas of international politics. Epistemic communities understood as transnational networks that not only improve the knowledge-base of global politics, but that also support the designing of policies can contribute to raising the output-oriented legitimacy of international governance, since the quality of problem solving in single issue areas would be worse without them (Haas 1992; Litfin 1994). Compared with normal citizens or with many nongovernmental actors, scientific experts have great potential to influence domestic and international policy making. They have more access to international and domestic political agendas, they participate in international and national bodies deciding on which issues will be considered as relevant for further management, and they are also usually more capable than normal citizens to frame public discourse. From the view of the deliberative ideal, experts can not only contribute to strengthening the rationality and quality of a discourse, but they also pose new problems regarding input-oriented legitimacy. As a consequence, a process-oriented research design of the study of regime consequences must establish to what extent the demand for scientific or other kind of expertise arising from international governance encourages the evolution of new forms of transnational rule and which differences are being made in allocating participation rights in political processes and in public discourses to domestic or transnational public actors. In this respect, the process-oriented investigation of the consequences of international governance also involves a historic long-term dimension. The growing empirical studies about the evolution of a world polity, about the evolving world culture, and about an all-embracing world environmental regime give reason to assume that a new sociology of transnational rule is emerging (Meyer et al 1997; Boli and Thomas 1999). This scholarship will establish to what extent world society has already been able to emancipate from governmental power and to reshape international governance according to the need of self-determination.

4. CONCLUSION

While the theoretical argument about the democratic deficit of international governance has led to a broad discussion in the last decade, it has yet to be proved by further empirical research. Not many efforts have been made to establish whether de-democratization is a result of international governance, or of domestic developments such as misgovernment, corruption, illegal donations to political parties that can be observed within many democracies, or whether developments on both levels account for the phenomenon equally. Empirical evidence is also lacking concerning the susceptibility of specific types of democracies for de-democratization caused by international governance. Only comparative case studies dealing with a larger number of states will prove whether national constitutions or distinctive features of national political cultures account for possible variances regarding de-democratization. The complexity involved with such comparison will be increased by the need to base the analysis on a larger number of governance systems.

The European Union and the UN system involving a widely branching network of international organizations and multilateral regimes are currently both referred to as main examples to support the argument for the democratic deficit of international governance. These contexts of international governance, however, differ concerning the degree of institutionalization and transference of sovereignty rights from the national to the supranational level. Therefore, empirical studies must also produce further knowledge concerning whether de-democratization can be observed in both contexts equally or whether it is more pronounced in the European Union. It is surprising that those consequences of international governance that contribute to the promotion of democratization in authoritarian political systems tend to be marginalized by the proponents of the de-democratization thesis. Empirical studies exploring de-democratization currently correlate the growing embeddedness of the nation state in international policy-making systems with de-democratizing effects occurring on the domestic level. From a methodological view, such correlations can hardly provide satisfying evidence, since they cannot describe causal pathways by which de-democratization will be established through international governance. Consequently, the development of such causal pathways is one of the most important requirements for future case study analysis. The need for a process-oriented study arises, inter alia, in connection with possible counterreactions of domestic democratic institutions to de-democratization. Process-tracing has also proven to be a very feasible method for identifying the contribution of nongovernmental actors toward domestic internalization of international human rights norms. Finally, it can be assumed that democratic polities or publics have begun to respond to the possible undermining of democratic decision making caused by international governance. However, we still lack sufficient knowledge about new mechanisms that could be used to change democratic constitutions in such a way that they will be able to cope with the challenges that arise for the democratic process from the internationalization of policy making.

NOTES

[1] I am grateful for comments on an earlier draft made by Jennifer Bailey, Oran R. Young, Arild Underdal and the participants of the workshop on "The Study of Regime Consequences: Methodological Challenges and Research Strategies" in Oslo on 19 – 20 November 1999.

REFERENCES

Abromeit, H. (2002) Wozu braucht man Demokratie? Die postnationale Herausforderung der Demokratietheorie, Leske + Budrich, Opladen.

Abromeit, H. (1998) Democracy in Europe: Legitimising Politics in a Non-State Polity, Berghahn Books, New York.

Andersen, S. S. and Burns, T. R. (1996) The European Union and the Erosion of Parliamentary Democracy: A Study of Post-parliamentary Governance, in S. S. Andersen and K. A. Eliassen (eds.) The European Union: How Democratic Is It? Sage, London, 227–251.

Andresen, S., Skodvin, T., Underdal, A., and Wettestadm, J. (eds.) (2000) Science in International Environmental Regimes: Between Integrity and Involvement, Manchester University Press.

Beisheim, M., Dreher, S., Wlater, G., Zangl, B. and Zürn, M. (1999) Im Zeitalter der Globalisierung? Thesen und Daten zur gesellschaftlichen und politischen Denationalisierung, Baden-Baden (Nomos).

Benhabib, S. (1997) Die gefährdete Öffentlichkeit, Transit, 13: 26–41.

Benhabib, S. (1992) Models of Public Space: Hannah Arendt, the Liberal Tradition, and Jürgen Habermas, in C. Calhoun, (ed.) Habermas and the Public Sphere, MIT Press, Cambridge, MA, 73–98.

Beyme, K. von (1997) Der Gesetzgeber: Der Bundestag als Entscheidungszentrum. Leske + Budrich, Opladen.

Bohman, J. (1998) Survey Article: The Coming Age of Deliberative Democracy, The Journal of Political Philosophy 6, 4: 400–425.

Boli, J. and Thomas, G. M. (eds.) (1999) Constructing World Culture: International Nongovernmental Organizations since 1875, Stanford University Press.

Breitmeier, H. and Rittberger, V. (2000) Environmental NGOs in an Emerging Global Civil Society, in P. S. Chasek (ed.) The Global Environment in the Twenty-First Century: Prospects for International Cooperation, 130–163.

Chatfield, C. (1997) Intergovernmental and Nongovernmental Associations to 1945, in J. Smith, Chatfield, C. and Pagnucco, R. (eds.) Transnational Social Movements and Global Politics. Solidarity beyond the State, Syracuse University Press, 19–41.

Cohen, J. (1997) Procedure and Substance in Deliberative Democracy, in J. Bohman and Rehg, W. (eds.) Deliberative Democracy: Essays on Reason and Politics, 407–437.

Dahl, R. A. (1994) A Democratic Dilemma: System Effectiveness Versus Citizen Participation, Political Science Quarterly 1, 109: 23–34.

De Yturriaga, J. A. (1997) The International Regime of Fisheries: From Unclos 1982 to the Presential Sea, Kluwer.
Ehrhart, W. (1998) Nicht im Rampenlicht, aber wirkungsvoll: Der Unterausschuß, Vereinte Nationen/Internationale Organisationen, des Deutschen Bundestages nach zwei Legislaturperioden, Vereinte Nationen 46, 4: 131–135.
Frank, D. J., Hironaka, A. and Schofer, E. (2000) The Nation-State and the Natural Environment Over the Twentieth Century, American Sociological Review 65, 1: 96–116.
Haas, P. M. (1992) Banning Chlorofluorocarbons: Epistemic Community Efforts to Protect Stratospheric Ozone, International Organization 46, 1: 187–224.
Habermas, J. (1962) Strukturwandel der Öffentlichkeit: Untersuchungen zu einer Kategorie der bürgerlichen Gesellschaft, Unveränd, nachdr. d. zuerst.
Habermas, J. (1998) Die postnationale Konstellation: Politische Essays, Frankfurt/Main.
Hall, C. (1998) Institutional Solutions for Governing the Global Commons: Design Factors and Effectiveness, Journal of Environment and Development 7, 2: 86–114.
Held, D. (1995) Democracy and the Global Order: From the Modern State to Cosmpolitan Governance, Stanford University Press.
Held, D. (1997) Democracy and Globalization, Global Governance 3, 3: 251–267.
Huntington, S. P. (1993) The Third Wave: Democratization in the Late Twentieth Century, University of Oklahoma Press.
Hyvarinen, J., Wall, E. and Lutchman, I. (1998) The United Nations and Fisheries in 1998, Ocean Development and International Law 29, 4: 323–338.
Inglehart, R. (1988) The Renaissance of Political Culture, American Political Science Review 82: 1202–1230.
Kaase, M. and Newton, K. (1995) Beliefs in Government, Oxford University Press.
Keck, M. E. and Sikkink, K. (1998) Activists Beyond Borders: Advocacy Networks in International Politics, Corenll University Press, Ithaca, New York.
Kittel, G. (1993) Demokratische Außenpolitik als Voraussetzung der Friedfertigkeit von Demokratien: Eine Untersuchung am Beispiel der "war powers" in den USA, Tübinger Arbeitspapiere zur Internationalen Politik und Friedensforschung, Tübingen.
Knight, J. and Johnson, J. (1994) Aggregation and Deliberation: On the Possibility of Democratic Legitimacy, Political Theory 22, 2: 277–296.
Krause, J. (1999) Der Bedeutungswandel parlamentarischer Kontrolle: Deutscher Bundestag und US-Kongreß im Vergleich, Zeitschrift für Parlamentsfragen 30, 2: 534–555.
Lijphart, A. (1989) Democratic Political Systems: Types, Cases, Causes, and Consequences, Journal of Theoretical Politics 1, 1: 33–48.
Litfin, Karen (1994) Ozone Discourses: Science and Politics in Global Environmental Cooperation, Columbia University Press, New York.
Meyer, J. W., Frank, D. J., Hironaka, A., Schofer, E. and Tuma, B. (1997) The Structuring of a World Environmental Regime, 1870-1990, International Organization 51, 4: 623–651.
Moravcsik, A. (1997) Warum die Europäische Union die Exekutive stärkt: Innenpolitik und internationale Kooperation. In Wolf, Klaus Dieter, ed., Projekt Europa im Übergang? Probleme, Modelle und Strategien des Regierens in der Europäischen Union, Baden-Baden, 211–269.
Nadelman, E. A. (1990) Global Prohibition Regimes: The Evolution of Norms in International Society, International Organization 44, 4: 479–526.
Peters, B. (1994) Der Sinn von Öffentlichkeit, in F. Neidhart (ed.) Öffentlichkeit, Öffentliche Meinung, Soziale Bewegungen: Kölner Zeitschrift für Soziologie und Sozialpsychologie, Sonderheft 34, Opladen, 42–76.

Peterson, M. J. (1993) International Fisheries Management, in P.M. Haas, R. O. Keohane and M. A. Levy (eds.) Institutions for the Earth: Sources of Effective International Environmental Protection, MIT Press, Cambridge, MA, 249–305.

Risse, T. and Ropp, S. C. (1999) International Human Rights Norms and Domestic Change: Conclusion, in T. Risse, S. C. Ropp, and K. Sikkink (eds.) The Power of Human Rights: International Norms and Domestic Change, Cambridge University Press, 234–278.

Risse, T., Ropp, S. C. and Sikkink, K. (eds.) 1999. The Power of Human Rights. International Norms and Domestic Change, Cambridge University Press.

Risse, T. and Sikkink, K. (1999) The Socialization of International Human Rights Norms into Domestic Practices: Introduction, in T. Risse, S. C. Ropp, and K. Sikkink (eds.) The Power of Human Rights: International Norms and Domestic Change, Cambridge University Press, 1–38.

Scharpf, F. W. (1991) Die Handlungsfähigkeit des Staates am Ende des zwanzigsten Jahrhunderts, Politische Vierteljahresschrift 32, 4: 622–634.

Scharpf, F. W. (1998) Interdependence and Democratic Legitimation, MPIfG Working Papers 98/2, September 1998, Max Planck Institute for the Study of Societies, Cologne.

Schmalz-Bruns, R. (1995) Reflexive Demokratie: Die demokratische Transformation moderner Politik, Baden-Baden.

Schmalz-Bruns, R. (1999) Deliberativer Supranationalismus, Demokratisches Regieren jenseits des Nationalstaats, Zeitschrift für Internationale Beziehungen 2, 6: 185–244.

Schmidt, M. G. (1995) Der Januskopf der Transformationsperiode, Kontinuität und Wandel der Demokratietheorien, in K. von Beyme, and C. Offe, (eds.) Politische Theorien in der Ära der Transformation, PVS-Sonderheft 26: 182–210.

Teubner, G. (1999) Polykorporatismus: Der Staat als „Netzwerk" öffentlicher und privater Kollektivakteure, in H. Brunkhorst and P. Niesen, (eds.) Das Recht der Republik. Frankfurt/Main, 346–371.

Tuchman, B. (1969) Der stolze Turm: Ein Porträt der Welt vor dem Ersten Weltkrieg 1890-1914, _____, Munich.

Vidas, D. and Ostreng, W. (eds.) (1999) Order for the Oceans at the Turn of the Century, The Hague.

Wolf, K. D. (1999) The New Raison d'État as a Problem for Democracy in World Society, European Journal of International Relations 5, 3: 333–363.

Wolf, K. D. (2000) Die Neue Staatsräson - Zwischenstaatliche Kooperation als Demokratieproblem in der Weltgesellschaft, Plädoyer für eine geordnete Entstaatlichung des Regierens jenseits des Staates, Baden-Baden.

Young, O. R. (1997) Rights, Rules and Resources in World Affairs, in O. R. Young (ed.) Global Governance: Drawing Insights from the Environmental Experience, MIT Press, Cambridge, MA, 1–23.

Zürn, M. (1998) Regieren jenseits des Nationalstaats: Globalisierung und Denationalisierung als Chance, Frankfurt/Main.

Chapter 12

INTO THE METHODOLOGICAL VOID
Researching Systemic Consequences of International Regimes

GREGOR WALTER, MICHAEL ZÜRN
Institute für Intercultural and International Studies, University of Bremen, Germany

1. INTRODUCTION

"We live in a world that is already in fact very different from the one which we have begun to comprehend, and by the time our comprehension has caught up with the new reality, the world is likely to be even more drastically different in ways that today seem unthinkable."

This aphorism by Zbigniew Brzewinski is used as an epitaph in a book about "Global Public Policy" (Reinicke 1998). It explicitly points to the speed of the changes in world politics and to the substantial difficulties in grasping it. It tells us that we live in a time of transformation, which is different from the past, but also different from the future. In the context of this volume one very significant element of contemporary change certainly is an unprecedented rise of international regimes. The overall number of multilateral treaties as deposited with the United Nations has grown in a linear fashion from less than 150 in 1960 to well over 400 in 1998 (Hirschi et al. 1999: 40). It seems fair to speak of a roughly comparable number of international regimes (Keohane 1993). This growth pattern is replicated on the level of different issue areas. The number of new international environmental treaties and agreements has grown continuously since the beginning of the century. While up until the 1970s, in average every five years brought about five new treaties, this number has increased to about 25 from the 1980s onwards (see Beisheim et al. 1999: 351). A very similar pattern applies to the development of new international economic treaties and agreements (ibid.: 353). Will this rise of international regimes lead to "systemic consequences"? Will it change the deep structure of international society? Will the identity and role of states change as a result of multi-level governance? Will a very dense set of resilient international regimes foster peace?

Our ability to comprehend changes and to answer these questions about the future of international relations may easily be outpaced by the transformation processes themselves. This is the methodological component of Brzewinski's aphorism. A closer look reveals that the problems of drawing inferences about systemic consequences of the rise of international regimes involves more than just the danger of being not fast enough. Implicitly, Brzewinski points to a methodological problem of significant proportions, which generally applies to the study of the broader consequences of ongoing changes. Investigations to this end can be called "research on the future consequences of ongoing transformations" (FCoT), which we want to set apart from standard research (StR). Idealtypical StR research would be interested in the (unknown) causes of a (known) outcome. Quite different, however, a question like the one about the "systemic consequences of the rise of international regimes", asks about the (unknown) consequences of a (known) but ongoing development. In other words: In FCoT, we are currently witnessing a "cause", and we want to know more about the future effect. This, however, is obviously methodologically much more challenging than StR.

While a rich tool-kit is available for conducting StR, FCoT in general faces at least two significant problems. First, statements about the effects of an ongoing transformation imply statements about the future. When asked about the future, however, social scientists are generally hard pressed. While historians confronted with this question might take refuge to the "lessons of history" (thereby undermining their own claims about the uniqueness of historical events), political scientists often resort to law-like relationships between so-called independent and dependent variables (propositions) and try to apply them to the future. The success of this endeavor, however, critically depends on the availability and quality of such propositions and in this respect the political scientist will generally not escape a gloating look from the eyes of historians (and other scientists). Second, in FCOT the issue is at the same time further complicated by the fact that the developments under consideration are ongoing processes of potentially far-reaching consequences. They themselves can thus be expected to undermine the (little) reliable theoretical knowledge we might have by changing the context. A changing context, however might change the way events have to be interpreted. For instance, the effects of the development of a very expensive new military technology is quite different in a power competition context such as the Cold War (effect: acceleration of the arms race) and in a societally and politically denationalized context such as the EU (effect: deepening of cooperation). The effects may thus vary drastically depending on changes in the context. Our theoretical comprehension of world politics might thus indeed lag behind the new reality, not least because we lack the methodology to study it.

These methodological restrictions stand in sharp contrast to the current demand for FCoT. Regime analysts are not the only ones to ponder on systemic changes. At present, a significant number of ongoing transformations are all assumed to have far reaching-consequences. Broad phenomena like the end of the Cold War, globalization and the rise of non-governmental organizations are expected to have the potential to fundamentally alter the basic entities of our theories: the state and the international system. In these times of transformation, we are particularly interested in increasing our knowledge about the world that will take shape after the transformation has taken place. The more we feel that changes are substantial and affect structures, the more we want to know their effects. For substantive reasons we are thus particularly interested in FCoT while the causes of these ongoing transformations are often neglected. Immediately after the downfall of the Berlin Wall, political scientists from different theoretical orientations sketched how the world would look like without the Cold War. Comparatively little effort was made to explain why the cold war has ended so suddenly. Most people ask about the consequences of globalization first, only few care about its causes. Most people ask how a world with a limited role for the nation state will look like, only few study how the rise of global governance and non-governmental actors could happen in the first place. In short, the demand for FCoT rapidly increases when there is the widespread feeling that major changes are underway. To be sure, there is no shortage of speculations about the future and the consequences of macro processes, but most of the time these contributions remained methodologically precisely this: speculations. The warnings methodologists would give—if asked—are hardly considered. As a consequence, debates like the one about the world after the Cold War often put the social sciences in a bad light. Their spin-offs were articles that were broadly read and received, yet often turn out to be devastatingly wrong.[i]

The study of the systemic effects of the current rise in international regimes is quite different from an exploration on the effects and the effectiveness of single or a small set of international regimes within a given issue area. Approaches to this research agenda are discussed in part one of this volume. The study of the systemic effects of international regimes, however, is an example of research on the future consequences of ongoing transformations: With regard to regimes it works on the aggregate (i.e. the institutionalization of world politics) rather than on individual regimes and it looks for possible large-scale transformations of the international system. It thus shares the dilemma FCoT faces in general: Whereas the demand for and the substantive interest in these studies is high, a substantive methodological tool-kit is hardly available. Sound knowledge about the effects of the ongoing transformative processes would require reliable theories and hypotheses, which are, however, largely absent especially because we have to deal with new and unknown phenomena of potentially far-reaching consequences. What to do in this predicament? Sticking to the principles of methodology and leaving the speculation to those who care about sales rather than about scientific principles does not seem satisfactory. In our view, it is more desirable to invest more efforts and imagination on methodological tools for FCoT, even if they will probably remain deficient compared to the ones that can be used for StR. This paper aims at contributing to such an effort. In section 2, we want to formalize the problem of research on FCoT to contribute to a better understanding of its characteristics. A brief look in section 3 at two recent major contributions to methodology in our field demonstrates that there really is what we call a "methodological void" with regard to FCoT. It therefore seems promising to inductively trace the methodological procedures of existing attempts to deal with FCoT (section 4). In the final section, we will summarize the results and discuss their implications for the study of systemic regime consequences.

2. THE PROBLEM OF CONSEQUENCES RESEARCH

Research on the future consequences of ongoing transformations has three features that are responsible for its specific methodological characteristics. The first two features have to do with the *position of the underlying variables in time*. A theory or model contains—among other things—an independent variable (IV) leading to some form of effect on a dependent variable (DV). Due to the fixed temporal direction of causality temporally the dependent variable will necessarily be placed ahead of the independent one. The relative position of these sets of independent and dependent variables in time, however, can vary. Schematically, we may distinguish three different constellations (see Figure 12.1).

| | (b) IV → DV | |
(a) IV → DV		(c) IV → DV
Past		Future
	Present	

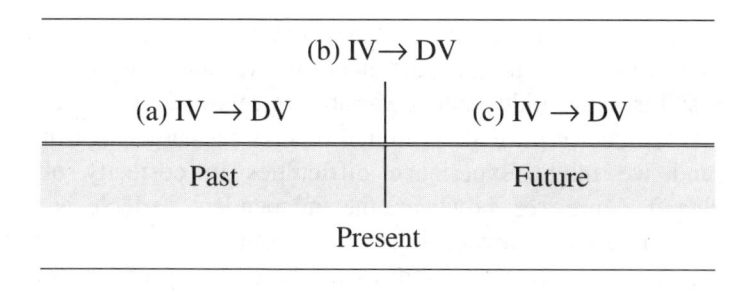

Figure 12.1. *Different constellations of research variables in time.*

Constellation (a) represents what we so far have referred to as "standard research" (StR): Independent and dependent variable lie in the past. For instance, we may be interested in the reasons of Great Power Wars. In this case, a comparative study of Great Power Wars since 1789 could be carried out. Possibly, an empirical correlation and a causal link (causal mechanism) between ideological competition of the major powers in Europe (independent variable) and the outbreak of Great Power Wars (dependent variable) could be identified. Similarly, in order to corroborate the theory according to which the creation of international regimes (dependent variable) can be explained by the underlying constellation of interests (independent variable), the study of existing regimes is recommended. This implies that we have to look at processes of regime formation and constellation of interests in the past. Procedures for this type of research are well established, methodologies abound.

When both the independent and the dependent variable lie in the future science gets a rather wobbly exercise. In constellation (c) the consequences of phenomena are explored that have not even taken place yet. In its pure form, constellation (c) could be labeled "futurology", since it would be an exercise in assessing the consequences of simply assumed (not concluded) factors in the future.[ii] Research on the question whether the creation of a world state (assumed independent variable in the future), will lead to eternal peace (assumed dependent variable in the future) falls into this category.

When major changes are unfolding, however, we might want to know about the consequences of these changes immediately. In this case we start out with an ongoing process that is presently taking place (independent variable) and ask about a dependent variable in the future (the consequences). This is formally represented by constellation (b), which we call "research on the future consequences of ongoing transformations" (FCoT). This label already describes two of the central features of FCoT: (1) The dependent variable of FCoT lies in the future and thus can empirically not be directly observed. (2) The causal agent under consideration (i.e. the independent variable) lies in the immediate past (carrying on into the present) and is assumed to have transformative potential. This creates two problems: First, the independent variable is relatively new. It is therefore rather likely that we have very limited theoretical knowledge on the causal agent and we might experience difficulties in correctly observing or measuring it. Moreover, however, the independent variable is assumed to have very far-reaching consequences in the sense of having the potential to transform the international system as a whole. The problems of FCoT are thus even more severe than those of "simple" prediction. It is helpful to recall Gilpin's (1981) differentiation between changes within a system and system changing transformations. Whereas the former leave the system intact the latter fundamentally alter the "rules of the game". FCoT deals with research on the latter type of changes, which undermine the applicability of established theories and our ability to correctly interpret events in a changing context. Research on the systemic consequences of international regimes shares these general features of FCoT: The rise of international regimes is an ongoing process we know relatively little about and which is assumed to have the potential to fundamentally affect the international system. Potential major shifts in the international system as its systemic consequence, however, will only unfold in the future (if at all).

The third feature of FCoT has to do with the *direction of reasoning*. As has been mentioned above theories or models are always presented as changes in an independent variable leading to a change in a dependent variable. The actual research process, however, most of the time works backwards. Within a more or less stable structure, researchers most often seem to be interested in the causes of a specific phenomenon, i.e. the factors that gave rise to a specific outcome. "Why did this happen?" seems to be the most important type of research question. Most StR thus traces the roots of an outcome (dependent variable) rather than evaluating the consequences of a causal agent (independent variable). To be sure, StR can also ask about the consequences of a certain phenomenon as the contributions to the first part of this volume demonstrate convincingly. They direct our attention to the effectiveness (i.e. the consequence) of a regime or a cluster of regimes thereby arguing "forward". Most StR, however, is driven by the impulse to explain a certain outcome. One implication of this research practice is that very often a single outcome (dependent variable) is linked to a multiplicity of explaining factors (i.e. independent variables). For instance, the above mentioned question about the reasons for Great Power Wars might be answered with "ideological competition" as a causally relevant factor but probably with "great power rivalry" or an "unbalanced distribution of power" as well. A general theory will then link "ideological competition",

INTO THE METHODOLOGICAL VOID 313

"rivalry" and the "distribution of power" to the outbreak of Great Power Wars.

By contrast, FCoT by its very nature does not have the opportunity to work backwards. Its starting point can not be the dependent variable since the dependent variable is what we want to get at as a result of our investigations. Rather, FCoT has to start out by focussing on the independent variable, i.e. the ongoing transformation. Therefore, in contrast to StR FCoT will very often look at one independent variable and link it to a multiplicity of consequences (i.e. changes in a number of dependent variables). The rise of international regimes in general, for instance, might simultaneously be linked to changes in the deep structure of international society, alterations of the identity and role of states and favorable conditions for international peace. Figure 12.2 summarizes these differences between StR and FCoT.

StR	FcoT
"Direction of reasoning"	*"Direction of reasoning"*
←	→
IV_1 ↘	↗ DV_1
IV_2 → DV_1	IV_1 → DV_2
IV_3 ↗	↘ DV_3
Time t_{-n-1} → Time t_{-n}	Time t_0 → Time t_{+n}

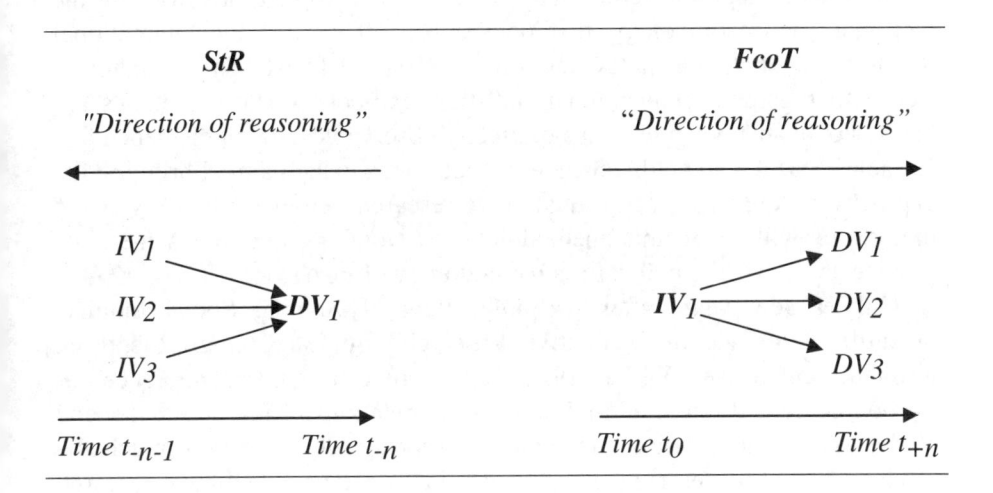

Figure 12.2. *Standard and consequences research compared.*

In sum, research on the consequences of ongoing transformations (FCoT) is characterized by three features:
1. an initial focus on a driving force or an independent variable that is new and just taking place and assumed to have transformative potential
2. an outcome or a dependent variable that has yet not come fully into existence or completely lies in the future
3. the logic of forward reasoning

Reversing these features yields an ideal type of Standard Research. Idealtypically, StR is characterized by an initial focus on a driving force or an independent variable that is well known and can be located in established theoretical models, an outcome or a dependent variable that took place in the past, and the logic of backward reasoning. To be sure, much real-world research is taking place between these two extremes. In our attempt to contribute to a tool-kit for FCoT (section 4), we will take advantage of this situation by reviewing research that comes close to the ideal type of FCoT.

3. THE METHODOLOGICAL VOID

There is no doubt about it: Even a superficial glance at the features of FCoT will lead us to expect that this kind of research is more complicated and, probably worse on the counts of validity and reliability than good StR. However, in times of transformation and change FCoT is of utmost importance. Society and politics demand knowledge about the changes that possibly will shape the future. The situation is worsened, however, by the fact that the methodology textbooks most often read by International Relations theorists are quite silent on situations of FCoT. This certainly is true with regard to conventional statistics textbooks—whose methods are hardly applicable when there is no directly observable data on the dependent variable—but it also holds for more recent books, which aim at bridging the gap between quantitative and qualitative research. An exemplary review of that genre will show this methodological "void", yet at the same time provide some starting points for a methodology of FCoT.

Only a few years after its publication, "Designing Social Inquiry: Scientific Inference in Qualitative Research" by Gary King, Robert O. Keohane and Sidney Verba (1994) has become a standard reference for methodological discussion in international relations. King, Keohane and Verba assume at the outset that qualitative research faces very much the same problems of descriptive and causal inference as quantitative research and thus that qualitative research with low Ns can and should be pursued following the same logic as quantitative research.[iii] Against this background, the book develops some essential recommendations for designing qualitative studies. One of the most important lessons of this book regards the selection of cases. The advice is to select cases allowing for variation in the dependent variable, or preferably to select cases based on variations in the independent variable. FCoT by definition cannot adhere to the first suggestion. A possible dependency between case selection and the dependent variable is uncontrollable since little is known about the *explanandum*. This, on the other hand, also translates into an advantage since such a design will hardly be biased against variation in the dependent variable. In this respect, FCoT might therefore do even better than much of StR, because it *necessarily* selects cases on the independent variable.

King et al. also specifically deal with the problem of the relative low numbers of cases available for qualitative studies and suggest a number of methods to make "many observations from few" (King et al. 1994: 217). Two of the strategies mentioned are of potential importance for FCoT. On the one hand, readers are advised to realize the potential for separate observations on the same empirical "case" as exhaustively as possible. This can be done by sub-dividing the case either across time or by looking for components of the case on lower levels of abstraction. Comparisons across time will probably be of limited use for FCoT because the novelty of the transformatory changes is one of its defining characteristics. A sub-division of the cases under investigation, however, especially combined with variations in the level of abstraction of the analysis could be used to transform FCoT into something that closer resembles StR. A question that "looks" like FCoT on a high level of abstraction could potentially be transformed into a number of more specific research questions on a lower level of abstraction thereby moving the dependent variable into the present or the immediate past. For instance, rather than looking at the overall number of regimes and pondering about its systemic consequences, researchers could break down the regimes by issue area and operationalize "systemic consequences" in a way that traces of systemic effects should be observable in the present or immediate past. "Has the recent surge of environmental regimes led to a changing role of states in this field?", for instance, as a question much closer resembles StR than "Will the rise of regimes change the deep structure of international society?". These issues will be taken up in greater detail below while looking at concrete examples of non-speculative FCoT. At this point, it is important to emphasize that despite the potential usefulness of some of their advice for FCoT, the concept of research used by King et al. is quite different from the one used in FCoT. In the view of the authors, observations constitute the "fundamental component of social science" (King et al. 1994: 217) and an observation is defined "as one measure of one dependent variable on one unit (and for as many explanatory variable measures as are available on that same unit)" (ibid.). In FCoT with its directly unobservable dependent variable, however, we will hardly have "observations" in this sense. The basic logic of "Designing Social Inquiry", is intimately connected to standard research which very much limits its usefulness as a tool-kit for FCoT.

As King and his colleagues, Charles Ragin (1987, 1994, 2000) also covers the middle ground between single case studies based on understanding and large n-studies geared towards the discovery of correlations between variables. Ragin (1994) calls the one approach case-oriented and the other variable-oriented. His "Qualitative Comparative Analysis" (QCA), which he characterizes as "diversity-oriented", aims at combining the advantages of the two approaches. Recently, he supplemented his QCA-method with fuzzy-set methods (FS) (Ragin 2000), which he considers to match perfectly with the notion of diversity-oriented research. In our context, others features of diversity-oriented research are most interesting. First, it views populations (or the universe of cases) as flexible, manipulable constructions and, secondly, it emphasizes a view of causation that is conjunctural and heterogeneous.

Whereas Ragin's approach certainly is conceived as a variant of standard research in that in all of his examples both the dependent and the independent variable are located in the past (or at least present), it also contributes to a better understanding of consequences research. FSQCA is extremely flexible in what constitutes a case in point. It emphasizes that, contrary to variable-oriented research, the case as such remains visible in the process of analyzing the data and thus views "populations" as flexible and manipulable. This feature is extremely important in our context, since any change of systemic effects implies a change in "populations". It relates directly to the second feature of FCoT mentioned above: The novelty and transformative potential of the independent variable. A case considered in one structure as a case of x, may be considered as a case of y in a newly emerging structure. For instance, the transfer of sovereignty to an international regime might be a significant event in a state-dominated international system. If the structure of the system, however, has changed, it might be nothing more than a routine procedure. Thus we have to keep in mind that a consequence as broad as a systemic effect might change the interpretation of variables.

Moreover, conjunctural causality is another feature of FSQCA that is interesting for FCoT. Looking for combinations or "conjunctures" of causal conditions to explain outcomes is equivalent to identifying "sufficient" conditions triggering a certain effect on the dependent variable. The distinction between necessary and sufficient conditions in turn reflects the difference between forward and backward reasoning. Conditions are "necessary" when for a dependent variable to be present a certain combination of independent variables must be present. In other words: When we "see" the outcome, we know that certain causal agents were in place, which reflects a line of reasoning from the dependent variables backwards to independent variables. Sufficiency tests on the other hand are based on forward reasoning and check whether certain combinations of independent variables always lead to a given outcome. Accordingly, these tests pay close attention to the variety of combinations of factors that can cause the same outcomes. The notion of conjunctural causation is thus based on forward reasoning, which is the third feature of FCoT identified in section 2. In a manner similar to a sufficiency test, FCoT asks about the effects of the change in a conjuncture of conditions by reasoning forward. Conjunctural causation does not claim that such a change is the only or the most pervasive to get this outcome. Thus, Ragin reminds us that a hypothesized consequence can also occur as a result of different independent variables than the transformatory changes under consideration. The proposition that the rise of international regimes will lead to a change in the deep structure of the international system, does not imply that the rise of international regimes is the only or the most important cause of this development. While scanning the "universe" of potential consequences of a transformation, we should take into account that effects could also be influenced by different factors than the changes under consideration.

We argued that most StR looks for those independent variables that preceded the effect to be explained, not caring so much about the question whether the outcome does not take place, if the independent variable is not there either. StR in practice thus aims at necessary conditions, if it follows the logic of selection on the dependent variable and backward reasoning. Contrary to this widespread research practice, both King et al. and Ragin advise putting more emphasis on the selection of the independent rather than on the dependent variable and thus reasoning forward. The question then is whether a change in the independent variables leads to a change in the outcome, that is, in a sense, the search for sufficient conditions. Contrary to most StR, FCoT *necessarily* has to work forward because there is not yet a clearly visible outcome that could be traced backwards. Quite remarkably then, FCoT is closer to the methodologists advice "select on the independent variable" than most of the practice of standard research.

In sum, the contributions by King et al. and Ragin show that the third feature of FCoT—i.e. the necessity to work on the basis of forward reasoning—actually translates into a methodological advantage rather than a problem, especially when compared to much of standard research. At the same time Ragin's approach, just as the one of King et al. is firmly situated within the logic of StR with regard to the location of the variables in time. Some of the advice geared at situations of StR might be useful for FCoT but by and large neither of these seminal textbooks on methodology offers a lot of help for dealing with the peculiarities for FCoT.

4. EXISTING METHODS OF RESEARCH ON FUTURE CONSEQUENCES OF ONGOING TRANSFORMATIONS (FCOT)

Given the methodological difficulties of FCoT, it is hardly surprising that studies that are primarily based on understanding, are most important when it comes to systemic consequences of international regimes (see *inter alia* H. Breitmeier and K. Litfin in this volume). There are very good reasons to emphasize "*idiographic methods*" when a very general process of change is taking place (see Eichengreen 1998, Ougaard 1999). An important element of such idiographic studies is the understanding by way of "causal process tracing". However, analyses of causal processes do in no way preclude the comparative and/or counterfactual, i.e. the explanatory logic.[iv] To the contrary, we believe that the logic of understanding and the logic of explanation[v] complement each other. In order to improve our understanding of systemic regime consequences, it seems worthwhile to survey the existing explanatory approaches.

Clearly—and despite a lack of any standard methodology for FCoT—there are a number of substantive explanatory studies that have, explicitly or implicitly, conducted approximations to FCoT and yet are certainly much more than informed speculations. In the remainder of this contribution, we want to look at two substantive fields that are more or less inevitably involved in FCoT in order to contribute inductively to the development of a tool-kit for FCoT. On the one hand, substantive research on the systemic consequences of the rise of institutions in world politics has already been carried out. It is worthwhile to survey these approaches to the methodological predicament of FCoT that were used so far.

On the other hand, there are many other fields where research comes very close to FCoT-type situations. Examples such as technology assessment, world modeling or world simulation come to mind. Very well-known, for instance, are the early studies of the Club of Rome (Meadows at al. 1972, Mersarovic/Pesterl 1975). Closer to the field of International Relations are the work of Hughes (1999)[vi] or the studies on the effects of environmental change (see e.g. IHDP 1999). These approaches, however, mainly take more or less "material" factors such as technological, demographic, economic and environmental change as their point of departure. The study of the systemic consequences of international regimes, in contrast, looks at rather broad macro variables resulting from very complex patterns of social interactions such as the "rise of international regimes". The flourishing debate on the social and political consequences of globalization appears very similar to research on regime consequences in this regard. Hence, a look at globalization studies might also yield methods that could more directly be brought to bear in the context of research on the systemic consequences of international regimes.

In this contribution we therefore want to focus on some examples of FCoT in studies about systemic regime consequences and in research on the far-reaching political consequences of globalization. The choice of these studies is no doubt extremely selective and largely driven by the perceptional limitations of the authors. We cannot claim these examples of "non-speculative FcoT" to be representative, let alone complete, but nevertheless we think they can contribute to the development of strategies and methods to reduce the methodological problems of FCoT.

4.1 The Rise of Institutions in World Politics

The study of international regimes focused for a long time on the conditions under which specific/single international regimes come into existence. Only in the 1990s have efforts to analyze regime consequences multiplied (Levy et al. 1995). Most of this work, however, has focused on regime effectiveness, that is, the question to what extent a single or a small set of regimes has helped to solve the problems that created the demand for them.[vii] Whereas the study of regime effectiveness has made some progress over the last decade, our understanding of the broader consequences of the rise of international institutions (institutionalization of world politics) is still underdeveloped.[viii] Broader consequences of international regimes take place beyond the issue area for which the regimes have been crafted for in the first place and affect fundamentals of the international system, be they constitutional institutions like sovereignty, the role of the state or the likelihood of the application of force. It is safe to assume that most of these systemic effects are non-intended outcomes of many instances of (more or less) intentional regime-building. It also seems safe to assume that systemic effects of international regimes are nothing that can be causally attributed to one, specific international regime. Therefore, the independent variable is the rise of international regimes as such, that is the institutionalization of deliberate conflict management and problem solving beyond the nation-state.

A first difficulty in evaluating the effects of the rise of international regimes has to do with the first feature of FCoT, i.e. the location of the independent variable in the present or the immediate past and its characteristic as an ongoing process. Up to know the collection of good data has been unable to catch up with the development of regimes. While we generally know that the number of international regimes has sharply risen of the last three decades, we lack more specific data that provides us with time-

, region-, and issue-area specific information. It seems fair to say that even something as broad as the measurement of globalization is more advanced than the measurement of international institutionalization.[ix] The provision of data that allows for a precise measuring of degrees of international institutionalization will be of utmost importance. However, even if this data were available, it would be still a major challenge to draw causal inferences between the rise of international regimes and their assumed systemic effects.

One strategy in this field is to look for *Historic Parallels*. While the overall amount of international regimes certainly is higher than in earlier historical periods, we may transform FCoT into StR by identifying comparable historical situations with similar degrees of institutionalization. This approach comes close to the ideal of a quasi-experiment, dependent on the degree of historical comparability and on the difference in the degree of institutionalization. Reinhard Wolf (1999), for instance, tackles the issue of the future of NATO in a world in which the enemy has dissolved that gave rise to the alliance in the first place.[x] As is well-known, different theories of international politics have quite different predictions about the future role of NATO. Wolf aims at obtaining additional insights by analyzing the post-war fate of cooperation between the members of successful war alliances in great power wars. A typical issue of FCoT, the future of NATO (dependent variable) as a result of a contemporary change (end of Cold War as independent variable) in absence of a broadly accepted theory, is thus successfully transformed into StR.[xi] Wolf concludes that it is neither the post-war international power distribution nor the institutionalization of cooperation that explains the persistence or decline of cooperation, but internal developments within the great powers.

The logic behind this imaginative methodological move is closely related to the general problems of FCoT. First, since we are interested in systemic effects of international regimes, the focus needs to be on situations that at least carry the potential for some fundamental and consequential changes in the international system. Given that the international system is by no measure older than 400 years and that this system has been considered relatively stable, it is extremely hard to identify a sufficient number of such cases. To put it differently, the approach of looking for historic parallels will always need to struggle with a low N problem and will thereby in most of the cases do worse than Wolf, who at least identified four cases. Second, the search for historical parallels in the international system is notoriously plagued by objections regarding comparability. Things in 1989 are quite different than things in 1815; therefore the search for historical parallels will almost by definition hamper the goal of varying the relevant independent variables only, while controlling for all others. The third problem may be the most relevant in our context and is due to the tendency that the demand for

FCoT is especially high in times of transformation. FCoT asks for the effects of a transformative process, thus for the effects of a new, historically unknown process. Therefore, there are inherent limits to the use of historical parallels. Some analysts would indeed consider the degree of institutionalization of the "war alliance" NATO as unprecedented. In this view, the future of NATO can be hard assessed by reference to older, much less institutionalized forms of security cooperation.

A second approach of interest may be labeled *Historic Contrasts*. In a number of case studies about East-West regimes, contributors to a volume edited by Rittberger (1990) looked for the robustness of international regimes during a time when the overall relationship between the US and the USSR was significantly deteriorating.[xii] Regimes established before the deterioration of overall East-West relations in the time between 1979 and 1984, such as the Baltic environmental protection regime, the Berlin and the intra-German trade regime, proved robust (Rittberger/Zürn 1990) while weakly institutionalized forms of cooperative relations such the regulations for the working conditions for foreign journalists broke down. The stability of relationships in issue areas with stronger forms of institutionalization can be taken as an indication of a stabilizing effect of regimes for overall relations. If the regimes would have failed, overall relations could be expected to have even further deteriorated. If this indicator is valid then the rise of international regimes could be expected to have a stabilizing systemic effect. In general this strategy suggests testing for a future consequence by looking at past or present examples in which the occurrence of such a consequence is *least likely*. If it can still be observed, it can be considered likely that the effect will be carried on into the future rather than being a spurious trend. Once again, FCoT is thus transformed into StR by moving the dependent variable into the past. However, a conclusion about the future implies an additional step of inference. In the example, it has only been shown that regimes help to stabilize cooperation within an issue area even in difficult times. Their future systemic impact, however, has to be additionally induced and of course can be criticized.

A third approach of interest here may be called *Analysis of Processes*. Although Helen Milner's (1988) work on global industries and the politics of international trade does not primarily address the issue of regime consequences, it is a good case in point for demonstrating rather broad effects of a single—though important—regime. Based on case studies on the US and France, Milner argues that to the extent that the GATT-regime has been implemented in the most industrialized countries, it has empowered the export sector of national industries and other agents of liberalism in OECD-countries. In this way, the GATT-regime has altered domestic structure in many countries, and paved the way for further liberalization.[xiii] The study proceeds by implicitly comparing observed processes with a notion of domestic trade politics without the international context of a trade regime. In general, the analysis of processes thus substitutes the problem of projections into the future (a) by looking at processes instead of outcomes and (b) by claims about counterfactuals. Looking at the effects of a regime on "politics" greatly increases the sensitivity in the measurement of the dependent variable as it can be assumed the changes in "politics" will translate into changes in "policies" in the future. Future effects on policies should be visible in processes first. Further, the effect of the regime is deduced from the comparison between the observable process and a counterfactual assumption. The validity of this comparison, however, depends on the correctness of the assumption about the counterfactual, i.e. the development in the absence of the regime under investigation. Only if assumptions about the counterfactuals hold, the difference between observed patterns and the counterfactual expectations can adequately describe the effects of regimes.[xiv] Clearly, the validity of counterfactual, in turn, depends on what is studied. At the same time, however, this approach has a huge advantage. It does not need to shift the dependent variable back in the past. Instead it relies on increasing the sensitivity of the respective measure.

4.2 Globalization Studies

Globalization usually depicts a process which "embodies a transformation on the spatial organization of social relations and transactions—assessed in terms of their extensity, intensity, velocity and impact—generating transcontinental or interregional flows and networks of activity, interaction, and the exercise of power" (Held et al. 1999: 16). Many analysts see globalization as extremely consequential. There is hardly any fundamental political institution of the western world—such as sovereignty, the welfare state, national political systems or democracy—that is not said to be severely affected, challenged or undermined by globalization. Accordingly, some authors see the process as a "nail in the coffin" of the sovereign democratic welfare state that has emerged in the post-war era. From this perspective, the current process implies nothing less than a fundamental change in the nature of the most prominent objects of international relations: the state and the international system at large. Clearly, research on globalization thus fits the blueprint of FCoT. The process itself is an ongoing transformation that is assumed to have very significant future consequences.

A first difficulty in evaluating these claims in a methodologically acceptable manner is due to the indeterminacy of the causal agent "globalization". Quite similar to research on the systemic consequences of regimes studies on the effects of globalization have to come to terms with the first feature of FCoT: globalization is currently unfolding and neither a very clear concept nor empirically easy to track. Some have even doubted that globalization is occurring at all by referring to earlier times in which the density of economic transactions across national borders has been similarly high. Moreover, globalization is a process, which may be measured with one scale or with a potentially extremely high number of different scales, all depending on its definition and operationalization. Whereas this difficulty is quite challenging, it is not insurmountable. The provision of data that allows for a concept-dependent, flexible measuring of globalization that takes into account different values of globalization dependent upon time, place and object of exchange has clearly improved in the last decade.[xv] The major challenge thus still is to draw inferences from globalization—that is a process taking place in the present and changing over time—to the assumed systemic effects in the future.

An obvious, first lesson that we can learn from non-speculative FCoT in this field is to apply *Trend Extrapolation*. Research on globalization has simultaneously applied trend extrapolation to both the causal agent (the independent variable) and the hypothesized outcome (the dependent variable). In applying this technique, both variables are moved into the present and FCoT thus gets transformed to something that is very close to StR. A good example of this strategy is Geoffrey Garrett's (1998a, 1998b) work on economic globalization and its impact on the welfare state.[xvi] The underlying question in the project is whether economic globalization has prompted a pervasive policy race to the neoliberal bottom among the OECD countries. The research strategy is to look at the most recent developments in economic globalization (foreign trade quotas, foreign direct investment and capital mobility) on the one hand and state activities on the other (in areas such as total government spending, spending on welfare, public sector deficit and tax policies). Implicitly, the findings are extrapolated into the future for that the study assumes that all of the forces of globalization are already in place and their effects already need to show somehow. Although the initial focus of this study has been on the independent variable—he asks for consequences of globalization –, the logic of forward reasoning is in this design more or less replaced by correlational tests. Garrett (1998a, 1998b) finds that the trend towards economic globalization is not accompanied by a neoliberal convergence of national economic policies. He concludes that "globalization has not prompted a pervasive policy race to the neoliberal bottom among the OECD-countries, nor have governments that have persisted with interventionist policies invariably been hampered by damaging capital flight." (Garrett 1998b: 823)

This approach successfully circumvents some of the general problems of consequences research. At the same time, it is dependent on a number of prerequisites that cannot be taken as given in all kinds of FCoT. We want to illustrate that by focusing on one element of Garrett's findings, that emphasizes that social spending has diverged rather than converged between social democratic and liberal countries. There are at least three requirements for the trend approach to work. First, it is of utmost importance to have very recent data available for both dependent and independent variables. Second, the sensitivity of the measures for especially the dependent variable must be extremely high. And third, it is important to have a very good understanding of the "inner workings" of the dependent variable. Although these conditions hold for Garrett's study amazingly well, probably better than in most comparable cases, the criticism of his work can be easily related to these problems. His conclusion is first criticized as premature, since the downward standardization of welfare spending has just started in the mid 1990s and has been delayed for a number of contingent reasons. This criticism can be translated into the argument that the data he is using is not recent enough and his measures are too insensitive to capture what is going on. Another criticism points to a lack of understanding of the European welfare state. To the extent that welfare policies are individual entitlements, the welfare spending necessarily goes up if unemployment rises. Therefore, the rise of expenditures in Scandinavian and some Continental countries is a consequence of older policies and does not indicate a lack of changes in current policies, which can be clearly traced, if, for instance, the level of spending for each individual receiver is looked at. This criticism amounts to the statement that a lack of understanding on the side of the dependent variable has led Garrett to a wrong conclusion.

A related, second lesson for FCoT that we can learn from non-speculative globalization studies is about the appropriate use of *Aggregation and Disaggregation*. Garrett in his work has strongly disaggregated the notion of "policy race to the neoliberal bottom", that is the dependent variable, by using different established measures for different national policies. Thereby the level of abstraction was significantly lowered for the purpose of empirical investigation. The debate about the future of state sovereignty could not built on such established conceptual distinctions. Therefore, the debate started out on a very general level. While "hyperglobalists" saw the coming global age as one with global enterprises, global civil society, dominance of market relations, and no place for sovereign states, globalization skeptics pointed to the rise of trading blocs, economies less interdependent than 100 years before, and state executives being more autonomous than ever. Progress in the study of the future of sovereignty did not become possible until the notion of sovereignty had been disaggregated. Janice Thomson (1995), for instance, has made an important contribution by distinguishing different dimensions of sovereignty such as "recognition", "state", "authority", "coercion", and "territoriality".[xvii] While empirical studies are still rare in the field, such a disaggregation of the concept is an important step in this direction for it allows "measuring sovereignty."

The work on sovereignty issues has been relatively silent on the side of the causal agents. Partially these studies refer to globalization processes, partially to processes of international institutionalization and global governance. This tendency to rather aggregate than disaggregate on the side of the independent variable is methodologically justifiable. However, for the more the causal agent is disaggregated, the smaller the impact of its components to the dependent variable will be. Thus, disaggregating the independent variable too much will make it hard to see any changes at all. It is unlikely that just the rise of world trade changes sovereignty as such. It is much more likely that a configuration of factors consisting of economic globalization, the rise of universal values, and the rise of international institutions will lead to changes of different dimension of sovereignty that are identifiable. In sum, while it is advisable to disaggregate in FCoT on the side of dependent variable, it makes sense to use more compound variables on the side of the independent variables.

Although the appropriate use of aggregation and disaggregation certainly helps to reduce the methodological problems of FCoT, it is again accompanied by a number of problems. First and most obvious, it assumes a trend, which will go on in the future. It is thus dependent on the assumption that no counterforces, either on the independent or the dependent forces, will set in. Second and also quite obvious, there are limits to aggregation and disaggregation. The aggregation of different possible causal agents into one independent variable leads in the extreme to a situation in which we assess a change on the side of the dependent variable, yet cannot identify the factor or the combination of factors that were the driving force behind the changes. It should be thus kept in mind that the aggregation of the independent variable is a *means* to attain the goal of *high values* on the side of the causal agent. The disaggregation of the dependent variable—a means to make it sensitive to trends—also has its limits, at least if we are interested in major, structural, systemic effects. Third, the most fundamental weakness of the disaggregation seems however to be that it ultimately depends on a configurational theory of the more general concept that relates the smaller component to the larger concept. If it is possible to show significant changes in one dimension of sovereignty, it does not seem sufficient to state that there are "core aspects of the institution of sovereignty which remain unchanged and there are core aspects of the institution which have changed dramatically over time" (Sørensen 1999: 591). This important finding will tell us about the future of sovereignty only, if we have a theory how the different dimension or aspects of sovereignty interact with each other. More often than not, we do not have such configurational theories.

A third approach for reducing the predicament of FCoT that has been used in globalization research may be called *Analysis of Processes In Crucial Cases*. It is very similar to what we have introduced as "analysis of processes" in the context of Milner's (1988) work on the GATT-regime. Applied in this context the approach starts from the assumption that globalization does certainly not directly translate into different outcomes (such as a decline of the nation state), but needs to cause different processes in the first place (eventually leading to different outcomes). Globalization implies challenges for the democratic welfare states and subsequently for international politics. These challenges are serious, yet the outcome is largely determined by political choices. Governments and other political organizations can respond to these challenges in a number of different ways. Against this background, a stylized version of old politics is compared with the politics that is triggered by extreme cases of globalization challenges. Then, it is asked to what extent the "politics of denationalization" differs from "national politics." (Zürn/Walter 2003). The central features of this approach from the perspective of FCoT are (a) the choice of clear examples of globalization for the case studies and (b) the observation of the political process within these examples instead of the future outcome. By means of (a) the independent variable of FCoT is turned into the unit of analysis. By focusing on processes instead of outcomes, the sensitivity of the observations on the dependent variable is increased in the same way as in Milner's work. Looking at crucial cases of globalization and at processes instead of outcomes can therefore also be seen as a way of designing research so that it is strongly sensitive to changes. This also explains the focus on the OECD-world that most studies on the consequences of globalization have taken. In a similar vein, the study of the future of sovereignty could benefit from taking into account those EU studies that describe the EU as a polity *sui generis*.[xviii] The logic is simple: Take an extreme case from the past and look at processes to learn something about the outcome of more regular cases in the future.

The analysis of processes in crucial cases also has weaknesses. First, any generalization on the basis of a choice of crucial cases is problematic. In the present context, the plausibility of such an approach at least depends upon trend studies that can establish the significance of the globalization process. Only if we know that globalization is a secular trend *and* how political actors have responded to significant cases of globalization in the past, it is possible to make meaningful conclusions about the overall consequences of globalization in the future. Second, the strategy of analyzing processes in crucial cases is also dependent on the quality of the conceptual theory that links the individual past occurrences of the independent variable to the overall concept of this causal agent. In a way, the analysis of processes applies the disaggregation approach to both the independent and dependent variable. Statements about the consequences of an aggregated independent variable are then only possible to the extent that it can be established that the crucial cases of the past are indeed conceptionally part and parcel of an ongoing overall process. Thus, the approach necessitates an intimate knowledge of the independent variable. The third weakness of such an approach is its dependence on a very good understanding of the dependent variable. If we want to draw conclusions from the responses of the political actors in the case studies for the overall consequences of globalization, it is also necessary to have an appropriate conceptual theory that links the concrete responses to a concept of the overall consequences. In other words: Analyses of processes are successful in simultaneously disaggregating the variables thus making them observable. However, they need to be supplemented by trend extrapolation and re-aggregations.

5. INSTEAD OF A CONCLUSION: IMPLICATIONS FOR REGIME ANALYSIS

This contribution has made two basic points. First, in times of transformation demand for something that we have labeled research on the future consequences of ongoing transformations (FCoT), and which differs in a number of respects from standard research, rises significantly. At the same time, meeting this demand faces a number of obstacles that seem insurmountable if one follows the methodological logic of standard research (StR). Our second point is that there are nevertheless a number of approaches and strategies that have been used to ameliorate the methodological predicaments of FCoT. These strategies can be seen as first signposts marking a third way between the *Scylla* of more or less informed speculation and the *Charybdis* of methodological purity rejecting demands for research that is considered as substantively important. We offered a *tour d'horizon* of available options for FCoT (see Figure 12.3) that was inductively guided by examples from the literature drawing on regime analysis as well as on the debate on globalization.

Approach	Independent Variable	Dependent Variable
Examples from Regime Analysis		
Historical Parallels (Wolf 1999)	Comparable Cases	Outcomes
Historical Contrasts (Rittberger 1990)	Crucial Outside Challenge	Outcome/Counter-factual Comparison
Analysis of processes (Milner 1988)	Crucial Case/Disaggregation	Processes/Counter-factual Comparison
Examples from Globalization Research		
Trend Extrapolation (Garrett 1998)	Trends	Trends/Disaggregation
(Des-) Aggregation (Thomson 1995)	Trends/Aggregation	Trends/Disaggregation
Analysis of processes in crucial cases (Zürn/Walter 2003)	Crucial Case as Challenge/ Disaggregation	Processes/Counter-factual Comparison

Figure 12.3. *Different approaches to the problems of FcoT.*

What is to be learned from this? Can we draw any lessons from reviewing existing methods of consequences research? Does it give indications about how to study systemic effects of international regimes? First and most important, all attempts reviewed here aim at transforming FCoT into StR by one or another methodological move in order to move the dependent variable into the observable past. Moreover, this admittedly limited survey of FCoT shows that some tools recur quite often. Four of these tools then seem to be especially important and could contribute to a core of any tool-kit of FCoT:

1. Trend extrapolation
2. The comparison between what is thought to be "normal" and very recent developments
3. Attempts to make the dependent variable as sensitive as possible (either by disaggregation or by looking at processes instead of outcomes) and
4. Attempts to make the independent variable as strong as possible (either by aggregation or by choosing extreme or crucial cases).

The analysis of systemic regime consequences so far seems to shy away from the use of trend extrapolation. This more or less most "natural" method to conduct FCoT has not been used in the study of international regimes. An important reason for this may be missing data on both the rise of international regimes and on systemic outcomes. The attempt to build up an International Regimes Database (see Breitmeier et al. 1996) may be instrumental in ameliorating this problem on the side of the dependent variable. With respect to systemic outcomes, there are attempts to systemize somewhat the array of conceivable dependent variables (Breitmeier/Wolf 1993, Zürn 1998), yet little has yet been done. The lack of any attempt to operationalize these systemic outcomes in a way that make it conducive to trend studies is largely lacking.[xix]

The studies on systemic regime consequences reviewed here are based on the comparison of crucial cases. Whereas the construction of crucial cases is quite different, all these studies have been successful in doing so and thus paved the way for similar attempts in the study of globalization consequences. However, none of these studies followed any explicit guidelines in constructing the crucial cases. The research designs were to some extent the by-product of more conventional StR: the Tübingen group studied different East-West regimes, mainly with an interest in the conditions of regime formation.[xx] Milner studied different national trade policies, mainly with an interest in accounting for the link between domestic and international politics; and Wolf studied different war alliances, mainly with an interest in evaluating the explanatory power of major IR theories. The conclusion from this is straightforward. Our knowledge about the construction of crucial cases needs urgently to be improved. Two developments are of special interest here. First, the already mentioned IRD may also prove useful to identify crucial cases, it "will help make the search for, and use of, crucial cases more rigorous end effective." (Breitmeier et al. 1996: 21). Second, the re-introduction of Bayesian thinking in qualitative social research through Ragin's QCA method points inevitably to the notion of crucial cases (see also Eckstein 1975).

Moreover, the study of systemic regime consequences seems not to be *en vogue*. What is more, conceptual thinking about systemic regime consequences is also not very developed. The number of studies on regime effectiveness however is still growing. Regime analysts, in our view, should rethink the given investment of resources.

NOTES

1 We leave it to the imagination of the reader to supplement the references for this footnote.
2 Most of the time, however, the constellation (c) type of research will take place as an "extension" of constellation (b). Having concluded that something will happen in the future researchers might become interested in consequences that lie even further ahead.
3 For a helpful review essay that emphasizes and criticizes exactly this point see McKeown (1999).
4 See the contribution by Lovi in this volume.
5 See Hollis/Smith (1991) for a still authoritative juxtaposition of these basic approaches.
6 See also the contribution of Hughes in this Volume.

7 The literature is by now rich and broad. For recent and influential contributions see Young 1999, Miles/Underdal 2000 and the contributions in the first part of this volume.
8 See however the contributions of Breitmeier and Litfin in this volume with regard to broad effects on democracy and sovereignty respectively.
9 This is for instance reflected in Beisheim et al. (1999: 331-355), where to some extent we had to use problematic indicators for international institutionalization (e.g. number of treaties overall and by issue area, development of regulatory output of exemplary regimes, membership in international organizations, etc), which are not very specific (e.g. with regard to the regulatory content of the regimes) and not very reliable (due to partially problematic sources).
10 For another example using a similar logic see Kennedy's (1989) bestseller on the "Rise and Fall of the Great Powers".
11 In a similar manner research on the effectiveness of economic sanctions (e.g. Galtung 1967 and Nossal 1989) tried to evaluate the past proficiency of these measures in order to draw conclusions about their future effectiveness.
12 The logic of this approach is similar to studies that try to compare national political systems by looking at the way they manage externally induced crises (See e.g. Gourevitch 1978, 1986; Katzenstein 1984, 1985).
13 A similar logic is pursued by studies like Rogowsky 1989, Frieden 1991.
14 See also the mounting literature on counterfactuals, e.g. Fearon 1991, Biersteker 1993.
15 See e.g. Hirst/Thompson 1996, Beisheim et al. 1999 or Held et al. 1999.
16 See Rodrik 1997, Bernauer 2000, Genschel 2001 for similar approaches.
17 For similar analyses see for instance contributions to Holm/Sørensen (1995), Krasner (1999), Liftin (1997), contributions to Lyons/Mastanduno (1995), Rosenau (1997), and Sørensen (1997, 1999).
18 See e.g. the work on the EU as a dynamic multi-level governance system by Jachtenfuchs/Kohler-Koch 1996, Marks et al. 1996.
19 See, however, the contribution of Hughes to this volume.
20 But see the current Tübingen project on regime robustness (Hasenclever at al. 1996) and the contribution of these authors to this volume.

REFERENCES

Beisheim, M., Dreher S., Gregor, W., Zangl, B., and Zürn, M. (1999) Im Zeitalter der Globalisierung? Thesen und Daten zur gesellschaftlichen und politischen Denationalisierung, Baden-Baden (Nomos).

Bernauer, T. (2000) Staaten im Wandel: Zur Handlungsfähigkeit von Staaten trotz wirtschaftlicher Globalisierung, Leske + Budrich, Opladen.

Biersteker, T. J. (1993) Constructing Historical Counterfactuals to Assess the Consequences of International Regimes: The Global Debt Regime and the Course of the Debt Crisis of the 1980s, in V. Rittberger, (ed.) Regime Theory and International Relations, Clarendon, Oxford.

Breitmeier, H. and Wolf, K. D. (1996) Analyzing Regimes Consequences: Conceptual Outcomes and Environmental Explorations, in H. Breitmeier, M. A. Levy, O. R. Young, and M. Zürn, Regime Theory and International Relations, Oxford University Press.

Eckstein, H. (1975) Case Study and Theory in Political Science, in F. Greenstein, N. W. Polby (eds.) Handbook of Political Science, Addison-Wesley Press, Reading, MA.

Eichengreen, B. (1998) Dental Hygiene and Nuclear Waste: How International Relations Looks from Economics, International Organization 52, 4: 993–1012.
Fearon, J. (1991) Counterfactuals and Hypothesis Testing in Political Science, World Politics 43, 2: 169–185.
Frieden, J. A. (1991) Invested Interests: the Politics of National Economic Policies in a World of Global Finance, International Organization 45, 4: 425–51.
Galtung, J. (1967) On the Effects of International Economic Sanctions: With Examples from the Case of Rhodesia, World Politics 19, 3: 378–416.
Garrett, G. (1998a) Partisan Politics in the Global Economy, Cambridge University Press.
Garrett, G. (1998b) Global Markets and National Politics: Collision Course or Virtuous Circle, International Organization 52, 4: 787–824.
Genschel, P. (2001) Globalization, Tax Competition, and the Fiscal Viability of the Welfare State, Max Planck Institute for the Study of Societies, Köln, Working Paper 01/1.
Gilpin, R. (1981) War and Change in World Politics, Cambridge University Press.
Gourevitch, P. (1978) The Second Image Reversed: the International Sources of Domestic Politics, International Organization, 32 4: 881–912.
Gourevitch, P. (1986) Politics in Hard Times: Comparative Responses to International Economic Crises, Cornell University Press, Ithaca, New York.
Hasenclever, A., Mayer, P. and Rittberger, V. (1996) Justice, Equality, and the Robustness of International Regimes, Tübinger Arbeitspapiere zur Internationalen Politik und Friedensforschung.
Held, D., McGrew, A., Goldblatt, D. and Perraton, J. (1999) Global Transformations: Politics, Economics and Culture, Polity Press, Cambridge.
Hirschi, C., Serdült, U. und Widmer, T. (1991) Schweizerische Außenpolitik im Wandel, in Schweizerische Zeitschrift für Politikwissenschaft 5, 1: 31–56.
Hirst, P. and Thompson, G. (1996) Globalization in Question. The International Economy and the Possibilities of Governance, Polity Press, Cambridge.
Hollis, M. and Smith, S. (1991) Explaining and Understanding International Relations, Clarendon Press, Oxford.
Holm, H.-H. and Sørensen, G. (eds.) (1995) Whose World Order? Uneven Globalization and the End of the Cold War, Westview Press, Boulder, Co.
Hughes, B. B. (1999) International Futures: Choices in the Face of Uncertainty, 3rd ed., Westview Press, Boulder, CO.
IHDP (International Human Dimensions Programme on Global Environmental Change) (1999) Institutional Dimenations of Global Environmental Change. Science Plan, IHDP Report No. 9, IHDP, Bonn.
Jachtenfuchs, M. and Kohler-Koch, B. (eds.) (1996) Europäische Integration, Leske + Budrich, Opladen.
Katzenstein, P. J. (1984) Corporatism and Change: Austria, Switzerland, and the Politics of Industry, Cornell University Press, Ithaca, New York.
Katzenstein, P. J. (1985) Small States in World Markets: Industrial Policy in Europe, Cornell University Press, Ithaca, New York.
Kennedy, P. M. (1989) The Rise and Fall of The Great Powers: Economic Change and Military Conflict From 1500 to 2000, Vintage Books, New York.
Keohane, R. O. (1993) The Analysis of International Regimes: Towards a European – American Research Programme, in V. Rittberger with the assistance of P. Mayer (ed.) Regime Theory and International Relations, Oxford University Press.
King, G., Keohane, R. O. and Verba, S. (1994) Designing Social Inquiry: Scientific Inference in Qualitative Research, Princeton University Press.

Krasner, S. (1999) Sovereignty: Organized Hypocrisy, Princeton University Press.
Levy, M. A., Young, O.R. and Zürn, M. (1995) The Study of International Regimes, European Journal of International Relations 1, 3: 267–330.
Litfin, K. (1997) Sovereignty in World Ecopolitics, Mershon International Studies Review 41, 2: 167–204.
Lyons, G. M. and Mastanduno, M. (eds.) (1995) Beyond Westphalia? State Sovereignty and International Intervention, John Hopkins University Press, Baltimore.
Marks, G., Schmitter, P. C., Scharpf, F. W. and Streeck, W. (eds.) (1996) Governance in the European Union, Sage, London.
McKeown, T. J. (1999) Case Studies and the Statistical Worldview: Review of King, Keohane, and Verba's Designing Social Inquiry: Scientific Inferences in Qualitative Research, International Organization 53, 1: 161–90.
Meadows, D. H., Meadows, D. L., Randers, J. and Behrens, W. W. (1972) The Limits to Growth. Potomac Associates, New York.
Mersarovic, M., and Pesterl, E. (1975) Mankind at the Turning Point, Hutchinson, London.
Miles, E., and Underdal, A. (eds.) (2000) Explaining Regime Effectiveness: Confronting Theory with Evidence, MIT Press, Cambridge, MA.
Milner, H. E. (1988) Resisting Protectionism: Global Industries and the Politics of International Trade, Princeton University Press.
Nossal, K. R. (1989) International Sanctions as International Punishment, International Organization 43, 2: 301–22.
Ougaard, M. (1999) The OECD in the Global Polity, paper prepared for workshop in SSRC Project "Globalization, Statehood, and World Order", Firenze, Italy, October 1 – 3, 1999.
Ragin, C. C. (1987) The Comparative Method: Moving Beyond Qualitative and Quantitative Strategies, University of California Press.
Ragin, C. (1994) Introduction to Qualitative Comparative Analysis, in T. Janows and A. Hicks, (eds.) The Comparative Political Economy of the Welfare State: New Methodologies and Approaches, Cambridge University Press.
Ragin, C. (2000) Fuzzy-Set Social Science, University of Chicago Press.
Reinicke, W. (1998) Global Public Policies: Governing without Governments, Brookings Institute, Washington, DC.
Rittberger, V. (ed.) (1990) International Regimes in East-West Politics, Pinter, London, New York.
Rittberger, V. and Zürn, M. (ed.) (1990) Towards Regulated Anarchy in East-West Relations, in V. Rittberger (ed.) International Regimes in East-West Politics, Pinter, London, New York.
Rodrik, D. (1997) Has Globalization Gone too Far? Institute for International Economics, Washington, DC.
Rogowski, R. (1989) Commerce and Coalitions: How Trade Affects Domestic Political Alignments, Princeton University Press.
Rosenau, J. N. (1997) Along the Domestic-Foreign Frontier: Exploring Governance in a Turbulent World, Cambridge University Press.
Sørensen, G. (1997) An Analysis of Contemporary Statehood: Consequences for Conflict and Cooperation, Review of International Studies 23, 3: 253–269.
Sørensen, G. (1999) Change and Continuity in a Fundamental Institution, Political Studies 47, 3: 590–604.
Thomson, J. E. (1995) State Sovereignty and International Relations: Bridging the Gap Between Theory and Empirical Research, International Studies Quarterly 39, 2: 213–33.

Volker R. and Mayer, P. (eds.) The International Regimes Database as a Tool for the Study of International Cooperation, working paper WP-96-160, International Institute for Applied Systems Analysis (IIASA), Oxford University Press.

Wolf, R. (1999) Partnerschaft oder Realität? Verbündete Großmächte nach Hegemonialkonflikten, Habilitation, Universität Halle.

Young, O. R, (ed.) (1999) The Effectiveness of International Environmental Regimes: Causal Connection and Behavioral Mechanisms, MIT Press, Cambridge, MA.

Zürn, M. (1998) The Rise of International Environmental Politics: A Review of Current Research, World Politics 50, 4: 617–649.

Zürn, M., Walter, G., Dreher, S. and Beisheim, M. (2000) Postnationale Politik? Über den politischen Umgang mit den Denationalisierungsherausforderungen Internet, Klima und Migration, Zeitschrift für Internationale Beziehungen 7, 2: 297–329.

Zürn, M., Walter, G. (ed.) (2003) Globalizing Interests: Pressure Groups and Denationalization, State University of New York Press.

Chapter 13

REGIMES AND SOCIAL TRANSFORMATION

BARRY B. HUGHES
Graduate School of International Studies, University of Denver

1. THE QUESTION AND AN APPROACH

Has the proliferation and strengthening of regimes in recent decades begun to have measurable consequences, not just in the specific arena of individual regimes, but more broadly? A premise of this book is that they almost certainly have, but that we have not yet developed empirical tools for identifying those consequences. The charge for this chapter is to consider how we might actually measure some of the "broad consequences" of regimes.

The methodological tasks are daunting, both at the conceptual and empirical levels. Although Young (Chapter 1) has already sketched some of them, we will begin with another inventory of them, as a preface to mapping an attack on at least of few of the more vulnerable. After those two foundational steps, we will actually risk a preliminary excursion into the measurement of broad consequences, using some indicators of social transformation, both attitudes and human conditions. We will argue that a combination of cross-sectional and longitudinal data on attitudes or opinions might be a particularly fruitful place to look for the footprints of regimes. Even in advance, however, it must be admitted that this chapter will scarcely begin the search for broad consequences of regimes.

2. METHODOLOGICAL BARRIERS

Figure 13.1 can help us organize our consideration of the methodological problems that we face. We will focus on four key problem areas.

Consequences of Regimes

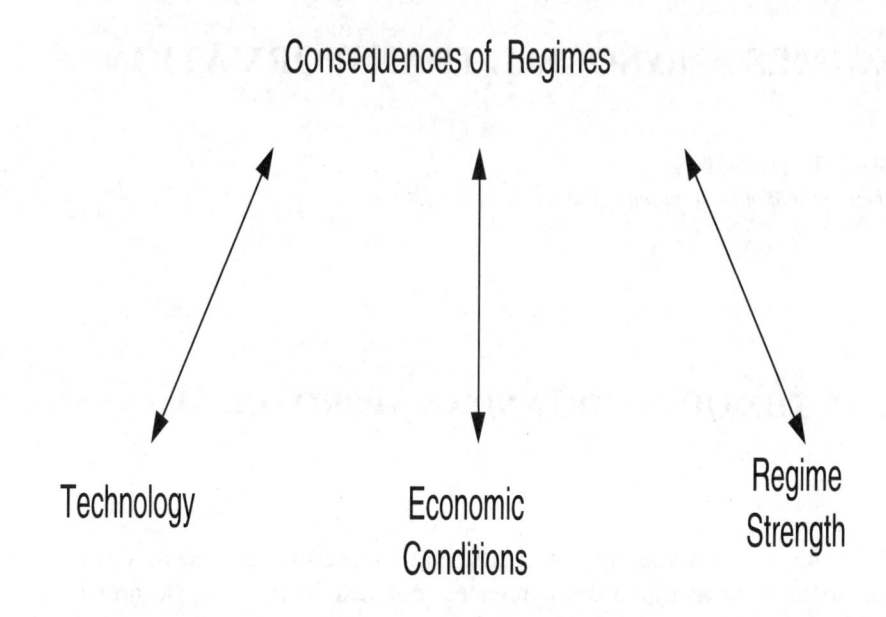

Technology — Economic Conditions — Regime Strength

Figure 13.1. *A schematic of causal links around regime consequences.*

The first and most obvious problem area is the one that Young (Chapter 1) gave the most attention, namely the definition of and measurement of the "dependent variable," namely regime consequences. What exactly do we think we might be looking for? Within the issue area of a very specific regime, such as the regime around protection of species against threats to their extinction, that can be fairly obvious (if not always easy to measure even when it is). What do we mean, however, by broader consequences? Presumably, one thing we mean is the impact that a regime around biological diversity could have in another area of environmental interest, namely tropical forest extent, or in one still more distant, the level of atmospheric carbon dioxide. But physical, biological, and specifically human systems are tightly linked. It is obvious that environmental and economic consequences flow jointly from even narrow issue areas such as protection of spotted owls, and potentially much more extensively from issue areas such as dampening of growth rates of atmospheric carbon. In such extensively linked systems (extensively in both geographic and issue terms), consequences could be extremely broad.

The second methodological problem concerns the independent variable. The International Regimes Database (Breitmeier, Levy, Young and Zürn 1996a; Breitmeier, Levy, Young and Zürn 1996b) has begun to organize comparative empirical data around regimes. Yet we do not yet have a longitudinal data base on the "strength" (somehow independent of consequences themselves) or even presence/absence of regimes by issue area.

Compare our situation on dependent and independent variables with that of those who study the outbreak of war or conflict short of war. The students of conflict can turn to several data sets around their dependent variable, including that from the long-running Correlates of War Project (COW; see Small and Singer, 1982). In terms of their independent variables, they also have extensive collections of aggregate data across countries on some of the characteristics reasonably hypothesized to give rise to higher probabilities of conflict. Further, they have considerable databases around the event sequences that can precede the outbreak of violence (including events data and data on militarized international disputes). In contrast, approaches to the study of both regime formation and regime consequence have typically been case studies using thick description.

A third methodological problem is the cluster of issues around consideration of causality in any empirical research. One of these issues is the reality that causality is very often bi-directional. This may be a more pronounced problem for analysis of regimes than in many areas of social research. In fact, as suggested above, it is not always even clear what we mean by the strength of a regime, independently from the strength of the consequences to which the regime gives rise in its issue area. Were regimes defined in terms of formal institutions, that would be less of a problem. Because they are defined as broader social structures, the boundaries between the regime and its impact become less clear-cut.

A second issue around causality is the role of third and potentially confounding variables. Two may be of special importance, as Figure 13.1 indicates. The first of these is technological change. If growth in renewable energy forms were ultimately associated with a slowing down or reversal of growth in atmospheric carbon levels, how would we understand the causality? Would technological developments in renewable energy be the "real" driving force? Or could we argue that one or more regimes provided the impetus for the development of technology? Note the bi-directional arrows around the link between technology and regime consequences in Figure 13.1, and the obvious oversight of omitting arrows directly linking regime strength, technology, and economic conditions. Given the complexity of causality around regimes, it is perhaps not surprising that case studies and thick description has been so prevalent.

The fourth problem area is in some respects simply an extension of the preceding three, but is more pronounced in the search for "broad" regime consequences than for narrow ones. What are the boundaries of the search? What is the issue domain of our analysis to be? There are arguably regimes now present in some form around every issue area of human interaction. Each of those could potentially be creating ripples of consequences that flow through every other issue domain. How, for instance, could we study the broader economic consequences of any given environmental regime without studying the consequences of all environmental regimes? In fact, would not regimes around security issues or around health care also be interacting in the unfolding of whatever we saw in economics?

3. THOUGHTS ON METHODOLOGICAL APPROACH

The first thought that may cross many minds is that this chapter has dug a very deep methodological hole, and that it might be prudent simply to give up. In particular, it would seem to make sense to insist on better clarity around independent and dependent variables before moving forward. Nonetheless, we shall try to suggest some directions that might demonstrate real and important consequences of regimes, in part by pursuing that clarity.

The first step in doing so will be to step back and ask again what we mean by regimes (a clearer consideration of the independent variable). One of the most often quoted definitions of a regime remains that of Stephen Krasner:

> Regimes can be defined as sets of implicit or explicit principles, norms, rules, and decision-making procedures around which actors' expectations converge in a given area of international relations. (Krasner 1983: 2).

Although the literature around international regimes focuses heavily on states and their behavior, many of the basic concepts upon which regimes are built, such as principles, norms, decision-making, and expectations of actors, suggest the foundational role that individuals and organizations based on individuals have in regime theory. The steady growth of attention to the place of ideas in global politics (Goldstein 1993; Goldstein and Keohane 1993) and of the constructivist or cultural perspective in international relations (Ruggie1998) reinforce this inherent tendency to look at people, individually and collectively, as the basic building blocks of regime theory.

So, even, does elaboration of the "new institutionalism" by scholars from the regimes literature. For instance, Oran Young defined institutions as

> sets of rules of the game or codes of conduct that serve to define social practices, assign roles to the participants in these practices, and guide the interactions among occupants of these roles..... institutions are social artifacts created by human beings—consciously or unconsciously—to cope with problems of coordination and cooperation that arise as a result of interdependencies among the activities of distinct individuals or social groups. (Young 1994: 3).

If regimes are social institutions built on individuals and social groups, and if principles, norms, and expectations of actors are central to the constitution of regimes, it suggests a possible revision/extension of our earlier schematic along the lines of Figure 13.2. That figure adds an important element, namely values and opinions. It connects that element to the "strength of regimes" by a relatively bold line, suggesting a somewhat complex linkage: a close relationship but one that falls definitively short of identity.

We do not mean to suggest here that the regimes consist only of the values and opinions of individuals. Clearly, there are formal institutional elements of most regimes; among other roles those elements play, they help structure the rules and decision-making procedures around which expectations converge. Moreover, it is the principles and norms held by a relatively small portion of populations, primarily those in leadership and decision positions, to which students of regimes primarily look.

At the same time, however, we do mean to suggest that values and opinions of individuals, including those of wide populations, are close to the heart of regime definition and are therefore very important intermediate variables between regime strength and broader regime consequences. Why has the global regime around atmospheric carbon emissions not begun to reduce those of the United States? Largely because the value that great many Americans place on personal mobility (and in many cases even the value they place on such mobility in large sports utility vehicles) is greater than that placed on reductions in carbon emissions.

In looking for the consequences of regimes, there is some real utility in focusing serious attention on values and opinions and on changes in them. In their role as a significant bridge between regimes and consequences, those values and opinions help us specify the pathway to regime impact. With respect to the latter, it is useful also to consider that values and opinions can be somewhat more independent of economic and technological change than are the ultimate and more material consequences of regimes. Consider again the possible reduction of carbon emissions through either substitution of renewable fuels or energy conservation. If carbon emissions fell for either reason, but values concerning carbon emissions did not change, it would strongly imply that technological advance had been a key independent force. At the same time it is (for our consideration of causality) unfortunately also true that if both technology advanced and values changed, it would be difficult to know that values did not shift largely because technology simplified once-complicated trade-offs.

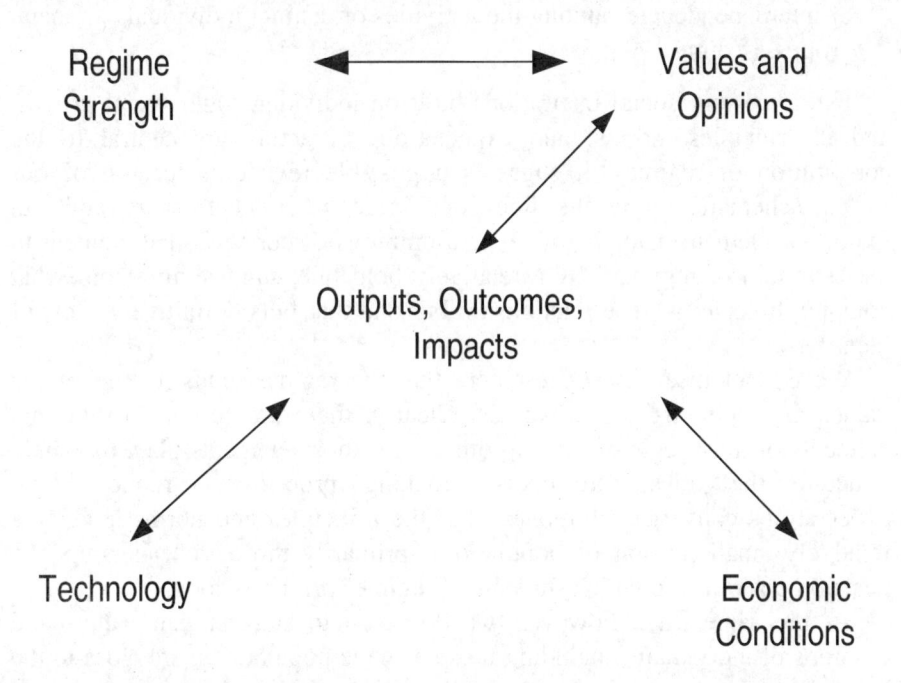

```
    Regime         <------>       Values and
    Strength                      Opinions
                         ↗↙
              Outputs, Outcomes,
                  Impacts
             ↗↙              ↖↘
    Technology                    Economic
                                  Conditions
```

Figure 13.2. *A revised schematic of causal links around regime consequences.*

Figure 13.2 has also replaced the abstract regime consequences item of Figure 13.1 with the elaborated listing of consequences that Young presented in Chapter 1. Although we will not do it here, it would be possible to break those consequences into separate items, hopefully with separate measurements, again with attention to which consequences are closest to the independent variable and which are most remote and therefore most likely to be affected separately by third variables.

So, can we after all hope to demonstrate the possibility of broad regime consequences? Given the great methodological challenges, we are unlikely to do provide strongly convincing cases for such consequences, but it would be useful to at least demonstrate some likelihood of, some significant space for their existence. This discussion suggests one approach to doing so.

It suggests more specifically that we would want to look for one or more issue areas in which values and opinions have changed fairly widely in a direction that is logically consistent with regimes in the same or related issue areas. We would, moreover, want to control for economic change in the societies that we examine so as to be confident that values have changed beyond what such economic change could reasonably explain. Although that control for economic change would simultaneously provide some check on the impact of technological change, and our attention to values and opinions itself provides some further check on its impact (as discussed above), we would want to consider further whether technology is likely to have caused the value change. If reasonably convinced of some value change that we could link to/explain by the presence of regimes, we would want next to look at changes in more substantive variables logically linked to the value changes. Again we would want to control for economic change and, if possible, independently control for technology change. Such a pattern of value change and related behavioral/systemic changes, seemingly independent of economic and/or technology change, would at least point to the potential of regime impact.

4. AN ISSUE DOMAIN: CHANGE IN SOCIAL CONDITIONS

Social change has been dramatic and widespread in the last century. For example, life expectancy was only about 50 years in even the richest Western European countries in 1900. Our attention to wide-spread data on social condition is, however, really a post-World War II phenomenon and truly dramatic global changes have occurred in recent decades. Since 1960, global life expectancy has increased from 55 to 66, the total fertility rate has dropped from 4.9 to 2.9, and food calories per capita have advanced globally by about 15 percent. In low income countries social change substantially exceeded the global rate on each of these measures and on others. Life expectancy advanced from 48 to 63 over the same period, the total fertility rate dropped from 6.1 to 3.3 births per women, calories per capita advanced by 25 percent, and literacy grew from under 30 percent to 65 percent.

There is some real value in distinguishing two aspects of social development: improvement of individual life condition and restructuring in social organization. The measures mentioned in the preceding paragraph portray individual life condition. But there has been great change in social organization also. Consider, for instance, both the second and third waves of world-wide democratic advance since World War II. Think also about the spread of female suffrage and of broader attention to rights of women.

What has driven this social change? There is a huge literature on social change or transformation, falling almost entirely within the complex development field. It would be impossible to summarize that literature here. Although all contributors recognize interconnected threads of the development process, they frequently emphasize one or another. On the social side, in spite of Parson's (1951) statement that a theory of change in social systems was then impossible, Lerner (1958) outlined the *Passing of Traditional Society*, while Moore (1963) and Amitai and Eva Etzioni (1964) elaborated the elements of social change. Lewis (1955) provided a theory of economic growth, Rostow (1960) described stages of economic growth, while Chenery and Syrquin (1975) and Chenery (1977) elaborated further the structural changes that mark economic transformation. Like Parsons on social change, Easton (1953) decried the absence of theory on political change, but Almond and Powell (1966) picked up the challenge, while Lipset (1959, 1960) and Huntington (1968, 1971) made seminal contributions to the literature on the development of democracy. Lipset's contributions included early empirical, cross-sectional analysis. McClelland (1961) and Inkeless and Smith (1974) explored the attitudinal changes that de Tocqueville (originally 1831) and Weber (1930) had suggested accompany development and that Inglehart (1997) continues to trace.

The now much maligned theory of modernization and the argument that change occurs simultaneously and interactively on all these dimensions emerged in the 1950s; Apter (1965) and Levy (1966, 1967) provided systematic discussions of it. Huntington (1968) presented a number of early critiques of the modernization argument, while Moore (1979) and many others explored the limitations to the thesis that there is convergence across countries in the development process. So (1990) and Jaffe (1990) presented good surveys of the theory and literature, emphasizing the social change of interest to us here. Many who have examined the linkages among dimensions of development have implicitly or explicitly looked to economic (or perhaps technological) change as the key driver, but others have appropriately recognized a complex web of reinforcing developments (Fedderke and Klitgaard 1998).

In general, however, the literature has, while maligning modernization, undertaking little investigation of alternative paths to social change. In particular, there has been minimal attention to the possibility that social change has been at least in part a result of regime development. That is quite surprising, because there has been extensive regime development around population control (including a series of global conferences on population issues and considerable financial assistance for family planning programs), the provision of heath care (consider the global effort to eliminate small pox alone), and the status of women (and other human rights issues). And, of course, there is what might be called a meta-regime on development, devoting particular attention to economic growth, but by no means ignoring the social side of development. Given the wide-spread commitment of many international and non-governmental organizations to these issues, the need for assessment of their impact, not just via their contributions to economic growth or technological change, but via attitudinal and behavior change would seem a nearly essential component of self-assessment activities.

In short, the area of social change appears to be a potentially important issue area for looking at the broad consequences of regimes (minimally for looking at the consequences of a very broadly defined regime). This chapter will not be able to do that in any depth; its primary purpose has been to identify some of the methodological problems in doing so. Nonetheless, we will provide some preliminary evidence that suggests the potential for such an investigation, and that will also suggest the very real possibility that regimes, in fact, are affecting social change. This is a very exploratory study of wide spread social transformation, part of a larger project on global social change (Hughes 1999, 2000).

The approach to analysis here also recognizes, however, another reality of research design. That is, regimes are highly interactive in their behavior and presumably in their consequences. It is not unreasonable to argue that it may never be possible to look at a single regime in a single issue-area of social change and fully gauge its impact. Looking instead an issue area and trying to estimate the affect of a broad range of regimes within it (and even "overlapping" with it) may be a useful strategy. We will look at social transformations that occur across several issue areas (including demographic fertility, medical care, education, and democracy) in an effort to look for possible regime effects (from regimes around health care, family planning, development, and democracy). In fact, we will attempt to use the multiple issue areas and multiple measures within them to distinguish between the effects of economic and technological change, on the one hand, and those of regimes on the other.

This second section of the chapter and Figure 13.2 provide our road map for the following discussion. We will, not, however, strictly follow the sequence of analysis suggested by that figure. Instead our discussion will develop that sequence in a fashion that begins more traditionally in its analysis of social change and then gradually elaborates the argument.

First, we will look briefly at the dependent variable of social transformation and at multiple and interacting indicators of it. Second, we will turn to the relationship between social transformation and economic condition, attempting to show that changes in economic condition can explain only a portion of the global social transformation that is well underway. Third, we will move into an analysis of that portion of social transformation that is not obviously linked to economic change. As part of that step in analysis, we will attempt "to control" for the contribution of technological change to that remaining portion. It would be foolish to attribute all of the residual social transformation (after removing what we can of economic and technology contributions) to the affect of regimes. If, however, there remains a significant residual transformation, and if we see no obvious alternative explanations, this analysis will at least suggest the possibility that the changing and growing strength of regimes could account for much of that residual. It will have created some space for regimes. Fourth and finally, we will turn to attitudinal data as a possible source of increased confidence in the speculation that regimes do have broad social consequences.

5. PRELIMINARY ANALYSIS : THE ECONOMIC AND TECHNOLOGICAL BASES OF SOCIAL CHANGE

Figure 13.3 is a common approach to demonstrating the clear relationship between economic condition and life or social condition. It indicates that relationship for a sample aspect of social condition, namely the fertility rate.

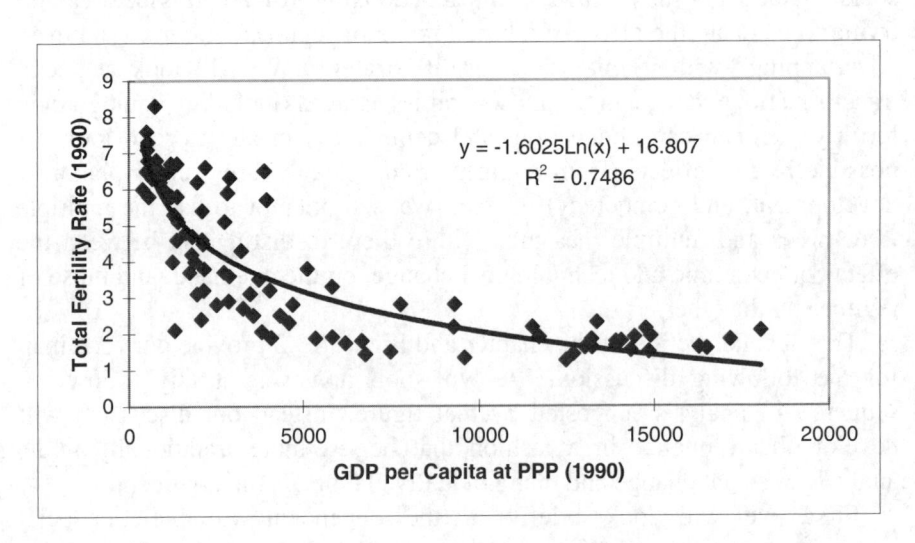

Figure 13.3. *Total fertility rate as a function of GDP per capita.*

$y = -1.6025\text{Ln}(x) + 16.807$
$R^2 = 0.7486$

Across countries in 1990 the total fertility rate (number of children that an average woman bears in a lifetime) drops with the GDP per capita at purchasing power parity. Using GDP per capita at purchasing power parity has two benefits: it increases accuracy in comparing economic condition and it "spreads' the large number of countries at lower GDP per capita levels.

This general pattern of relationship proves remarkably consistent across a very wide range of indicators of social indicators and attitudes. In a related analysis Hughes (2000) called the rapid change in the range below $5,000 per capita (PPP) the "sweet spot" of social transformation, in contrast to the "steady slog" that we see above that level of GDP per capita. The same pattern appears clearly in other social indicators such as literacy rate, life expectancy, malnutrition rate, urbanization, and access to safe water. The same pattern appears again with respect to the level of democracy in societies (as measured by the Freedom House). With respect to many social variables that tend to capture social organization, rather than individual life condition or beliefs, the pattern tends to flatten or to become linear (suggesting a longer-term "steady slog" for aspects of social condition that require development of institutional structures or wide-spread value change). This is true, for example, with respect to the place of women in society and the level of corruption.

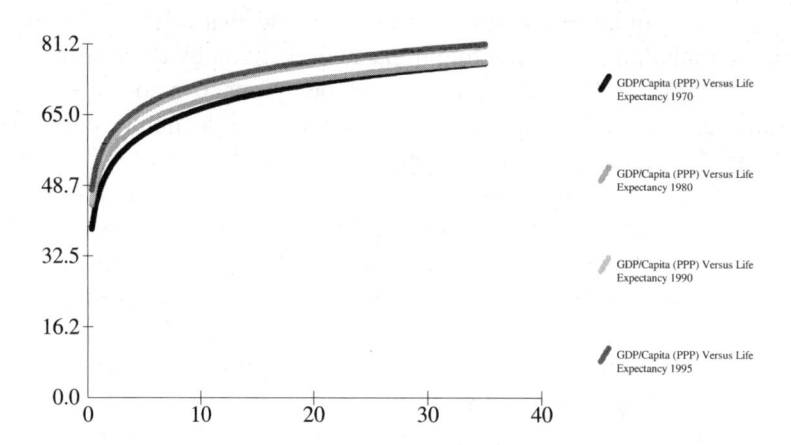

Figure 13.4. *Systemic shift in the relationship between GDP per capita (thousand dollars at PPP) and life expectancy (years).*

When we move from cross-sectional analysis to comparative cross-sectional analysis (a form of longitudinal analysis) built upon it, we see something more, something important for the study of regime consequences. Figure 13.4 shows that life expectancy exhibits the same kind of cross-sectional relationship that characterizes fertility rate, with the same type of sweet spot at lower levels of GDP per capita and steady slog at higher ones. Figure 13.4 shows four relationships, however, using data from 1970, 1980, 1990, and 1995. Note that there has been an upward shift in the cross-sectional relationship. People around the world now have higher life expectancies than in earlier years, even at the same real GDPs per capita. That is, there has been a "systemic shift" in life expectancy that economic condition cannot explain.

This shift clearly suggests that we need to turn to other variables to help us explain changes in life expectancy (and potentially other social conditions). An obvious additional variable is advance in medical technology (see again the schematic in Figure 13.2). Is there, however, some room for the possibility that regime development also plays a role? There is a global regime around the diffusion of medical technology and the extension of life expectancy. The World Health Organization is an institutional manifestation of that regime, but many governmental and nongovernmental organizations contribute to it. The fact that the function shifts upward across the range of GDP per capita (not just at the upper end, representing countries where most medical technology is developed) gives added credibility to the potential impact of that regime.

As this example demonstrates, however, it will be very hard to distinguish among bases for social change beyond that of increases in GDP per capita, including the interacting impacts of technology and regimes. How might we do that? One approach would be to make some a priori, but hopefully reasonable assumptions about the impact of technology on various indicators of social change and to attempt to "control" for technology on that basis. Of course, it would still not be possible to attribute definitively any residual social change (after controlling for both changes in real GDP per capita and for technology) to regime change, even in the absence of obvious alternative explanations. If, however, we were to find no such residual social change, it would suggest strongly that regimes were not significantly affecting social change. If we were to find residual change, the strength of regimes remains a possible explanation for it.

Table 13.1 shows a range of variables and indicators related to social change for which we have data. It ranks them from most likely to reflect technological change to least likely. As the comments in the Table indicate, there are a number of social variables on which we would expect the impact of technological change to be rather low.

The International Futures (IFs) modeling project (Hughes 1999) provides a tool for the exploration of considerable historic data, as well as for exploring alternative possible global futures.[1] Historic data on the variables in Table 13.1 exist in International Futures, as does the ability to undertake both the cross-sectional analyses of Figure 13.3 and comparative, across-time analyses like that in Figure 13.4. We can therefore use that tool to investigate social change in selected variables/indicators of Table 13.1. To do so we look at selected variables in Table 13.1. Ideally, we would want to select variables from Table 13.1 that fall into the lower cells and may be less subject to technological change. Ideally, also, we would want to select variables for which we might have some data on changes in values and opinions. One reason for this being a preliminary study is that data limitations preclude our pursuing the ideal empirical analysis.

Table 13.1. *Social condition and attitudes: assumptions and comments.*

Variable/Indicator	Assumed Impact of Technology	Comments
Life Expectancy, Infant Mortality	High	Medical technology clearly affects these variables over time; a regime effect might still be evident at lower levels of GDP per capita, where diffusion of technology (with the help of regimes), rather than its development is critical.
Contraception Use, Total Fertility Rate	Medium	Improved contraceptive technology clearly has an impact here; but methods for limiting family size predate modern technology, suggesting considerable room for a regime effect.
Literacy Rate	Low	Educational technology has not historically changed rapidly; once we control for the economic ability to use existing technology, there is much room for a regime effect.
Democracy; Gender Empowerment	Low	Although various technologies, including communications, affect these elements of social organization, there is much room for regime effects.

Although technology greatly affects mortality patterns (and the systemic shift over time in infant mortality is at least as pronounced as that for life expectancy), it has less affect on fertility. Obviously, the technology of modern contraceptive methods does influence both the use of those methods and the fertility rates of society. It seems reasonable to posit, however, that on the fertility side (relative to the mortality side) there is a much stronger element of variation in human choice: many individuals and many societies have been very slow to embrace the options for reducing fertility. Figure 13.5 shows that there has been a systemic shift in the percentage of married couples using contraception as a function of GDP per capita. In 1975 the use was so limited at low levels of GDP per capita that the form of the best-fitting line was linear. In subsequent years (1980, 1985, and 1990) usage has steadily risen across all levels of GDP per capita. It seems unlikely that the pattern can be attributed only to improved potential for family planning and likely that it reflects a "regime" that has developed and strengthened around the value of family planning (as reflected in the global population conferences in Bucharest, Mexico City, and Cairo).

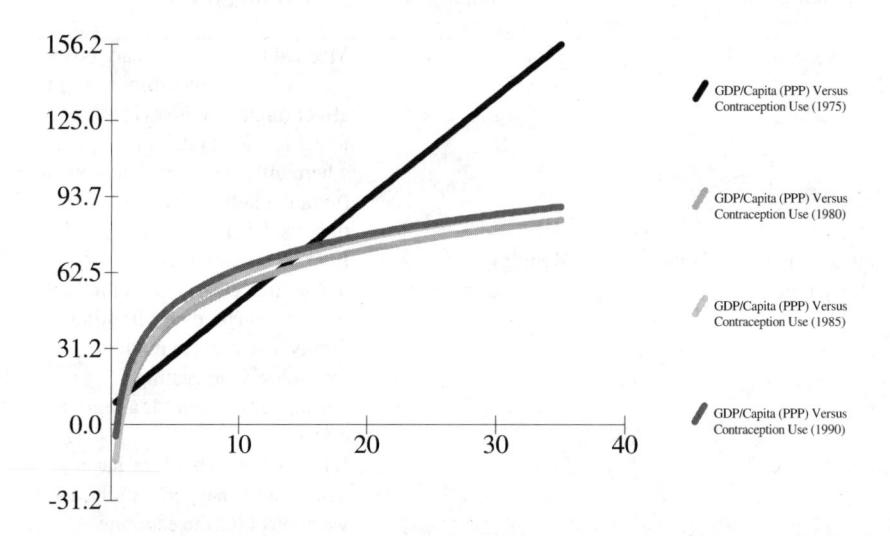

Figure 13.5. *Systemic shift in the relationship between GDP /capita (thousand dollars PPP) and contraception use (%).*

Figure 13.6 shows that the systemic shift in fertility rates is even more dramatic than that in use of modern contraceptives. At each succeeding time point the curve has shifted to lower fertility rates. It is interesting to note that the curve for 1995 hints at an accelerating shift at the lowest levels of GDP per capita. Over the 25-year period, fertility rates have dropped by about 1.5 births per woman across the entire range of GDP per capita. Again, this shift seems unlikely to be an affect that technology alone can explain. It appears likely that the regimes around family planning and economic/social development can take very considerable credit. (Although some might point out that modern communication technologies have made the work of that regime possible, such technology is instrumental to the working of regimes, not directly determinative of the shift in fertility rates.)

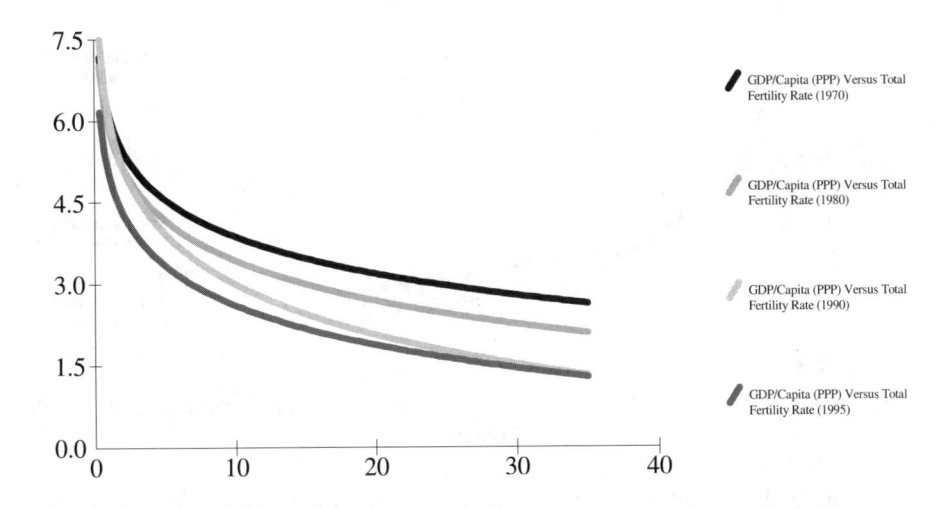

Figure 13.6. *Systemic shift in the relationship between GDP /capita (thousand dollars PPP) and total fertility rate.*

Let us continue to move down the list of variables in Table 13.1. Technology can again affect literacy rates; both the educational technologies of classrooms and the proliferation of the printed word throughout societies around the world could be at work. Nonetheless, learning to read requires clear and costly individual and social choices with respect to the use of such technology. Figure 13.7 shows still again the steady systemic shift in literacy (captured by percentages of adults who remain illiterate) as a function of GDP per capita.

It is important to point out that the pattern of shift in Figure 13.7 is neither as dramatic nor as regular as that in previous figures. Although the lines for 1970 and 1995 represent the highest and lowest rates of illiteracy, respectively (at least at moderate to high levels of GDP per capita), some of the intervening lines do not fall into the anticipated sequence over time. The fact that there appears to have been less systemic shift at the lowest levels of GDP per capita than in previous figures interacts with this reduction in sharpness of the systemic shift. It may be that the societal organization required for improvements in literacy has been harder to achieve at the lowest levels of GDP per capita than has the individual commitment to use of medical technology or family planning options.

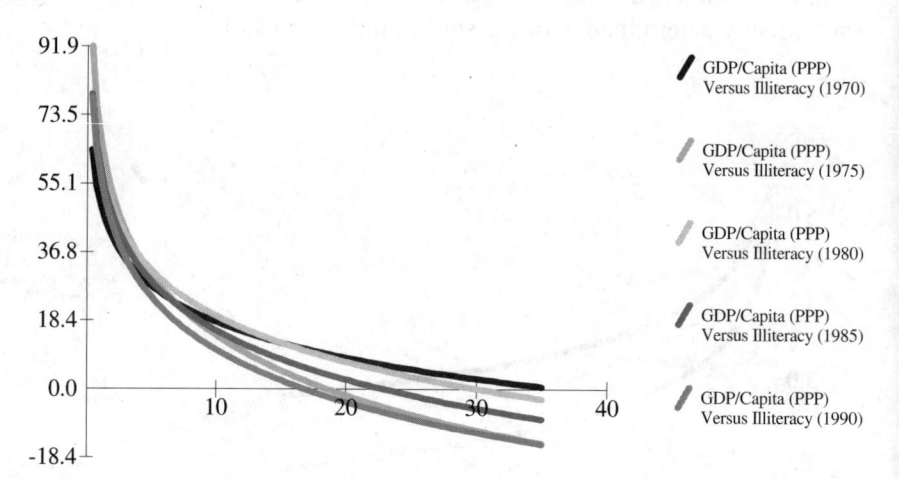

```
                91.9
                                                                    ╱ GDP/Capita (PPP)
                                                                      Versus Illiteracy (1970)
                73.5

                                                                    ╱ GDP/Capita (PPP)
                55.1                                                  Versus Illiteracy (1975)

                                                                    ╱ GDP/Capita (PPP)
                36.8                                                  Versus Illiteracy (1980)

                18.4                                                ╱ GDP/Capita (PPP)
                                                                      Versus Illiteracy (1985)

                 0.0
                        10      20      30      40                 ╱ GDP/Capita (PPP)
                                                                      Versus Illiteracy (1990)
               -18.4
```

Figure 13.7. *Systemic shift in the relationship between GDP /capita (thousand dollars PPP) and illiteracy rate.*

Figure 13.8 shifts our focus more clearly to a societal/organizational variable, one that cannot even be measured at the individual level. The Freedom House measure of democracy (on a scale from 2 to 14, most to least democratic) also shows a clear systemic shift between 1975 and 1992. As with the shift in most other measures we have examined, the movement is consistently unidirectional across time. We would not, however, expect that pattern to prevail over much longer periods of time, because the phenomenon of long historic waves in the progression of democracy is well documented. In fact, it is a bit surprising to see it over at full 17-year period. Again, however, the reasonable assumption that technology has little explanatory power here (except as an instrumental conveyor of values via, for example, communications media) leaves room for an explanation based on a developing regime around democratic forms and processes.

Ideally we would want to examine measures of additional variables that are more sharply societal in their character (as opposed to social indicators of individual life conditions). The Gender Empowerment Measure (GEM) of the United Nations Development Programme and Transparency International's measures of corruption are logical candidates. Although data is accumulating for such measures, the length of time series available to us is unfortunately short for most of them.

Returning our attention to the schematic of Figure 13.2, we have now "created a space" for the possible impact of regimes on social change. More specifically, we have demonstrated that economic advance or development alone does not explain it--there is a systemic shift as well as a move by

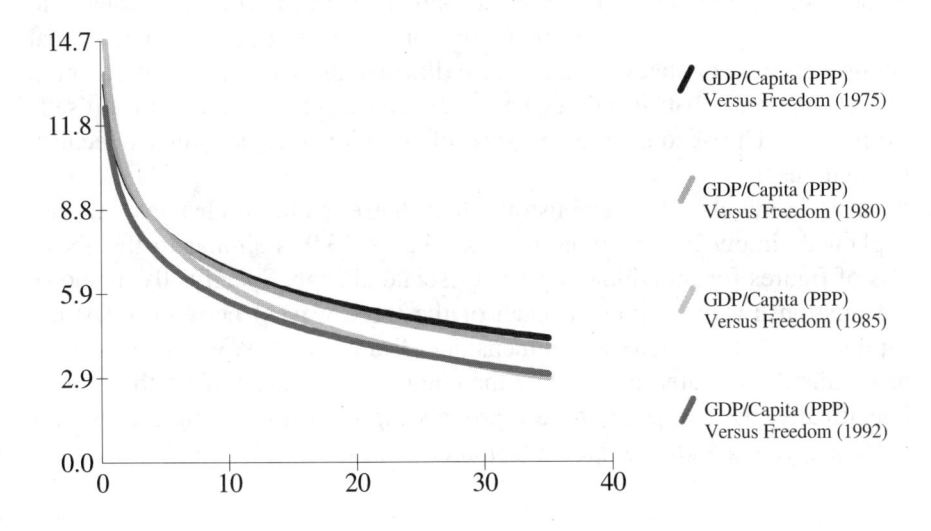

Figure 13.8. *Systemic shift in the relationship between GDP /capita (thousand dollars PPP) and democracy (freedom).*

societies up an economic development curve. Nor does technological change, either through its indirect impact on economic condition or through its specific affect on aspects of social change, appear to explain it--there is systemic shift even in arenas of social change like literacy that technological advance seems unlikely to explain.

Although we have demonstrated the space for regime impact, we have not demonstrated it. Much else might account for social change. Figure 13.2 suggested, however, that one way of better demonstrating the consequences of regimes would be to demonstrate also a transformation in values and opinions in the relevant issue area. Can we do that with social change?

There is, unfortunately, very little systematic cross-sectional and/or longitudinal data on values and opinions with respect to social issues. There is, however, one major research project that has provided such data, the World Values Survey (WVS) of Ronald Inglehart (1997). That project has now completed three waves of surveys in more than 60 societies and is undertaking a fourth wave that will be still more comprehensive. The first three waves provide data from roughly 1981, 1990, and 1995, respectively. Inglehart was very generous in provision of data from the project for analysis with the International Futures modeling system.

Inglehart (1997) has demonstrated very clearly that cultural changes are occurring around the world. He has aggregated his analysis of those cultural changes into three dimensions of cultural change. The first is a general scale called materialism/postmaterialism (or sometimes modernism/postmodernism). The second and third cultural scales are roughly orthogonal to each other and jointly help identify major global cultural clusters of states. One of those dimensions is a measure of attention in the answers that it aggregates to survival versus attention to self-expression. The second is a measure of traditional values versus secular-rational ones.

It is easy also to demonstrate that these cultural changes are not explained simply by economic change. Figure 13.9 is similar to the above sets of figures for individual aspects of social change. Specifically, it shows the relationship over time (in each of the three waves) between GDP per capita and the general dimension from the WVS project of materialism/postmaterialism. Note the complex systemic shift in that figure. Specifically, there appears to be a progressing flattening of the curves over time, suggesting a kind of globalization of values.

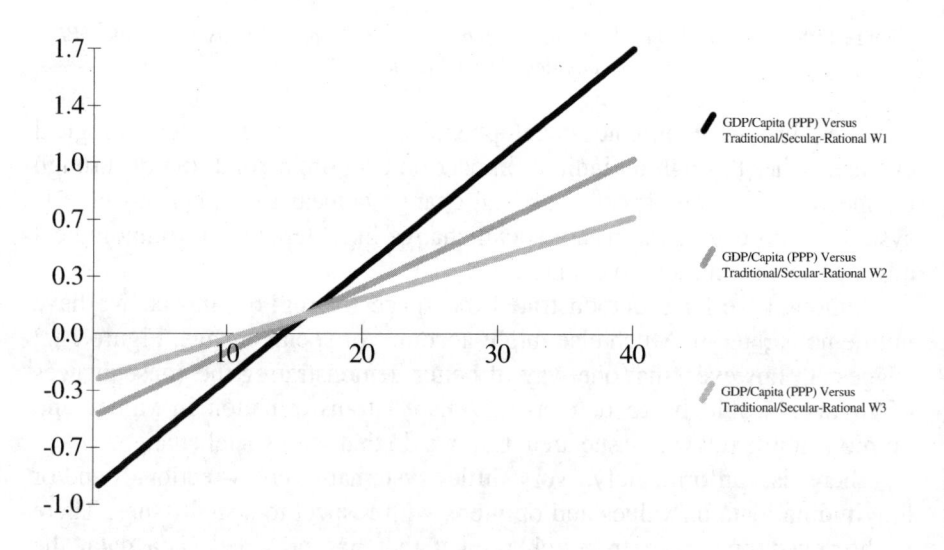

Figure 13.9. *Systemic shift in the relationship between GDP /capita (thousand dollars PPP) and traditionalism/rationalism.*

Some caution must be urged in interpreting Figure 13.9. One of the complications of analysis is that progressive waves of the survey have included more societies at lower levels of GDP per capita. We might have expected, however, that such inclusion would lead to a line of steeper slope as greater numbers of poorer countries in the data set anchored a "third

REGIMES AND SOCIAL TRANSFORMATION

world" attitudinal orientation; instead we see the reverse. That result actually reinforces a conclusion that less economically developed societies may have become less traditional across time at fixed levels of GDP per capita. Although caution is warranted, the overall pattern significantly reinforces the notion that some kind of global development regime may be having a substantial impact on principals, norms, and rules, perhaps especially in economically less-developed countries

Unfortunately, even the WVS project does not yet have data over time on many of the variables that would be most useful to us here or in the broader evaluation of regime consequences. For instance, the third wave of surveys was the first to include a significant battery of questions focused on attitudes around environmental issues. After completion of the fourth wave it will be possible to analyze cross-society change in such attitudes.

Even now, however, the WVS data can be very useful to us. For instance, Figure 13.10 shows the systemic shift in the one environmental question that was asked across all three of the first waves: Do you belong to an environmental organization? Although the vast majority of people in all countries answer that they do not (a value of 3), it is very interesting that between Wave 2 and Wave 3 (a small period in the early 1990s), there was a noticeable global shift towards membership.

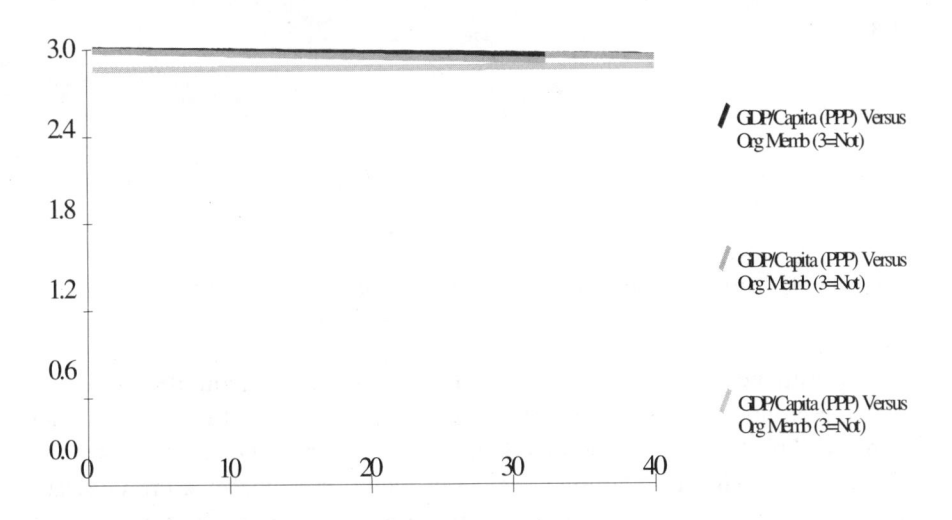

Figure 13.10. *Systemic shift in the relationship between GDP /capita (thousand dollars PPP) and membership in environmental organizations.*

Similarly, Figure 13.11 shows the systemic shift in attitudes about family size between the first and second waves. Given the dramatic shifts over time in total fertility rates, it is not surprising to see a downward shift over time in the relationship between GDP per capita and desired family size. This nonetheless reinforces our earlier conclusion that the drops in fertility reflect values and norms, not just new or expanded availability of family planning methods. In fact, a quick comparison of the desired family sizes in Figure 13.10 with the actual ones in Figure 13.6 hint at still further reductions in global fertility to come, because of the low desired family sizes at low levels of GDP per capita. (Be careful, however, because the number of less-developed societies in the WVS is limited and that end of the curve still has relatively few societies in which to anchor it.)

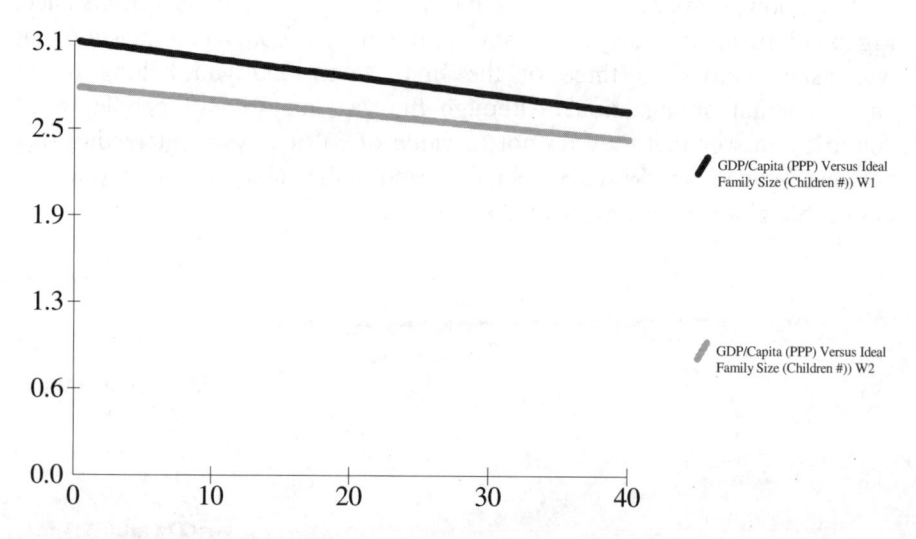

Figure 13.11. *Systemic shift in the relationship between GDP /capita (thousand dollars PPP) and desired family size (children).*

Unfortunately, we do not have responses to questions about democracy at multiple points in time. We nonetheless include Figure 13.12, based on data from the Third Wave. Respondents to a question about whether democracy is the best system of government (most of whom presumably were unaware of the quip attributed to Winston Churchill about it being the worst except for all the others) could choose responses ranging from strongly agree (coded 1) to strongly disagree (coded 4). The remarkably heavy concentration of responses near the pole of strong agreement, even in economically less-developed societies, attests to a global normative attachment to democracy. That is, it suggests the potential power of a regime around democracy.

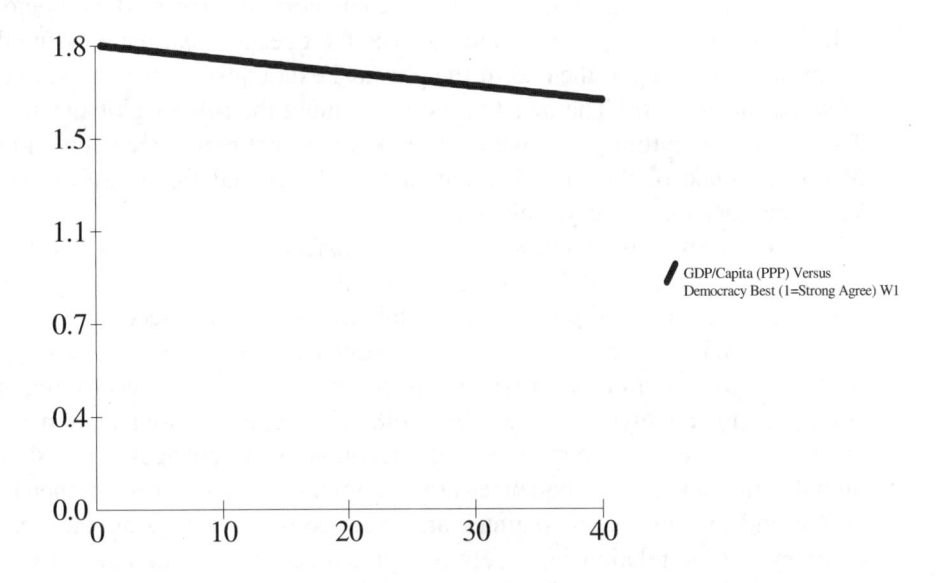

Figure 13.12. *Relationship between GDP /capita (thousand dollars PPP) and support for democracy.*

6. FINAL THOUGHTS

This chapter began by asking whether the proliferation and strengthening of regimes in recent decades has begun to have measurable consequences, not just in the specific arena of individual regimes, but more broadly. It went on to document the nearly insuperable obstacles that we face methodologically in trying to answer that question. In spite of the obstacles, it sketched an approach to exploring the question. That approach involves improved specification of our independent as well as dependent variables, notably some attention to value and opinion change, and it involves serious efforts to control for at least two of the most confounding additional variables, notably economic and technological change. It went on to suggest that social change would be an appropriate area to investigate broad regime consequences and to provide a preliminary investigation using the databases and tools of the International Futures modeling project and of the World Values Survey project.

There is, however, at least one important element of challenge to an endeavor like this that we have not yet addressed. It is so important, and we have left it for so long, that it fits into the category of what medical doctors call the "door knob" question. That is, it is the question that patients finally get around to asking at the end of the physical exam, just as they are starting to walk out the door. The question is, what about the role of globalization? That is, has everything we have been looking at here really been some kind of consequence of the globalization of trade, financial flows, information flows and just about everything else?

There are two quick answers, both unsatisfactory. The first is that, yes, global value changes and changes in global social condition clearly have been dramatically influenced by globalization. The second is that globalization itself is a broad regime consequence, linked not just to changes in the regime(s) around international political economy, but to regime strengthening on myriad issues. In addition, of course, globalization is a result of dramatic economic and technological changes. In short, globalization and its consequences are as complicated a set of phenomena to define and explain as are regimes and their consequences. And there is a complex set of relationships between globalization and regimes that we really do need to sort out. So, take two aspirin and come back tomorrow for some tests.

In the meantime, we should reiterate what we have accomplished here, not just in exploring the methodological issues, but in tackling them. This chapter has taken a first cut at distinguishing the possible affects of changes in economic development level, of advance in global technology, and "other" affects. We did so by systematically controlling for GDP per capita and by making a priori assumptions about the realms in which technological change would be most powerful. The remaining "other" category potentially incorporates many other factors, very probably including the strength of global regimes. The "other" category proved qualitatively significant. The demonstration of the change in attitudes around social condition reinforces the likelihood that regimes have been important influences in that unexplained social change. Thus the analysis strongly suggests, even if it cannot prove, that regimes do have important and broad consequences.

NOTES

1 The professional edition of International Futures (IFs), Version 4, provided the data, analysis, and graphics for this paper. The data files of IFs draw from a wide variety of

sources, but we should note especially the World Value Survey data from Inglehart (1997), GDP per capita (PPP) data from the CIA, and assorted data from the World Bank's World Development Indicators.

REFERENCES

Almond, G. A. and Bingham Powell, Jr., G., (1966) Comparative Politics: A Developmental Approach, Little, Brown, Boston.
Apter, D. E. (1965) The Politics of Modernization, The University of Chicago Press.
Breitmeier, H., Levy, M. A., Young, O.R. and Zürn, M. (1996a) International Regimes Database (IRD): Data Protocol, IIASA WP-96-154.
Breitmeier, H., Levy, M. A., Young, O.R. and Zürn, M. (1996b) The International Regimes Database as a Tool for the Study of International Cooperation, IIASA WP-96-160.
Chenery, H. (1979) Structural Change and Development Policy, Oxford University Press, New York.
Chenery, H. and Syrquin, M. (1975) Patterns of Development 1950-1970, Oxford University Press.
De Tocqueville, A. (1945) [1831] Democracy in America, Vintage Books, New York.
Easton, D. (1953) The Political System: An Inquiry into the State of Political Science, University of Chicago Press.
Etzioni, A. and Etzioni, E. (eds.) (1964) Social Change: Sources, Patterns, and Consequences, Basic Books, New York.
Fedderke, J. and Klitgaard, R. (1998) Economic Growth and Social Indicators: An Exploratory Analysis, Economic Development and Cultural Change 46, 3 (April): 455-490.
Fukuyama, F. (1999) The Great Disruption, The Atlantic Monthly 283, 5 (May): 55-80.
Goldstein, J. (1993) Ideas, Interests, and American Trade Policy, Cornell University Press, Ithaca, New York.
Goldstein, J. and Keohane, R. O. (eds.) (1993) Ideas and Foreign Policy: Beliefs, Institutions, and Political Change, Cornell University Press, Ithaca, New York.
Hughes, B. B. (1999) International Futures, 3rd edition, Westview Press, Boulder, CO.
Hughes, B. B. (2000) Global Social Transformation: The Sweet Spot, the Steady Slog, and the Systemic Shift, Economic Development and Cultural Change, forthcoming.
Huntington, S. P. (1968) Political Order in Developing Societies, Yale University Press, New Haven, CT.
Inkeles, A. and Smith, D. (1974) Becoming Modern: Individual Change in Six Developing Countries, Harvard University Press, Cambridge, MA.
Inglehart, R. (1997) Modernization and Postmodernization, Princeton University Press.
Jaffe, D. (1990) Levels of Socio-Economic Development Theory, Praeger, New York.
Krasner, S. D. (1983) Structural Causes and Regime Consequences: Regimes as Intervening Variables, in S. D. Krasner, ed., International Regimes, Cornell University Press, Ithaca, New York, 1-21.
Lerner, D. (1958) The Passing of Traditional Society: Modernizing the Middle East, The Free Press, New York.
Levine, R. and Renelt, D. (1992) A Sensitivity Analysis of Cross-Country Regressions, The American Economic Review 82, 4 (September): 942-963.
Levy, Jr., M. J. (1966) Modernization and the Structure of Societies, Princeton University Press.

Levy, Jr., M. J. (1967) Social Patterns (Structures) and Problems of Modernization, in W. Moore and Cook, R. M. (eds.) Readings on Social Change, Prentice-Hall, Englewood Cliffs, NJ, 189-208.

Lewis, W. A. (1955) The Theory of Economic Growth, Allen and Unwin, London.

Lipset, S. M. (1959) Some Social Requisites of Democracy: Economic Development and Political Legitimacy, American Political Science Review 53 (March).

Lipset, S. M. (1960) Political Man: the Social Bases of Politics, Doubleday, New York.

McClelland, D. (1961) The Achieving Society, Free Press, New York.

Moore, W. E. (1963) Social Change, Prentice Hall, Englewood Cliffs.

Moore, W. E. (1979) World Modernization: The Limits of Convergence, Elsevier, New York.

Parsons, T. (1951) The Social System, The Free Press, New York.

Rostow, W.W. (1960) The Stages of Economic Growth, A Non-Communist Manifesto. Cambridge University Press, London.

Ruggie, J. G. (1998) Constructing the World Polity: Essays on International Institutionalization, Routledge, London and New York.

Small, M. and Singer, J. D. (1982) Resort to Arms: International and Civil Wars, 1816-1980, Sage Publications, CA.

So, A. Y. (1990) Social Change and Development, Sage Publications, London.

Weber, M. (1930) The Protestant Ethic and the Spirit of Capitalism, Allen and Unwin, London.

Young, O. (1994) Institutional Governance: Protecting the Environment in a Stateless Society, Cornell University Press, Ithaca, New York.

PART III

CONCLUSION

Chapter 14

RESEARCH STRATEGIES FOR THE FUTURE
Where Do We Go from Here?

ARILD UNDERDAL AND ORAN R. YOUNG
Department of Political Science, University of Oslo; Donald Bren School of Environmental Science and Management, University of California (Santa Barbara)

Studies of regime consequences wrestle with a wide range of more or less complex questions. Some of these pertain to single regimes, others to sets or even universes of regimes. Most studies focus on consequences defined in terms of success in coping with the specific problem that a particular regime has been designed to solve or alleviate. But analysts as well as policy-makers have come to recognize that many international regimes have important consequences well beyond their designated domains. These broader consequences can be traced in other substantive issue-areas as well as in the nature of domestic political institutions and processes and in the structure of the international political system. Table 14.1 offers a crude map of the field.

1. THE STATE OF THE ART

At the most general level, the methodological problems we encounter are largely similar across the entire field. Yet, there can be no doubt that the *complexity* of these challenges increases substantially as we move from the upper left hand cell ("simple effectiveness") toward the bottom right hand corner. The more complex the unit of analysis, the more complex become both a regime's "signal" and the causal mechanisms through which it generates consequences. Once we move from studying the consequences of a single regime to mapping consequences brought about by a set of regimes, we have to examine the possibility of regime interplay. In cases of interplay, the consequences of a set of regimes cannot be determined merely by adding up the effects that each of them would have produced had it been operating in isolation. We also have to measure positive or negative synergy, and that

Table 14.1. *The field of regime consequences.*

		Scope: Consequences *For*			
		Regime domain	Other issue-area(s) or regime(s)	Party (state, society, individual)	The interna-tional system
Units: Conse-quences *of*	Single regime	Effective-ness, robustness	Externali-ties, interplay	---	---
	Cluster of regimes	Effective-ness, robustness	Externa-lities, interplay	Political system; actor identity; human welfare.	Struc-ture and proc-esses. State of affairs (e.g. peace).
	Uni-verse of regimes	♦	♦	Political system; actor identity; human welfare.	Struc-ture and proc-esses. State of affairs.

--- Questions rarely asked
♦ Not applicable

can be a demanding exercise. If we extend the scope even further—to some *universe* of regimes—we may even have a hard time identifying the population; inventories of regimes exist only for certain issue-areas and/or regions. Moreover, the further we move beyond designated domains, the weaker will be the signal of regimes and the more difficult it will be to distinguish that signal from the "noise" generated by a wide range of other factors—some of which may well be more important.

As a result, it should come as no surprise that more energy has been invested and more progress made in analyzing simple effectiveness than in tracing and understanding what we have called broader consequences. We can easily see that tasks such as determining the net effect of the universe of international regimes upon aggregate human welfare or the peacefulness of the international system represent daunting challenges that only the boldest (or most naïve) scholars would dare to confront. Still, students of international regimes can hardly afford to ignore the more complex questions. There is no good reason to assume that the questions that are most easily addressed will also be the most important. In this volume, therefore, we have broadened our scope to explore these new and admittedly somewhat fuzzy frontiers of regime analysis.

1.1 Simple Effectiveness

Over the past decade or two, significant progress has been made in conceptualizing, measuring and explaining what we have called simple effectiveness. At this stage, we can point to several important achievements, including:

- A *common* and focused research agenda, centered on a limited range of related questions all having to do with the capacity or success of a particular regime in solving or alleviating the problem(s) that motivated its establishment. Moreover, we see a transnational research community emerging that shares this agenda and is capable of working together in joint projects as well as in looser networks.
- A fair amount of conceptual convergence, at least as far as the *dependent* variables are concerned. Although different definitions of key concepts are still in ample supply, we can at least begin to speak about a common core. Perhaps as important, we are making progress in specifying how different concepts—such as "strength", "robustness," and "effectiveness"—relate to each other. This is an essential prerequisite for cumulative research, as well as for encouraging dialogue between law and political science.
- A move toward more complex and sophisticated explanatory frameworks. While many of the first generation studies tended to focus on one-factor explanations—such as those of "hegemonic stability" or particular game-theoretic payoff structures—recent research is at least

beginning to work with more complex causal models that build bridges between different islands of theory. For example, instead of asking whether "power" generally accounts for more of the variance in effectiveness than "interests" or "knowledge," we are beginning to combine multiple elements and to recognize that their relative significance varies systematically with the nature of the problem and the stage of the political process.

– Intensive case studies being supplemented with more extensive modes of analysis. The creation of new databases containing standardized information about increasing numbers of cases will enable us to engage in more extensive and rigorous comparative research and eventually to bring statistical methods to bear on the study of international regimes. We are in a better position now than ever before to draw upon a wider repertoire of methodological approaches. Moreover, we have seen the first systematic and comprehensive efforts at comparing and contrasting approaches and findings (see e.g. Levy, Young and Zürn 1995; Hasenclever, Mayer and Rittberger 1997). Such reviews and assessments are important tools for integrating existing knowledge, identifying gaps and inconsistencies, and guiding future research.

In other respects, the present state of the art leaves much to be desired. Suffice it here to point to four problems that we believe warrant particular concern:

– Even when the dependent variable is clearly defined at the conceptual level, *operational measurement* is by and large crude and non-transparent. Not surprisingly, this problem seems to pertain particularly to ordinal level ("qualitative") measurement; the few bold attempts that have been made at creating interval scales (Sprinz and Helm 1999) offer more transparent tools (but raise some hard questions about validity). We do think there is considerable scope for improvement when it comes to specifying how the scales are constructed and how we arrive at a specific score for a particular case. Without greater transparency, it is hard to determine how the conclusions obtained in one study compare with those reported in another. And in the absence of a common yardstick, we have no basis for assuming that common-sense labels such as "low" or "high" are used in a consistent manner in different studies and by different authors.

– Attributing consequences to a regime involves some kind of *causal inference*. As we have seen, students of international regimes use a wide range of different techniques for this purpose, ranging from in-depth mapping of causal pathways and mechanisms to attempts at controlling for other factors through some kind of comparison with other cases that differ in one or more critical respects. Barred from experimental research

and without sufficiently rich databases, causal inference often hinges on some kind of counterfactual reasoning. This kind of analysis is a very demanding; in principle, it requires nothing less than a well-specified causal model of the system of activities under consideration. It can be no surprise that transparent and rigorous counterfactual analysis is still rare. But in the absence of such analysis there is a real risk that a strong preoccupation with *regime* mechanisms and signals could lead us to neglect or underestimate the impact of other factors. In a worst-case scenario, the field at large could be systematically biased in favor of findings exaggerating the effectiveness of international regimes.
- We know a number of things about the determinants of regime effectiveness. Yet, it is abundantly clear that we do not have a well-developed causal model identifying the most potent independent variables and specifying how they work and interact under different circumstances. Except for so-called "interest-based" explanations, which have been specified and structured by game-theoretic tools, other main categories of causal factors, such as "power" and "knowledge," are still wide baskets of more or less poorly defined variables. To be fair, we should point out that there are individual studies that do specify a causal framework and make laudable efforts at defining and measuring their independent variables. But the field at large still has a long way to go before it can claim to have a common model that is sufficiently precise and well specified to serve as a guide to research and as a framework for integrating findings.
- In the absence of such a common framework, *accumulation* of knowledge becomes an inefficient and somewhat erratic process. As we have seen, crude and non-transparent measurement of key variables adds to the difficulties. This complex problem has no easy solution, but we believe that research in this field has reached a stage where systematic and comprehensive efforts at comparing and contrasting findings could pay off handsomely. Such efforts are likely to be most productive if undertaken by carefully selected *teams* rather than individual scholars.

1.2 Broader Consequences

By comparison, the field of broader consequences is characterized by, inter alia:
- The absence of a common and well-defined research agenda. This explains why most of the contributions to this section of the volume devote much of their energy to mapping poorly charted terrain and developing distinctions and taxonomies that can help guide and focus future research. Given the diversity of the field, we suspect that progress

toward a common agenda and a common conceptual framework for research can be made only within more narrow subfields. We see some encouraging progress in this direction, perhaps most clearly in the study of regime externalities and interplay—the area that is closest to that of simple effectiveness.
- Longer and more complex causal chains. As the contributions of Hughes and Walter and Zürn to this volume make clear, tracing the impact of international regimes on target variables such as human welfare or the transformation of the international system confronts us with intriguing methodological challenges that call for bold and innovative approaches. It is easy to question the validity of some of these approaches. But there is no easy way out. We find ourselves on the horns of a dilemma between declaring such questions non-researchable (at least at the present stage) and trying to make the best of the most promising approaches and tools available to us. We would argue in favor of the latter.

2. A RESEARCH AGENDA FOR THE FUTURE

We turn now to the future with the aim of identifying cutting-edge questions and growth areas for the study of regime consequences during the next phase. Our purpose is not to establish a unified agenda. Individual scholars are likely to find such an agenda overly restrictive and unnecessarily directive, and it would be inappropriate and undesirable to hinder the play of individual creativity in this field of study. Nonetheless, the discussion at the Oslo Workshop and the subsequent interactions concerning revisions of the papers included in this volume have produced a relatively clear picture regarding critical issues and growth areas in this field. In this section, we offer our own judgments regarding the way forward for students of regime consequences. The result is a set of research priorities, starting as before with simple effectiveness and moving on to the range of issues included under the heading of broader consequences.

2.1 Simple Effectiveness

Even in the comparatively well-defined realm of simple effectiveness, there is much to be done in the next phase of research on regime consequences. We would single out three topics for particular attention: sharpening the dependent variables, improving causal inference, and integrating hypotheses and findings about a range of independent variables into a coherent body of knowledge.

Sharpening the dependent variables. As we have noted already, there are encouraging signs of convergence regarding the target of analysis for studies of regime effectiveness. And there is no need to force consensus around a single conception of institutional effectiveness. Even so, there are several issues relating to the dependent variables that students of regime effectiveness do need to address. Among these, three strike us as requiring particular attention during the next phase of research in this field.

- Behavioral change and problem-solving. Spurred by the old controversy over the importance of institutions in international relations, students of international regimes have geared much of their effort toward examining the role of regimes in guiding or channeling behavior. This is a no-regret option in the sense that any assessment of effectiveness will have to involve some analysis of behavioral change. The ultimate concern of decision-makers and stakeholders, however, will most often be the role of regimes in solving or alleviating particular problems. This directs attention to effects measured in terms such as economic growth or the state of the environment ("impact"). Studying effectiveness in such terms is a more demanding exercise in at least two respects. First of all, it no longer suffices to determine whether and how a regime influences behavior; we must also understand the relationship between actor behavior and the state of the economy or the health of the environment. Second, we now need two points of reference instead of one. Measuring behavioral change requires that we determine what would have happened in the absence of the regime. If our ultimate concern is problem-solving, we must in addition determine what qualifies as a "good" or "optimal" solution. There are ways of dealing with both of these challenges, but at the present stage we clearly have a better grasp on effectiveness defined in terms of behavioral change. In order to be able to respond constructively to the ultimate concern of decision-makers and stakeholders, we need to develop better procedures for assessing impact on the basic problem itself.
- Constructing general and integrated measures of effectiveness. In studies focusing on one single regime or one particular issue-area, regime consequences are often described in terms specific to that particular domain. For some purposes this approach makes perfect sense. When it comes to comparing and contrasting findings, however, we need a measurement tool that is generally applicable across a wide range of issue-areas, from marine pollution to arms control and international trade. Despite the progress that has been made over the past decade in terms of defining such basic standards in the abstract, some hard questions remain concerning the feasibility of translating these constructs into reliable operational tools. The challenge becomes even more complex when we

realize that a general measure of effectiveness should meet, ideally, two other requirements. First, it should enable us to produce integrated assessments, aggregating the various effects arising from the operation of individual regimes into a single and coherent measure of effectiveness. Second, a general index of effectiveness should be applicable at the micro as well as at the macro level; that is, it should enable us to assess effects at the level of individual actors as well as for the system at large. Most of our colleagues may find that this is asking for too much. We have some sympathy for that view, and we certainly have to admit that we do not have such an elegant and powerful tool at this stage. It is, equally clear, however, that comparative research could benefit substantially from having in its toolbox a conceptually sound and operationally manageable measure of effectiveness that can be applied across a wide range of cases.

– Broader normative assessments. The interest in regime effectiveness seems to be premised, at least in part, on the assumption that effectiveness is a good thing. This is a reasonable assumption, but only in a narrow sense: an effective regime solves or alleviates a particular problem for its members as a group. The costs incurred in establishing and operating the regime, and the externalities—effects on other issues or for other parties—it produces are simply left out of the equation. So is the internal distribution of costs and benefits. Clearly, analysts as well as decision-makers sometimes want to evaluate regimes in broader normative terms. They may ask, for instance, whether a regime produces outcomes that are efficient or fair. Moreover, they may want to answer these questions with reference also to a larger group of stakeholders, including non-members. These questions point toward new frontiers of research. At the very least, the fact that a regime may be highly effective and yet inefficient or unfair means that great caution is required in using assessments of effectiveness as the basis for broader normative evaluation.

Making causal inferences. Any study of regime consequences must make causal inferences. We therefore need to find credible and manageable procedures for distinguishing developments brought about by a regime's existence or operation from changes caused by other factors.

There are at least two main strategies for coping with this challenge. One aims at maximizing the mileage we can get out of comparing *consequences*. By means of focused comparisons or statistical analysis of patterns of variance, we can to some extent control for other factors or measure their effects. Focused comparisons require, first of all, that cases be selected on the basis of their scores on the critical variables. However, as Andresen and Wettestad point out in their contribution to this volume, in actual practice the

RESEARCH STRATEGIES FOR THE FUTURE 369

choice of cases is often made primarily on the basis of other, more pragmatic criteria, such as data availability and research costs. For its part, statistical analysis requires that we increase the number and expand the range of cases available for study. Recent progress in building up regimes databases will provide new and interesting opportunities. To take full advantage of such facilities we will need to bring a wider range of tools for comparative and statistical analysis to bear on the data available. The chapters by Mitchell and Stokke explore some of the techniques that seem particularly promising in this context.

Even with new databases and more sophisticated tools, however, the limits on the uses of the variation-finding approach in this field are such that we cannot expect studies that rely merely on measures of association to produce fully satisfactory conclusions about the role regimes play in altering behavior or solving problems. We therefore need to supplement these studies with approaches that can help to identify and examine in depth the causal mechanisms at work and to trace in detail the pathways through which particular effects come about. Fortunately, a number of other analytic procedures are available for this purpose—from intensive process-tracing to formal modeling—and we have just begun to use them effectively in the study of regime consequences.

None of these procedures will suffice *on its own* as a means of determining the direction, strength, and form of causal links. We therefore need to combine two or more of them in a coordinated fashion that enables us to draw upon the comparative advantages of each. When analyses using several distinct procedures yield similar or compatible results, there are grounds for optimism regarding the conclusions we reach. But discordant conclusions may prove useful as well. In cases where different procedures lead to significant divergences in our understanding of the causal significance of regimes, it will be apparent that something is going on that we do not understand properly. Such anomalies can prove useful in guiding research towards an effort to solve important puzzles. Naturally, the use of this strategy will require a conscious effort to coordinate the work of many members of the research community interested in regime effectiveness, a point to which we will return in the next section.

Toward an integrated causal model. The study of international regimes has identified a set of independent variables that seem to be important determinants of effectiveness. Moreover, we have a fair amount of research examining how many of these factors have affected regime formation and implementation in particular cases. But at this stage most of our findings and propositions exist in the form of disconnected bits and pieces rather than a coherent body of knowledge. We clearly have a long way to go before we can claim to have an integrated causal model identifying the important independent variables and specifying how they affect—jointly as well as individually—the performance of international regimes.

Understandably, we began the study of effectiveness with an effort to pick one or a few critical variables and to think of them in terms of necessary or sufficient conditions for effectiveness. The ideas that the presence of a hegemon is necessary for a regime to succeed and that a good match between regime attributes and the biogeophysical properties of the ecosystems involved is sufficient to guarantee success are examples of such propositions. Everything we have discovered so far, however, suggests that simple generalizations—and especially those framed in the form of bivariate statements about necessary or sufficient conditions for regime effectiveness—are not likely to get us very far. Again and again, empirical research points to cases that fail to conform to such expectations. This does not mean that the factors identified are unimportant, merely that the relations involved are too complex to support simple generalizations of this type. We need a framework that can deal also with contingencies, interplay and functional equivalents.

This points towards a research strategy that incorporates at least two "new" elements. One of these focuses on *combinations* of independent variables that are *jointly* necessary or sufficient to ensure high effectiveness. The importance of combinations cannot be fully understood in additive terms. Sometimes, the importance of a particular combination lies in the *configuration* of factors that it puts in place. This is the case when particular variables *interact* to produce positive synergy. To illustrate, the role of social learning and knowledge in general seems to be enhanced by the presence of formal or informal leadership (Underdal 2002). Boolean logic, as used in Charles Ragin's (1987) approach to qualitative comparative analysis, seems particularly useful as a tool for identifying combinations of conditions that are jointly necessary or sufficient (see Stokke's chapter). The other response is to think in terms of *contingent* relationships or, in other words, propositions that indicate that a particular variable is more important under some conditions than others. Simple examples would include the ideas that the presence of a dominant actor is more important in large groups than in small groups (Olson 1965), that well-developed compliance mechanisms are important in dealing with collaboration problems but not coordination problems (Stein, 1983), and that flexibility and social learning processes are important in dealing with cases featuring high levels of uncertainty but not in other circumstances (Young 2002: Ch. 7). These examples all refer to bivariate relationships differentiated by one single contingency factor, but it is easy to see that much more complex forms of contingent relationships may be identified and analyzed systematically once we move away from thinking of necessary and sufficient conditions in terms of single variables.

Many of the phenomena we are interested in (e.g. climate change, marine pollution, biological diversity) are affected, at one and the same time, by numerous driving forces. In some cases, the role of a regime in determining the behavior of key dependent variables will be truly marginal. For example, the operation of the climate change regime can at best explain only a small proportion of the variance in rates of greenhouse gas emissions into the Earth's atmosphere over time. To be able to separate the effect of a regime from consequences brought about by a suite of other factors, we will need a more comprehensive model identifying also the most important *non-institutional* driving forces and specifying how they shape particular outcomes. In other words, regime effectiveness can be determined only in the context of a more holistic understanding of the system of activities in which a regime operates. This is arguably the most important challenge that students of regime consequences are facing. And it is a challenge that calls not merely for more focused and concerted efforts on the part of the regime studies community itself, but also for broader interdisciplinary collaboration.

2.2 Broader Consequences

Research on the broader consequences of international regimes is in its infancy. Whereas researchers have been working intensively on the problems involved in analyzing simple effectiveness for the last decade, the research agenda relating to broader consequences is just now coming into focus. In one respect, this is good news. It means that virtually any serious research endeavor can add significantly to the existing stock of knowledge about broader consequences. At the same time, it means that the issues confronting this line of analysis are more preliminary or primitive than the issues addressed in the preceding subsection. We are convinced that the study of broader consequences is destined to become a growth area for regime analysis over the coming decade. In this subsection, therefore, we seek to identify the principal methodological challenges associated with this endeavor and to indicate what strike us as attractive targets for research in this field.

Methodological challenges. In the final analysis, the methodological challenges facing students of simple effectiveness and broader consequences are the same. We need to demonstrate causal links between the operation of regimes and the behavior of our dependent variables and, in the process, to find ways to answer questions about the proportion of the variance in the dependent variables we select for analysis that can be accounted for in terms of the impact of institutional arrangements. As in the case of simple effectiveness, we can make use of alternative analytic procedures, such as treating regime consequences as such as the dependent variable or focusing on some other dependent variable(s) and treating institutions as one of a set of driving forces. It makes sense as well to explore the causal mechanisms through which institutions produce broader consequences.

That said, however, the study of broader consequences introduces a number of methodological concerns that can be expected to make this field of study particularly demanding. Broader consequences are typically *external* in the sense that they extend beyond the specific behavioral complex or issue area that a regime addresses and *indirect* in the sense that the length of the causal chain linking regimes and broader consequences is likely to be longer than the causal chains involved in simple effectiveness (Young 1999). Take the regimes for ozone depletion, climate change, and biological diversity as cases in point. It is perfectly possible that these regimes will, in time, have significant impacts on the nature of state sovereignty over and above their effects with regard to the specific environmental problems that led to their creation. But these broader consequences will take time to show up in an unambiguous fashion and will be mediated by a stream of other forces at work in international society at the same time. This is not to say that the broader consequences of the regimes in question will be insignificant in their impact. But it does mean that it will be difficult to trace these impacts in a convincing manner and to separate out the broader consequences of regimes from the impacts of other drivers.

Additionally, the study of broader consequences frequently centers on the impacts of *collections* of regimes in contrast to the effects produced by individual regimes. When we ask whether the recent growth in the number and variety of regimes operating in international society has caused problems for the practice of democracy at the domestic level (see Breitmeier's chapter in this volume) or contributed to global social transformation (see the chapter by Hughes in this volume), for instance, the challenge is to find ways to understand the impacts of institutions *in the aggregate* in contrast to asking about the success of specific regimes in solving the problems that led to their creation. This move poses methodological issues of an altogether different and more difficult nature. Instead of treating the properties of individual regimes (or regime components) as the independent variables, we now want to treat some aggregate measure of institutionalization or the growth of regimes at the international level as the independent variable. Not only is it harder to operationalize this variable for purposes of empirical research, but it is also more difficult to isolate its impacts from those of a wide range of other processes occurring in international society. As Hughes' chapter on global social transformation indicates, there is a tendency to interpret the broader consequences of the growth of regimes as a residual variable in this setting.

It is apparent that this is not an entirely satisfactory procedure. But it is easy to understand why analysts resort to it in seeking to pinpoint the broader consequences of collections of regimes.

Attractive targets. Despite these methodological difficulties, we believe the study of broader consequences is destined to become a growth area for regime analysis. The issues at stake are simply too important to ignore just because the methodological problems they pose are difficult to solve. Because the potential agenda is extremely broad and because this line of research is just getting underway, however, it is particularly important to select targets for research at this stage that are both reasonably tractable and likely to produce results whose significance is apparent to all observers. There is ample scope for judgment in this realm, and others may come to conclusions about such matters that differ from ours. In our view, however, three topics seem particularly attractive as targets for the study of broader consequences during the next phase of regime analysis. For purposes of analysis, we can call these topics: institutional interplay, the consequences of institutional structures, and the role of institutions as underlying causes.

As Gehring and Oberthür make clear in their chapter, *institutional interplay* arises when two or more regimes that deal with discrete problems and have distinct histories interact with one another. The resultant interactions may be horizontal in the sense that they involve regimes operating at the same level of social organization or vertical in the sense that they involve cross-scale interactions (Young et al. 1999, Young 2002). These interactions may differ in the extent to which they involve de facto links arising from biogeophysical or socioeconomic interdependencies or, alternatively, reflect conscious efforts to design complex institutional arrangements that link a number of separate elements in such a way as to maximize the attainment of various goals. Such interactions may vary also in the degree to which they are symmetrical or reciprocal. Some interactions between or among regimes involve links that cut across broad functional areas. The rising concern about interactions between environmental regimes and trade regimes exemplifies this case. Other cases of interplay center on links between regimes that operate in the same functional realm. Prominent examples include interactions between the regimes dealing with ozone depletion and climate change and between regimes dealing with marine pollution and marine living resources.

In our judgment, the study of institutional interplay should start with comparatively simple cases and emphasize the development of tools needed to understand these broader consequences. To be specific, we believe it makes sense to focus on cases involving horizontal interplay arising from functional interdependencies. An appropriate research agenda might include cases of environmental interplay (e.g. the interactions among the various regimes dealing with atmospheric issues) and of economic interplay (e.g. the interactions between the international regimes governing trade and monetary matters) as well as cases involving interplay that cuts across issue areas (e.g. the interactions between the international trade regime and environmental regimes dealing with matters like trade in endangered species, transboundary movements of hazardous wastes, and trade in ozone-depleting substances). Although these cases constitute only a subset of the larger domain of institutional interplay, they have the virtue of presenting the phenomenon of interplay in its clearest form, and the methodological innovations developed in exploring these examples will prove useful in extending the analysis to other cases. Of course, research in this realm may well lead to the identification of situations where there are good reasons to engage in institutional design either to mitigate the effects of negative interactions or to ensure the continuation of positive interactions. But the initial thrust of this line of enquiry should concentrate on particularly prominent cases of interplay arising from functional interdependencies.

Although we have tended to treat international regimes as discrete entities, it is apparent that many institutional arrangements function as elements of *interlocking structures* or networks of regimes that operate in broad issue areas. Thus, it makes sense to talk about a structure of economic regimes encompassing trade arrangements operating at the global and regional levels along with monetary arrangements that have direct consequences for trade flows. Similarly, it is possible to identify structures of or families of international regimes dealing with matters of public health and human rights. This concern for structures of regimes parallels the analytic concerns underlying the new institutionalism in studies of political economy. Douglass North, for example, argues that a substantial proportion of the high rates of economic growth occurring in the West over the last 500-1000 years is attributable to the development of an interlocking network of institutional arrangements—including private property rights, contractual procedures, liability rules, and credit systems—that promoted the growth of dynamic markets (North and Thomas 1973). Mancur Olson develops a parallel argument in his effort to explain the superior economic performance of democratic systems in comparison with authoritarian systems (Olson 2000).

North and others who focus on domestic institutions have a significant advantage arising from the fact that it is possible to compare and contrast a sizable number of economic and political systems that differ in institutional terms. In seeking to explain the "rise of the western world," for instance, we can compare and contrast developments in Europe with events unfolding in other parts of the world during the same time period. Although the scope for such comparisons at the international level is limited, it is by no means nonexistent. In thinking about the role of postwar international regimes governing trade and monetary relations as determinants of long-term economic growth and globalization, for instance, we can compare this institutional structure with the parallel arrangements governing trade and monetary affairs at other periods of time. As Konrad von Moltke has observed, moreover, there are striking differences between the institutional structure governing international trade and the parallel network of arrangements that have emerged over the last three decades governing environmental affairs (von Moltke 1997). As a result, it is possible to compare and contrast the consequences of institutional structures across functional areas as well as across time periods.

Many analysts see international institutions as proximate causes or, to put it differently, intervening variables whose character is influenced profoundly by the operation of underlying forces, such as demographic and technological developments (Krasner 1983). Some even go so far as to view institutions as epiphenomena, prone to changing as a result of fluctuations in underlying causes, including shifts in the distribution of power in the material sense and the rise of new technologies (Strange 1983; Mearsheimer 1994/1995). But what about the role of institutions themselves as underlying causes? Consider the well-known I = PAT formula as a case in point (Ehrlich and Holdren 1971). Institutions play a role in determining both rates of population growth and shifts in the spatial distribution of populations by structuring incentives (e.g. offering rewards or penalties for acquiring additional dependents) or even by the promulgation of direct regulations (e.g. the establishment of wilderness areas in which most human activities are banned). Institutions in such forms as taxes or subsidies and safety regulations play major roles as determinants of investment patterns and consumer choices in most societies. The rules of the game also have obvious consequences for the development and diffusion of technologies through the effects of systems of subsidies, patents, and liability rules.

This is not to deny that institutions sometimes function as proximate causes and that other drivers can have substantial impacts on the performance and evolution of institutions in a wide range of social settings. But it appears to us that the relationship between institutions and other driving forces is a complex one and that this is just as true at the international level as it is in other social settings. To understand the broader consequences of international institutions, therefore, we need to examine the interactions between institutions and a variety of demographic, economic, political, and technological forces at work both at the global level and in various parts of international society. Certainly, efforts to meet this challenge will require us to venture into what Walter and Zürn call the "methodological void." In this connection, we may once again have to start with a program of in-depth case studies. But an examination of the role of institutions as underlying causes and of their interactions with other driving forces may contribute over time to a deeper understanding of the nature of institutions and the roles they play as determinants of the course of human affairs.

3. A STRATEGY FOR THE FUTURE

If this is the research agenda for the next phase of the study of regime consequences, what strategy should we adopt in tackling this agenda? Clearly, several options are well worth exploring, and it is not our place to dictate the choice for members of the research community. Yet, we are convinced that this field of study faces a challenge that is familiar to natural scientists working in a variety of areas but that is only beginning to come into focus among social scientists. In essence, the goal is to devise a common structure that integrates the work of many individuals, while leaving all participants ample scope for the exercise of individual creativity and the development of personal niches. Any effort that is perceived as overly directive or top down will backfire; herding social scientists is undoubtedly even harder than herding cats. But any approach that leaves each participant entirely to his or her own devices will yield a loose collection of studies that do not contribute effectively to the growth of cumulative knowledge even though they bear a family resemblance to one another. What is needed, then, is a strategy that creates *opportunities* for concerted action and *encourages* the growth of a vibrant community of researchers working on issues relating to regime consequences which stimulates individual creativity but at the same time guides the efforts of creative individuals toward the pursuit of common goals. In our judgment, this strategy must include both a substantive component and a procedural component.

3.1 The Substantive Component

The substantive component of the strategy should address a range of conceptual and analytic matters as well as the creation and management of common data sets. There is no need for everyone to focus on the same dependent variable(s). There is, for example, certainly room for systematic work dealing with behavioral change as well as problem solving. But it would help to reach consensus within the community on *definitions* of the variables in common use. A particularly significant challenge in this regard concerns the matter of devising a common index of regime effectiveness that is both widely recognized as meaningful and easy to use. The jury is still out regarding the feasibility of devising such an index (Young 2001), but the debate about the issue of index construction is obviously a community-wide concern; the introduction of a usable index could have far-reaching implications for every member of the research community involved in the study of regime consequences. Similar comments are in order regarding the use of various procedures for demonstrating causal connections in this field. There is no need for everyone to use the same procedures. In fact, too much conformity in these terms would probably be a bad thing for the field at this juncture. Yet it is important to make sure that we have a common understanding regarding such matters as the construction and use of counterfactuals, the concept of causal mechanisms, or the requirements of qualitative comparative analysis. The important point, then, is to ensure that we understand the potential as well as the limitations of the various tools included in our tool kit and agree on how to use them.

As we move toward more systematic comparative analyses using a larger number of cases, the need for common or at least compatible data sets arises as a growing concern. A number of efforts are currently underway to build data sets of use to students of regime consequences. Some confine themselves to relatively straightforward factual matters (e.g. How many members does a regime have? What is the nature of a regime's formal decision rule?). Others—including the International Regimes Database—extend to more complex factors and include qualitative information as well as observations that are essentially matters of judgment. The key issues here center on quality control, compatibility, and access. How do we guarantee the internal validity of the data included in these data sets? How do we harmonize or maximize the compatibility of data sets created by different individuals or groups for their own purposes? How can we manage access to these data sets to ensure that they are available to all accredited users on efficient terms? There are no simple answers to these questions. But it may well be that we are approaching the point at which it would be useful to establish an international data management group for the field of regime analysis.

3.2 The Procedural Component

Research communities, like all other communities, thrive on multiplex interactions that occur on a regular and ongoing basis. The good news, in this connection, is that the study of regime consequences - and regime analysis more generally - has spread rapidly so that the ranks of those interested in such matters are substantial in Europe and North America and growing rapidly in Asia and other parts of the world. But the dispersed nature of this community also poses a challenge. How can we promote the level of interaction among the members of this community needed to engender a clear sense of membership in a common enterprise and to stimulate the right mix of cooperation and competition to maximize the production of cumulative knowledge? Modern information technologies surely provide part of the answer. The advent of electronic means of communication - email, the Internet - has undoubtedly played a role in the remarkable spread of regime analysis. There are good reasons to believe that these technologies will become even more important as both data sets and the results of previous studies become accessible online.

Important as they are, however, these instruments are not sufficient to ensure the growth of a strong and productive community. Part of the strategy for the next phase in studies of regime consequences, therefore, must involve the creation or strengthening of mechanisms that allow for face-to-face interaction among members of this community. A number of mechanisms of this sort are already in place. We think, in this connection, of the annual meetings of the International Studies Association, the activities of the European Concerted Action on the Effectiveness of International Environmental Agreements, and the periodic open meetings of the community of scholars interested in the human dimensions of global environmental change. But more may be required at this juncture. The exact nature of the mechanisms needed to promote face-to-face interaction among the members of a dispersed community remains to be determined. Yet it is clear that we can benefit from combining arenas for open exchanges of ideas and information with focused collaborative efforts to address the more complex challenges that no individual researcher or local team can cope with on its own.

Finally, there is the matter of devising appropriate arrangements for the dissemination of research results on regime consequences. Almost certainly, electronic publication will become an important feature of our strategy in this connection. Yet there is still a place for print media in this field. A traditional strategy for dispersed research communities desiring to exchange results on a regular basis is to create a specialized journal to serve their purposes. We are skeptical about the need for such a journal to serve the needs of those working on regime consequences. The most active members of the community will not need a journal to exchange information with one another. Among those interested in environmental regimes in particular, the advent of two new journals—*International Environmental Agreements* and *Global Environmental Politics*—should go a long way toward providing outlets for the publication of results. And other, existing journals are available to serve as vehicles for the publication of results that go beyond the realm of environmental regimes. On the other hand, there may be something to be said for the initiation of a newsletter or digest—distributed electronically and/or in hard copy—as a means of facilitating and improving the exchange of information and ideas within the research community. An interesting example in a neighboring field is *The Common Property Resource Digest*, which has evolved into a useful vehicle linking the widely dispersed community of individuals interested in common-pool resources.

4. A CONCLUDING OBSERVATION

We realize that the suggestions we have made add up to a long and demanding agenda. It would be foolish to think of this agenda as a work program that can be completed in five, ten, or even twenty years. In fact, many of the problems we have identified have no *Endlösung*; they are inherent in the questions we ask and will have to be addressed again and again as we embark upon new projects. Yet we are convinced that none of these problems is so intractable that we cannot learn to do better. In offering this long list of suggestions, we implicitly express our confidence that the field at large is reaching a stage where further progress can legitimately be expected.

REFERENCES

Ehrlich, P. R., and Holdren, J. P. (1971) Impact of Population Growth, Science, 171: 1212–1217.

Hasenclever, A., Mayer, P. and Rittberger, V. (1977) Theories of International Regimes, Cambridge University Press.

Krasner, S. D. (1983) Structural Causes and Regime Consequences: Regimes as Intervening Variables, in S. D. Krasner, (ed.) International Regimes, Cornell University Press, Ithaca, New York, 1 – 21.

Levy, M., Young, O. R. and Zürn,M. (1995) The Study of International Regimes, European Journal of International Relations, 1: 267–330.

Mearsheimer, J. J. (1994/1995) The False Promise of International Institutions, International Security, 19: 5–49.

North, D. C. and Thomas, R. P. (1973) The Rise of the Western World, Cambridge University Press.

Olson, M., Jr. (2000) Power and Prosperity: Outgrowing Communist and Capitalist Dictatorships, Basic Books, New York.

Ragin, C. (1987) The Comparative Method, University of California Press.

Sprinz, D. Helm, C. (1999) The Effect of Global Environmental Regimes: A Measurement Concept, International Political Science Review, 20: 359–369.

Stein, A. A. (1983) Coordination and Collaboration: Regimes in an Anarchic World, in S. D. Krasner (ed.) International Regimes, Cornell University Press, Ithaca, New York, 115 – 40.

Strange, S. (1983) Cave! Hic Dragones: A Critique of Regime Analysis, in S. D. Krasner (ed.) International Regimes, Cornell University Press, Ithaca, New York, 337–354.

Underdal, A. (2002) Conclusions: Patterns of Regime Effectiveness, in E. L. Miles et al., Explaining Regime Effectiveness, MIT Press, . Cambridge, MA, 433 – 65.

Von Molthe, K. (1997) Institutional Interactions: The Structure of Regimes for Trade and the Environment, in O. R. Young (ed.) Global Governance, MIT Press, Cambridge, MA, 247–72.

Young, O. R. (ed.) (1999) The Effectiveness of International Environmental Regimes: Causal Connections and Behavioral Mechanisms, MIT Press, Cambridge, MA.

Young, O. R. (2001) Inferences and Indices: Evaluating the Effectiveness of International Environmental Regimes, Global Environmental Politics, 1: 99–121.

Young, O. R. (2002) The Institutional Dimensions of Environmental Change: Fit, Interplay, and Scale. MIT Press, Cambridge, MA.

Young, O. R. with contributions from Agrawal, A., King, L. A., Sand, P. H., Underdal, A. and Wasson, M. (1999) Institutional Dimensions of Global Environmental Change (IDGEC) Science Plan, IHDP Report No. 9, IHDP, Bonn.

Index

access procedures, 60
acid precipitation, 133
actor attributes, 18
advocacy networks, 220, 243, 305
Africa, 228, 252, 270, 272, 288
aggregation, 138, 234, 237, 253, 271, 305, 324, 325, 328
America (USA), 54, 66, 85, 165, 168, 174, 243, 305, 321
American Endangered Species Act, 75
analysis of processes, 321, 322, 326–328
 in crucial cases, 326, 328
analytic/methodological challenges, 4, 11, 12, 19, 27, 36, 40, 42, 44, 52, 64, 65, 144, 149, 179, 304, 340, 366, 371
analytical Marxism, 72
analytical reduction, 87, 104, 111
annual percentage change scores (APCs), 133–135, 139
Antarctic/Antarctica, 6, 47, 69, 75, 79, 86, 89, 101, 102, 118, 119, 242, 278, 300
Antarctic Treaty System (ATS), 69, 75, 79, 86, 118, 119
APCs, *see* annual percentage change scores
argumentative discourses, 289, 290
arms race, 80, 308
Asia, 288, 377
Atlantic Ocean, 300
Atlantic tuna regime, 137
ATS, *see* Antarctic Treaty System
availability of data, 139

Baltic Sea, 68, 250, 252, 253, 300
Barents Sea, 33, 88, 97–100, 104, 114, 115, 118, 300
 cod, 97, 100, 104
 fisheries regime, 33, 300
bargaining theory, 161, 180

Basel Convention, 247, 252
behavioral mechanisms/pathways, 11, 16, 22, 75, 78, 83, 84, 86, 119, 149, 246, 333, 380
behavioural change, 34, 35, 45, 56, 57, 96, 97, 104, 106, 108, 110, 116, 121, 126, 131, 134, 135, 144, 146, 262, 264, 272, 367, 376
Belgium, 133, 134, 141, 142
Berlin Wall, 309
black box, 71, 72, 91
Boole, George, 88, 115
Boolean:
 algebra, 17, 88
 analysis, 87, 91, 94, 106
 minimization, 105, 107
 sets, 87, 88, 92, 111, 112, 115
boomerang effect, 289
bounded rationality, 153, 161, 163–165, 174, 181
broad/broader consequences, 4, 7, 10–14, 19, 20, 217, 219–227, 229–235, 237–241, 308, 319, 335, 336, 343, 356, 361, 363, 365, 366, 371–373, 375
Bundestag, 294–297, 304, 305
bureaucratic organizations, 90

Canada, 100, 101, 295
carbon lobby, 165
case-driven narrative analyses, 96
case-oriented leads, 102
case-oriented research, 87, 88, 96, 118
case selection, 49–51, 54, 55, 57, 58, 60–63, 96, 211, 314
case study, 17, 18, 37, 43, 46, 49, 51-53, 55, 57-59, 61-63, 81, 87-89, 94, 111, 112, 114, 122, 124, 131, 140, 192, 193, 210, 288-292, 301, 303, 315, 321, 326, 327, 337, 338, 376
case study approach, 52, 58

382

INDEX

catch levels, 37, 98
causal:
   candidate, 92, 105
   chains, 7, 72, 73, 76, 77, 83, 234–237, 272, 273, 366, 372
   conjunctures, 42, 111
   connections, 14, 17, 20, 22, 48, 86, 119, 149, 182, 246, 249, 269, 273, 333, 377, 380
   explanation, 72, 86, 89, 118, 189, 251, 271, 273
   inference, 12, 15, 16, 34, 35, 45, 51, 69, 89, 112, 143, 169, 276, 314, 320, 364–366, 368
   links, 14, 30, 90, 249, 311, 336, 340, 369, 371
   strength, 369
   mechanisms, 39, 42, 46, 71, 72, 77, 81, 83, 85, 89, 179, 185, 200, 211, 212, 229, 236, 239, 249, 269, 273–276, 288–290, 294, 299, 311, 361, 369, 372, 377
   generalized, 249, 269, 273, 274, 276
   model, 93, 102, 147, 237, 364, 365, 369
   integrated, 369
   pathways, 44, 51, 56, 77, 95, 104, 105, 229–231, 234–237, 249–251, 253, 255, 256, 258–260, 262–264, 268–273, 275, 276, 289, 303, 364
   relationships, 50, 77, 79, 83, 108, 112, 123, 145, 185, 200
causality, 88, 89, 92, 112, 148, 216, 237, 249, 269–271, 276, 310, 316, 337, 338, 340
causation, 12, 49, 51, 52, 55, 57, 58, 62, 64, 72, 88, 91, 105, 112, 113, 194, 211, 225, 234, 235, 241, 271, 316, 317
CBD, *see* Convention on Biological Diversity
CCAMLR, *see* Conservation of Antarctic Marine Living Resources, and *see* International Regime to Conserve Marine Resources in the Southern Ocean
CFCs, *see* chlorofluorocarbons
chemical fertilizers, 9
Chernobyl, 99
chlorofluorocarbons (CFCs), 5, 250, 252, 257, 263, 264
CICERO, Project on Science and Politics in International Environmental Regimes, 53, 61, 71
CITES, *see* Convention on International Trade in Endangered Species
Clean Development Mechanism, 74
climate change, 7, 47, 53, 61, 67, 69, 132, 133, 146, 162, 165, 166, 168, 171, 173–175, 177, 178, 180–182, 226, 228, 229, 231, 232, 234, 235, 247, 250, 251, 257, 263, 264, 267, 278, 302, 371–373
CLRTAP, *see* Convention on Long-range Transboundary Air Pollution
co-evolution processes, 225, 249, 251, 275
CO_2 emissions, 133, 336
Cold War, 80, 143, 145, 198, 199, 206, 215, 308, 309, 320, 331
collective action failure, 151, 152, 154, 156
collective action models, 14
collective governance, 29
collective optimum, 13, 35, 36, 45, 55, 131
commensurability, 194, 195, 209
comparators, 125, 126
compliance, 12, 17, 20–22, 29, 32, 34, 44–46, 60, 68, 95, 99, 103, 104, 110, 117, 122, 126, 130, 138, 145, 147, 148, 157, 159, 175, 178, 184, 195, 199, 206, 207, 224, 228, 230, 250, 262, 264, 287, 289–291, 370
compound justice, 202, 213
Comprehensive Test-Ban Treaty (CTBT), 206, 207
concentration of pollutants, 37

concept formation, 12
conceptual clarification, 93
conceptual systems, 74
conditional hypotheses, 186, 210, 211
configurative analysis, 95
consequences research, 143, 220, 221, 225, 227, 232–235, 237, 241, 310, 313, 315, 316, 324, 328, 371
Conservation of Antarctic Marine Living Resources (CCAMLR), 55, 101, 102, 109, 114, 115
conservationists, 6, 102
consistent behavior, 291
constitution of cases, 96
constructive adaptation, 30
contraception use, 347, 348
Convention on Biological Diversity (CBD), 8, 247, 263, 266
Convention on International Trade in Endangered Species (CITES), 75, 227, 247, 267
Convention on Long-range Transboundary Air Pollution (CLRTAP), 58, 60, 61, 65, 66, 125, 267
cooperative outcome, 201
Correlates of War project (COW), 337
correlational hypotheses, 185, 210
counterfactual emissions, 127
counterfactual reasoning, 51, 365
co-variation, 92, 123, 125–128, 132, 137, 145
COW, *see* Correlates of War project
crisp sets, *see* Boolean sets,
cross-case analysis, 94
cross-country comparisons, 57
CTBT, *see* Comprehensive Test-Ban Treaty
CVs, *see* variables

data:
    collection, 12, 18, 55, 64, 138, 140
    gathering, 49, 51, 61, 62
    management, 19, 377
decision making, 29, 60, 92, 95, 124, 204, 213, 219, 222, 223, 227, 238, 253, 264–267, 269, 274, 281, 284, 285, 294, 296, 297, 303, 338, 339
decision making rules, 60
decision rules, 29, 43, 45, 377
de-democratization, 282, 286, 291, 292, 297, 303
deductive approach, 196, 198
deductive-nomological model, 187, 188
degree-of-freedom problem, *see* small-N problem
democracy, 59, 186, 231, 237, 246, 281–286, 292, 293, 298, 304–306, 322, 330, 342, 343, 345, 347, 350, 351, 354, 355, 357, 358, 372
    deliberative, 282–285, 298, 304
    post-national, 285
democratic polity, 282, 284, 285, 291, 292, 297, 299
democratic process, 282, 283, 285, 286, 289, 291, 294, 297, 304
democratic theory, 282, 286, 291, 292
democratization, 282, 286–288, 291, 292, 297, 303, 305
demographic shifts, 9
denationalization, 281, 282, 299, 326, 333
de-parliamentarization, 286, 291–294, 296
desertification, 5, 133, 302
dichotomous variable, 108, 109
differentiation, 41, 92, 285, 293, 312
direction of reasoning, 312, 313
disaggregation, 233, 235–237, 250, 324, 325, 327, 328
discursive structure, 175, 283, 298
disruption, 256–259, 266, 357
dissimilarities, 96, 201

distribution of power, 41, 198, 210, 212, 312, 313, 375
distributive bargaining, 163
distributive justice, 183, 184, 186, 191–193, 199–205, 208–210, 212–214
domestic implementation, 52, 53, 56–58, 64, 66–68, 273
domestic internalization, 286, 288, 289, 291, 303
domestic publics, 286, 293, 298, 299, 301
DVs, *see* variables

Earth's climate system, 11, 15
Eastern Europe, 101, 109, 288
Eastern Pacific Ocean, 300
East-West relations, 46, 102, 231, 245, 321, 332
economic conditions, 18, 337, 340, 343–346, 351
economic fluctuations, 51
economic (in)equality, 10
effective action, 54
effectiveness:
  and implementation, 64
  as efficiency, 157–160
  community, 54
  index of, 13, 157, 368
  simple, 4, 5, 7–9, 11–14, 19, 20, 221, 222, 225–227, 233, 241, 253, 254, 270, 361, 363, 366, 371, 372
Efficiency Limit Theorems, 163
embeddedness, 34, 292–294, 303
emission volumes, 37
emissions, 34, 39, 51, 69, 126-128, 131-133, 145, 168, 173, 232
  carbon, 247, 263, 336, 337, 339, 340
  CO_2, 133, 336
  greenhouse gas, 8, 15, 16, 39, 132, 250, 257, 263, 371
  NO, 133-135
  ODS, 132, 133, 138
  SO_x 126

sulfur, 127, 133-135, 141
sulfur dioxide, 6, 57, 127, 133
VOC, 6, 133
empirical analysis, 81, 125, 137, 255, 269, 347
empirical mapping, 234, 268, 276
empirical methods, 269, 288, 294, 299
empirically observed combinations, 93
EMS, *see* European Monetary System
endangered species, 8, 75, 133, 227, 247, 267, 277, 374
endogeneity problems, 142, 143
energy switching, 51
enforcement, 99, 129, 140, 178, 243
environmental cost-benefit analysis, 159
environmental Kuznets curves, 126, 130, 136, 148
environmental NGOs, 10, 22, 166, 224, 242, 245, 304
epistemic communities, 170–172, 177, 179, 181, 220, 231, 243, 302, 305
equality and reciprocity, 304
ETH, *see* Swiss Federal Institute of Technology
EU, *see* European Union
European Court of Justice, 267
European Monetary System (EMS), 75, 292, 293
European Union (EU), 57, 221, 229, 230, 242, 243, 272, 285, 292, 295, 299, 300, 303, 304, 332
EU Commissioners, 168
EU environmental policy, 174, 276
EU Parliament, 168
Exchange Rate Mechanism, 74
Exclusive Economic Zones, 97, 252
exogenous shock, 184, 188, 193–199, 209, 212, 213
experimental design, 92, 105, 201
explanandum, 72, 76–80, 83, 90, 187–189, 314

explanans, 77, 90, 187, 188
explanatory model, 43, 96, 110
extensiveness, 91
external validity, 50, 55, 88, 94, 114
extra-institutional adaptation, 262, 264, 270

facts of life, 257
farming, 9
FCoT, *see* future consequences of ongoing transformations
feasibility, 38, 49, 54, 62–65, 115, 367, 377
feasibility concerns, 49, 63, 64
fertility rates, 10, 341, 344, 345, 347–349, 354
first differences, 133
fishing, 9, 97–104, 109, 115, 118, 163
Folk theorem, 155
formal organisation, 41
formal theory, 151
France, 213, 295, 321
Freedom House measure of democracy, 345, 350
freeriding, 154, 157
full employment, 80
functional conflict, 258, 274
functional linkage, 257
fur seals, 133
future consequences of ongoing transformations (FCoT), 308–328
futurology, 311
fuzzy sets, 22, 87, 92, 103, 109, 111, 112, 115, 118, 316, 332

game-theoretical model, 151, 153, 154, 165
game theory, 151–153, 156, 161, 162, 171, 177, 196, 363, 365
GATT/WTO regime, 5, 8, 10, 220, 226–228, 230, 231, 240, 245, 247, 257, 260
GDP per capita, 344–349, 352–354, 356, 357

GEM, *see* Gender Empowerment Measure
Gender Empowerment Measure (GEM), 350
Germany, 294, 295, 307
Global Environment Facility, 267, 277, 279
globalization, 8, 10, 220, 241, 295, 296, 305, 309, 318–320, 322–329, 331, 332, 352, 356, 375
global juridification, 286–288
global warming, 54, 177, 180, 182, 245
global welfare, 28
government of the people, 281
grandfathering, 173
Great Power Wars, 311–313, 320
green golden rules, 160
greenhouse gases, 8, 15, 16, 39, 132, 250, 257, 263, 279, 371
emissions, 132, 279, 371
grey boxes, 90

habitualization, 290
Hanf/Underdal acid rain project, 53, 56, 57, 66, 68
hard-soft approach, 63
heterogeneity, 15, 93, 137, 140
HFCs, *see* hydrofluorocarbons
high-probability criterion, 188, 189, 211
historical analysis, 81
historic contrasts, 321
historic parallels, 320
holism, 80, 81
homogeneity, 91, 97, 107, 108, 169
cross-case, 91
human interactions with marine animals, 6
human rights, 9, 10, 37, 46, 220, 227, 231, 237, 240, 242, 244, 286–291, 303, 306, 342, 374
human rights NGOs, 220
hydrofluorocarbons (HFCs), 250, 265
hyperglobalists, 324

hypothesis development, 12

IAEA, *see* International Atomic Energy Agency
Iceland, 97, 100, 115, 133, 134, 141, 142
ideological competition, 311, 312
IIASA, *see* International Institute for Applied Systems Analysis
IIASA/IEC project, 56
impacts, 3, 5, 8, 9, 11, 12, 14, 56, 109, 144, 159, 283, 286, 288, 296, 340, 346, 372, 375
implementation review, 17, 250
indeterminacy, 73, 322
indexing, 133
India, 207, 213
individual decision-making, 29
inductive analysis, 267
inductive approach, 196, 198
inductive-statistical model, 188, 189
industry emissions, 34
ineffectiveness, 152, 168
inefficient outcomes, 162
infant mortality, 347
inflation, 80, 81
input-oriented legitimacy, 281, 283, 286, 302
institutional design, 56, 59, 61, 62, 68, 69, 274, 374
institutional interplay, 8, 9, 278, 373, 374
institutionalization, 290, 303, 309, 319–321, 325, 330, 358, 372
institutional specification, 60
instrumental adaptation, 289, 290
interaction:
   among regimes *see*, regime interaction
   human, 6
   institutional, 8, 10, 22, 227
   of states, 78, 80, 154, 176
   terms, 125, 130, 145
inter-group conflict, 258

internal politics, 75
internal validity, 50, 51, 63, 88, 91, 94, 114, 377
International Atomic Energy Agency (IAEA), 206
International Convention for the Prevention of Pollution from Ships (MARPOL), 253
International Council for the Exploration of the Sea (ICES), 98, 99
international environmental regimes, 8, 21–23, 47–49, 52, 53, 61, 68, 69, 71, 86, 119, 121, 144, 148, 149, 179, 181, 182, 227, 242, 245–247, 277, 304, 333, 380
International Futures (IF) modeling project, 346, 356
international human rights, 46, 242, 244, 286–291, 303, 306
International Institute for Applied Systems Analysis (IIASA), 19, 53, 56, 58, 59, 65, 139
international regimes, 3–6, 9–11, 15, 17–21, 28, 31, 32, 42–44, 47, 52, 55, 62, 65, 68, 69, 71, 72, 74, 75, 77, 81, 83, 89, 93–95, 110, 111, 114, 119, 139, 145, 147, 151, 164, 179, 182, 183, 188, 193, 194, 198, 199, 209, 214–216, 219–245, 247, 248, 250–252, 254–256, 266, 270, 271, 274, 275, 277, 278, 281, 282, 286, 293, 296–301, 303, 305, 307–309, 311–313, 316–321, 328, 330–333, 337, 338, 357, 361, 363–367, 369–371, 374, 375, 377, 379, 380
   consequences of, 3–6, 11, 15, 19, 20, 147, 221, 225, 230–233, 241, 242, 277, 282, 307, 312, 318, 319, 330, 371
      boundaries among types, 4
      types, 4
International Regimes Database, (IRD), 19,

145, 329
International Regime to Conserve Marine Resources in the Southern Ocean (CCAMLR), 55, 101, 102, 109, 114, 115, 118
International Relations (IR) theory, 54, 152, 159, 164, 167, 175, 176, 329
international resource management, 68, 93, 94
international society, 3, 4, 7, 8, 10, 13, 16, 48, 203, 209, 213, 215, 216, 231, 242, 246, 279, 289, 298, 305, 308, 313, 315, 372, 375
International Tropical Timber Agreement (ITTA), 8
International Whaling Commission (IWC), 59, 61, 66, 95, 102, 115, 116, 228
internationalization, 220, 241, 244, 292, 294, 296, 297, 304
intra-institutional adaptation, 263, 264, 273
intra-institutional response, 266
IRD, *see* International Regimes Database
IR, *see* International Relations theory
Israel, 207
issue-interlinkages, 157
Italy, 295, 332
IVs, *see* variables
IWC, *see* International Whaling Commission

Japan, 95, 101, 102, 115, 118, 119, 213, 295
Joint Fisheries Commission, 98, 99
jurisdictional disputes, 6
justice hypothesis, 184–186, 188, 191–193, 199, 200, 202, 204, 205, 209–212

Kazakhstan, 207
krill, 101–103, 109
Kyoto Protocol, 74, 244, 245, 247, 263, 264, 266, 278

large-N comparisons, 122
Latin America, 244, 288
Law of the Sea Convention (1982), 98
learning, 15, 32, 64, 75, 111, 151, 152, 160, 171, 172, 178, 212, 215, 262, 349, 370
legitimacy, 29, 30, 41, 47, 69, 86, 117–119, 281–284, 286, 294, 302, 305, 358
levels of emissions, 133
life expectancy, 10, 226, 237, 341, 345–347
literacy rate, 345, 347, 349, 350
literature, 28, 31, 36, 46, 51, 68, 71, 72, 74, 75, 77, 81, 82, 85, 89, 91, 124, 127, 130, 136, 145, 152, 163, 164, 170–172, 176, 184, 196, 212, 220, 221, 225, 228, 241, 253, 254, 257, 259, 262, 276, 327, 330, 338, 339, 342, 380
lock-in mechanism, 90
logic of appropriateness, 14, 16, 175, 239
London dumping regime, 58
long-range transboundary air pollution (LRTAP) regime, 6, 34, 58, 60, 61, 65, 66, 125–127, 133, 139, 143, 226–229, 267
Loophole case, 100, 103, 118
LRTAP, *see* long-range transboundary air pollution regime

macrolevel, 81, 90
macroreduction, 81
marine living resources, 55, 88, 101, 300, 373
marine pollution, 55, 226, 367, 371, 373
MARPOL, *see* International Convention for the Prevention of Pollution from Ships
mechanical systems, 74

mechanism-oriented regime effectiveness research, 104
mechanisms:
  of international regulation, 75
  reductionist, 152
  utilitarian, 152
mesh-size, 98, 99, 103
methodological:
  approach, 31, 38, 42, 49, 63, 65, 301, 338, 364
  challenges, 4, 11, 12, 19, 27, 36, 40, 42, 44, 52, 64, 65, 144, 149, 179, 304, 340, 366, 371
  individualism, 72, 76, 79, 80, 83
  malaise, 44
  strategies, 42
  strength, 40
  void, 307, 310, 314, 375
Mexico, 295, 348
microlevel, 81
microreduction, 81
Miles/Underdal model, 59, 61, 330
Miles projects, 53, 62, 66
Mill, John Stuart, 88, 92, 112, 113, 116, 118, 215
minimization, 94, 104–107, 109, 110, 116
miscodings, 108
model-based estimates, 39
model construction, 12, 110
modeling, 121, 124–126, 128, 136, 140, 147, 244, 318, 346, 351, 356, 369
  a single regime, 125
multinational corporations, 10, 231
multiple-value variables, 112, 116

NAFTA, *see* North American Free Trade Area
NAFO, *see* Northwest Atlantic Fisheries Organization
Nash equilibria, 153, 170, 175, 197
  bargaining model, 162, 165, 175, 180
NATO, *see* North Atlantic Treaty Organization

North Atlantic Treaty Organization (NATO), 198, 259, 299, 320, 321
natural experiment, 92
necessary conditions, 29, 30, 34, 50, 93, 104, 106, 107, 110, 183–191, 193, 202, 206, 209, 214, 317
  hypothesis, 184–191, 193, 202, 206, 209
  approach, 184, 185
negative cases, 92, 105, 109, 110
neo-institutionalist, 152, 161, 175
network-state approach, 293, 294, 296
NGOs, *see* non-governmental organisations
nitrogen oxides, 6, 133–135, 141, 148, 158
NNWS, *see* non-nuclear weapon states
noncompliance, 17, 224, 228, 250, 264
non-co-operative outcome, 35, 36, 46, 156
non-governmental organisations (NGOs), 10, 22, 55, 59, 166, 220, 224, 239, 242, 245, 304, 318
non-modelled, 92, 96, 97, 112
  antecedent variable, 92, 96
  conditions, 96, 97
  causality, 112
non-nuclear weapon states (NNWS), 206, 208
non-regime:
  factors, 143
  IVs, 125, 136
  situations, 239, 240
  variables, 130, 144
norm, strength, 207
North American Free Trade Area (NAFTA), 8
North Atlantic Marine Mammal Organization (NAMMCO), 228
North Atlantic, 100, 228, 242, 300
  salmon, 300,
North Korea, 207, 213
North Sea, 55, 58, 59, 61, 65, 66, 69, 226, 268

Northwest Atlantic Fisheries Organization (NAFO), 100, 101, 117
Norway, 19, 57, 66, 68, 95, 97–100
NPR, *see* nuclear nonproliferation regime
NPT, *see* Treaty on the Non-Proliferation of Nuclear Weapons
nuclear bargain, 208
nuclear nonproliferation regime (NPR), 205–210, 213, 184
nuclear weapon states (NWS), 206, 208, 209, 213
NWS, *see* nuclear weapon states

ODSs, *see* ozone depleting substances
OECD-countries, 252, 292, 294, 295, 321, 323, 326, 332
open interviews, 51
openness, 298
operationalisation, 5, 129, 184, 192, 193, 200, 212, 323
operational measurement, 364
operation of social institutions, 281
operation of social roles, 75
OSCON, *see* Oslo Dumping Convention
Oslo commission, 55
Oslo conference, 20
Oslo Dumping Convention (OSCON), 50, 55, 60, 236, 251
outcomes, 12–16, 18, 34–36, 46, 52, 61, 65, 75, 80, 82, 88–94, 97, 101, 103–107, 111, 112, 114–116, 122, 127, 131, 146, 152, 156, 158, 159, 161, 162, 164, 165, 167–169, 172, 173, 176, 184, 186, 187, 191, 196, 197, 202, 203, 209–211, 213, 222, 234, 239, 248, 262, 263, 270, 290, 293, 296, 308, 312, 313, 316, 317, 319, 322, 323, 326, 328–330, 340, 368, 371
output-oriented legitimacy, 281, 282, 294
outputs, 12, 14, 53, 54, 100, 340

overfishing, 97–99, 103, 104
ozone depleting substances (ODSs), 132, 133, 138, 261, 263, 267, 374
ozone-friendly HFCs, 265
ozone loss, 133

Pacific Ocean, 306
Pacific salmon, 300
Pakistan, 207, 213, 214
panel data, 122, 140–144, 147
PARCON, *see* Paris Convention on Land-based Marine Pollution
PARCON/North Sea Conferences, 50, 60, 61
Paretian welfare economics, 159
Pareto:
    efficient, 156, 159, 177, 197
    frontier, 156, 157, 159, 161–163, 168, 179
    optimum, 157, 197
Paris Convention on Land-based Marine Pollution (PARCON), 55, 60, 61
participation issues, 59, 60
payoff, 153–157, 162, 163, 167, 173, 175, 176, 196, 297, 363
per unit effort (PUE), 132, 134, 135, 139, 146
pesticides, 9
philosophy of science literature, 72, 75, 117, 188, 215
polar bears, 133, 139
polarisation, 43, 66
policy diffusion, 262
policy significance, 128
political oppression, 81
pollutants, 6, 9, 37, 127, 132, 133, 139
    persistent organic (POP), 6, 9, 127, 129
pollution, 6, 7, 9, 10, 39, 55, 58, 68, 69, 121, 122, 125, 127, 133, 134, 136, 139, 146, 148, 156, 159, 226, 227, 234, 252, 253, 267, 367, 371, 373

POP, *see* pollutants
Portugal, 101, 277
post-parliamentary governance, 295, 304
potential falsifier, 190–192, 206, 209–211
prescriptive status, 290
preservationists, 6, 102
Prisoner's Dilemma, 154, 157, 167, 175, 181, 196–198
  supergame, 154, 167
problem-related behavior, 87, 91, 95
problem solving capacity, 54, 56, 59, 229, 281, 299
problem structure, 18, 54, 56, 59, 60, 64
procedural component, 29, 376, 377
process-orientation, 58, 222, 223, 235, 290, 296, 301, 302
process tracing, 17, 43, 51, 56–58, 64, 81, 269, 290, 303, 318, 369
protection of:
  Antarctica, 242
  Baltic sea, 250
  environment, 245
  global climate, 235
  human rights, 287
  individuals, 287
  juveniles, 98
  North Sea, 268
  ozone layer, 226, 228, 247, 250
  sharks, 75
  species, 336
  spotted owls, 336
  whales, 6
public choice theory, 72
PUE, *see* per unit effort

QCA, *see* Qualitative Comparative Analysis
qualitative approach/method, 17, 18, 51, 57, 121–123, 234, 237, 276
Qualitative Comparative Analysis (QCA), 87, 88, 92–94, 96, 97, 102–112, 115, 116, 315, 316, 329
  strength, 110
qualitative research, 16, 21, 47, 68, 86, 88, 117, 118, 122, 123, 148, 179, 214, 215, 278, 314, 331, 332
  scientific inference in, 16, 21, 47, 68, 86, 118, 148, 179, 215, 278, 314, 331
qualitative techniques, 121, 143
qualitative versus quantitative approaches, 49, 51
quantitative approach/method, 49, 51, 64, 111, 113, 121–124, 137, 144, 214, 268
quantitative study design, 122
quantitative techniques, 122, 143

rational choice, 72, 151–154, 160, 161, 163, 164, 166, 167, 173–175, 178, 180, 182, 239
rational players, 151, 152
rational self-interest, 75
realism, 76, 81–83, 178, 215, 242
realist, 82, 83, 85, 86, 113, 117, 135, 152, 161, 162, 164, 165, 167, 178, 239
reasonableness, 284
reduced emissions, 51
regime(s):
  acid rain, 55, 57, 58, 139
  analysis, 18, 37, 39, 46, 48, 89, 91, 201, 220, 222, 233, 234, 240–242, 254, 279, 327, 328, 363, 371, 373, 377, 378, 380
  arms control, 34, 215
  as social systems, 225
  Baltic, 58
  bargaining, 162, 165, 168–170, 172
  consequences, 5, 7–9, 11–14, 16–20, 27, 49, 65, 122, 123, 143, 144, 149, 179, 215, 221, 225, 231, 233, 237, 244, 249, 282, 285, 286, 288, 298, 299, 301, 302, 304, 310, 318, 319, 321,

328, 329, 336–340, 345, 353, 355–357, 361, 362, 366–369, 371, 376–379
density, 227, 247
effectiveness,16, 18, 21, 22, 27, 28, 31–33, 36, 37, 40–42, 45, 47, 49–51, 68, 75, 78, 79, 87, 89, 92, 104, 106, 112, 114, 116, 118, 119, 121, 124, 132, 148, 149, 151–154, 156, 159, 161, 164, 166, 169, 170, 173, 174, 179–182, 220, 225, 245, 275, 319, 329, 332, 365, 367–371, 376, 380
    assessing, 31
effects or impacts of, 9
features, 16, 128, 129, 131, 135, 140, 141
fisheries, 33, 45, 137, 139, 301
habitat, 133, 134
human rights, 37, 227, 240, 288, 289
ideal, 157, 159, 162
interaction, 2, 53, 219, 221, 225, 253, 262
irrational, 151
linkages, 45, 49, 64, 245, 279
North Sea, 58
ozone, 5, 38, 60, 61, 132, 138, 139, 191, 229, 233, 250, 257, 261, 264
pollutant/pollution, 133, 134, 159
robustness, 183, 184, 186, 191, 193–195, 210, 215, 330
Schengen, 260, 272, 274
shock – strength 195, 196, 199
solution, 35
source, 53, 65, 69, 228, 229, 236, 249–253, 255–257, 259–263, 265–271, 273, 275, 276
strength, 17, 20, 28, 29, 31, 336, 337, 339, 340, 344, 346, 356
target, 228, 229, 232, 233, 236, 249–253, 255–257, 259–273, 275, 276
theorists, 204
theory, 147, 152, 154, 155, 170, 172, 180, 214–216, 242–244, 277, 278, 330, 331, 338
transnational, 272
whaling, 21, 55, 58, 67
wildlife, 133, 134
regime effort units (REUs), 134, 135
regime-related:
    behavioral change, 56
    factors, 125
    issues, 300
    IVs, 125, 132, 134, 135, 141
    processes, 45
regression analysis, 16, 122, 132, 138, 143
relevant acreage, 133
relevant effectiveness projects, 53
rent-seeking, 165, 177
research strategies, 19, 20, 42, 110, 144, 149, 179, 192, 221, 304, 323, 361, 370
REU, *see* regime effort units
rhetorical moves, 173
rivalry, 312, 313
river and ocean pollutants, 133, 139
River Rhine, 226
    regime, 226, 228
robustness, 28, 30, 31, 45, 47, 109, 181, 184–186, 188, 191–196, 199, 205–207, 209–212, 214, 215, 321, 330, 331, 362, 363
role of the secretariat, 60
Russia, 68, 97–100, 213

sample size, 137
sanctions, 73, 74, 91, 121, 122, 129, 130, 135, 146, 148, 171, 243, 257, 260, 289, 298, 330–332
science-politics interface, 59–61, 69
scientific measurement, 37
Seattle-Oslo project, 55
semiotic systems, 74
Serbia, 73

set-theoretic algebra, 92, 93, 112
set theory, 92
shaming, 91, 93–101, 103–110, 114, 116
similarities, 96, 144, 146, 201
simplifying assumptions, 90, 94, 106–108, 111, 112, 114
situation-specific causes and effects, 256, 258, 267
situation-structural approach, 196, 197, 199
skews, 51, 188
small-N problem, 88, 111
social:
    capital, 41, 47
    conditions, 341, 344–347, 356
    context, 14, 18
    development, 341, 348
    learning, 32, 75, 370
    mechanisms, 72, 73, 79, 80, 85, 86, 117
    norms, 75, 152, 227
    phenomena, 73, 80, 184, 249, 267
    psychology, 72, 201
    transformation, 9, 325, 343–345, 357, 372
    welfare, 28, 44
social-practice models, 14, 22
source regime actors, 259–262, 266
South Africa, 207, 243
Southern Ocean, 55, 89, 101, 109, 278
Soviet Union, 80, 97, 99, 101, 102, 118, 198, 207, 213, 215, 231
SO_X emissions, 126
Spain, 101
specificity, 76, 83, 91, 136, 287
spiral model of human rights change, 290, 291
Sprinz and Helms formula, 37
standardisation, 18, 19, 63, 67, 269, 324
standardised indicators, 37
standard of evaluation, 35, 199, 200
standard research (StR), 308, 310–317, 320, 321, 323, 327–329
State Committee on the Environment, 99
static cost-benefit analysis, 159
statistical significance, 128, 146
statistical techniques, 11, 51, 137
strategic bargaining, 289, 290
structuring of the agenda, 60
substantive component, 376
sulfur dioxide, 6, 127, 133–135, 143, 148, 158
sulfur emissions, 127, 134, 135, 141
Sulfur Protocol, 125, 126
supply of instrumental leadership, 41
surveys, 47, 51, 148, 245, 278, 304, 318, 328, 342, 351–353, 356, 357
sustainability, 8, 9, 21, 28, 99, 160, 161, 172, 177–179, 245, 263, 266, 276
Svalbard, 6
Sweden, 57, 66
Swiss Federal Institute of Technology (ETH), 112
synergy, 254, 256–259, 266–268, 276, 277, 362, 370
    functional, 258, 268
    membership-induced, 258
systemism, 80, 81
systems-theoretic (systemic):
    approach, 81
    consequences/effects, 8–10, 13, 102, 228, 231, 232, 237, 238, 307–310, 312, 315, 316, 318–323, 325, 328, 329, 341
    research, 228
    shift, 345–354, 357

tactical concessions, 290
target regime actors, 256, 259–261, 263, 269
technology, 11, 53, 88, 91, 99, 112, 127, 136, 144, 206, 281, 286, 308, 318, 336, 337, 340, 341, 344, 346–350, 356, 375, 378

tendency-finding analysis, 16
terrestrial resources, 6
textbook ideals, 49, 50, 54, 55, 63, 64
theoretical constructs, 51
theory of institutions and organisations, 72
Trade Policy Review Mechanism, 74
transnational publics, 298–302
Transparency International, 350
treaty congestion, 227, 248
Treaty on the Non-Proliferation of Nuclear Weapons (NPT), 206, 207, 213
trend extrapolation, 323, 327, 328
truth table, 18, 93, 95, 97, 102–105, 114–116
t-statistic, 127–129, 132, 134
two-level games, 165, 180
two-stage least squares model, 143

Ukraine, 207
UNCLOS III, see UN Convention on the Law of the Sea
unemployment, 81, 324
UN Conference on Environment and Development (1992), 130
UN Conference on the Human Environment (1972), 130
UN Convention on the Law of the Sea (UNCLOS III), 5, 252, 253, 305
UN Development Programme (UNDP), 350
UNDP, see UN Development Programme
UNFCCC, see UN Framework Convention on Climate Change
UN Framework Convention on Climate Change (UNFCCC), 7
United Kingdom (UK), 296
United States, see America

unit of analysis, 33, 52, 123, 137, 138, 236, 249, 326, 361
unit of effectiveness, 37
Universal Declaration of Human Rights (1948), 287
UV-B radiation, 5

values, 3, 27, 32, 37, 50, 51, 60, 88, 92, 95, 99, 104, 111, 112, 116, 123–125, 128–131, 139, 141, 145, 160, 161, 185, 186, 189, 195, 201, 205, 206, 210, 211, 213, 214, 235, 256, 274, 285, 291, 294, 323, 325, 339–341, 345, 347, 348, 350–357
variable(s):
  control, (CVs), 50, 51, 123–126, 137, 141, 142, 144
  dependent (DVs), 12, 13, 15, 16, 18, 20, 38, 40, 50, 54, 59, 61, 73, 77, 88, 96, 97, 112, 114, 123, 125, 128, 131–135, 138, 141, 143, 144, 146, 164, 169, 185, 210, 211, 221, 225–234, 236, 237, 241, 249, 250, 282, 308, 310–317, 319–329, 336–338, 340, 343, 355, 363–367, 369–372, 376
  independent (IVs), 18, 38, 40, 50, 54, 112, 123, 125, 128, 135, 141, 146, 169, 185, 210, 221, 225–228, 230–234, 236, 237, 241, 249, 310–314, 316, 317, 319, 320, 323–328, 337, 338, 340, 365, 366, 369, 370, 372
  non-regime, 130
  individual time-invariant, 141
  individual time-varying, 141
  strength, 137
variable-oriented data matrix, 94
variable-oriented research, 88, 97, 118, 316
variation-finding procedures/techniques, 15, 16, 276, 369

verification and compliance mechanisms, 60, 190, 208
VOC, *see* volatile organic compounds
volatile organic compounds (VOC), 6, 133

War Powers Resolution (1972), 297, 305
Warsaw Pact, 259
waste brokers, 270, 272
waste producing industries, 270, 272
WCO, *see* World Customs Organization
wetlands, 133
whales/whaling, 6, 21, 55, 58, 61, 66, 67, 95, 102, 114–116, 132, 133, 139, 228, 242, 273, 300
World Commission on Environment and Development (1992), 130
World Customs Organization (WCO), 261
world heritage sites, 133
World Trade Organization (WTO), 5, 8, 10, 220, 226–228, 230, 231, 240, 245, 247, 250, 257, 260
World Values Survey (WVS), 351–354
WTO/GATT regime *see* GATT/WTO regime